Joint Workshop on Multiword Expressions and Electronic Lexicons (MWE-LEX 2020)

Held online due to COVID-19

Barcelona, Spain
13 December 2020

ISBN: 978-1-7138-2833-4

Joint Workshop on Multiword Expressions and Electronic Lexicons (MWE-LEX 2020)

Held online due to COVID-19

Barcelona, Spain
13 December 2020

MWE-LEX 2020

Joint Workshop on Multiword Expressions and Electronic Lexicons

Proceedings of the Workshop

December 13, 2020
Barcelona, Spain (Online)

Introduction

The Joint Workshop on Multiword Expressions and Electronic Lexicons (MWE-LEX 2020)[1] took place in an online format on December 13, 2020 in conjunction with COLING 2020.

This was the 16th edition of the Workshop on Multiword Expressions (MWE 2020). The event was organized and sponsored by the Special Interest Group on the Lexicon (SIGLEX)[2] of the Association for Computational Linguistics (ACL) and by ELEXIS[3] - European Lexicographic Infrastructure.

The joint MWE-LEX workshop addressed two domains – multiword expressions and (electronic) lexicons – with partly overlapping communities and research interests, but divergent practices and terminologies.

Multiword expressions (MWEs) are word combinations, such as in *the middle of nowhere*, *hot dog*, *to make a decision* or *to kick the bucket*, displaying lexical, syntactic, semantic, pragmatic and/or statistical idiosyncrasies. Because of their unpredictable behavior, notably their non-compositional semantics, MWEs pose problems in linguistic modelling (e.g. treebank annotation, grammar engineering), NLP pipelines (notably when orchestrated with parsing), and end-user applications (e.g. information extraction).

Because MWE-hood is a largely lexical phenomenon, appropriately built electronic MWE lexicons turn out to be quite important for NLP. Large standardised multilingual, possibly interconnected, NLP-oriented MWE lexicons prove indispensable for NLP tasks such as MWE identification, due to its critical sensitivity to unseen data. But the development of such lexicons is challenging and calls for tools which would leverage, on the one hand, MWEs encoded in pre-existing NLP-unaware lexicons and, on the other hand, automatic MWE discovery in large non-annotated corpora.

In order to allow better convergence and scientific innovation within these two largely complementary scientific communities, we called for papers on joint topics on MWEs and e-lexicons, on the one hand, and on MWE-specific topics, on the other hand.

Joint topics on MWEs and e-lexicons

- Extracting and enriching MWE lists from traditional human-readable lexicons for NLP use

- Formats for NLP-applicable MWE lexicons

- Interlinking MWE lexicons with other language resources

- Using MWE lexicons in NLP tasks (identification, parsing, translation)

- MWE discovery in the service of lexicography

- Multiword terms in specialized lexicons

- Representing semantic properties of MWEs in lexicons

- Paving the way towards encoding lexical idiosyncrasies in constructions

---

[1] http://multiword.sourceforge.net/mwelex2020
[2] http://alt.qcri.org/siglex/
[3] https://elex.is/

MWE-specific topics

- Computationally-applicable theoretical work on MWEs and constructions in psycholinguistics, corpus linguistics and formal grammars

- MWE and construction annotation in corpora and treebanks

- Processing of MWEs and constructions in syntactic and semantic frameworks (e.g. CCG, CxG, HPSG, LFG, TAG, UD, etc.), and in end-user applications (e.g. information extraction, machine translation and summarization)

- Original discovery and identification methods for MWEs and constructions

- MWEs and constructions in language acquisition and in non-standard language (e.g. tweets, forums, spontaneous speech)

- Evaluation of annotation and processing techniques for MWEs and constructions

- Retrospective comparative analyses from the PARSEME shared tasks on automatic identification of MWEs

We received 25 submissions (14 long and 11 short papers). We selected 6 long papers and 7 short ones. All 13 accepted papers were presented orally. The overall acceptance rate was 52 %.

In addition to the oral sessions, the workshop featured an invited talk that given by Roberto Navigli from Sapienza University of Rome.

The workshop also organized the PARSEME Shared Task on Semi-Supervised Identification of Verbal MWEs (edition 1.2). This was a follow-up of editions 1.0 (2017), and 1.1 (2018). Edition 1.2 featured (a) improved and extended corpora annotated with MWEs, (b) complementary unannotated corpora for unsupervised MWE discovery, and (c) a new evaluation methodology focusing on unseen MWEs. Following the synergy with Elexis, our aim was to foster the development of unsupervised methods for MWE lexicon induction, which in turn can be used for identification.

Seven teams submitted 9 system results to the shared task (some teams made 2 submissions): 2 to the closed track (where only the data provided by the organizers could be used on input) and 7 to the open track (where external data were also allowed). Out of these 9 results, 4 covered all 14 languages for which data were made available by the organizers. Six teams also submitted systems description papers, all of which were accepted and presented orally.

We are grateful to the paper authors for their valuable contributions, the members of the Program Committee for their thorough and timely reviews, all members of the organizing committee for the fruitful collaboration, and all the workshop participants for their interest in this event. Our thanks also go to the COLING 2020 organizers for their support, as well as to SIGLEX and ELEXIS for their endorsement.

Stella Markantonatou, John McCrae, Jelena Mitrović, Carole Tiberiu, Carlos Ramisch, Ashwini Vaidya, Petya Osenova, Agata Savary

Organizers:

Stella Markantonatou, Institute for Language and Speech Processing, R.C. "Athena" (Greece)
John McCrae, National University of Ireland Galway (Ireland)
Jelena Mitrović, University of Passau (Germany)
Carole Tiberius, Dutch Language Institute in Leiden (Netherlands)
Carlos Ramisch, Aix Marseille University (France)
Ashwini Vaidya, Indian Institute of Technology in Delhi (India)
Petya Osenova, Institute of Information and Communication Technologies (Bulgaria)
Agata Savary, University of Tours (France)

Program Committee:

Tim Baldwin, University of Melbourne (Australia)
Verginica Barbu Mititelu, Romanian Academy (Romania)
Archna Bhatia, Florida Institute for Human and Machine Cognition (USA)
Francis Bond, Nanyang Technological University (Singapore)
Tiberiu Boroș, Adobe (Romania)
Marie Candito, Paris Diderot University (France)
Helena Caseli, Federal University of Sao Carlos (Brazil)
Anastasia Christofidou, Academy of Athens (Greece)
Ken Church, IBM Research (USA)
Matthieu Constant, Université de Lorraine (France)
Paul Cook, University of New Brunswick (Canada)
Monika Czerepowicka, University of Warmia and Mazury (Poland)
Béatrice Daille, Nantes University (France)
Gerard de Melo, Rutgers University (USA)
Thierry Declerck, DFKI (Germany)
Gaël Dias, University of Caen Basse-Normandie (France)
Meghdad Farahmand, University of Geneva (Switzerland)
Christiane Fellbaum, Princeton University (USA)
Joaquim Ferreira da Silva, New University of Lisbon (Portugal)
Aggeliki Fotopoulou, ILSP/RC "Athena" (Greece)
Francesca Frontini, Université Paul-Valéry Montpellier (France)
Marcos Garcia, CITIC (Spain)
Voula Giouli, Institute for Language and Speech Processing (Greece)
Chikara Hashimoto, Yahoo!Japan (Japan)
Kyo Kageura, University of Tokyo (Japan)
Diptesh Kanojia, IITB-Monash Research Academy (India)
Dimitris Kokkinakis, University of Gothenburg (Sweden)
Ioannis Korkontzelos, Edge Hill University (UK)
Iztok Kosem, Jožef Stefan Institute (Slovenia)
Cvetana Krstev, University of Belgrade (Serbia)
Malhar Kulkarni, Indian Institute of Technology, Bombay (India)
Eric Laporte, University Paris-Est Marne-la-Vallee (France)
Timm Lichte, University of Duesseldorf (Germany)
Irina Lobzhanidze, Ilia State University (Georgia)

Ismail el Maarouf, Adarga Ltd (UK)
Yuji Matsumoto, Nara Institute of Science and Technology (Japan)
Nurit Melnik, The Open University of Israel (Israel)
Elena Montiel-Ponsoda, Universidad Politecnica de Madrid (Spain)
Sanni Nimb, Det Denske Sprog- og Litteraturselskab (Denmark)
Haris Papageorgiou, Institute for Language and Speech Processing (Greece)
Carla Parra Escartín, Unbabel (Portugal)
Marie-Sophie Pausé, independent researcher (France)
Pavel Pecina, Charles University (Czech Republic)
Scott Piao, Lancaster University (UK)
Alain Polguère, Université de Lorraine (France)
Alexandre Rademaker, IBM Research Brazil and EMAp/FGV (Brazil)
Laurent Romary, INRIA & HUB-ISDL (France)
Mike Rosner, University of Malta (Malta)
Manfred Sailer, Goethe-Universität Frankfurt am Main (Germany)
Magali Sanches Duran, University of São Paulo (Brazil)
Nathan Schneider, Georgetown University (USA)
Sabine Schulte im Walde, University of Stuttgart (Germany)
Kiril Simov, Bulgarian Academy of Sciences (Bulgaria)
Ranka Stanković, University of Belgrade (Serbia)
Ivelina Stoyanova, Bulgarian Academy of Sciences (Bulgaria)
Stan Szpakowicz, University of Ottawa (Canada)
Shiva Taslimipoor, University of Wolverhampton (UK)
Arvi Tavast, Qlaara, Tallinn (Estonia)
Beata Trawinski, Institut für Deutsche Sprache Mannheim (Germany)
Zdeňka Urešová, Charles University (Czech Republic)
Ruben Urizar, University of the Basque Country (Spain)
Lonneke van der Plas, University of Malta (Malta)
Veronika Vincze, Hungarian Academy of Sciences (Hungary)
Jakub Waszczuk, University of Duesseldorf (Germany)
Eric Wehrli, University of Geneva (Switzerland)
Seid Muhie Yimam, Universität Hamburg (Germany)

Invited Speaker:

Roberto Navigli, Sapienza University of Rome

Table of Contents

Workshop Program

Sunday, December 13, 2020

14:00–14:10 *Welcoming and preparation*

14:10–14:40 *Session 1: MWE Resources and Linguistics*

CollFrEn: Rich Bilingual English–French Collocation Resource
Beatriz Fisas, Joan Codina-Filbá, Luis Espinosa Anke and Leo Wanner

Filling the ___-s in Finnish MWE lexicons
Frankie Robertson

Hierarchy-aware Learning of Sequential Tool Usage via Semi-automatically Constructed Taxonomies
Nima Nabizadeh, Martin Heckmann and Dorothea Kolossa

Scalar vs. mereological conceptualizations of the N-BY-N and NUM-BY-NUM adverbials
Lucia Vlášková and Mojmír Dočekal

14:40–14:50 *Break*

14:50–15:20 *Session 2: Verbal Multiword Expressions*

Polish corpus of verbal multiword expressions
Agata Savary and Jakub Waszczuk

AlphaMWE: Construction of Multilingual Parallel Corpora with MWE Annotations
Lifeng Han, Gareth Jones and Alan Smeaton

Annotating Verbal MWEs in Irish for the PARSEME Shared Task 1.2
Abigail Walsh, Teresa Lynn and Jennifer Foster

VMWE discovery: a comparative analysis between Literature and Twitter Corpora
Vivian Stamou, Artemis Xylogianni, Marilena Malli, Penny Takorou and Stella Markantonatou

Sunday, December 13, 2020 (continued)

15:20–15:30 *Break*

15:30–16:30 *Session 3: Invited Talk*

Generationary or: "How We Went beyond Sense Inventories and Learnedto Gloss"
Roberto Navigli

16:30–16:40 *Break*

16:40–17:10 *Session 4: Processing Multiword Expressions*

Multi-word Expressions for Abusive Speech Detection in Serbian
Ranka Stankovic, Jelena Mitrović, Danka Jokic and Cvetana Krstev

Disambiguation of Potentially Idiomatic Expressions with Contextual Embeddings
Murathan Kurfalı and Robert Östling

Comparing word2vec and GloVe for Automatic Measurement of MWE Compositionality
Thomas Pickard

Automatic detection of unexpected/erroneous collocations in learner corpus
Jen-Yu Li and Thomas Gaillat

17:10–17:20 *Break*

17:20–18:00 *Session 5: Shared Task*

Edition 1.2 of the PARSEME Shared Task on Semi-supervised Identification of Verbal Multiword Expressions
Carlos Ramisch, Agata Savary, Bruno Guillaume, Jakub Waszczuk, Marie Candito, Ashwini Vaidya, Verginica Barbu Mititelu, Archna Bhatia, Uxoa Iñurrieta, Voula Giouli, Tunga Gungor, Menghan Jiang, Timm Lichte, Chaya Liebeskind, Johanna Monti, Renata Ramisch, Sara Stymne, Abigail Walsh and Hongzhi Xu

HMSid and HMSid2 at PARSEME Shared Task 2020: Computational Corpus Linguistics and unseen-in-training MWEs
Jean-Pierre Colson

Seen2Unseen at PARSEME Shared Task 2020: All Roads do not Lead to Unseen Verb-Noun VMWEs
Caroline Pasquer, Agata Savary, Carlos Ramisch and Jean-Yves Antoine

ERMI at PARSEME Shared Task 2020: Embedding-Rich Multiword Expression Identification
Zeynep Yirmibeşoğlu and Tunga Gungor

TRAVIS at PARSEME Shared Task 2020: How good is (m)BERT at seeing the unseen?
Murathan Kurfalı

MTLB-STRUCT @Parseme 2020: Capturing Unseen Multiword Expressions Using Multi-task Learning and Pre-trained Masked Language Models
Shiva Taslimipoor, Sara Bahaadini and Ekaterina Kochmar

MultiVitaminBooster and MultiVitaminRegressor at PARSEME Shared Task 2020: Combining Window- and Dependency-Based Features with Multilingual Contextualized Word Embeddings for Detecting Verbal Multiword Expressions
Sebastian Gombert and Sabine Bartsch

18:00–18:10 *Break*

18:10–19:10 *Session 6: Section reporting, panel discussion*

CollFrEn: Rich Bilingual English–French Collocation Resource

Beatriz Fisas[1], Luis Espinosa-Anke[2], Joan Codina-Filbà[1], Leo Wanner[3,1]
[1]NLP Group, Pompeu Fabra University, Barcelona
[2]School of Computer Science and Informatics, Cardiff University, UK
[3]Catalan Institute for Research and Advanced Studies (ICREA)
`firstname.lastname@upf.edu, espinosa-ankel@cardiff.ac.uk`

Abstract

Collocations in the sense of idiosyncratic lexical co-occurrences of two syntactically bound words traditionally pose a challenge to language learners and many Natural Language Processing (NLP) applications alike. Reliable ground truth (i.e., ideally manually compiled) resources are thus of high value. We present a manually compiled bilingual English–French collocation resource with 7,480 collocations in English and 6,733 in French. Each collocation is enriched with information that facilitates its downstream exploitation in NLP tasks such as machine translation, word sense disambiguation, natural language generation, relation classification, and so forth. Our proposed enrichment covers: the semantic category of the collocation (its *lexical function*), its vector space representation (for each individual word as well as their joint collocation embedding), a subcategorization pattern of both its elements, as well as their corresponding BabelNet id, and finally, indices of their occurrences in large scale reference corpora.

1   Introduction

Collocations in the sense of idiosyncratic lexical co-occurrences of two syntactically bound words are central to second language (L2) learning (Hausmann, 1984; Bahns and Eldaw, 1993; Granger, 1998; Lewis and Conzett, 2000; Nesselhauf, 2005; Alonso Ramos et al., 2010) and various NLP applications – including, e.g., word sense disambiguation (Maru et al., 2019), parsing and machine translation (Seretan, 2013), and natural language generation (Wanner and Bateman, 1990; Smadja and McKeown, 1991). However, manually compiled and semantically annotated large scale collocation datasets are scarce.[1] Even more scarce are aligned multilingual collocation resources, which are instrumental for any cross-language application. In what follows, we present a manually compiled and semantically annotated bilingual (English–French) collocation resource. In order to facilitate its uptake in different applications, we enrich the collocations in this resource with additional information: each collocation is assigned its semantic category in terms of a lexical function (Mel'čuk, 1996) and its corresponding relation embedding (Espinosa-Anke et al., 2019). The individual collocation elements are also embedded using Mikolov et al. (2013)'s skipgram algorithm. The functional head of each collocation is furthermore disambiguated against BabelNet (Navigli and Ponzetto, 2012), which facilitates the alignment between the equivalent English and French heads (as, e.g., between Eng. *charges* and Fr. *accusations* in *dismiss the charges* and *rejeter les accusations*). To allow for the consultation of the use of a collocation in context (be it for second language learning or model training), for each collocation, sentences from large scale English and French corpora in which they occur are also released.

The remainder of the paper is structured as follows. In Section 2, we provide some background on the notion of collocation, point to some of the available collocation (or, in more general terms, *multiword expression*) resources, and introduce the concept of lexical function. Section 3 outlines the types of information by which we enrich each collocation in our English and French collocation lists. Section 4

---

[1]To the best of our knowledge, the largest datasets of this kind are currently the *Lexical Systems* developed at the ATILF Laboratory for several languages `https://perso.atilf.fr/apolguere/projects/`; cf. (Polguère, 2014) for the theoretical background.

Joint Workshop on Multiword Expressions and Electronic Lexicons, pages 1–12
Barcelona, Spain (Online), December 13, 2020.

describes how the resource is organized. Section 5 finally, draws some conclusions from the presented resource and outlines several tasks that we are about to tackle in order to enhance and further enrich it.

2 Background

Despite the fact that an increasing number of works addresses the challenge of collocation extraction and classification, the diverging interpretations of the term "collocation" that underline these works call for a clear statement of what we mean by "collocation", before providing any further details on our resource. In what follows, we thus fist define the notion of "collocation" as we use it. In the following subsections we then review the available resources of multiword expressions, of which collocations are one type, and introduce the *lexical function*-based categorization in terms of which the collocations in our resource are classified.

2.1 On the notion of collocation

The interpretation of the phenomenon of collocation underlying the presented resource is that of an idiosyncratic binary word combination of two syntactically bound and semantically related lexical elements (Kilgarriff, 2006), such that the meaning of one of the elements (the *collocate*) is determined by its co-occurrence with the other element (the *base* or semantic head of the collocation). For instance, in *give [an] advice*, *take [a] walk*, or *deliver [a] speech*, the meaning of *give*, *take* and *deliver* (namely 'perform') is determined by *advice*, *walk* and *speech* respectively. Analogously, the meaning 'intense' of *heavy*, *big*, and *strong* in *heavy storm*, *big surprise* and *strong argument* is determined by *storm*, *surprise* and *storm* respectively.

In the light of the dependence of the meaning of the collocate on the base (e.g., in the collocation *hot topic hot* stands for 'relevant' or 'prominent', in the collocation *hot debate* for 'intense' and in the free combination *hot surface* for 'high temperature'), the value of semantically tagged (or disambiguated) collocation resources for human and machine has been repeatedly emphasized and taken up both in lexicography and in NLP. Collocation dictionaries, such as the Oxford Collocations Dictionary or the MacMillan Collocations Dictionary group collocations in terms of semantic categories to facilitate that language learners can easily retrieve the collocate that expresses the meaning they want to express – even if the categories are not always homogeneous. For instance, in the MacMillan Dictionary, the entries for *admiration* and *affinity* contain the categories 'have' and 'show'; in the entry for *ability*, collocates with the meaning 'have' and 'show' are grouped under the same category; in the entries *problem* and *admiration*, the categories 'cause' and 'show' are explicitly distinguished; and so on.

In computational lexicography, on the other hand, semantic categories of different granularity have been used for automatic classification of collocations; cf., e.g., Wanner et al. (2016), who use 16 categories for automatic classification of verb+noun collocations and 5 categories for the classification of adj+noun collocations; Moreno et al. (2013), who work with 5 broader categories for verb+noun collocations, or Chung-Chi et al. (2009), who also use very coarse-grained semantic categories of the type 'goodness', 'heaviness', 'measures', etc. In contrast, for instance, Wanner (2004), Wanner et al. (2006), Gelbukh and Kolesnikova (2012), and Garcia et al. (2019) use the most fine-grained semantic typology of collocations available in the field: the typology of lexical functions (LFs) developed in the context of the Explanatory Combinatorial Lexicology (ECL) (Mel'čuk, 1996). LFs have the advantage that due to their level of detail, they can be used as semantic units in semantic structures and, if needed, for particular applications they can be generalized.[2] Moreover, their cross-language consistency has been validated on a large number of language families. Following the tradition in ECL, in the resource we introduce, collocations are categorized according to their LF.

2.2 A glance at available collocation resources

Printed LF dictionaries of limited coverage are available for French (Mel'čuk *et al.*, 1984 1988 1992 1999; Mel'čuk and Polguère, 2007) and Russian (Mel'čuk and Žolkovskij, 1984). For

---

[2]As a matter of fact, the broader categories used in (Wanner et al., 2016) have been obtained by the generalization of the LF typology.

French `https://www.ortolang.fr/market/lexicons/lexical-system-fr` and Spanish `http://www.dicesp.com`, online resources are available, which can be consulted via dedicated web interfaces, but not downloaded for NLP use. Experiments on enriching WordNet with LFs have been reported earlier in the literature (Wanner et al., 2004; Espinosa-Anke et al., 2016). Alonso Ramos et al. (2008) discuss the compilation of an LF-based collocation resource from the FrameNet corpus `https://framenet.icsi.berkeley.edu/`, but do not make any resource available. In the context of learning Spanish as second language, Alonso Ramos et al. (2015) facilitate web interface-based retrieval of Spanish LF instances extracted from a large newspaper corpus, but, again, without providing any collocation resource. Similarly, for English learners, a number of works discuss the extraction of (semantically unlabeled) collocations from corpora; cf., e.g., (Chang et al., 2008; Liu et al., 2009).

Semantically unlabeled collocation databases have been compiled for a number of languages using Sketch Engine[3]; cf.: `https://www.lexicalcomputing.com/language-databases-tools-solutions/collocation-databases/`.

Apart from general collocation databases, some resources are available that focus on specific types of multiword expressions, such as, e.g., phrasal verbs (Tu and Roth, 2012) or Light Verb Constructions (Tu and Roth, 2011).

To the best of our knowledge, no resources as proposed in this paper are available.

2.3 Lexical Functions

Formally, a *lexical function* (LF) can be interpreted as a function that provides, for a given lexical item (referred to as 'keyword' or 'base'), the set of its values (= 'collocates') that express the meaning of this LF. In total, about 60 "simple" LFs (including, e.g., 'perform', 'cause', 'realize', 'terminate', 'intense', and 'positive') are distinguished. Simple LFs can be combined into "complex" LFs; see (Kahane and Polguère, 2001) for the mathematical apparatus of this combination. For the sake of brevity and transparency, each LF is labeled by a Latin acronym: 'perform' ≡ "Oper(are)", 'realize' ≡ "Real(is)", 'intense' ≡ "Magn(us)", etc. Consider, for illustration, a few examples of notably frequent LFs in English. Indices indicate the subcategorization patterns of the collocate+base structures ('1': the first semantic argument of the base is realized as the grammatical subject, '2': the second semantic argument of the base is the grammatical subject, etc.).

Magn ('intense'):

Magn(*thought*) = {*deep, profound*}
Magn(*wounded*) = {*sorely, heavily*}

Oper$_1$ ('do', 'perform', 'have'):[4]

Oper$_1$(*lecture*) = {*give, deliver*}   Oper$_1$(*decision*) = {*make*}
Oper$_1$(*search*) = {*carry out, conduct, do, make*}   Oper$_1$(*idea*) = {*have*}

Real$_1$ ('realize/ do what is expected with B')[5]

Real$_1$(*temptation*) = {*succumb* [to ∼],
                          yield [to ∼]}
Real$_1$(*exam*) = {*pass*}
Real$_1$(*piano*) = {*play*}

IncepOper$_1$ ('begin to do B', 'begin to have B')

IncepOper$_1$(*fire$_N$*) = {*open*}
IncepOper$_1$(*debt*) = {*run up, incur*}

CausOper$_1$ ('do something so that B is performed/done')

CausOper$_1$(*opinion*) = *lead* [to ∼]

Note that the set of simple LFs contains *syntagmatic* and *paradigmatic* LFs. A syntagmatic LF captures a specific idiosyncratic relation between the keyword and the value such that both co-occur with each other. In other words, syntagmatic LFs are genuine collocations. Magn, Oper$_1$, Real$_1$, InceptOper$_1$

---

[3] https://www.sketchengine.eu/
[4] As already pointed out above, the index indicates the syntactic structure of the collocation. 'i' stands for a structure in which the i-th semantic actant of the base is realized as grammatical subject.
[5] Here and henceforth 'B' stands for "base" or "keyword".

and CausOper₁ cited above are typical syntagmatic LFs. A paradigmatic LF captures a specific idiosyncratic relation between the keyword and the value, such that one can substitute the other. Examples of paradigmatic LFs are Syn(onymy): **Syn**(*car*) = *automobile*, Mult(itude): **Mult**(*player*) = *team*, Gener(al): **Gener**(*car*) = *vehicle*, and others. In our resource, we currently capture only syntagmatic LFs since we are interested in collocations.

3 Composition of the collocation resource

As shown by Maru et al. (2019)'s experiments with (Espinosa-Anke et al., 2016)'s ColWordNet,[6] the mere annotation of collocational information with LF tags is already useful for word sense disambiguation. However, LF-tagged collocations can be further enriched to be even more useful for state-of-the-art NLP applications. For instance, instead of lexical items as such, it is very common to use their embeddings. Espinosa-Anke et al. (2019) have also shown that the embedded relation vectors of collocations differ from the embedded vectors of other perhaps better known semantic relations such as hypernymy or meronymy. Furthermore, the sentential contexts of the occurrences of collocations in corpora is an additional signal that can (and should) be used, even more so with the breakthrough of language models and their capacity to generate better multiword expression representations thanks to, precisely, observing their textual context. Our goal is thus to provide a bilingual collocation resource that is enriched with all of this information.

3.1 Collocation lists and corpora

The base of our collocation resource are lists of English and French collocations manually tagged with LFs as well as reference corpora for both languages.

3.1.1 Collocation Lists

We start from lists of syntagmatic lexical function instances, i.e., collocations, with the LF labels assigned to them (see Section 2.3), in English and French, retrieved manually over a number of years by I. Mel'čuk from different online sources and printed material. The English list contains in total 7,480 syntagmatic LF instances, almost evenly distributed between verb+noun (50.1%) and noun+adjective/adverbial+verb (49.9%) collocations. Among verb+noun collocations, Oper₁/₂/₃ are the most frequent (accounting for 32.9% of all captured verb+noun collocations) and among the noun+adjective/adverbial+verb collocations, Magn (accounting for 74,2% of all captured noun+adjective/adverbial+verb collocations) are the most frequent.

The French list contains 6,733 syntagmatic LF instances, with a distribution 53.6%:45.5%:0.9% between verb+noun, noun+adjective/adverbial+verb, and preposition+noun collocations. Similar to the English list, Oper₁/₂/₃ and Magn dominate (with 41% of Operᵢ and 76,7% of Magn in the respective syntactic pattern).[7] Table 1 lists the frequencies of the collocations of the 10 most frequent syntagmatic LFs (with their semantic glosses) in both English and French and their "density", i.e., the ratio between the distinct bases that appear in collocations tagged with a specific LF and the total number of distinct bases in our dataset (2,277 for English and 2,444 for French).[8]

Table 2 displays the distribution of the number of collocates across bases for both English and French LF instances in our resource.

3.1.2 Reference corpora

Reference corpora serve us, on the one hand, to obtain the collocation embedding vectors with which we enrich the collocation lists (see Subsections 3.2.2, and 3.2.3 below), and, on the other hand, as source of collocations in use: both the English and French LF instances are linked to their occurrences in such corpora. The occurrence contexts can be used for illustration of the contextualized use of a collocation in

---

[6]ColWordNet is an extended WordNet enriched with information of eight different LFs.

[7]In addition, the lists contain 2626 English paradigmatic LF instances and 2110 French paradigmatic LF instances. As pointed out above, they are not included so far in our resource; see also future work in Section 5.

[8]Note that '#' and 'ρ' are different because a single base can co-occur with different collocates with the meaning of the same LF. Real₁ and Real₂ have the same meaning, namely 'fulfil (the role) assigned by the semantic frame of the base'; only that their syntactic structure is different. Cf., Real₁(*law*) = [*to*] *enforce*, Real₂(*law*) = *abide*.

	LF gloss	English		French	
		#	ρ	#	ρ
Magn	'intense'	2,758	0.37	2,366	0.35
Oper1	'perform'	1,040	0.14	1,258	0.19
Real1	'fulfil'	316	0.04	277	0.04
AntiMagn	'weak'	304	0.04	207	0.04
IncepOper1	'begin to perform'	221	0.03	265	0.04
AntiBon	'negative'	210	0.03	228	0.03
Oper2	'undergo'	187	0.03	216	0.03
CausFunc0	'cause existence of'	150	0.02	150	0.02
Real2	'fulfil'	144	0.02	99	0.01
Bon	'positive'	137	0.02	113	0.02

Table 1: Most frequent LFs in our resource. 'ρ' stands for "density" of an LF.

#collocates	English (% bases)	French (% bases)
1	44	46.5
2	19.4	15.5
3	10.6	8.9
4	6.6	5.1
5	4.1	4.2
6–10	9.9	8.5
>10	5.5	3

Table 2: Distribution of the collocates across the different bases in the English and French LF instances lists

second language teaching contexts or in online collocation dictionaries. They can also serve as targeted training material to fine-tune language models. In other words, they allow for a more varied use of the occurrence contexts than sample sentence copies, as, e.g., in the Spanish online collocation dictionary DiCE http://www.dicesp.com/.

Not all corpora are equally suited for our purposes. For example, it is likely to expect more occurrences of collocations in general discourse than in encylopedia-like corpora such as Wikipedia. This intuition has been evaluated in the past, where two separate vector spaces were learned for bases and collocates, and showed that indeed a less constrained corpus is likely to produce better collocation representations (Rodríguez Fernández et al., 2016). Thus, we use Gigaword for the English portion of our resource, and for French the spoken language corpus ORFÉO (Benzitoun et al., 2016), the Corpus Est Républicain http://redac.univ-tlse2.fr/corpus/estRepublicain.html analyzed with Talismane (Urieli, 2013) and the newspaper corpus frWaC corpus from the Wacky corpus collection (Baroni et al., 2009). The English corpus contains about 150 million sentences, while the French corpora contain 62 million of sentences in total.

In total, 6,528 different LF instances from the English list (88% of coverage) and 5,731 different LF instances from the French one (85% of coverage) occur in these corpora. Table 3 summarizes the distribution of the occurrences across the most common 10 LFs. In the English corpus, we have found an average of 4,026 sentences for each collocation, totaling 26.6 million sentences, while in the French corpora we found 1,094 sentences for each collocation, totaling 5 million sentences.

3.2   Enriching lists of collocations

In what follows, we describe the information with which the lists of English and French LF-tagged collocations are enriched.

LF	English	French
Magn	30,0%	15,6%
Oper1	31,2%	52,5%
Real1	4,6%	6,2%
AntiMagn	2,5%	1,3%
IncepOper1	5,9%	4,16%
AntiBon	0,7%	0,5%
Oper2	4,6%	3,7%
CausFunc0	2,8%	2,9%
Real2	1,4%	2,6%
Bon	1,2%	1,1%

Table 3: The distribution of the instances of the most common 10 LFs in the reference corpora.

3.2.1 Subcategorization information

The base or the collocate of a collocation may imply idiosyncratic subcategorization restrictions, which constitute useful information. For instance, in *go [for] [a] walk* the collocate *go* requires the preposition *for*, and the base *walk* an indefinite article.[9] In our resource, the subcategorization restrictions of the collocation elements are captured; cf. a few French and English examples (the information following the following pattern: 'b(ase) | bpos | c(ollocate) | c.subcat'):

boast | ART | *feed* | –
brake | ART | *step* | *on*
habit | ART | *fall out* | *of*
hope | ART | *feed* | *of* ARG1

. . .

bataille 'battle' | ART | *se lancer*, 'launch o.s.' | *dans* 'in'
observation 'observation' | NULL | *être* 'be' | *sous* 'below'
sommeil 'sleep' | ART | *sortir*, lit. 'exit' | *de* 'from'
virus 'virus' | *le* 'the' | 'catch' | –

. . .

Such refined information may have an impact, for instance, on the treatment of function words by downstream NLP tasks, better multiword expression single-tokenization, and certainly on a more accurate collocation classification in the context of second language learning.

3.2.2 Embedding of collocation elements

Embeddings are the most common representations of lexical items in modern NLP applications. Therefore, we provide word embedding models for the vocabulary of this resource (all bases and collocates for both languages) obtained using the skip-gram algorithm (Mikolov et al., 2013).

The main idea is to enable further research in NLP and computational lexicography by providing distributional semantic models for individual collocation elements. We anticipate that this can be useful, for example, for improving word-level representations based on how well they capture their relational properties. This could be done, for example, by predicting relation (pairwise) vectors from two individual word embeddings, similarly as it was proposed by Camacho-Collados et al. (2019b).

3.2.3 Collocation relation vectors

Intuitively, a natural representation of a collocation could be the result of a vector composition operation which is applied to the word embeddings of its base and its collocate. Such a vector composition operation is typical for modeling semantic relations in the distributional semantics literature, where well-known operations are vector difference (Mikolov et al., 2013; Vylomova et al., 2015) and concatenation (Roller et al., 2014), and which have been investigated for capturing, among others, hypernymy and

---

[9]Verbal collocates and their subcategorization restrictions are often referred to as "phrasal verbs".

meronymy. More formally, let us assume w_b and w_c are the two words forming a collocation, i.e., a base and a collocate, and $\mathbf{v}_b$ and $\mathbf{v}_c$ their corresponding vector representations for some predefined word embedding model. Then, their composition can be given either by their average $\frac{\mathbf{v}_b + \mathbf{v}_c}{2}$, component-wise multiplication $\mathbf{v}_b \odot \mathbf{v}_c$, or vector difference $\mathbf{v}_b - \mathbf{v}_c$, among others.

However, it is unclear if such a composition would capture the idiosyncratic properties of collocations. For example, a conflated vector for *heavy* will not account for its different meanings if paired with different head nouns (e.g., *rain*, *metal* or *table*). More importantly, the idiosyncratic (collocational) relation between *heavy* and *rain* (as opposed to the other examples) is not captured in models based on co-ocurrence statistics, and explicit encodings seem necessary to complement the semantic properties of the individual vectors. This phenomenon is discussed by Espinosa-Anke et al. (2019), who show that representing a collocation's context in a dedicated vector space is more desirable (and leads to better results in the relation classification task) than simply operating with individual word vectors.

Based on these findings, we construct a *relation vector* model where each collocation is represented as a dedicated vector. Representing pairs of words is bound to become a popular problem in general, as joint embeddings can complement word representations and make them more powerful in downstream tasks such as lexical semantics modeling, text categorization or textual inference (Joshi et al., 2018; Camacho-Collados et al., 2019a). Our relation vector model of choice is SEVEN (Espinosa-Anke and Schockaert, 2018), where each collocation is represented as a vector $\mathbf{r}_{bc}$ condensing left, middle and right contexts of sentences in which its base and its collocate occur (also in reversed order). This is achieved by averaging their corresponding word embeddings. Specifically, given a sentence s and some context $\mathcal{C}$, we compute

$$\mathcal{C}^s_{v_b v_c} = \frac{1}{k} \sum_{r=1}^{k} \mathbf{v}_{a_r} \tag{1}$$

where a is a word appearing in a sentence in which w_b and w_c are mentioned within a predefined window and k is the number of words in that context ($\mathcal{C}$). We consider six different contexts: 'before w_b' (*pre*), 'between w_b and w_c' (*mid*), and 'after w_c' (*post*) for the occurrence $w_b + w_c$ and 'before w_c' (*pre**), 'between w_c and w_b' (*mid**), and 'after w_b' (*post**) for the reverse occurrence $w_c + w_b$. Thus, we obtain $\mathbf{r}_{bc} \in \mathbb{R}^{6d}$, where d is the dimensionality of the pre-trained word vectors. We then average $\mathcal{C}$ over the set S_{bc} of all sentences mentioning w_b and w_c:

$$\mathcal{C}_{w_b w_c} = \frac{1}{|S_{bc}|} \sum_{s \in S_{bc}} \mathcal{C}^s_{w_b w_c} \tag{2}$$

Finally, the collocation vector $\mathbf{r}_{bc}$ is given by:

$$\mathbf{r}_{bc} = \mathcal{C}^{pre}_{w_b w_c} \oplus \mathcal{C}^{mid}_{w_b w_c} \oplus \mathcal{C}^{post}_{w_b w_c} \oplus \mathcal{C}^{pre*}_{w_b w_c} \oplus \mathcal{C}^{mid*}_{w_b w_c} \oplus \mathcal{C}^{post*}_{w_b w_c} \tag{3}$$

However, simply weighted averages based on frequencies, as is the case in this model, may ignore the fact that some words contribute more to the relation. For example, in the case of **Magn** we are interested in modeling the notion of intensity, and assuming this is something that can be captured from corpora, not all co-occurring words provide this information equally. Therefore, we apply a *conditional autoencoder* that serves two purposes: (1) dimensionality reduction; and (2) purification of the relation vector, putting less weight on words relevant to the meaning of base and collocate alone, and more on those that refer to the relation[10].

Space properties and size A comprehensive assessment of the intrinsic properties of this collocational embedding space is beyond the scope of this paper. We provide, however, a piece of analysis based on exploring semantic clusters. In Table 4, we list the nearest neighbours for selected target collocation vectors in both English and French. Note that the semantic clusters that emerge group collocations of the same lexical function nearby in the space (e.g., *tragic mistake* and *terrible tragedy* are both **Magn**

---

[10]We refer to the original SeVeN publication for details of the autoencoder architecture. We used the implementation available at `https://bitbucket.org/luisespinosa/seven`.

MAGN		REAL1		QSYN	
EN	**FR**	**EN**	**FR**	**EN**	**FR**
tragic-mistake	**réputation-solide**	**follow-line**	**balle-loger**	**irritate-annoy**	**pluie-ondée**
terrible-tragedy	faible-densité	smoke-pipe	cérémonie-tenir	efficiently-expeditiously	élections-tenir
great-achievement	riche-carrière	buy-store	différence-fair	brazen-brash	sueur-suer
bad-mistake	large-victoire	eat-restaurant	victoire-donner	scorn-disdain	geste-poser
wonderful-person	forte-hausse	aim-goal	lutte-poursuivre	uncouth-rude	fumée-dégager
great-honor	lourde-responsabilité	return-save	crise-désamorcer	evergreen-deciduous	vote-faire

Table 4: Nearest neighbours in English and French for selected relation vectors belonging to three lexical functions.

collocations). However, in those cases where this regularity is not preserved, obvious word-level semantics are prevalent, which suggests that these embeddings could be effectively exploited in downstream applications where either relational or word-level semantics or both are required. In terms of space size, we encode embeddings for all collocations for which sufficient examples have been encountered in the reference corpora. These are 5,844 collocations in English and 4,156 in French.

3.2.4 BabelNet senses

The bases of the collocations in our lists are assigned their BabelNet senses (Navigli and Ponzetto, 2012). This ensures, on the one hand, the disambiguation of the bases, and, on the other hand, the alignment of the bases across the English and French collocation lists. For instance, Eng. *reception* and Fr. *accueil* are both assigned bn:00066506n, Eng. *purchase* and Fr. *achat* bn:00065265n, Eng. *death* and Fr. *mort* bn:00100948a, etc. However, not all bases have a BabelNet id; cf., e.g., *shadow* in the sense of Fr. *ombrage* or *ascendant*.[11] In this case, no cross-language linkage is currently provided. Note that the current version of our resource does not contain the BabelNet senses of the collocates either.

3.2.5 References to the occurrences in the corpora

A great number of sentences in our reference corpora contain collocations; cf. Section 4. Consider five of them for illustration (subcategorization patterns are not highlighted):

(1) Fr. **AntiMagn**: *Une mince$_{\text{Coll}}$ chance$_{\text{Base}}$ de qualification existe encore . . .*
(2) Eng. **AntiVer**: *The White House still continues its baseless$_{\text{Coll}}$ accusations$_{\text{Base}}$ against . . .*
(3) Eng. **Oper1**: *The legendary Olympia Music Hall in Paris bid$_{\text{Coll}}$ adieu$_{\text{Base}}$ to French music . . .*
(4) Fr. **Oper2**: *Il va se trouver$_{\text{Coll}}$ sous le feu$_{\text{Base}}$ de l'actualité pugilistique*
(5) Eng. **Real1**: *The plane crashed because of a problem with lowering$_{\text{Coll}}$ its landing gear$_{\text{Base}}$ or had . . .*

In order to facilitate the illustration of the use of collocations in context and also to provide more targeted material for collocation-related model training, we assign to each collocation the indices of its occurrences in the reference corpora.

4 Corpus Preparation

The development of this resource consisted of a two-step procedure: first, corpus processing and indexing; and second, collocation matching and assembling the resource in the desired output format. In the first step, we apply a syntactic parser to obtain the Part-of-Speech (PoS) tags and dependency relation information for the sentences in the corpus. Once processed, the sentences are indexed in a Solr search engine. In the second step, each collocation is searched for in the index. PoS tags and dependencies are used to retrieve the sentences in which the base and the collocate co-occur distribution-wise and are related syntactically. For this purpose, first, a query is applied to search for a specific syntactic relation between the base and the collocate (e.g., verb-object or head-modifier). This query guarantees a high precision, but could result in a low recall for some collocations due to, e.g., parsing errors or difficulty to

---

[11] For English, out of the 3065 different bases, 27 do not have a BabelNet id; for French, 262 out of 3148 bases do not have it.

L.id	b	BN.id	bpos	c	LF	st.	end	q	s	sentence fragment
EN	wrong	bn:00104880a	A	terribly	Magn	5	6	4	1	he knew something was terribly wrong .
EN	wreath	bn:00017726n	N	lay	CausFunc2	4	5	4	1	prince charles to lay wreath at graves
EN	wrath	bn:00081680n	N	incur	Oper2	5	7	4	1	the foundation has also incurred the wrath of many in the exile ...
EN	_cold feet_	bn:00020546n	N	get	IncepOper1	9	11	1	1	but in the white house , some are getting cold feet
EN	_turn out_	bn:00085376v	V	well	Bon	3	5	1	1	when things turned out well , they walked away with huge bonuses
...	...	...	...	...	...	...	...	...	...	...

Table 5: The format of the codification of the English and French corpora we release as part of CollFrEn.

determine the head of a multiword base or collocate. To increase the recall, a second query is performed searching for a sequence that combines the lemmas and POS tags of the base and collocate. If both queries do not retrieve any results, a third and fourth queries may also be applied where the conditions are further relaxed (e.g., in terms of the search for words and search for the base and collocate lexical items at a maximum distance of six tokens). It is obvious that the chance to retrieve co-occurrences that do not form a collocation increases as we relax the conditions. In order to ensure the transparency in this respect, each of the retrieved sentences indicates the most restrictive query that was used to obtain it, such that it is straightforward to retain only high precision sentences.

The English corpus is composed of 9,272,395 sentences. 83.1% of it have been obtained with the first query, 16% with the second one, and less than 1% applying more relaxed queries. The French corpus is composed of 3,474,134 sentences, with 86% being retrieved with the first query, 11.7% with the second, 2.1% with the third, and 0.1% with more relaxed queries. Further details about the format of the resulting corpora (which is the same in both English and French) can be found in Table 5.

5 Conclusions

We presented a bilingual English–French collocation resource in which the collocations are tagged with respect to lexical functions and enriched by information that is commonly used by state-of-the-art NLP applications. This information concerns, in particular, subcategorization patterns, embeddings of the collocation elements and embeddings of the collocation relations and indices of the collocation occurrences in the reference corpora. For disambiguation and interlinking of the bases in the English and French collocation lists, we use BabelNet senses.

The presented resource can be used either as an input to NLP applications or as an online collocation dictionary. In this latter interpretation it resembles the online collocation dictionary DiCE of Spanish http://www.dicesp.com/. As our resource, DiCE classifies collocations in terms of lexical functions, provides the subcategorization information of both the base and the collocate and cites examples of the use of each collocation extracted from a large scale corpus. However, while DiCE includes only some selected examples of the occurrence of each collocation, in our resource, each collocation is indexed with all of its occurrences in the corpus. Furthermore, DiCE does not contain any embedding-related information on the collocation elements or the collocational relations. The resource is available at https://github.com/TalnUPF/CollFrEn.

As part of future work, we plan to align the French and English collocation equivalents (not only the bases), completing the lists when no equivalent is available in the present list. Furthermore, we plan to automatically extend the resource using state-of-the-art collocation extraction and semantic classification techniques, also for other languages than English and French. In this context, the resources created in the PARSEME Cost Action https://typo.uni-konstanz.de/parseme/ will be also explored.

Acknowledgements

Many thanks to Igor Mel'čuk for making the original lists of the English and French LF instances available to us. We would also like to thank the three anonymous reviewers whose comments helped to significantly improve the paper. This work has been supported by the European Commission in the context of its H2020 Program under the contract numbers 870930-RIA, 825079-STARTS, and 779962-RIA.

References

Margarita Alonso Ramos, Owen Rambow, and Leo Wanner. 2008. Using semantically annotated corpora to build collocation resources. In *Proceedings of LREC*, pages 1154–1158, Marrakesh, Morocco.

Margarita Alonso Ramos, Leo Wanner, Orsolya Vincze, Gerard Casamayor, Nancy Vázquez, Estela Mosqueira, and Sabela Prieto. 2010. Towards a Motivated Annotation Schema of Collocation Errors in Learner Corpora. In *Proceedings of the 7th International Conference on Language Resources and Evaluation (LREC)*, pages 3209–3214, La Valetta, Malta.

Margarita Alonso Ramos, Roberto Carlini, Joan Codina-Filbà, Ana Orol, Orsolya Vincze, and Leo Wanner. 2015. Towards a learner need-oriented second language writing assistant. In *Proceedings of the European Conference on Computer Assisted Language Learning (CALL)*, Padova, Italy.

J. Bahns and M. Eldaw. 1993. Should we teach EFL students collocations? *System*, 21(1):101–114.

M. Baroni, S. Bernardini, A. Ferraresi, and E. Zanchetta. 2009. The WaCky Wide Web: A Collection of Very Large Linguistically Processed Web-Crawled Corpora. *Language Resources and Evaluation*, 43(3):209–226.

Christophe Benzitoun, Jeanne-Marie Debaisieux, and Henri-José Deulofeu. 2016. Le projet ORFÉO : un corpus d'étude pour le français contemporain. *Corpus*, 15.

Jose Camacho-Collados, Luis Espinosa-Anke, Shoaib Jameel, and Steven Schockaert. 2019a. A latent variable model for learning distributional relation vectors. In *International Joint Conferences on Artificial Intelligence*.

Jose Camacho-Collados, Luis Espinosa Anke, and Steven Schockaert. 2019b. Relational word embeddings. In *Proceedings of the 57th Annual Meeting of the Association for Computational Linguistics*, pages 3286–3296, Florence, Italy, July. Association for Computational Linguistics.

Y.C. Chang, J.S. Chang, H.J. Chen, and H.C. Liou. 2008. An Automatic Collocation Writing Assistant for Taiwanese EFL learners. A case of Corpus Based NLP Technology. *Computer Assisted Language Learning*, 21(3):283–299.

H. Chung-Chi, T. Chiung-hui, K.H. Kao, and J.S. Chang. 2009. A thesaurus-based semantic classification of english collocations. *Computational Linguistics and Chinese Language Processing*, 14(3):257–280.

Luis Espinosa-Anke and Steven Schockaert. 2018. Seven: Augmenting word embeddings with unsupervised relation vectors. In *Proceedings of the 27th International Conference on Computational Linguistics*, pages 2653–2665.

Luis Espinosa-Anke, José Camacho-Collados, Sara Rodríguez-Fernández, Horacio Saggion, and Leo Wanner. 2016. Extending wordnet with fine-grained collocational information via supervised distributional learning. In *Proceedings of COLING*, pages 3422–3432. ACL.

Luis Espinosa-Anke, Steven Schockaert, and Leo Wanner. 2019. Collocation classification with unsupervised relation vectors. In *Proceedings of the 57th Annual Meeting of the Association for Computational Linguistics*, pages 5765–5772.

M. Garcia, M. Garcia-Salido, S. Sotelo, E. Mosqueira, and M. Alonso-Ramos. 2019. Pay attention when you pay the bills. a multilingual corpus with dependency-based and semantic annotation of collocations. In *Proceedings of the 57th Annual Meeting of the Association for Computational Linguistics*, pages 4012–4019, Florence, Italy.

A. Gelbukh and O. Kolesnikova. 2012. *Semantic Analysis of Verbal Collocations with Lexical Functions*. Springer, Heidelberg.

Sylviane Granger. 1998. Prefabricated patterns in advanced EFL writing: Collocations and Formulae. In A. Cowie, editor, *Phraseology: Theory, Analysis and Applications*, pages 145–160. Oxford University Press, Oxford.

F.-J. Hausmann. 1984. Wortschatzlernen ist Kollokationslernen. Zum Lehren und Lernen französischer Wortwendungen. *Praxis des neusprachlichen Unterrichts*, 31(1):395–406.

Mandar Joshi, Eunsol Choi, Omer Levy, Daniel S Weld, and Luke Zettlemoyer. 2018. pair2vec: Compositional word-pair embeddings for cross-sentence inference. *arXiv preprint arXiv:1810.08854*.

S. Kahane and A. Polguère. 2001. Formal foundation of lexical functions. In *Proceedings of the ACL '01 Workshop COLLOCATION: Computational Extraction, Analysis and Exploitation*, Toulouse, France.

A. Kilgarriff. 2006. Collocationality (and how to measure it). In *Proceedings of the Euralex Conference*, pages 997 1004, Turin, Italy. Springer-Verlag.

Michael Lewis and Jane Conzett. 2000. *Teaching Collocation. Further Developments in the Lexical Approach.* LTP, London.

A. Li-E. Liu, D. Wible, and N.-L. Tsao. 2009. Automated suggestions for miscollocations. In *Proceedings of the NAACL HLT Workshop on Innovative Use of NLP for Building Educational Applications*, pages 47–50, Boulder, CO.

Marco Maru, Federico Scozzafava, Federico Martelli, and Roberto Navigli. 2019. Syntagnet: Challenging supervised word sense disambiguation with lexical-semantic combinations. In *Proceedings of EMNLP*, pages 3525–3530. ACL.

Igor Mel'čuk and Alain Polguère. 2007. *Lexique actif du français*. De Boeck Supérieur, Brussels.

Igor Mel'čuk and Alexander Žolkovskij. 1984. *Explanatory Combinatorial Dictionary of Modern Russian.* Wiener Slawistischer Almanach, Vienna.

Igor Mel'čuk *et al.* 1984, 1988, 1992, 1999. *Dictionnaire explicatif et combinatoire du français contemporain, Volumes I–IV*. Presses de l'Université de Montréal, Montreal.

Igor Mel'čuk. 1996. Lexical functions: a tool for the description of lexical relations in a lexicon. *Lexical functions in lexicography and natural language processing*, 31:37–102.

Tomas Mikolov, Wen-tau Yih, and Geoffrey Zweig. 2013. Linguistic regularities in continuous space word representations. In *HLT-NAACL*, pages 746–751.

Pol Moreno, Gabriela Ferraro, and Leo Wanner. 2013. Can we determine the semantics of collocations without using semantics? In I. Kosem, J. Kallas, P. Gantar, S. Krek, M. Langemets, and M. Tuulik, editors, *Proceedings of the eLex 2013 conference*, Tallinn & Ljubljana. Trojina, Institute for Applied Slovene Studies & Eesti Keele Instituut.

Roberto Navigli and Simone Paolo Ponzetto. 2012. Babelnet: The automatic construction, evaluation and application of a wide-coverage multilingual semantic network. *Artificial Intelligence*, 193:217–250.

Nadja Nesselhauf. 2005. *Collocations in a Learner Corpus.* Benjamins Academic Publishers, Amsterdam.

Alain Polguère. 2014. From writing dictionaries to weaving lexical networks. *International Journal of Lexicography*, 27(4):396–418.

Sara Rodríguez Fernández, Luis Espinosa-Anke, Roberto Carlini, and Leo Wanner. 2016. Semantics-driven recognition of collocations using word embeddings. In *Proceedings of the 54th Annual Meeting of the Association for Computational Linguistics; 2016 Aug. 7-12; Berlin (Germany).[place unknown]: ACL; 2016. Vol. 2, Short Papers; p. 499-505.* ACL (Association for Computational Linguistics).

Stephen Roller, Katrin Erk, and Gemma Boleda. 2014. Inclusive yet selective: Supervised distributional hypernymy detection. In *Proceedings of COLING 2014, the 25th International Conference on Computational Linguistics: Technical Papers*, pages 1025–1036.

V. Seretan. 2013. On collocations and their interaction with parsing and translation. *Informatics*, 1(1):11–31.

F. Smadja and K.R. McKeown. 1991. Using collocations for language generation. *Computational Intelligence*, 7(4):229–239.

Yuancheng Tu and Dan Roth. 2011. Learning English light verb constructions: Contextual or statistical. In *Proceedings of the Workshop on Multiword Expressions: From Parsing and Generation to the Real World*, pages 31–39. Association for Computational Linguistics.

Yuancheng Tu and Dan Roth. 2012. Sorting out the most confusing english phrasal verbs. In **SEM 2012: The First Joint Conference on Lexical and Computational Semantics – Volume 1: Proceedings of the main conference and the shared task, and Volume 2: Proceedings of the Sixth International Workshop on Semantic Evaluation (SemEval 2012)*, pages 65–69. Association for Computational Linguistics.

Assaf Urieli. 2013. *Robust French syntax analysis: reconciling statistical methods and linguistic knowledge in the Talismane toolkit*. Ph.D. thesis, Université de Toulouse II le Mirail.

Ekaterina Vylomova, Laura Rimell, Trevor Cohn, and Timothy Baldwin. 2015. Take and took, gaggle and goose, book and read: Evaluating the utility of vector differences for lexical relation learning. *arXiv preprint arXiv:1509.01692*.

Leo Wanner and John Bateman. 1990. A collocational based approach to salience-sensitive lexical selection. In *Proceedings of the Fifth International Workshop on Natural Language Generation*, Dawson, PA.

Leo Wanner, Margarita Alonso Ramos, and Antonia Martí. 2004. Enriching the Eurowordnet by Collocations. In *Proceedings of LREC*, Lisbon. ELDA.

Leo Wanner, Bernd Bohnet, and Mark Giereth. 2006. Making sense of collocations. *Computer Speech and Language*, 20(4):609–624.

Leo Wanner, Gabriela Ferraro, and Pol Moreno. 2016. Towards distributional semantics-based classification of collocations for collocation dictionaries. *International Journal of Lexicography, doi:10.1093/ijl/ecw002*.

Leo Wanner. 2004. Towards automatic fine-grained semantic classification of verb-noun collocations. *Natural Language Engineering Journal*, 10(2):95–143.

Filling the ___-s in Finnish MWE lexicons

Frankie Robertson
University of Jyväskylä
frankie@robertson.name

Abstract

This paper describes the automatic construction of FinnMWE: a lexicon of Finnish Multi-Word Expressions (MWEs). In focus here are syntactic frames: verbal constructions with arguments in a particular morphological form. The verbal frames are automatically extracted from FinnWordNet and English Wiktionary. The resulting lexicon interoperates with dependency tree searching software so that instances can be quickly found within dependency treebanks. The extraction and enrichment process is explained in detail. The resulting resource is evaluated in terms of its coverage of different types of MWEs. It is also compared with and evaluated against Finnish PropBank.

1   Introduction

This paper describes the automatic construction of a lexicon of Finnish Multi-Word Expressions (MWEs) derived from data in English Wiktionary[1] and FinnWordNet (Lindén and Carlson, 2010). A specific issue which is pronounced in — but by no means unique to — Finnish is is that of government. Consider the following examples:

(1) a. *Minä pidä-n   kaku-sta*
     I   hold-1SG cake-ELA

   'I like cake'

  b. *Minä rakasta-n kakku-a*
     I   love-1SG   cake-PAR

   'I love cake'

  c. *Minä pidä-n   kaku-n*
     I   hold-1SG cake-GEN

   'I keep (the) cake'

Contrasting 1a & 1b, we see that a particular verb may dictate the case of its argument. Conversely, contrasting 1a & 1c, we see that different cases of an argument can alternate with different senses of the same verb.

The perspective taken here is that such governance restrictions can be treated as simply another type of multiword. One justification for this approach is to consider an English transliteration of 1a where the elative case ending is translated using the preposition "from", i.e. the literal "I hold from cake". If we consider a hypothetical dialect of English where this was synonymous with "I like cake", then we could conceive of "hold from" as a prepositional verbal multiword.

[1]https://en.wiktionary.org/

Joint Workshop on Multiword Expressions and Electronic Lexicons, pages 13–21
Barcelona, Spain (Online), December 13, 2020.

These types of multiwords can be presented to humans in multiple ways, for example "pitää ___-sta" (to like), given just there in the author's preferred form of a gapped multiword, would commonly be presented in one of two other forms in a typical dictionary of Finnish. The first is as part of a headwords, where gaps would instead be rendered with an inflected pronoun e.g. "pitää jostakin", (jostakin = something-ELA). Alternatively, the gap might be specified in a grammar notes next to a particular word sense, in which case the entry under the headword pitää corresponding to "to like" would have a note "~ + elative" where ~ indicates the headword. Given this information is already specified in dictionaries, the focus of this paper is upon extracting it, alongside other types of Finnish multiwords, and making them machine readable so as to interoperate with other resources and systems.

The type of specifications given alongside individual definitions on Wiktionary go beyond simply verb-predicate argument-case associations, and include other types of morphological valency information, as well as constituent words, syntactic valency information (e.g. transitive/intransitive), fine-grained POS information (e.g. auxiliary), and occasionally semantic valency information.

A complimentary view on these these lexical items is that they are dependency tree templates, since, excepting semantic valency information, all this information is available within a Universal Dependencies (de Marneffe et al., 2014) parse tree. This perspective makes the simplifying assumption that a verb's arguments are its descendants within a dependency tree, which is not always the case.

Beside these syntactic frames, and more straightforward multiwords, the resource also includes inflections as another form of non-lemma idiomatic construction. Of interest is whether an inflected form is given a definition. If it is, this is a reasonable indication of idiomatic usage.

2   Related work

Related to this work are verb oriented semantic valency, or predicate-argument structured, Lexical Knowledge Bases (LKBs) such as PropBank (Palmer et al., 2005) and FrameNet (Baker et al., 1998). For Finnish, in this category there are Finnish PropBank (Haverinen et al., 2015), FinnFrameNet (Lindén et al., 2017) and FinnTransFrameNet (Lindén et al., 2019). The verbal frames within these resources do not concern themselves with syntax or morphology and can to some extent be preserved across languages, and so information about language specific issues such as the case in which a nominal argument appears are only visible through corpora annotated with these schemes.

In contrast, VerbNet is a fairly language specific formalism. Its frames give a great deal of specific semantic information about verbs, and also include syntactic restrictions on the parts of speech of arguments. In the case of the Basque Verb Index (Estarrona et al., 2016), which was inspired by the VerbNet formalism, this includes case information on arguments. Outside of VerbNet inspired formalisms, but within the Uralic languages, Wiechetek (2018) created a resource for Northern Saami, with both morphological and semantic category restrictions upon arguments, allowing identification of situations when the incorrect case had been used within a grammar checking application.

The approach in this paper is novel in its selection of initial data and the extent to which it is exploited. English Wiktionary gives definitions for words from many languages in English. Focussing in on the definitions of Finnish words on English Wiktionary, it can be seen as a unidirectional Finnish-English bilingual dictionary. As such, while it is written for everyday usage by a general audience, it is directed somewhat towards second language learners. The level of grammatical detail is thus driven by this intended audience, rather than by a specific linguistic formalism. While previous work in automatic creation of LKBs from existing resources such as DBnary (Sérasset, 2015), ConceptNet (Speer et al., 2017), and BabelNet (Navigli and Ponzetto, 2012) have made heavy use of Wiktionary, for the most part, detailed information about grammatical constructions has been neglected.

3   Method

The overall pipeline of linguistic data resulting in the FinnMWE resource is shown in Figure 1. The processing is performed with Python. For accessing FinnWordNet, NLTK (Bird et al., 2009) is used, while Wiktionary data is processed from the raw MediaWiki XML dumps using mwparserfromhell[2].

---

[2]https://github.com/earwig/mwparserfromhell

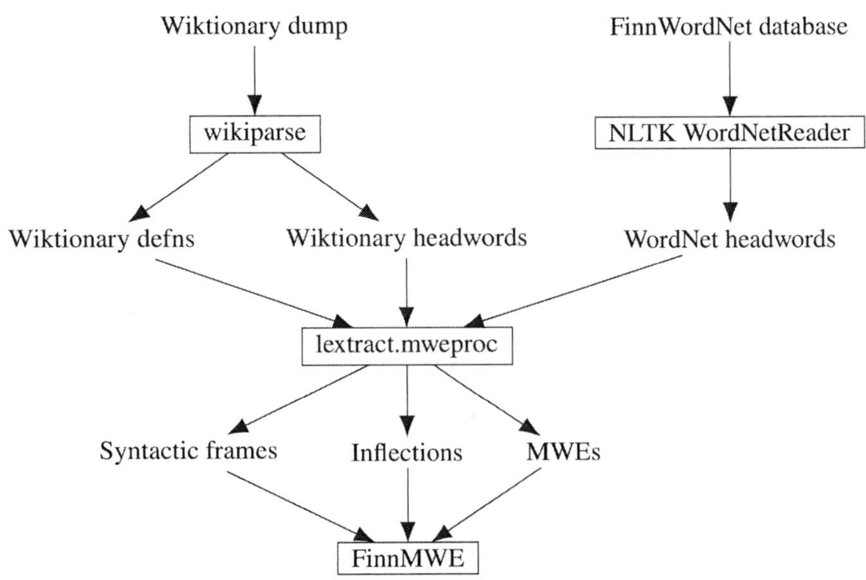

Figure 1: Diagram showing the data flow of linguistic data to create FinnMWE.

Figure 2: Pipeline to parse grammatical usage notes within Wiktionary definitions.

3.1 Sources

MWEs are obtained from two sources: FinnWordNet (Lindén and Carlson, 2010) and English language Wiktionary. Both Wiktionary and FinnWordNet contain data which can be used to create syntactic frames.

Within Wiktionary, there are multiple places MWEs can occur:

- The headword itself can be a multiword.

- The derived terms section of a page can contain MWEs expressed as headwords which are either links to other Wiktionary pages, or links which have not yet been created (known colloquially as redlinks).

- A word sense/definition entry within a page can contain a syntactic frame. On Wiktionary, the data is included within the text of a definition, for example, the headword pitää has the entry "(transitive + elative) To like, be fond of". In this case, the syntactic frame "pitää ___-sta" is extracted and associated with this definition.

    - The usage examples section can also contain MWEs, which can be extracted in a similar way to definitions.

MWEs in FinnWordNet are found only in headwords. When there is valency information in FinnWord-Net, it is marked using abbreviated forms of pronouns. For example in the headword "pitää_kiinni_jstak" (hold onto something) jstak is short for jostakin (kiinni is a postposition with jostakin as its head), allowing the syntactic frame "pitää kiinni ___-sta" to be extracted.

Extraction of syntactic frames from collocation notes in Wiktionary word senses is more involved. The rule based information extraction pipeline is outlined in Figure 2. As the first step, spans which contain grammar notes are identified. These are typically visually separated from the definition text itself, e.g. by being bracketed. The main indicator that a bracketed part may contain a grammar note is the presence of certain words e.g. a case name "elative" or a tidle ~, which indicates the position of the headword.

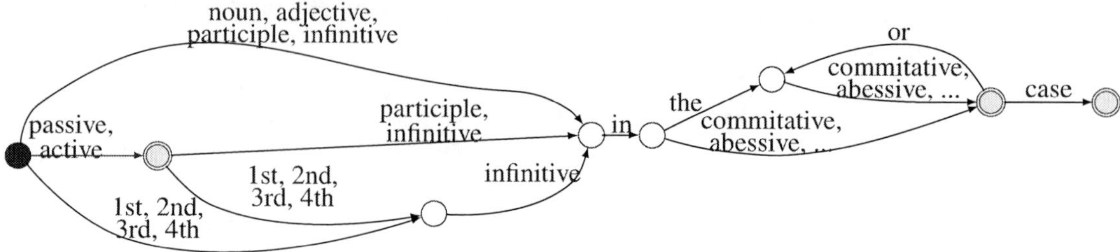

Figure 3: Fragment of a finite state automaton accepting grammar notes about Finnish nominal and nominalisation collocates. The black node is the starting state and the yellow nodes are accepting states.

Once a potential note is found, the lexing process maps surface tokens consisting of a mix of English words and MediaWiki markup to an intermediate set of normalised, type-tagged tokens. It is driven by an FST specified using the xfst language (Beesley and Karttunen, 2003) as implemented in HFST (Lindén et al., 2009). The input side of a fragment of the FST handling English language specifications of Finnish nominals and nominalised collocates is given in Figure 3.

The parsing step is implemented as a recursive descent Pratt (1973) parser. A Pratt parser extends the traditional recursive descent approach to context free parsing with a table-driven approach to operator precedence. For an example of where this is important consider the following headword-note pairs and their interpretation as bracket gapped MWEs.

yltää: intransitive + allative or illative ↔ yltää (___-lle OR ___-hin)

tulla: elative + 3rd person singular + noun/adjective in nominative or partitive **or** personal + translative

↔ (___-sta tulee (___ OR ___-ta)) OR (tulla ___-ksi)

In this case, it becomes apparent that *or* has a different precedence depending upon whether it is bold or not. The descending operator precedence order is: "/", "or", "+", "**or**", ";".

The interpretation step uses a cascade of heuristics to try and obtain MWEs from the final parse tree. The aim is to transform the tree into a state where it has a single root and consists only of plus-nodes and or-nodes, and finally to ensure that some node is marked as being the headword.

1. Merge directly adjacent (not separated by +) word features into word units.

2. Find or create a root, typically consisting of a plus-node, and abort if there is not exactly one.

3. Find all features outside the root, and merge them.

4. Ensure there is a word corresponding to the headword within each plus-node:

    (a) Features derived from certain strings such as "3rd pers. singular" and "personal" are always chosen as the headword node, even in preference to ~ (this is because sometimes ~ is misused as a generic blank).

    (b) Otherwise if there is a ~, which indicates the headword.

    (c) Otherwise if there is only one word, and it has the same part of speech as the head, assume it is the head.

    (d) Otherwise if there is any place where an empty node has been created in the parse tree, such as when there is nothing present on one side of a binary operator such as "+ elative" or "elative +" then pick one of these as the head node.

      i. If the first node in a plus-node is an empty node, pick this.

      ii. Otherwise if the last node in a plus-node is an empty node, pick this.

      iii. Otherwise just pick the first empty node left to right.

(e) Otherwise insert a new node as the headword at the beginning of the plus-node.

5. Merge all the merged features outside the root with the headword.

3.2 Finding the head

Finding which part of the MWE is the head can be helpful for identifying it in dependency trees, since if we make the argument constituency assumption, it will be at the root of the tree containing its arguments. For a Wiktionary definition or a usage example, it is clearly the case that the head is the same as the head of the title of the Wiktionary page. For a MWE Wiktionary headword, the head is sometimes explicitly specified in the etymology section, e.g. it may be formatted bold. Failing this, if the MWE occurs within the derived terms section of another page, we can assume that the head of the title of this page is its head.

For the remaining title derived Wiktionary definitions, the head must be guessed. This is, however, always necessary for FinnWordNet. In both cases, the guessing is done with the same procedure, based on the head and the MWE having the same part of speech, shown in detail in Algorithm 1.

Function FIND-HEAD(multi-word expression mwe from LKB lkb)
returns head h or **fails**
> $cand :=$ empty list
> **for** constituent word w in mwe **do**
>> **if** w is a surface word **then**
>>> $w_{pos} :=$ all parts of speech of w in lkb
>>> **if** $|w_{pos} \cap mwe_{pos}| > 0$ **then**
>>>> push w onto $cand$
>>> **end**
>> **end**
> **end**
> **if** $|cand| = 1$ **then**
>> **return** $cand_0$
> **else**
>> **fail**
> **end**

end

Algorithm 1: The Find-Head procedure to find the head of an MWE.

3.3 Normalisation

As a normalisation step, all morphological information is converted into Universal Dependency features. For valency information, this means all information about case, infinitive, participles and so on are converted from the grammar usage note descriptions on the Wiktionary pages or the case abbreviation in a FinnWordNet headword into features on the consistent word. For part of speech tags, this means conversion from Wiktionary and WordNet part of speech to Universal Dependencies part of speech.

3.4 Storage, formatting and identification within text

Next, the normalised MWEs are saved as an SQLite database as an intermediate format for downstream applications. There are a series of formatters which directly make use of the collection of MWEs. The human readable formatters produce either a gapped MWE or one using pronoun abbreviations such as jstk. as in many Finnish dictionaries. In both cases, this is done by mapping from Universal Dependency features to normalised surface morphemes.

Another formatter exists for the purposes of creating search queries for SETS dependency tree search engine (Luotolahti et al., 2015). Since this is also based on universal dependencies, the mapping is mostly straightforward. However, one minor obstacle is Finnish's marginal accusative case. In Finnish this case only has a unique realisation for pronouns e.g. minä $\rightarrow$ minut, for other words it is realised as genitive e.g. kakku $\rightarrow$ kakun. This means that within corpora, the accusative is only annotated for

	Number	Proportion
Total multiwords	218 807	
...of which are syntactic frames within Wiktionary definitions	7726	3.5 %
...of which are extracted from Wiktionary titles	97 007	44.3 %
...of which are inflections	93 173	96.0 %
...of which are from a page without definitions	62 283	66.8 %
...of which are from a page with definitions	30 890	33.2 %
...of which are multiwords	3834	4.0 %
...of which are are a redlink	183	4.8 %
...of which are have a Wiktionary page	3651	95.2 %
...of which are extracted from FinnWordNet titles	114 074	52.1 %
...of which are syntactic frames	348	0.3 %
...of which are inflections	56 068	49.2 %
...of which are multiwords	57 658	50.5 %

Table 1: Table summarising contents of FinnMWE.

pronouns. Thus we map the accusative case within MWEs to the SETS dependency search language string `(PRON&Case=Acc)|(!PRON&Case=Gen)`, that is to say either a pronoun in the accusative, or something other than a pronoun in the genitive.

The FinnMWE toolkit also contains tools for extracting matches in morphologically analysed text by assuming they are contiguous or directly from Universal Dependencies trees without requiring an indexing step.

4 Evaluation

Table 1 gives basic information about the number of different types of multiwords in FinnMWE. The breakdown shows specifically how many Wiktionary inflections contain sense data, indicating they may be some kind of idiomatic usage, as well as how many multiwords come from redlinks, indicating they can only be found in the derived terms area.

Table 2 shows the results of comparing syntactic Wiktionary derived frames and semantic Finnish PropBank frames in its accompanying corpus. Since for a given hit for a headword, multiple MWEs can match, we use the powerset construction to make a discrete probability distribution of independent events. This distribution is compared against the distribution of PropBank frames found in the PropBank corpus using the entropy (in bits), mutual information and normalised mutual information (equivalent to the V-measure) defined as:

$$H(X) = -\sum_i p_i \log_2(p_i), \quad \text{MI}(X;Y) = \sum_{y \in \mathcal{Y}} \sum_{x \in \mathcal{X}} p_{(X,Y)}(x,y) \log_2 \left(\frac{p_{(X,Y)}(x,y)}{p_X(x)\, p_Y(y)} \right),$$

$$\text{NMI}(X;Y) = \frac{2\,\text{MI}(X;Y)}{H(X) + H(Y)}$$

For headwords with high normalised mutual information, the syntactic frame information from Wiktionary and the semantic frames of Finnish PropBank co-alternate. This means that the syntactic frames under this headword correspond to different senses according to the held-out LKB of PropBank.

5 Conclusion

This paper has introduced a large MWE and syntactic construction resource for Finnish based on FinnWordNet and English Wiktionary. The full extraction and processing pipeline is made available under the Apache v2 license at `https://github.com/frankier/wikiparse` and

Headword	Gloss	Freq	Wiktionary			PropBank		Agreement	
			Frames	Combs	Entropy	Frames	Entropy	MI	NMI
kannattaa	to support	54	3	2	0.69	2	0.68	0.61	0.88
vastata	to answer	104	6	7	1.31	3	1.06	0.93	0.79
pitää	to hold	442	18	18	1.78	14	1.72	1.09	0.62
ottaa	to take	324	3	2	0.69	21	1.94	0.49	0.38
käydä	to visit	151	11	15	1.94	18	2.10	0.72	0.36
lisätä	to add	102	2	2	0.69	4	1.13	0.30	0.33
saada	to obtain	688	11	5	0.63	11	1.40	0.31	0.30
tulla	to come	63	7	4	0.91	19	1.08	0.30	0.30
koskea	to touch	245	4	4	0.29	2	0.14	0.06	0.29
päästä	to reach	155	6	7	1.42	5	0.31	0.18	0.21
seurata	to follow	61	4	4	0.86	2	0.63	0.16	0.21
näyttää	to show	81	2	2	0.68	3	0.71	0.14	0.20
katsoa	to look	158	5	9	1.55	3	0.98	0.19	0.15
voida	to be able to	825	3	2	0.01	2	0.08	0.01	0.15
tehdä	to make/do	602	16	3	0.34	9	0.94	0.09	0.14
mennä	to come	165	4	4	0.90	11	0.97	0.07	0.08
todeta	to state	103	2	2	0.22	2	0.65	0.03	0.07
kuulua	to belong	131	2	3	0.56	3	0.17	0.02	0.06
antaa	to give	351	13	2	0.04	5	0.45	0.01	0.06
lukea	to read	86	4	2	0.11	5	1.01	0.03	0.05
päättää	to device	95	2	2	0.69	2	0.26	0.02	0.05
laskea	to calculate	96	3	2	0.06	6	1.37	0.02	0.02
istua	to sit	54	2	2	0.31	2	0.31	0.01	0.02
olla	to be	7866	33	4	0.01	25	1.45	0.00	0.00

Table 2: Table comparing distributions of syntactic frames from Wiktionary with frames from Finnish PropBank in its accompanying annotated corpus. Headwords with less than 50 results are excluded.

`https://github.com/frankier/lextract`. The final SQLite database is available to browse online, as well as to download at `https://github.com/frankier/finnmwe`.

Currently, the most fragile part of the processing pipeline is the extraction of information given within the body of Wiktionary pages, in particular the syntactic frame data. The reason is that this information is given as free text, and is only as consistent as it is by-convention, and so a Wiktionary editor could decide to introduce new conventions at any time. Therefore, one reasonable direction is to introduce more structure upstream. On more the conservative side, the current conventions on Wiktionary could be encoded into official template tags. A longer term solution would be to make sure this type of data can be encoded within the lexicographical data section of Wikidata.

Acknowledgements

Thank you to the reviewers for their valuable comments.

References

Collin F Baker, Charles J Fillmore, and John B Lowe. 1998. The berkeley framenet project. In *Proceedings of the 17th international conference on Computational linguistics-Volume 1*, pages 86–90. Association for Computational Linguistics.

Kenneth R Beesley and Lauri Karttunen. 2003. *Finite-state morphology: Xerox tools and techniques.* Center for the Study of Language and Information.

S Bird, E Loper, and E Klein. 2009. *Natural language processing with Python.* O'Reilly media.

Marie-Catherine de Marneffe, Timothy Dozat, Natalia Silveira, Katri Haverinen, Filip Ginter, Joakim Nivre, and Christopher D. Manning. 2014. Universal stanford dependencies: A cross-linguistic typology. In *LREC*.

Ainara Estarrona, Izaskun Aldezabal, Arantza Díaz de Ilarraza, and María Jesús Aranzabe. 2016. A methodology for the semiautomatic annotation of epec-rolsem, a basque corpus labeled at predicate level following the propbank-verbnet model. *Digital Scholarship in the Humanities*, 31(3):470–492.

Katri Haverinen, Jenna Kanerva, Samuel Kohonen, Anna Missilä, Stina Ojala, Timo Viljanen, Veronika Laippala, and Filip Ginter. 2015. The finnish proposition bank. *Language Resources and Evaluation*, 49(4):907–926.

Krister Lindén, Heidi Haltia, Juha Luukkonen, Antti Olavi Laine, Henri Roivainen, and Niina Väisänen. 2017. Finnfn 1.0: The finnish frame semantic database. *Nordic Journal of Linguistics*, 40:287–311.

Krister Lindén, Heidi Haltia, Antti Laine, Juha Luukkonen, Jussi Piitulainen, and Niina Väisänen. 2019. Finntransframe: translating frames in the finnframenet project. *Language Resources and Evaluation*, 53:141–171.

Krister Lindén and Lauri Carlson. 2010. Finnwordnet–finnish wordnet by translation. *LexicoNordica–Nordic Journal of Lexicography*, 17:119–140.

Krister Lindén, Miikka Silfverberg, and Tommi Pirinen. 2009. Hfst tools for morphology—an efficient open-source package for construction of morphological analyzers. In *International Workshop on Systems and Frameworks for Computational Morphology*, pages 28—47.

Juhani Luotolahti, Jenna Kanerva, Sampo Pyysalo, and Filip Ginter. 2015. Sets: Scalable and efficient tree search in dependency graphs. In *Proceedings of the 2015 Conference of the North American Chapter of the Association for Computational Linguistics: Demonstrations*, pages 51–55.

Roberto Navigli and Simone Paolo Ponzetto. 2012. Babelnet: The automatic construction, evaluation and application of a wide-coverage multilingual semantic network. *Artificial Intelligence*, 193:217–250.

Martha Palmer, Daniel Gildea, and Paul Kingsbury. 2005. The proposition bank: An annotated corpus of semantic roles. *Computational Linguistics*, 31(1):71–106.

Vaughan R Pratt. 1973. Top down operator precedence. In *Proceedings of the 1st annual ACM SIGACT-SIGPLAN symposium on Principles of programming languages*, pages 41–51.

Gilles Sérasset. 2015. Dbnary: Wiktionary as a lemon-based multilingual lexical resource in rdf. *Semantic Web*, 6(4):355–361.

Robyn Speer, Joshua Chin, and Catherine Havasi. 2017. Conceptnet 5.5: An open multilingual graph of general knowledge. In *Proceedings of the Thirty-First AAAI Conference on Artificial Intelligence*, AAAI'17, page 4444–4451. AAAI Press.

Linda Wiechetek. 2018. *When grammar can't be trusted-Valency and semantic categories in North Sámi syntactic analysis and error detection*. Ph.D. thesis, University of Tromsø.

Hierarchy-aware Learning of Sequential Tool Usage via Semi-automatically Constructed Taxonomies

Nima Nabizadeh
Institute of
Communication Acoustics,
Ruhr University Bochum,
Germany
`nima.nabizadeh`
`@rub.de`

Martin Heckmann
Aalen University of
Applied Sciences,
Honda Research
Institute Europe GmbH,
Germany
`martin.heckmann`
`@hs-aalen.de`

Dorothea Kolossa
Institute of
Communication Acoustics,
Ruhr University Bochum,
Germany
`dorothea.kolossa`
`@rub.de`

Abstract

When repairing a device, humans employ a series of tools that corresponds to the arrangement of the device components. Such sequences of tool usage can be learned from repair manuals, so that at each step, having observed the previously applied tools, a sequential model can predict the next required tool. In this paper, we improve the tool prediction performance of such methods by additionally taking the hierarchical relationships among the tools into account. To this aim, we build a taxonomy of tools with hyponymy and hypernymy relations from the data by decomposing all multi-word expressions of tool names. We then develop a sequential model that performs a binary prediction for each node in the taxonomy. The evaluation of the method on a dataset of repair manuals shows that encoding the tools with the constructed taxonomy and using a top-down beam search for decoding increases the prediction accuracy and yields an interpretable taxonomy as a potentially valuable byproduct.

1 Introduction

Humans perform various tasks that have an inherent sequential nature comprising several steps; repairing a device is one of them. An AI agent serving as a cooperative assistant in such a task should be provided with contextual knowledge about the pertinent sequence of steps. The importance of such knowledge in cooperative situations has been shown in (Salas et al., 1995; Marwell and Schmitt, 2013). An example of using sequential context knowledge in a cooperative situation is found in Whitney et al. (2016). Here, it can be seen that learning the dependencies among the ingredients in cooking recipes helps with resolving the user's request for ingredients, since the system can anticipate what may be needed next.

There have been numerous efforts to acquire task knowledge from available sources of instructional data, for instance from the web. Related work on extracting the workflow from instructional text, such as (Maeta et al., 2015; Yamakata et al., 2016), have not built a sequential model for generalizing the obtained knowledge to unseen tasks. Working on data collected from the wikiHow website as the resource, Chu et al. (2017) and Zhou et al. (2019) developed models that learn the temporal order of steps but only take one previous step into account and ignore the higher-order dependencies.

Nabizadeh et al. (2020a) compared sequence learning methods for modeling long-term dependencies among the used tools in various steps of repair tasks, showing the advantage of Recurrent Neural Network (RNN) models for this purpose. Their results revealed that the similarity among the sequence of used tools in different repair manuals makes it possible to predict the next required tool on unseen repair tasks. In their approach, each tool is represented as a distinct class, while the relationships among the related types of the tools are not considered. As a result, the input does not provide the model with any information about different types associated with a class of tool. For instance, the model has no clue that different types of screwdrivers, such as Phillips and Torx, are all screwdrivers, and that different sizes of Phillips screwdrivers belong to the same category of Phillips screwdrivers. Such information is

Joint Workshop on Multiword Expressions and Electronic Lexicons, pages 22–26
Barcelona, Spain (Online), December 13, 2020.

also missing in calculating the cross-entropy loss of the RNN. However, we posit that for instance the penalty for predicting a 4mm Nut Driver instead of a 5mm Nut Driver should be less than the penalty of predicting a hammer, instead.

This paper, therefore, extends their work by taking such missing information into account. Specifically, we develop a sequential model for predicting the tool usage in unseen repair tasks, where we encode the tools using a semi-automatically constructed taxonomy. Previous work has shown the advantage of hierarchy-aware neural networks for different tasks, such as audio event detection (Jati et al., 2019) and entity type classification (Xu and Barbosa, 2018), which both benefit from predefined hierarchies.

The tool names in repair tasks are often compound nouns, containing information about the main class of the tool and its detailed attributes. We use the arrangement of words in the tool names for building a tool taxonomy, with different types and sizes of a parent node tool arrayed as its child nodes. Applying a binary classifier for predicting each node in the taxonomy, i.e., predicting the main class of the tool and its details separately, we show the advantages of hierarchy-aware prediction model over the flat one.

2 Method

This section introduces the proposed approach for producing the tool taxonomy from data and modeling the dependencies among the used tools in the steps of the repair tasks.

2.1 Semi-automatic Construction of Tool Taxonomy

The head-modifier principle (Spärck Jones, 1983) inspired our approach for constructing a taxonomy, stating that the linear arrangement of the elements in a compound reveals the kind of information it conveys. The head of a compound, which is usually the right-most word for compound nouns in the English language, serves as the general (semantic) category to which the entire compound belongs. Other elements, i.e., modifier, distinguish this member from other members of the same category. The automatic process of constructing the taxonomy contains two main stages: 1- branching and 2- merging. In the branching stage, we split the head and the modifier of the multi-word tool names and arrange the modifiers as the child nodes of the node corresponding to the head of the compound noun. In the merging step, a constructed node with only one child is merged with its child node, making a single node for both. E.g., the node "1.5mm Hex" in Figure 1, is produced by merging the parent node "Hex" and its child node "1.5mm". The inherent structure of the tool names in the repair tasks allows us to perform the above process for more than one level. The multi-word tool names usually follow the pattern <size, type, main class>, as is the case, for example, in "t6 Torx screwdriver." However, we still needed to apply several handcrafted rules, e.g. via regular expressions, to standardize the tool names that were entered with a different pattern. For instance, "Phillips #00 screwdriver" was changed to the equivalent and normalized name "Ph00 Phillips screwdriver" to follow a unified pattern of left-branching compounds. It is worth mentioning that on the iFixit website, the instructors usually link the tools to the iFixit tool store; therefore, in most cases, different manuals use a unique name for a specific tool. In the process of constructing the taxonomy, the single-word tool names, and the heads of the multi-word tool names are grouped under the root node with the compound modifiers as the child nodes. This process is repeated for creating a taxonomy with up to three levels. Figure 1 shows the instances of the produced taxonomy, where the leaves, i.e., terminal nodes, are marked in gray. The constructed taxonomy is a non-ultrametric tree, i.e., the distance between the leaves and the root node is not the same for all leaves.

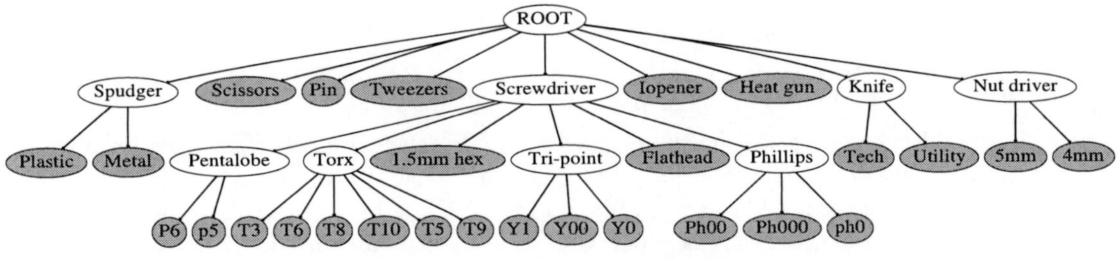

Figure 1: Instances of the tool taxonomy constructed from the MyFixit dataset

2.2 Sequential Models of Tool Usage

A repair manual can be understood as a list of steps; each step might require a different tool. Moreover, each tool is a node in the constructed taxonomy, with one or more parent nodes representing the more general categories of the tool. Let $\mathcal{O}$ denote the set of all nodes in the taxonomy except for the root node. The model is trained to predict the probability of observing each node from $\mathcal{O}$ in the following step, based on the sequence of prior, observed tools, i.e., based on the sequence of the taxonomy nodes seen in the preceding steps. We represent each node in the set $\mathcal{O}$ with a one-hot vector. A tool is then encoded by the sum of its active node vectors. The resulting multi-hot vector is later used as the input of the sequential model at each timestep. Our sequential model consists of a Long-Short-Term Memory (LSTM) (Hochreiter and Schmidhuber, 1997) layer with state size 256, followed by a Fully Connected (FC) hidden layer of the same size. The LSTM layer takes the encoded tools from the input and generates a representation of the used tools at each step. The LSTM output is fed to a fully-connected hidden layer with a hyperbolic tangent activation function while its parameters are shared among all the timesteps. The output layer has $|\mathcal{O}|$ neurons and a sigmoid activation function that estimates the probability of observing each node in $\mathcal{O}$. The model takes the multi-hot vector of the next tool as the ground truth during training. Its parameters are learned by minimizing the binary cross-entropy loss in Equation (1) using the Adam optimizer (Kingma and Ba, 2015) with a learning rate of 0.001.

$$\mathrm{H}(y, \hat{y}) = -\frac{1}{|\mathcal{O}|} \sum_{i \in \mathcal{O}} y_i \cdot \log(\hat{y}_i) + (1 - y_i) \cdot \log(1 - \hat{y}_i) \tag{1}$$

Here, $\hat{y}_i$ denotes the probability of i-th node in the model output and y_i is the corresponding target value. Figure 2 illustrates the unrolled graph of the proposed sequential model.

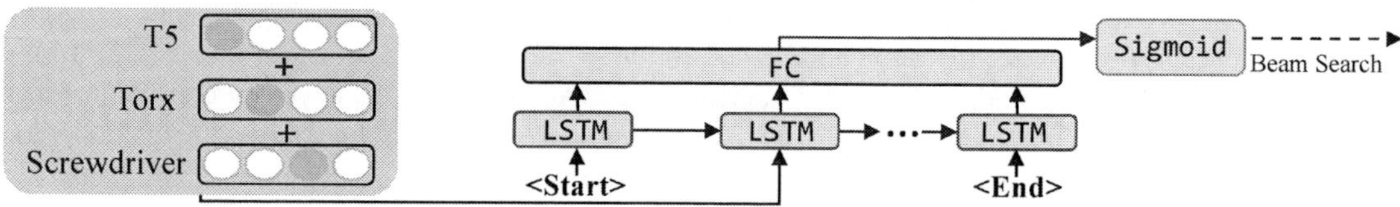

Figure 2: Proposed sequential model for learning the sequence of tools in repair tasks with an example of an encoded tool input.

2.3 Inference

To infer the required tool from the model's predicted distribution of taxonomy nodes, we used beam search, a search algorithm that generates the sequence of nodes one-by-one while keeping a fixed number of active candidates, the *beam size*, denoted by m. For each example in the test set, starting from the root node, we take m child nodes of the root node with the highest probability scores. For each node candidate, we expand it if it is not a leaf node and take its m child nodes with the highest probability. This process continues until we have expanded all the non-leaf-node candidates. Finally, the tool with the highest probability is returned as the prediction for the next step. The probability associated with a tool prediction is the average of the probabilities of its corresponding nodes in the taxonomy.

3 Experiment

3.1 Dataset Description

MyFixit is a collection of repair manuals collected by Nabizadeh et al. (2020b) from the iFixit website. The manuals are divided into several steps by the instructors, where at each step, the user should typically detach a specific component of the device under repair. Each step of the manuals in the "Mac Laptop" category is manually annotated with the required tools of the steps. In total, 1,497 manuals with 36,973 steps are annotated with the required tools. The authors also proposed an unsupervised method for the automatic annotation of tools from each step description. Their method utilizes the Jaccard similarity

Model	Annotation	Taxonomy Levels			
		1	2	3	Total
Flat	Manual	50.56 ± 2.0	83.69 ± 1.1	78.90 ± 1.3	76.30 ± 0.8 [1]
	Automatic	29.31 ± 1.6	72.08 ± 0.9	65.68 ± 1.9	62.39 ± 0.9
Hierarchy-aware	Manual	49.97 ± 1.0	86.29 ± 0.6	88.33 ± 0.5	81.78 ± 0.5
	Automatic	30.68 ± 0.9	72.87 ± 0.9	80.97 ± 1.0	70.42 ± 0.8

Table 1: Average accuracy of the tool prediction (%) with standard deviation, using the flat and hierarchy-aware model trained on automatically and manually annotated data.

between the bags of n-grams of the text description of steps and each tool name to return the tool with the highest similarity as the required tool of the step. The automatically annotated tools were reported to be correct in 94% of the steps. In addition to the sequential model trained on human-annotated data, we also evaluate the models trained on automatically annotated tools but tested on human annotations. This allows us to investigate the effect of hierarchy-aware prediction in the presence of annotation errors. Among the total steps of the annotated data, 51.8% of the used tools have three levels, 38.1% have two levels, and 10.1% have only one level in the constructed taxonomy.

3.2 Baseline Model

We compare the result of our proposed hierarchy-aware prediction to the baseline flat prediction of (Nabizadeh et al., 2020a). In this model, each tool is independently encoded with a one-hot vector, and the model is trained to reduce the cross-entropy loss between the predicted and ground-truth distribution.

3.3 Evaluation

To evaluate the proposed methodology in Section 2 we used ten folds of cross-validation; in each fold, we randomly split the data into 70% training, 20% test, and 10% development set. The development set is used for an early stopping mechanism. In our experiments, the best result is achieved with beam size 3. For the evaluation metric, we report the per-level leaves' accuracy, standard deviation, and total accuracy of the leaf nodes. The accuracy of each level is the number of correct predictions of leave nodes in a taxonomy level, divided by the total number of tools having leaf nodes at that level in the test set. Per-level leaves' accuracy can be calculated similarly for the flat predictor. The total accuracy is the count of all correct predictions divided by the size of the test set. Table 1 shows the result of our evaluation. It can be seen that the hierarchy-aware model improves the total accuracy by 5.48% for the manually annotated tools and 8.03% for the automatically extracted ones. The accuracy improvement achieved for predicting the tools with three levels in taxonomy is considerably higher than for the tools with a lower number of levels. Moreover, the hierarchy-aware model has a lower average standard deviation, and using this model helps the most for the prediction with automatically annotated data. This could be due to the fact that in the hierarchy-aware encoding of the tools, even if the annotation of the tool's detailed characteristics is wrong, the model can still be provided with correct information about the more general category of the tool. In 36.6% of the automatic annotation errors, the automatically and manually annotated tools have a common parent in the taxonomy.

4 Conclusion

In this paper, we utilize the head-modifier principle to decompose the multi-word expressions of tool names and build a taxonomy for the used tools in a dataset of repair manuals. We noted that utilizing the constructed taxonomy in sequential modeling of the used tools improves the tool prediction performance, especially when the data is annotated automatically and includes annotation errors. We imagine that hierarchy-aware modeling also helps when we have an imperfect observation of the used tools, e.g., when the model is uncertain about the size of used screwdrivers in the past. In the future, we plan to study the effect of such observation uncertainty on the prediction performance.

---

[1]Compared to (Nabizadeh et al., 2020a), we achieved a slightly higher accuracy for the flat predictor, due to the standardization of the tool names that led to a lower number of unique tools.

References

Cuong Xuan Chu, Niket Tandon, and Gerhard Weikum. 2017. Distilling task knowledge from how-to communities. In *Proceedings of the 26th International Conference on World Wide Web*, pages 805–814. ACM.

Sepp Hochreiter and Jürgen Schmidhuber. 1997. Long short-term memory. *Neural computation*, 9(8):1735–1780.

Arindam Jati, Naveen Kumar, Ruxin Chen, and Panayiotis Georgiou. 2019. Hierarchy-aware loss function on a tree structured label space for audio event detection. In *In Proceedings of IEEE International Conference on Acoustics, Speech and Signal Processing (ICASSP)*, pages 6–10. IEEE.

Diederik P. Kingma and Jimmy Ba. 2015. Adam: A method for stochastic optimization. In *3rd International Conference on Learning Representations, ICLR*.

Hirokuni Maeta, Tetsuro Sasada, and Shinsuke Mori. 2015. A framework for procedural text understanding. In *Proceedings of the 14th International Conference on Parsing Technologies, IWPT*, pages 50–60. ACL.

Gerald Marwell and David R Schmitt. 2013. *Cooperation: An experimental analysis*. Academic Press.

Nima Nabizadeh, Martin Heckmann, and Dorothea Kolossa. 2020a. Target-aware prediction of tool usage in sequential repair tasks. In *Proceedings of The Sixth International Conference on Machine Learning, Optimization, and Data Science*, pages 869–880. Springer.

Nima Nabizadeh, Dorothea Kolossa, and Martin Heckmann. 2020b. Myfixit: An annotated dataset, annotation tool, and baseline methods for information extraction from repair manuals. In *Proceedings of Twelfth International Conference on Language Resources and Evaluation*, pages 2120–2128. European Language Resources Association.

Eduardo Salas, Carolyn Prince, David P Baker, and Lisa Shrestha. 1995. Situation awareness in team performance: Implications for measurement and training. *Human factors*, 37(1):123–136.

Karen Spärck Jones. 1983. Compound noun interpretation problems. Technical report, University of Cambridge, Computer Laboratory.

David Whitney, Miles Eldon, John Oberlin, and Stefanie Tellex. 2016. Interpreting multimodal referring expressions in real time. In *Proceedings of International Conference on Robotics and Automation (ICRA)*, pages 3331–3338. IEEE.

Peng Xu and Denilson Barbosa. 2018. Neural fine-grained entity type classification with hierarchy-aware loss. *arXiv preprint arXiv:1803.03378*.

Yoko Yamakata, Shinji Imahori, Hirokuni Maeta, and Shinsuke Mori. 2016. A method for extracting major workflow composed of ingredients, tools, and actions from cooking procedural text. In *Proceedings of International Conference on Multimedia & Expo Workshops (ICMEW)*, pages 1–6. IEEE.

Yilun Zhou, Julie Shah, and Steven Schockaert. 2019. Learning household task knowledge from wikihow descriptions. In *Proceedings of the 5th Workshop on Semantic Deep Learning*, pages 50–56. ACL.

Scalar vs. mereological conceptualizations of the N-BY-N and NUM-BY-NUM adverbials

Lucia Vlášková
Masaryk University
Brno, Czech Republic
l.vlaskova@gmail.com

Mojmír Dočekal
Masaryk University
Brno, Czech Republic
docekal@phil.muni.cz

Abstract

The multiword adverbials N-BY-N and NUM-BY-NUM (as English *brick by brick* and *one by one*, respectively) are event modifiers which require temporal sequencing of the event they modify into a linearly ordered series of sub-events. Previous studies unified these two constructions under a single semantic analysis and adopted either a mereological or a scalar approach. However, based on a corpus study examining new Slavic language material and a binomial logistic regression modelling of the manually annotated data, we argue that two separate analyses are needed to account for these constructions, namely a scalar analysis for the N-BY-N construction and a mereological one for the NUM-BY-NUM construction.

1 Background

Sentences in (1) both contain constructions traditionally analyzed as adverbials consisting of multiple words. In (1-a), it is a so-called N-BY-N construction, where two identical nouns are connected by a preposition; in (1-b), a so-called NUM-BY-NUM construction, where a preposition connects two numerals. It is these multiword adverbials, their semantic analysis and a new formal description that will be the focus of this paper.

(1)   a.   The workers built the house *brick by brick*.   N-BY-N

         b.   They laid the bricks *one by one*.   NUM-BY-NUM

1.1 Previous analyses

Formal semantic descriptions of both N-BY-N and NUM-BY-NUM constructions are of the two general types: a mereological and a scalar one.

The mereological approach assumes a division of the main event into a sequence of temporally ordered sub-events, either with the help of a particular syntactic structure at the LF level (Beck and von Stechow, 2007) or by utilizing relevant θ-roles (Brasoveanu and Henderson, 2009). In result, both events and participating pluralities are simultaneously divided and linked together in a distributive manner.

On the other hand, the scalar approach developed mainly by Henderson (2013) and also Braginsky and Rothstein (2008) formalizes the contribution of the adverbial as a fixation of a scalar change. More precisely, the adverbials in question require the event to be divided into a plurality of temporally sequenced sub-events, just like the mereological accounts, but the sub-events here are distinguished by the scalar interval that sets the unit of the scalar change (the N in N-BY-N) that the theme of the main verb undergoes, without necessarily dividing the theme itself. Furthermore, Henderson (2013) ties the N-BY-N modification closely to the verbs of scalar change, that is, incremental theme verbs (*John ate the pie*), change of state verbs (*The crack widened*) and inherently directed motion verbs (*John walked to the store*), arguing for their unified scalar semantics based on the accessible N-BY-N modification.

Although sometimes differences between the N-BY-N and NUM-BY-NUM construction are acknowledged, the usual tacit assumption of both mereological and scalar approaches is that one framework is

Joint Workshop on Multiword Expressions and Electronic Lexicons, pages 27–31
Barcelona, Spain (Online), December 13, 2020.

expressive enough to describe both types of constructions. We challenge this assumption and claim that a realistic description of the N-BY-N and the NUM-BY-NUM constructions must be both mereological *and* scalar.

1.2 New data

Our empirical arguments for a new analysis come from a corpus query, manual annotation, and binomial logistic regression modelling of the tagged data.

We worked with Czech, a West Slavic language with around 13 million native speakers and rich morphology that reveals some properties obscured in English. Let us look more closely on the Czech equivalent of the previous example in (2).

(2) a. Dělníci postavili dům   cihlu   po cihle.
         workers built.PL house.MASC.A brick.FEM.A after brick.FEM.LOC
         'The workers built the house brick by brick.'   N-BY-N
     b. Ukládali cihly   jednu   za druhou.
         laid.3PL bricks.A one.FEM.A after second.FEM.INST
         'They laid the bricks one by one.'   NUM-BY-NUM

Firstly, it is important to note that there are two alternative realizations of the prepositions in either N-BY-N or NUM-BY-NUM construction: the preposition *po* "after", seen in (2-a), and the preposition *za* "after", seen in (2-b), which will be the focus of our research, although both variants behave similarly with respect to their frequency and collocations. The existence of alternative prepositions is recognized also in English where the possible candidates are: *by, after, upon, over, within* (Beck and von Stechow, 2007).

Due to relatively transparent morphology, we see that the case on the nouns and numerals is assigned by the respective preposition. Moreover, the gender agreement of the relevant expressions (nouns/numerals) is active only in the NUM-BY-NUM construction where it is guided by the corresponding noun (*bricks* in (2-b)) and applies to both numerals, hence a mix of two genders within a single construction is not grammatical.

The most noticeable distinctive property in (2-b) is the usage of different lemmas within the construction, i.e. *jeden* "one" and *druhý* "second", as opposed to English *one* repeated in both slots. In this respect, the Czech construction is similar to English *one after the other*, which is considered to be semantically closely related to the NUM-BY-NUM construction (Beck and von Stechow, 2007), but contrary to English, the Czech adverbial with the same lemma, **jeden za jedním*, is not grammatical.

2 Excerpting and modelling

In this section, we will focus on the excerpting and further handling of the data, as well as describing the process of statistical modelling.

We worked with the Czech National Corpus (Křen et al., 2015), which has approximately 120 million tokens. Firstly, all the N-BY-N and NUM-BY-NUM occurrences were extracted via CQL and regex queries[1] which resulted in 2 264 and 537 hits, respectively. An example of two such occurences is in (3). The occurrences were randomized and then a manageable number of them was selected to be annotated later. Overall, we were working with 300 NUM-BY-NUM and 600 N-BY-N constructions (the unequal number of selected constructions illustrates the unequal number of natural occurences).

(3) a. Ubíral   se blok   za blokem   dál.
         walked-on.3SG REFL block.MASC.A after block.MASC.INST farther
         'He walked on block by block.'   N-BY-N
     b. Němci   zapalovali bloky   jeden   za druhým.
         Germans lit.on.fire.PL blocks.MASC.A one.MASC.N after second.MASC.INST
         'The Germans lit the blocks on fire one by one.'   NUM-BY-NUM

---

[1]Search for N-BY-N: 1: `[tag="N.*"] [lemma="za"] 2:[tag="N.*"] & 1.lemma=2.lemma`; and for NUM-BY-NUM: `[lemma="jeden"] [lemma="za"] [lemma="druhý"]`.

The annotation was carried out manually and each sentence was judged by 4 criteria listed below, all with their respective factor names used later in the statistical model.

1. ANTECEDENT: Is there a local antecedent for the adverbial, such as *bloky* "blocks" for *jeden za druhým* "one by one" in (3-b)? (the mereological approaches decompose the local argument)

2. PREDICATETYPE: Is the predicate scalar? (scalar approaches work with the incremental degree change, δ)

3. ACCOMPLISHMENTSTATUS: Is the main verb an accomplishment? (Braginsky and Rothstein (2008) claim that the N-BY-N/NUM-BY-NUM modification is eligible only with accomplishments)

4. PLURACTIONALITYSTATUS: Is the main verb pluractional?

After the tagging, we fitted a logistic regression model[2] and a generalized linear model[3] to recognize which of the 4 factors that differentiate between the two constructions are really distinctive.

Our hypothesis was that speakers choose between using either the N-BY-N or the NUM-BY-NUM adverbial on the basis of their conceptualization of the given event. If they view the sequence of sub-events from the mereological perspective, they tend to use the NUM-BY-NUM construction. On the other hand, the N-BY-N construction is chosen for scalar perspectives.

In both logistic models, the response variable was CONSTRUCTION and the 4 criteria were the predictors (of factor type). The `lrm()` model reported outstanding discrimination: the concordance index $C = 0.902$. Table 1 displays the log odds of coefficients, standard errors, p-values and the exponentiated values of the coefficients for each predictor. The coefficients and the p-values show that only two conditions, ANTECEDENT and PREDICATETYPE, were statistically significant. The two other conditions, ACCOMPLISHMENTSTATUS and PLURACTIONALITYSTATUS do not show significant differentiation between the N-BY-N and NUM-BY-NUM construction. This is also confirmed by the 95 % confidence interval visualised in Table 2.[45]

Conditions	Coef	S.E.	*p*-value	Exp. Coefs
INTERCEPT	−1.49	0.65	0.02	0.22
ANTECEDENT=no-antecedent	3.63	0.24	< 0.0001	37.86
PREDICATETYPE=scalar	3.60	0.28	< 0.0001	36.92
ACCOMPLISHMENTSTATUS=not-accomplishment	−0.31	0.65	0.63	0.73
PLURACTIONALITYSTATUS=pluractional	−0.28	0.40	0.48	0.75

Table 1: Statistical results of the linear regression model

The two distinguishing predictors, ANTECEDENT and PREDICATETYPE, show very similar strength. Moreover, the odds of the N-BY-N vs. NUM-BY-NUM construction (the latter was the reference level) in sentences without an antecedent are approximately 38, and in sentences with scalar verbs are approximately 37, thus the odds are similar as well. This shows us that in sentences with clear antecedent and non-scalar verb, speakers strongly tend to select the NUM-BY-NUM construction, whereas in sentences with a scalar verb and without antecedent they strongly prefer the N-BY-N adverbial. The two other factors are statistically non-significant.

---

[2] We used the `lrm()` function from the R add-on package rms (Harrell Jr., 2020) and the following formula: `m.lrm ← lrm(Construction ~ Antecedent + PredicateType + AccomplishmentStatus + PluractionalityStatus, data = NzaN)`

[3] We used the `glm()` function from the R base package (R Core Team, 2013) and the following formula: `m.glm ← glm(Construction ~ Antecedent + PredicateType + AccomplishmentStatus + PluractionalityStatus, data = NzaN, family = binomial)`

[4] The values here are retrieved by the `confint(m.glm)` function. `m.glm()` resulted in similar coefficients and other values as `m.lrm`.

[5] In both Table 1 and Table 2, we report the intercept values which (as usually both in linear and logistic models) represent the expected value of the response variable CONSTRUCTION when all the predictors are at their reference levels.

Conditions	2.5 %	97.5 %
INTERCEPT	-2.75	-0.21
ANTECEDENT=no-antecedent	3.18	4.12
PREDICATETYPE=scalar	3.07	4.19
ACCOMPLISHMENTSTATUS=not-accomplishment	-1.60	0.93
PLURACTIONALITYSTATUS=pluractional	-1.05	0.49

Table 2: 95 % confidence interval of the generalized linear model

3 Analysis and discussion

In this section, we turn to the formal semantic analysis of the constructions in question, which was modified on the basis of the statistical modelling of the corpus data. We will introduce the essential pieces of instruments which can deal with the new Slavic data and by hypothesis can scale-up to analogical types of constructions and other natural languages, too.

First, we claim, unlike previous authors, that speakers of natural language differentiate between the two constructions and conceptualize linearly ordered pluralities of events either as mereological (resulting in NUM-BY-NUM preference) or as scalar (preferring the N-BY-N construction).

For mereological semantics we follow Brasoveanu and Henderson (2009) and for the NUM-BY-NUM construction in example (2-b), we propose the semantics in (4-a). The contribution of the adverbial is highlighted with the $\ulcorner \ldots \urcorner$ notation and it essentially requires: i) the sub-events e' (of the plural event e) to be temporally sequenced; ii) each sub-event (lay) to have its own patient and there to be a plurality of them; iii) each sub-event to be individuated by a particular brick.

For the scalar semantics we assume basically Henderson's (2013) scalar analysis, but we add to it an incrementality requirement formalized in (4-c). (4-b) exemplifies a scalar semantics for the N-BY-N construction, demonstrated here with (2-a), and requires: i) a plurality of events; ii) a linear order; iii) for each increase in the difference function over the θ-role ($^{\mathrm{th}}_{\delta}$) to measure exactly one brick; iv) each sub-event to be smaller than the main event; v) each event e'' in the time following any event e', to properly contain the event e' (indicated by **incr** in (4-c)).

The incrementality addition is our contribution, and we intend it as a fix for too weak truth conditions of Henderson's (2013) scalar semantics, because for Henderson, the incrementality of events is not mapped from the difference function over degrees. That means that (2-a) would be true, for example, if the house was built brick after brick without creating the whole structure. The incrementality is partially inspired by Braginsky and Rothstein (2008), but it is weaker in order to avoid their accomplishment incrementality prediction, which turns out to be empirically wrong.

(4)   a. $\exists e_{\epsilon}(\mathrm{LIE}(e) \wedge$
$\mathbf{pat}(e) = \sigma x.{}^{*}\mathrm{BRICKS}(x) \wedge$
$\ulcorner \mathbf{linear.order}(\{e' \leq e : \mathbf{atom}(e')\} \wedge$
$|\{\mathbf{pat}(e') : e' \leq e \wedge \mathbf{atom}(e')\}| > 1 \wedge$
$\forall e' \leq e(\mathbf{atom}(e') \rightarrow \mathrm{BRICK}(\mathbf{pat}(e')^{\urcorner})$

        b. $\exists e[\mathrm{BUILD}(e) \wedge$
$\mathbf{ag}(e) = x \wedge$
$\mathbf{th}(e) = \sigma x.{}^{*}\mathrm{HOUSE}(y) \wedge$
$\ulcorner |\mathbf{atoms}(e)| > 1 \wedge$
$\mathbf{linear.order}(\mathbf{atoms}(\mathbf{e})) \wedge$
$\forall e' \sqsubseteq e[\mathbf{atom}(\mathbf{e'}) \rightarrow \mathrm{BRICK}(\mathrm{BUILD}^{\mathbf{th}}_{\delta})(\mathbf{e'})) = \mathbf{1}] \wedge$
$\forall e' \sqsubset e[\mathrm{BRICK}(\mathrm{BUILD}^{\mathbf{th}}_{\delta}(e')) < \mathrm{BRICK}(\mathrm{BUILD}^{\mathbf{th}}_{\delta}(e)]] \wedge$
$\mathbf{incr}(\mathrm{BUILD}, e))^{\urcorner}]$

        c. $\mathbf{incr}(P, e) \leftrightarrow \forall e', e'' \sqsubseteq e[(P(e') \wedge P(e'') \wedge \tau(e') \prec \tau(e'')) \rightarrow e' \sqsubset e'']$

4   Summary

The aim of this paper was to show that native speakers prefer the NUM-BY-NUM construction when conceptualizing the sequence of sub-events as divided into the parts corresponding to the relevant objects, and that they choose the N-BY-N construction if they conceptualize the main event as a plurality of sub-events developing along a scalar dimension. Theoretically speaking, we propose that both mereological and scalar approaches to NUM-BY-NUM and N-BY-N are correct, but each for a different type of data. In Czech, the difference between the theories maps to the two discussed constructions. In the future, we want to investigate whether this approach can scale up to a wider range of data (such as reciprocal constructions or reduplicative event modifiers like *time after time*) discussed by Beck & von Stechow (2007). Nevertheless, the mereological approach of Beck & von Stechow (2007) yields the wrong truth conditions if applied to degree achievements and verbs of motion, as shown convincingly by Henderson (2013).

Still, the linguistic work on these adverbials is far from concluded, since several other aspects remain to be clarified. It would be worth examining, for example, what is the relationship between the alternating prepositions and whether they differ somehow in their semantic contribution to the construction. Future research could also try to answer the question whether the proposed analyses can scale up to a wider variety of cross-linguistic data.

References

Sigrid Beck and Arnim von Stechow. 2007. Pluractional adverbials. *Journal of Semantics*, 24(3):215–254.

Pavel Braginsky and Susan Rothstein. 2008. Vendlerian classes and the Russian aspectual system. *Journal of Slavic linguistics*, pages 3–55.

Adrian Brasoveanu and Robert Henderson. 2009. Varieties of distributivity: 'One by One' vs 'Each'. In *Semantics and Linguistic Theory*, volume 19, pages 55–72.

Frank E. Harrell Jr., 2020. *rms: Regression Modeling Strategies*. R package version 6.0-1. Available from https://CRAN.R-project.org/package=rms.

Robert Henderson. 2013. Quantizing scalar change. In *Semantics and Linguistic Theory*, volume 23, pages 473–492.

M. Křen, V. Cvrček, T. Čapka, A. Čermáková, M. Hnátková, L. Chlumská, T. Jelínek, D. Kováříková, V. Petkevič, P. Procházka, H. Skoumalová, M. Škrabal, P. Truneček, P. Vondřička, and A. Zasina. 2015. SYN2015: Reprezentativní korpus psané češtiny. Praha: Ústav Českého národního korpusu, FF UK.

R Core Team, 2013. *R: A Language and Environment for Statistical Computing*. R Foundation for Statistical Computing. Vienna, Austria. Available from https://www.R-project.org/.

Polish corpus of verbal multiword expressions

Agata Savary
University of Tours, LIFAT
France
`first.last@univ-tours.fr`

Jakub Waszczuk
Heinrich Heine Universität Düsseldorf
Germany
`waszczuk@phil.hhu.de`

Abstract

This paper describes a manually annotated corpus of verbal multi-word expressions in Polish. It is among the 4 biggest datasets in release 1.2 of the PARSEME multiligual corpus. We describe the data sources, as well as the annotation process and its outcomes. We also present interesting phenomena encountered during the annotation task and put forward enhancements for the PARSEME annotation guidelines.

1 Introduction

Multiword expressions (MWEs), such as ***at times***, ***red tape*** or ***take off***, are word combinations with idiosyntactic behaviour, notably non-compositional semantics. Therefore, they constitute a challenge for linguistic modelling and semantically-oriented text processing. Verbal MWEs (VMWEs), like *to **bear** sth **in mind***, are particularly challenging due to their partly regular and partly idiosyncratic morphosyntactic flexibility, and their frequent discontinuity in texts (Savary et al., 2018). These challenges are even harder in languages like Polish, with rich inflectional morphology and a relatively free word order.

In order to bring progress to MWE modelling and processing, the PARSEME initiative has been co-ordinating multilingual efforts towards annotating VMWEs in corpora and their automatic identification in texts (Ramisch et al., 2018). This paper describes the most recent version of the Polish corpus, which is the 4th biggest dataset in edition 1.2 of the PARSEME suite (Ramisch et al., 2020). We show how the basic definitions from the PARSEME methodology apply to Polish (Sec. 2), we analyse the state of the art in Polish MWE-annotated corpora (Sec. 3), we describe the construction of our corpus (Sec. 4) and its outcomes (Sec. 5). We evoke some challenging phenomena and lessons learned from manual annotation (Sec. 6) and on this basis we put forward some recommendations for enhancing the PARSEME annotation guidelines (Sec. 7). Finally, we conclude and sketch perspectives for future work (Sec. 8).

2 Verbal multiword expressions in Polish

The Polish VMWE dataset is integrated in the PARSEME corpus annotation methodology. The latter increasingly relies on (version 2 of) Universal Dependencies (UD), a *de facto* standard for morphosyntactic annotation (Nivre et al., 2020). Thus, we largely follow the definitions of both initiatives.

Firstly, we differentiate *words* (linguistically motivated units undergoing syntactic relations) from *tokens* (technical items resulting from corpus segmentation). This difference is notably visible in multiword tokens (MWTs), highly productive in some Polish verb forms like *widziałlem* 'I saw' (cf. Sec. 6).

We further understand MWEs as combinations of words which: (i) have at least two lexicalized components, i.e. components always realized by the same lexemes, (ii) display lexical, morphological, syntactic or semantic idiosyncrasies. For instance, in ***postawić*** *kogoś* ***w stan*** *gotowości* (lit. 'put sb into state of-readiness') 'to put sb on alert',[1] the object *stan* 'state' must receive a complement (here: *gotowości*

---

[1]Henceforth, the lexicalized components of MWEs are highlighted in bold, an asterisk (*) means ungrammaticality, while a dash (#) signals a substantial change in meaning with respect to the original expression.

Joint Workshop on Multiword Expressions and Electronic Lexicons, pages 32–43
Barcelona, Spain (Online), December 13, 2020.

'of-readiness'). This is idiosyncratic since such a complement is not required in non-idiomatic constructions, like *postawić miotłę w kąt* 'put the broom in the-corner'. However, this complement, even if com-
pulsory, is not lexically fixed: ***postawić** kogoś **w stan** gotowości/pogotowia/oskarżenia/upadłości/etc.*
(lit. 'to-put sb into state of-readiness/emergency/accusation/bankruptcy/etc.'). Therefore, only the words
postawić w stan count as lexicalized components.

VMWEs are MWEs whose *canonical form*, i.e. the least syntactically marked form keeping the idiomatic reading, is such that its syntactic head is a verb V and its other lexicalized components form
phrases directly dependent on V. This means that a canonical form is a weakly connected graph (i.e.
fully connected if directions of the dependencies are disregarded). Consider the example *obiektywna*
***rola**, jaką uczelnie **odgrywają** w Polsce* 'objective role which universities play in Poland'. Here, the
noun *rola* 'role' heads the verb *odgrywają* 'play' rather than vice versa. Since a construction with a relative clause is syntactically more marked than without it, we have to transform it into a canonical form,
e.g. *uczelnie **odgrywają** obiektywną **rolę** w Polsce* 'universities play an objective role in Poland'. This is
why we can consider this candidate as headed by the verb and passing the light verb construction tests.

Five out of the ten VMWE (sub)categories from the PARSEME guidelines v 1.2 are relevant to Polish:

- *Inherently reflexive verbs* (IRV) are combinations of a verb v and a reflexive clitic (RCLI) r, such
  that at least one of the non-compositionality conditions holds: (i) v never occurs without r, as
  in ***gapić się*** (lit. 'stare RCLI') 'stare'; (ii) r distinctly changes the meaning of v, like in ***stać się***
  (lit. 'stand RCLI') 'become'; (iii) r changes the subcategorization frame of v, like in ***dziwić się***
  takim reakcjom (lit. 'surprise RCLI such reactions.DAT') 'be surprised by such reactions'[2]
- *Light verb constructions* (LVCs) are combinations of a verb v and a noun n (with an optional
  preposition) in which v is semantically void or bleached, and n is a predicate, i.e. it is abstract and
  has semantic arguments. Two subcategories are defined. In an *LVC.full*, v's subject is n's semantic
  argument. For instance, in ***wezmę odwet*** 'I-will-take revenge' the (pro-dropped) subject of the verb
  ('I') is the agent of the revenge and the verb adds no meaning to the noun. In an *LVC.cause*, n is
  no semantic argument of but adds a causative meaning to v. For instance, in *Ela **podsunęła** Janowi*
  *tę **myśl*** (lit. 'Ela moved Jan this thought') 'Ela suggested this thought to Jan', Jan might have a
  thought without any intervention of Ela (i.e. she is not a semantic argument of the thought). But in
  this precise sentence, Ela is the cause of Jan's thought.
- *Verbal idioms* (VIDs) are verb phrases of various syntactic structures which contain cranberry words
  or exhibit lexical, morphological or syntactic inflexibility. For instance, in ***nosić** kogoś **na rękach***
  (lit. 'carry sb on hands') 'to give special care to sb', when the noun is inflected in number or replaced
  by a semantically related word, the idiomatic meaning is lost (#*nosić kogoś na ręku/ramionach*
  'carry sb on hand/shoulders').

Another category potentially pertaining to Polish are *inherently adpositional verbs* (IAVs), defined as
combinations of a verb v and an adposition a (i.e. a preposition in Polish), such that: (i) v never occurs
without a, as in ***polegać na** kimś* 'to rely on someone', or (ii) a significantly changes v's meaning, as in ***o***
co tu chodzi? (lit. 'about what here goes') 'what is the matter here?'. IAVs were to be experimentally and
optionally annotated in PARSEME corpora since version 1.1. In Polish, we performed this annotation
in edition 1.1 but IAVs proved too hard to distinguish from 'regular' verbal valency with the current
annotation guidelines. Therefore, we abandoned the IAV annotation in edition 1.2 of the Polish corpus.

3 Multiword expressions in Polish treebanks

In previous work on modelling and annotating Polish MWEs, lexicon, grammar and treebank construction efforts have often been closely related.

Głowińska and Przepiórkowski (2010) and Głowińska (2012) present the manual shallow syntactic
annotation of the National Corpus of Polish (NKJP).[3] The whole corpus follows multilayer annotation

---

[2]When the verb *dziwić* 'surprise' takes a regular non-reflexive object, it admits a complement in instrumental but not in
dative (*dziwiła go swoim zachowaniem/*swojemu zachowaniu* 'she-surprised him her behavior.INST/DAT').

[3]http://clip.ipipan.waw.pl/NationalCorpusOfPolish

principles. In particular the layer of syntactic groups (roughly chunks), builds upon the layer of the so-called syntactic words, which in turn builds upon the layer of tokens. The layer of syntactic words includes a number of (mostly) continuous MWEs such as multiword prepositions (*w duchu* *czegoś* 'in the spirit of sth'), adverbs (*do czysta* 'completely') or conjunctions (*a zatem* 'that is'). Those are not explicitly marked as MWEs but can be queried by looking for word nodes which point at least two token nodes.[4] All MWEs delimited in this way are decorated with their parts of speech. Verbal MWEs are not covered. NKJP is released with a shallow grammar developed for its automatic pre-annotation. Among the 1,187 grammar rules, 350 are lexicalized rules describing MWEs.

Fragments of the NKJP corpus have been transformed into the constituency treebank Składnica. On top of the previous morphosyntactic annotation described above, the constituency parser *Świgra* produced candidate trees, which were then manually disambiguated (Świdziński and Woliński, 2010). A recent version of Składnica (Woliński et al., 2018) integrates data from a valency dictionary Walenty.[5] Walenty has a rich phraseological component (Przepiórkowski et al., 2014; Hajnicz et al., 2016) and a semantic layer. On the morphosyntactic level, verbal MWEs are represented as valency frames in which some arguments are lexically fixed, e.g. *zobaczyć coś na własne oczy* (lit. 'to see sth on own eyes') 'to see sth for oneself' receives a frame with the head verb *zobaczyć* 'see', a free subject and object, and a lexicalized complement *na własne oczy* 'on own eyes'. On the semantic level, adverbial, nominal, adjectival and other MWEs can appear as lexicalized elements of verbal frames, e.g. a multiword adverb *w trupa* 'into a dead body' occurs as a possible lexicalized realization of the semantic role of manner in the verbal frame of *upić się* 'get drunk', the whole combination meaning 'to get totally drunk'. The latest dowloadable Walenty version (from 2016) contains notably over 60,000 syntactic verbal frames, 14,295 of which have lexicalized arguments, i.e. correspond to VMWEs entries. Walenty frames were integrated into the Świgra's grammar, which was then used to enhance Składnica. The latter does not seem to explicitly indicate which tree nodes correspond to lexicalized components of VMWEs from Walenty.

Such efforts of making MWE occurrences in Składnica explicit were undertaken in two Polish UD treebanks. In the Polish Dependency Bank (PDB), Wróblewska (2012) automatically converted the continuous MWEs into dependency chains using the mwe relation (pertaining to UD version 1). Later, PDB was enlarged with new texts and converted into UD version 2, with the fixed and flat dependencies marking morphologically fixed MWEs and named entities, respectively. The number of both types of labels in PDB version 2.5 is 3,850 and 5,525, respectively. Later the whole NKJP corpus[6] was enriched with dependencies, using a parser trained on PDB, and manually correcting major flaws (Wróblewska, 2020). There, the fixed and flat dependencies most probably follow the same principles as in PDB, but no statistics of these specific labels were available at the time of writing. It is also unclear if any fixed MWEs were marked except those predicted by the parser, i.e. the coverage of MWEs is unclear.

In parallel to the above treebanking efforts involving Świgra, Walenty and UD conversion, similar work was done in the Lexical Functional Grammar framework. Patejuk and Przepiórkowski (2014) developed an LFG grammar of Polish, integrated with Walenty, parsed texts stemming mainly from NKJP, and manually disambiguated them to obtain an LFG treebank. They further performed an automatic conversion of this treebank into the UD version 2 (Przepiórkowski and Patejuk, 2020), including the so-called enhanced dependencies[7] The resulting UD-LFG treebank contains 144 and 884 fixed and flat dependencies, respectively. Like in PDB, the former are limited mostly to continuous morphosyntactically fixed MWEs, and the latter to named entities, i.e. the information about verbal MWEs from Walenty is not propagated to the treebank, and nominal/adjectival MWEs are neglected.

An effort focused on explicitly marking occurrences of large classes of MWEs in Składnica was undertaken by Savary and Waszczuk (2017). They used 3 resources: (i) Walenty, (ii) the named entity annotation layer of the NKJP corpus, and (iii) SEJF, an electronic lexicon of Polish nominal, adjectival and adverbial MWEs, with 4,700 multiword lemmas, 160 inflection graphs and 88,000 automatically gener-

---

[4]Such a query will however also return multi-token words which are no MWEs, for instance analytical forms of verbs.

[5]http://zil.ipipan.waw.pl/Walenty

[6]More precisely, the manually annotated 1-million-token subcorpus of NKJP, called NKJP1M is concerned here.

[7]Enhanced dependencies enable overt marking of some relations which are implicit in the basic UD format, notably arguments which are ellipted or shared by conjuncts. A syntactic graph containing enhanced dependencies is not a tree.

ated inflected forms (Czerepowicka and Savary, 2018). These 3 resources were automatically mapped on Składnica, and the outcome was manually validated, which resulted in the SkładnicaMWE treebank with explicit marking of over 1,300 named entities, as well as 450 verbal and 400 nominal/adjectival/adverbial MWEs.[8] Differently from the previous efforts, this time, the treebank remains in its original constituency format, and information about MWEs is added to selected tree nodes as additional features, together with pointers to those lexical nodes which represent lexicalized components of the MWEs. This is in sharp contrast with the UD encoding, where dependencies indicating the MWE status potentially compete with those marking the syntactic relations. SkladnicaMWE is also the first Polish treebank with an explicit marking of verbal, nominal and adjectival MWEs. This resource would be worth extending with entries from VERBEL, a more recent grammatical e-lexicon of verbal MWEs.[9]

In the context of this state of the art, we describe the first attempt towards systematic annotation of Polish verbal MWEs in running text. We do not use any pre-annotation methods so as to avoid bias. The resulting resource is fully integrated into the PARSEME suite of multilingual treebanks annotated for verbal MWEs (Savary et al., 2018; Ramisch et al., 2018; Ramisch et al., 2020). It follows the cross-lingually unified and validated annotation guidelines and the centralized quality insurance methodology.

4 Constructing the Polish VMWE-annotated corpus

All the manual annotations of VMWEs were performed on texts coming from one of three (more or less overlapping) sources (cf. Sec. 3): (i) NKJP1M, a 1-million word manually annotated subcorpus of NKJP; (ii) PCC, Polish Coreference Corpus (Ogrodniczuk et al., 2015); (iii) PDB (cf. Sec. 3). From the first two sources we only took newspaper texts, while PDB provided a mixture of news, periodicals, literature, fiction, popular science, social media, parliamentary debates and manuals. The source corpus and the text genre of each sentence are indicated in its comment, as documented in the corpus repository.[10]

Like all corpora in the PARSEME suite v 1.2, the Polish dataset is released in the `.cupt` format,[11] an instance of the CoNLL-U Plus format[12] defined for annotations built upon UD corpora. Fig. 1 shows the first sentence of a corpus file. The first line is global to the whole corpus and gives the headings of the 11 columns. The first 10 stem from the CoNLL-U format, and the 11th contains the VMWE annotations. Here, tokens 1–2 belong to an IRV *postarać się* (lit. 'try RCLI') 'try hard', which overlaps with another IRV encompassing tokens 2–5 *się pogodzić* (lit. 'RCLI reconcile') 'make it up (with someone)'.

```
# global.columns = ID FORM LEMMA UPOS XPOS FEATS HEAD DEPREL DEPS MISC PARSEME:MWE
# text = Postaraj się z tym pogodzić.
# source_sent_id = http://hdl.handle.net/11234/1-3105 UD_Polish-PDB/pl_pdb-ud-train.conllu train-s11054
1 Postaraj   postarać  VERB   impt:sg:sec:perf       Aspect=Perf|Mood=Impl...        1 root      _ _                  1:IRV
2 się        się       PRON   part                   PronType=Prs|Reflex=Yes         1 expl:pv   _ _                  1;2:IRV
3 z          z         ADP    prep:inst:nwok         AdpType=Prep|...                4 case      _ _                  *
4 tym        to        PRON   subst:sg:inst:n:ncol   Case=Ins|Gender=Neut|...        1 obl:arg   _ _                  *
5 pogodzić   pogodzić  VERB   inf:perf               Aspect=Perf|VerbForm=Infl...    1 xcomp     _ SpaceAfter=No    2
6 .          .         PUNCT  interp                 PunctType=Peri                  1 punct     _ _                  *
```

Figure 1: First sentence of a corpus, with two overlapping VMWEs.

Henceforth, the first 10 columns of a `.cupt` file will be referred to as morphosyntactic annotation. By morphological annotation alone we mean columns 3–6 (LEMMA, UPOS, XPOS and FEATS) and by syntactic annotation alone, columns 7–8 (HEAD and DEPREL). Morphosyntactic annotation is considered compatible with UD (in version 1 or 2) if is follows the UD annotation guidelines (in the corresponding version).[13] It is further considered compatible with a certain release of UD, e.g. with UD 2.5 if, for the same sentences, it contains the same data as this release or if it is automatically generated using a parser trained on this release.

---

[8] http://zil.ipipan.waw.pl/SkładnicaMWE

[9] http://uwm.edu.pl/verbel

[10] https://gitlab.com/parseme/parseme_corpus_pl

[11] http://multiword.sourceforge.net/cupt-format

[12] https://universaldependencies.org/ext-format.html

[13] See https://universaldependencies.org/guidelines.html for version 2, and https://universaldependencies.org/docsv1/ for version 1.

The corpus in version 1.2 extends and enhances the one in version 1.1. Firstly, we annotated new texts and made the previous and the new annotations mutually consistent (Sec. 4.1). Secondly, we updated the morphosyntactic annotation to make it compatible with the UD version 2.5 (see Sec. 4.2). Finally, we provided a companion raw corpus, automatically annotated for morphosyntax (Sec. 4.3) and meant for automatic discovery of unseen VMWE.

4.1 Manual annotation

To increase the size of the manually annotated corpus, we selected new sentences from PDB. The manual annotation, based on the PARSEME guidelines v 1.2,[14] was performed by one native annotator with the PARSEME-customized online annotation platform FLAT.[15] No automatic pre-annotation had been performed, but all verbal tokens were underlined in the FLAT interface, so as to easily spot potential VMWEs. In hard cases, the decision process was supported by an NKJP concordancer,[16] Polish online dictionaries[17] and, sporadically, the valence e-dictionary Walenty (cf. Sec. 3). All the resulting manual annotations, both the new ones and those from version 1.1, were checked for consistency, by the same annotator, with a PARSEME tool (Savary et al., 2018), grouping annotated and non-annotated instances of the same lemma sets. At the same time, known errors from edition 1.1 were manually corrected. Finally, 900 sentences taken from the newly annotated texts were double-annotated by another native expert for the sake of inter-annotator agreement estimation (cf. Sec. 5). Some interesting phenomena, hard challenges and decisions taken during manual annotation are documented in Sec. 6.

4.2 Updating the morphosyntactic annotation

New VMWE annotations were performed on UD-2.5-compatible files, while the corpus in version 1.1 used an older UD tagset. Therefore, upgrades to UD 2.5 were performed for the sake of consistency.

We first split the entire dataset (excluding the part with new annotations) into three parts based on sentence origin: PDB, NKJP1M or PCC. Next, each of the three parts was processed separately, paying attention to their different characteristics. Sentences originating from PCC (which does not contain manual morphosyntactic annotations) were re-parsed with UDPipe using the latest Polish model.[18] For the NKJP1M part, with the manually annotated morphological layer, we first performed a morphological tagset conversion using conversion tables specifically (semi-automatically) compiled for the task. This was necessary because the morphological layer of NKJP1M uses a different tagset than the remaining, UD-compliant part of the dataset. After that, we used UDPipe to re-parse the NKJP1M part at the syntactic level only (dependencies are not manually annotated in NKJP1M). Finally, in PDB, all annotations result from the conversion of manual annotations in Składnica (see Sec. 3). Hence, for this part of the dataset it was only necessary to update the morphosyntactic layer of the corpus with respect to the latest version of PDB.

4.3 Companion "raw" corpus

Together with the main corpus, manually annotated for VMWEs, we prepared a large (159,115,022 sentences, 1,902,279,431 tokens) UD-2.5-compliant raw corpus automatically annotated for morphosyntax and dependencies with UDPipe.[19] The raw corpus is released in the CoNLL-U format and does not contain any VMWE annotations. It is meant to facilitate automatic discovery of unseen VMWEs, i.e. VMWEs with no occurrences in the (training) corpus. Unseen VMWEs are known to be hard to capture with purely supervised methods, due to their Zipfian distribution and the particular nature of their idiosyncrasies, which show at the level of types (sets of occurrences) rather then tokens (single occurrences) (Savary et al., 2019). Edition 1.2 of the PARSEME shared task brought unseen VMWEs into focus and raw corpora, accompanying manually annotated corpora, were released for all participating

---

[14]`https://parsemefr.lis-lab.fr/parseme-st-guidelines/1.2/`

[15]https://github.com/proycon/flat

[16]`http://www.nkjp.pl/poliqarp/`

[17]Wikisłownik (`https://pl.wiktionary.org/`, Słownik PWN (`https://sjp.pwn.pl/`), and Wielki Słownik Języka Polskiego (`https://wsjp.pl/index.php`)

[18]polish-pdb-ud-2.5-191206

[19]Using the same model as for the automatically tagged parts of the manually annotated corpus.

languages. The Polish raw corpus is based on the CoNLL 2017 shared task raw corpus[20] (Zeman et al., 2017), which we upgraded to UD-2.5 for the sake of compatibility with the main corpus.

5   Results

The resulting UD-2.5-compatible corpus, manually annotated for VMWEs, comprises 23,547 sentences, 396,140 tokens, and 7,186 manually annotated VMWEs in total. 12,187 sentences originate from PDB-UD, 9,241 from NKJP1M and 2,119 from PCC. Morphological annotation is manually performed in the first two sources[21] and automatically in the third one. Syntactic annotation is manual only in PDB. 7,426 new sentences from PDB-UD were added in edition 1.2.

While the corpus covers a rather broad spectrum of different genres (cf. Sec.4), a large majority (over 68% sentences) are newspaper texts. Double annotation performed over 900 newspaper sentences, new in edition 1.2, resulted in inter-annotator agreement (IAA) scores of $F_{\text{span}} = 77.4\%$ (F-measure between annotators), $\kappa_{\text{span}} = 73.2\%$ (agreement on the annotation span) and $\kappa_{\text{cat}} = 90.7\%$ (agreement on the VMWE category).[22] See (Savary et al., 2017) for the definitions of these three IAA measures.

Table. 1 presents the statistics of the corpus concerning the different VMWE categories as well as the fine-grained VMWE phenomena – discontinuity, one-token length and overlapping – as defined by Savary et al. (2018) – in comparison with version 1.1 of the corpus. The number of overlapping VMWE tokens decreased since version 1.1 most likely due to the removal of IAVs (annotated experimentally in version 1.1), which often co-occur with other VMWEs. Figure 2 (a) illustrates the variability of the different categories of VMWEs in the Polish corpus. We follow the PARSEME-based definition of a variant: it is a sequence of words starting from the first VMWE component and ending on the last VMWE component, including the non-lexicalized words in between. The linear regression models fitted to the numbers of different variants of various categories suggest that LVC.cause and LVC.full VMWEs are the most variable, followed by VIDs, which in turn are more variable than IRVs. Figure 2 (b) on the other hand shows the variability of VMWEs in the Polish corpus in general, in contrast with several other PARSEME 1.2 corpora. It shows that, even though morphologically rich and with relatively free word order, VMWEs in Polish are not as variable as those in Chinese or Turkish, and have a similar level of variability as VMWEs in German or Basque. Interestingly, the variant-of-traindev F-scores[23] achieved by the two best systems, in both the open and the closed track of the PARSEME shared task 1.2, are higher for Polish than for any other language. However, it can be stipulated that the variability captured by the PARSEME definition is influenced by non-related factors such as the average length of the (non-lexicalized) gap,[24] which is in particular significantly higher in the German (average gap length 2.06) than in the Polish corpus (average gap length 0.55).[25]

6   Findings from the manual annotation

This section describes selected interesting phenomena, challenging cases, as well as findings and lessons learned from the manual annotation, across all 3 versions of the Polish PARSEME corpus.

6.1   Interactions with tokens, lemmas, morphology and syntax

The PARSEME definitions and annotation methodology heavily rely on the underlying morphosyntactic annotation (Sec. 2), inherited from the source corpora or from tools, most often trained on UD treebanks.

---

[20] http://hdl.handle.net/11234/1-1989

[21] PDB-UD has priority over NKJP regarding sentences which belong to the overlap of the two corpora.

[22] All three scores improved in comparison with edition 1.1 of the corpus, where a similar IAA estimation based on 2079 sentences resulted in $F_{\text{span}} = 61.9\%$, $\kappa_{\text{span}} = 56.8\%$ and $\kappa_{\text{cat}} = 88.2\%$.

[23] According to edition 1.2 of the PARSEME shared task, the variant-of-traindev evaluation metrics is the MWE-based F-measure calculated only on those VMWEs which occur in the test corpus and: (i) are seen, i.e. their multisets of lemmas occur, as annotated VMWEs, in the training or in the development corpus, (ii) are not identical to their training/development occurrences, when the strings between the first and the last lexicalized component (including the non-lexicalized elements in between) are compared.

[24] Gap length is defined as the number of non-lexicalized elements in a VMWE's variant (Savary et al., 2018).

[25] Note also that the ratio of discontinuous VMWEs (with a gap) is higher in DE (42.74%) than in PL (28.68%).

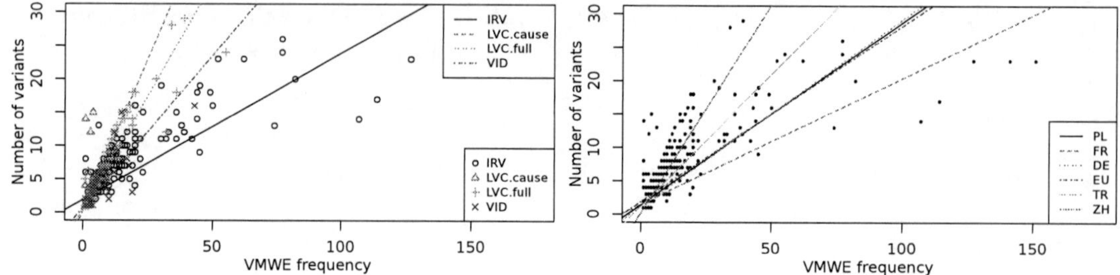

Figure 2: (a) Number of different variants per VMWE frequency for various VMWE categories in Polish, together with the corresponding linear regression fit. (b) Number of variants per VMWE frequency (only displayed for Polish) together with the corresponding linear regression fit for different languages.

The impact of these pre-existing choices on the VMWE annotation is seen in Polish in at least three cases.

Firstly, since a VMWE, by definition, contains at least two words, we have to conform to the definition of a word stemming from the pre-existing corpora. This imposes a careful annotation of some multiword tokens (MWTs). In Polish, contracting two words into one token is very productive in past tense verbal forms like *widziałem* 'I saw' or *widzieliśmy* 'we saw'.[26] According to the so-called flexemic tagset (Przepiórkowski and Woliński, 2003), such forms are regular combinations of a past participle form common for all persons of the same number and gender (*widział*.PRAET:SG:M1, *widzieli*.PRAET:PL:M1) and of a 'floating' form of the auxiliary 'to be' specific for the given person and number (*em*.SG:PRI, *śmy*.SG:PRI).[27] Therefore, while annotating a VMWE like **na własne oczy widziałem** (lit. 'on own eyes I-saw') 'I saw sth for myself', we should not include the auxiliary *em* since the same VMWE can appear without it, as in **na własne oczy widział** (lit. 'on own eyes he-saw') 'he saw sth with his own eyes'.[28]

The UD tagset does not fully standardize the annotation of some verb forms, like gerunds and participles, which share properties of nouns and adjectives. For instance, Polish gerunds stem from verbs by regular inflection but they behave like nouns (e.g. they inflect for number and case, and have gender). Therefore, in the Polish UD corpora, a gerund like *rzucanie* 'throwing.SG:NOM:N' is tagged as NOUN but receives a verbal lemma, here *rzucać* 'throw'.[29] This means that many Polish VMWEs contain no word tagged as VERB.[30] It should, therefore, be kept in mind that the guidelines apply to the canonical form instead of the actual occurrence of a VMWE candidate. Without the canonical form, examples such as **rzucanie czarów** 'casting spells' could not be considered headed by a verb.

	Nb. of categories			Fine-grained phenomena		
VID	**IRV**	**LVC**		**Discon-**	**Single-**	**Over-**
		full	cause	tinuous	token	lapping
1.2 826	3,629	2,420	311	28.68	0.0	0.87
1.1 487	2,275	1,837	246	29.76	0.0	2.92

Table 1: Statistics of the Polish corpus in version 1.2 in comparison with version 1.1.

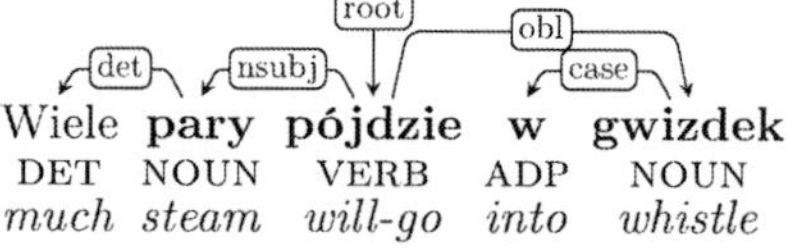

Figure 3: A VMWE with a numeral phrase.

Another phenomenon related to canonical forms shows the usefulness of the UD annotation scheme for the PARSEME methodology. A major UD principle is that dependencies hold between content words, and the latter head function words. This approach has received criticism (Osborne and Gerdes, 2019), and in Polish there is, indeed, strong evidence that many function words, such as numerals and determiners,

---

[26]A similar analysis concerns conditional forms of verbs.

[27]The Polish-specific morphological tags stemming from the NKJP corpus are documented at `http://nkjp.pl/poliqarp/help/ense2.html`.

[28]FLAT shows both the contracted and the split versions of MWTs in the annotation interface, and only the split version should be used.

[29]Similarly, all present and past participles, like *rzucająca* 'throwing.SG:NOM:F' and *rzucane* 'thrown.SG:NOM:N', receive the UPOS value of ADJ but their lemma is a verb, here *rzucać* 'throw'.

[30]The morphological features `VerbForm=Part` and `VerbForm=Vnoun` do indicate the verbal stem.

determine the grammatical forms of content verbs (Przepiórkowski and Patejuk, 2020). However, the UD assumption helps keep the PARSEME definition of a VMWE (cf. Sec. 2) relatively simple. Consider the example and its UD-style dependency tree in Fig. 3, meaning 'one's efforts will bring no result'. According to Savary et al. (2018), this form is canonical (the head verb occurs in a finite non-negated form and all its arguments are in singular and realized with no extraction).[31] Note that the numeral *wiele* 'a-lot-of' is not lexicalized. In Polish formal linguistics, e.g. in the HPSG framework (Przepiórkowski, 1999), *wiele pary* 'much steam' is seen as a numeral phrase headed by the indefinite numeral *wiele* 'much'. If this principle were not overridden by the content word primacy, the dependency arc between *wiele* 'much' and *pary* 'steam' would be inverted and the lexicalized components of this VMWE would be disconnected, conversely to PARSEME's definition of a VMWE.

6.2 IRV-specific phenomena

IRVs are, by far, the most frequent VMWE category in Polish (cf. Sec. 5). Hard cases include those verbs which are much more frequent with than without a RCLI. For instance, *delektować* 'to-delight' is found 563 times by a NKJP concordancer with a RCLI, as in **delektować się** *piwkiem* (lit. 'delight RCLI beer.INST') 'enjoy a beer', and only 3 times without it, as in *delektuje nas znakomitymi zdjęciami* 'delights us with great photos'. The latter use can easily be missed by the annotator, who then concludes that the verb never occurs without the RCLI (test IRV.1), i.e. it is an IRV, although the former use is simply a reflexive variant of the latter (IRV.6).

Another specificity of Polish (and Czech), is the so-called haplology of the RCLI (Kupść, 1999; Rosen, 2014): a single occurrence of RCLI can satisfy several requirements for this item. For instance, in the sentence from Fig. 1 two IRVs co-occur: **postarać się** (lit. 'try RCLI') 'try hard' and **pogodzić się** (lit. 'reconcile RCLI') 'reconcile' and share the RCLI.[32]

We also found that many Polish simple verbs can be simultaneously preceded by the prefix *na-* and accompanied by the RCLI, to express the fact that the given action has been performed frequently or for a long time, as in *czytał* 'he-read' → **naczytał się** 'he-has-read-a-lot', *siedziała* 'she-sat' → **nasiedziała się** 'she-has-sat-a-lot', *zamiatali* 'they-swept' → **nazamiatali się** 'they-have-swept-a-lot', etc. This phenomenon is productive, and should, intuitively, not be considered idiomatic. However, all the above examples have to be annotated as IRVs, according to the PARSEME guidelines (due to test IRV.3).

Let us also mention that the RCLI in Polish (and other Slavic languages) does not inflect for person and number, as in **boję się** 'I am afraid', **boicie się** 'you are afraid'.[33] However, it does inflect for case. Even if its accusative form *się* is predominant, the IRVs with its dative form *sobie* should not be omitted, e.g. **wyobrazić sobie** (lit. 'imagine RCLI') 'imagine', **poradzić sobie** (lit. 'advise RCLI') 'cope'.

6.3 LVC-specific phenomena

LVCs are the second most frequent VMWE type in Polish. A major challenge was to distinguish LVC.full and LVC.cause when the cause belongs to the semantic arguments of the noun. In example (1), *stwarzać* 'create' is a typical causative verb. It also occurs in several LVC.cause expressions, e.g. **stwarzać** *okazję/szansę/warunki* 'to create an occasion/chance/conditions'. Here, however, the predicative noun *zagrożenie* 'danger' requires an agent/cause, i.e. *produkty* 'products' belong to its semantic arguments. Since the test for being a semantic argument of the noun (LVC.2) is placed earlier in the decision flowchart then the one for being its cause (LVC.5), this expression has to be tagged as an LVC.full.

(1)   Produkty te   **stwarzają zagrożenie** dla zdrowia konsumenta.
     products these create   danger   for health   consumers.GEN

    'These products constitute a danger for the health of the consumers.'

---

[31]One might argue that a form omitting the determiner *wiele* 'much' is canonical instead. Recall, however, that a canonical form is to be constructed in context, while keeping the meaning of the whole expression possibly unchanged. Omitting the determiner would contradict this principle.

[32]Repeating RCLI would be ungrammatical here: **postaraj się z tym pogodzić się*. The annotators have to be careful with such cases, so as not to miss the overlapping annotation.

[33]This is in contrast e.g. with Romance languages, where the RCLI agrees for person and number with the subject of the verb, as in (FR) *je* **me trouve** 'I find myself', *vous* **vous trouvez** 'you find yourself', etc.

(2) **umożliwili**   mi **preprowadzenie badań**
     they-allowed me carrying-out   researches
     'They allowed me to carry out research.'

Another interesting, even if quantitatively minor, question is how to annotate LVCs in which the direct object of the verb is itself a light verb. In example (2), ***przeprowadzenie badań*** 'carrying-out research' is clearly an LVC.full. The other verb *umożliwili* 'allowed', has a causative meaning but one may hesitate as to the choice of its predicative noun. One natural candidate is the syntactic object *przeprowadzenie* 'carrying-out'. Since, however, it is a nominalisation of a light verb *przeprowadzić* 'carry-out', it is dubious to establish its semantic arguments (needed in tests LVC.2 and LVC.5). Another choice would be to consider ***umożliwić badania*** 'allow research' as an LVC.full but the structural tests (S.1 to S.4) require the predicative noun to be a dependent of the verb. The problem lies, truly, in not knowing how to establish the canonical form of such nested LVCs. The nominalisation needs to be converted to a finite form, e.g. ***przeprowadziłam badania*** 'I-carried-out research'. But then, the finite verb *przeprowadziłam* 'I-carried-out' can no longer be the object of *umożliwili* 'allowed'. One solution is not to annotate *umożliwili* 'allowed' at all. Another one would consist in a more elaborated definition of a canonical form, so as to yield strong reformulations, e.g. ***przeprowadziłam badania***, *oni* ***umożliwili te badania***. 'I-carried-out research, they allowed my research.'

6.4 VMWEs and peripheral phenomena

As discussed by Savary et al. (2018), the VMWE-ness has fuzzy borders with related phenomena, and we encountered them while annotating Polish texts. Firstly, VMWE are often hard to discriminate from collocations, defined by PARSEME as word combinations whose idiomaticity is of statistical nature only. Thus, word combinations like *stawiać stopnie* (lit. 'put grades') 'to-grade' or *zapuścić wąsy* 'grow a mustache', look idiomatic because the mutual lexical selection between both components is statistically strong (i.e. test VID.2 based on component replacement seems likely to be passed). Corpus searches often help to invalidate this hypothesis but doubts remain if: (i) the verb selects only a small class of nouns (*zapuścić wąsy, brodę, włosy, paznokcie* 'grow a mustache, beard, hair, nails'), (ii) it has several close senses[34] (iii) the variants stemming from lexical replacement are infrequent in corpora.

Metaphor is another challenging peripheral phenomenon, because most VMWEs are lexicalized metaphors. It seems, therefore, that the only difference between the two is the degree of lexicalization, which is however hard to establish, even with corpus studies, for the same reasons as with collocations. Particularly testing are those metaphors which are collocations at the same time. For instance, *pękać ze śmiechu* 'burst with laughter' is a frequent metaphor in NKJP. Luckily, some rare examples do reveal that *pękać* 'burst' can be used metaphorically with many emotions (*z dumy/bólu/przemęczenia/migreny/etc.* 'with pride/pain/fatigue/fatigue/etc.'). Other examples of metaphors judged as non-VMWE include: *nabrzmiewać ironią* (lit. 'swell with irony'), *omiatać (horyzont) spojrzeniem* (lit. 'sweet (the horizon) with a glance'), *znaleźć kij na prawicę* (lit. 'find a stick against the right wing'), etc.

Finally, MWEs are particular cases of grammatical constructions, i.e. conventional associations of lexical, syntactic and pragmatic features, such as *the-Adj-the-Adj* (*the more the merrier, the higher the better*, etc.). In the corpus we encountered examples of Polish constructions which are no VMWEs but contain non-lexicalized verbs, e.g. *mało nie V*, as in *mało nie zwariował* (lit. 'little not went-crazy') 'he almost went crazy', *V.INF V*, as in *rozumieć rozumiem* (lit. 'understand.INF I-understand') 'I do understand', or *nie sposób V.INF*, as in *nie sposób zapomnieć* (lit. 'not way to-forget') 'one cannot forget'.

Attending constructions led us to detecting a minor flaw in the IRV tests. Namely, examples like *bać się* (lit. 'fear RCLI') 'be-afraid' are tagged as IRVs because the verb can never appear without the RCLI (test IRV.1). There are, however, some constructions which contain a slot for any IRV, and a duplication of its verb alone, without the RCLI. Examples include: *V RCLI, oj V*, as in ***działo się***, *oj działo* (lit. 'happened RCLI, oh happened') 'there was really a lot going on' and *V.INF RCLI nie V*, as in ***bać się*** *nie bał* (lit. 'to-fear RCLI not he-feared') 'as to being afraid, he was not'. These constructions

---

[34]*Zapuścić korzenie* 'take root' might be an instance of the same or a different sense than *zapuścić wąsy* 'grow a mustache', which is or is not an evidence of lexical flexibility, respectively.

are productive and omitting the RCLI is clearly licensed by the duplication. Therefore, they should not be considered counterexamples in the IRV decision process.

7   Towards enhanced PARSEME guidelines

Several enhancements in the PARSEME annotation guidelines can be proposed based on our experience.

Firstly, nesting of VMWEs should be more accurately accounted for. Currently, the verb in an LVC is allowed to only have one lexicalized dependent (test S.2), which excludes inherently reflexive light verbs, as in *nosić się z zamiarem* (lit. 'carry RCLI with intention') 'to have an intention'. Such examples can only be annotated as VIDs, although they function like LVCs. We might therefore allow for more than one lexicalized dependent of the verb in test S.2, provided that all but one of them belong to a previously annotated VMWE. This would also allow verb-particle constructions (VPCs)[35] to be nested in IRVs, as in (DE) *er [[stellt]$_{VPC}$ sich [vor]$_{VPC}$]$_{IRV}$* (lit. 'he puts RCLI forward') 'he imagines' (now such cases are formally VIDs).

Secondly, the reciprocal uses of the RCLI listed in test IRV.8 do not accurately cover Slavic languages. The test checks if a plural or coordinated subject can be distributed over two occurrences of the same verb. For instance *Jan i Ela się całują* (lit. 'Jan and Ela RCLI kiss') 'Jan and Ela kiss each other' can be transformed into *Jan całuje Elę, a Ela całuje Jana* 'Jan kisses Ela and Ela kisses Jan'. Therefore, *całować się* (lit. 'kiss RCLI') is a reciprocal use of *się* and not an IRV. But in Polish, there is another reciprocal form with a singular subject and an oblique: *Jan całuje się z Elą* 'Jan kisses RCLI with Ela'. Adding this case to IRV.8 is necessary, at least for language-specific variants of this test. But this is not sufficient since the verb alone does not admit the same subcategorization: **Jan całuje Elę z Eleną* (lit. 'Jan kisses Ela with Elena'). Thus, test IRV.3 is always passed, and such cases have to be annotated as IRVs, although they are productive. A possible solution would be to change the order of the IRV tests so that those checking non-idiomatic uses of the RCLI (currently IRV.4 to IRV.8) are placed first.

Thirdly, specific constructions with duplicated verbs invalidate some genuine IRVs (cf. Sec. 6.4). Language-specific lists of such constructions, to be neglected by test IRV.1, could be proposed.

Finally, an open problem is how to ensure that the decision diagrams always yield the same outcome for the same sense of a verb, whatever its non-lexicalized arguments. In *stawiam sobie/komuś cel* (lit. 'I-put myself/someone a goal') 'set a goal to myself/someone', the outcome of test LVC.2 depends on the indirect object. With a reflexive object *sobie* 'myself', the subject of the verb (I) is the agent/beneficiary of the noun *cel* 'aim', which suggests the LVC.full status. But with another object, the verb's subject does not fill any semantic role of the noun, which leads to LVC.cause. We would of course like both of these uses to be annotated in the same way, here as LVC.cause. But this would imply applying the test to all possible instances of the (non lexicalized) object, rather than to the precise example being annotated. With such a major difference in the annotation strategy, the decision replicability might be jeopardized.[36]

8   Conclusions

We described the construction of the Polish corpus of VMWEs, which is the 4th biggest dataset in the PARSEME suite. We presented some details of the annotation process and its outcomes. We also discussed some Polish-specific phenomena, interpreted in the light of the PARSEME annotation guidelines. We displayed several drawbacks of these guidelines and put forward suggestion for their enhancements. We believe that these observations can help continuous enhancement of the PARSEME methodology, and can be useful to annotators of other languages, linguists studying the MWE phenomenon, as well as authors of VMWE identification tools.

Acknowledgements

This work was partly funded by the French PARSEME-FR grant (ANR-14-CERA-0001). We are grateful to the anonymous reviewers for their useful comments.

---

[35] VPC is a PARSEME VMWE category, pervasive notably in Germanic languages but non-existent in Polish.

[36] A similar issue, recently raised on the PARSEME discussion forum, concerns IRV tests for supposedly middle passive uses of the RCLI, like *ograniczać się* (lit. 'limit itself') 'be limited to'. See guidelines Gitlab issue #98 for details.

References

Monika Czerepowicka and Agata Savary. 2018. SEJF - A Grammatical Lexicon of Polish Multiword Expressions. In Zygmunt Vetulani, Joseph Mariani, and Marek Kubis, editors, *Human Language Technology. Challenges for Computer Science and Linguistics*, pages 59–73, Cham. Springer International Publishing.

Katarzyna Głowińska and Adam Przepiórkowski. 2010. The design of syntactic annotation levels in the National Corpus of Polish. In *Proceedings of the Seventh International Conference on Language Resources and Evaluation, LREC 2010*, Valletta, Malta. European Language Resources Association (ELRA).

Katarzyna Głowińska. 2012. Anotacja składniowa. In Adam Przepiórkowski, Mirosław Bańko, Rafał L. Górski, and Barbara Lewandowska-Tomaszczyk, editors, *Narodowy Korpus Języka Polskiego*, pages 107–127. Wydawnictwo Naukowe PWN, Warsaw.

Elżbieta Hajnicz, Anna Andrzejczuk, and Tomasz Bartosiak. 2016. Semantic layer of the valence dictionary of Polish *Walenty*. In Nicoletta Calzolari, Khalid Choukri, Thierry Declerck, Marko Grobelnik, Bente Maegaard, Joseph Mariani, Asuncion Moreno, Jan Odijk, and Stelios Piperidis, editors, *Proceedings of the Tenth International Conference on Language Resources and Evaluation, LREC 2016*, pages 2625–2632, Portorož, Slovenia. European Language Resources Association (ELRA), European Language Resources Association (ELRA).

Anna Kupść. 1999. Hapology of the polish reflexive marker. In Robert D. Borsley and Adam Przepiórkowski, editors, *Slavic in Head-Driven Phrase Structure Grammar*. CSLI Publications, Stanford, CA.

Joakim Nivre, Marie-Catherine de Marneffe, Filip Ginter, Jan Hajic, Christopher D. Manning, Sampo Pyysalo, Sebastian Schuster, Francis Tyers, and Daniel Zeman. 2020. Universal Dependencies v2: An Evergrowing Multilingual Treebank Collection. In *Proceedings of The 12th Language Resources and Evaluation Conference*, pages 4034–4043, Marseille, France, May. European Language Resources Association.

Maciej Ogrodniczuk, Katarzyna Głowińska, Mateusz Kopeć, Agata Savary, and Magdalena Zawisławska. 2015. *Coreference in Polish: Annotation, Resolution and Evaluation*. Walter De Gruyter.

Timothy Osborne and Kim Gerdes. 2019. The status of function words in dependency grammar: A critique of Universal Dependencies (UD). *Glossa: a journal of general linguistics*, January.

Agnieszka Patejuk and Adam Przepiórkowski. 2014. Synergistic development of grammatical resources: A valence dictionary, an LFG grammar, and an LFG structure bank for Polish. In Verena Henrich, Erhard Hinrichs, Daniël de Kok, Petya Osenova, and Adam Przepiórkowski, editors, *Proceedings of the Thirteenth International Workshop on Treebanks and Linguistic Theories (TLT 13)*, pages 113–126, Tübingen. Department of Linguistics (SfS), University of Tübingen.

Adam Przepiórkowski and Agnieszka Patejuk. 2020. From Lexical Functional Grammar to enhanced Universal Dependencies: The UD-LFG treebank of Polish. *Language Resources and Evaluation*, 54:185–221.

Adam Przepiórkowski and Marcin Woliński. 2003. A flexemic tagset for Polish. In *Proceedings of* Morphological Processing of Slavic Languages, *EACL 2003*.

Adam Przepiórkowski, Elżbieta Hajnicz, Agnieszka Patejuk, and Marcin Woliński. 2014. Extended phraseological information in a valence dictionary for NLP applications. In *Proceedings of the Workshop on Lexical and Grammatical Resources for Language Processing (LG-LP 2014)*, pages 83–91, Dublin, Ireland. Association for Computational Linguistics and Dublin City University.

Adam Przepiórkowski. 1999. *Case Assignment and the Complement-Adjunct Dichotomy: A Non-Configurational Constraint-Based Approach*. Ph.D. dissertation, Universität Tübingen.

Carlos Ramisch, Silvio Ricardo Cordeiro, Agata Savary, Veronika Vincze, Verginica Barbu Mititelu, Archna Bhatia, Maja Buljan, Marie Candito, Polona Gantar, Voula Giouli, Tunga Güngör, Abdelati Hawwari, Uxoa Iñurrieta, Jolanta Kovalevskaitė, Simon Krek, Timm Lichte, Chaya Liebeskind, Johanna Monti, Carla Parra Escartín, Behrang QasemiZadeh, Renata Ramisch, Nathan Schneider, Ivelina Stoyanova, Ashwini Vaidya, and Abigail Walsh. 2018. Edition 1.1 of the PARSEME Shared Task on Automatic Identification of Verbal Multiword Expressions. In *Proceedings of the Joint Workshop on Linguistic Annotation, Multiword Expressions and Constructions (LAW-MWE-CxG-2018)*, pages 222–240. Association for Computational Linguistics.

Carlos Ramisch, Agata Savary, Bruno Guillaume, Jakub Waszczuk, Marie Candito, Ashwini Vaidya, Verginica Barbu Mititelu, Archna Bhatia, Uxoa Iñurrieta, Voula Giouli, Tunga Güngör, Menghan Jiang, Timm Lichte, Chaya Liebeskind, Johanna Monti, Renata Ramisch, Sara Stymne, Abigail Walsh, and Hongzhi Xu. 2020. Edition 1.2 of the PARSEME shared task on semi-supervised identification of verbal multiword expressions. In *Proceedings of the Joint Workshop on Multiword Expressions and Electronic Lexicons (MWE-LEX 2020)*. Association for Computational Linguistics.

Alexandr Rosen. 2014. Haplology of reflexive clitics in Czech. In Elżbieta Kaczmarska and Motoki Nomachi, editors, *Slavic and German in Contact: Studies from Areal and Contrastive Linguistics*, pages 97–116. Slavic Research Center, Hokkaido University, Sapporo, Japan.

Agata Savary and Jakub Waszczuk. 2017. Projecting multiword expression resources on a Polish treebank. In *Proceedings of the 6th Workshop on Balto-Slavic Natural Language Processing*, pages 20–26, Valencia, Spain, April. Association for Computational Linguistics.

Agata Savary, Carlos Ramisch, Silvio Cordeiro, Federico Sangati, Veronika Vincze, Behrang QasemiZadeh, Marie Candito, Fabienne Cap, Voula Giouli, Ivelina Stoyanova, and Antoine Doucet. 2017. The PARSEME Shared Task on automatic identification of verbal multiword expressions. In *Proceedings of the 13th Workshop on Multiword Expressions* , MWE '17, pages 31–47. Association for Computational Linguistics.

Agata Savary, Marie Candito, Verginica Barbu Mititelu, Eduard Bejček, Fabienne Cap, Slavomír Čéplö, Silvio Ricardo Cordeiro, Gülşen Eryiğit, Voula Giouli, Maarten van Gompel, Yaakov HaCohen-Kerner, Jolanta Kovalevskaitė, Simon Krek, Chaya Liebeskind, Johanna Monti, Carla Parra Escartín, Lonneke van der Plas, Behrang QasemiZadeh, Carlos Ramisch, Federico Sangati, Ivelina Stoyanova, and Veronika Vincze. 2018. PARSEME multilingual corpus of verbal multiword expressions. In Stella Markantonatou, Carlos Ramisch, Agata Savary, and Veronika Vincze, editors, *Multiword expressions at length and in depth: Extended papers from the MWE 2017 workshop*, pages 87–147. Language Science Press., Berlin.

Agata Savary, Silvio Cordeiro, and Carlos Ramisch. 2019. Without lexicons, multiword expression identification will never fly: A position statement. In *MWE-WN 2019*, pages 79–91, Florence, Italy. ACL.

Marcin Woliński, Elżbieta Hajnicz, and Tomasz Bartosiak. 2018. A new version of the Składnica treebank of Polish harmonised with the Walenty valency dictionary. In Nicoletta Calzolari, Khalid Choukri, Christopher Cieri, Thierry Declerck, Sara Goggi, Koiti Hasida, Hitoshi Isahara, Bente Maegaard, Joseph Mariani, Hélène Mazo, Asuncion Moreno, Jan Odijk, Stelios Piperidis, and Takenobu Tokunaga, editors, *Proceedings of the Eleventh International Conference on Language Resources and Evaluation (LREC 2018)*, pages 1839–1844, Paris, France. European Language Resources Association (ELRA).

Alina Wróblewska. 2012. Polish Dependency Bank. *Linguistic Issues in Language Technology*, 7(1).

Alina Wróblewska. 2020. Towards the Conversion of National Corpus of Polish to Universal Dependencies. In *Proceedings of the 12th Language Resources and Evaluation Conference*, pages 5308–5315, Marseille, France. European Language Resources Association (ELRA).

Daniel Zeman, Martin Popel, Milan Straka, Jan Hajič, Joakim Nivre, Filip Ginter, Juhani Luotolahti, Sampo Pyysalo, Slav Petrov, Martin Potthast, Francis Tyers, Elena Badmaeva, Memduh Gokirmak, Anna Nedoluzhko, Silvie Cinková, Jan Hajič jr., Jaroslava Hlaváčová, Václava Kettnerová, Zdeňka Urešová, Jenna Kanerva, Stina Ojala, Anna Missilä, Christopher D. Manning, Sebastian Schuster, Siva Reddy, Dima Taji, Nizar Habash, Herman Leung, Marie-Catherine de Marneffe, Manuela Sanguinetti, Maria Simi, Hiroshi Kanayama, Valeria de Paiva, Kira Droganova, Héctor Martínez Alonso, Çağrı Çöltekin, Umut Sulubacak, Hans Uszkoreit, Vivien Macketanz, Aljoscha Burchardt, Kim Harris, Katrin Marheinecke, Georg Rehm, Tolga Kayadelen, Mohammed Attia, Ali Elkahky, Zhuoran Yu, Emily Pitler, Saran Lertpradit, Michael Mandl, Jesse Kirchner, Hector Fernandez Alcalde, Jana Strnadová, Esha Banerjee, Ruli Manurung, Antonio Stella, Atsuko Shimada, Sookyoung Kwak, Gustavo Mendonça, Tatiana Lando, Rattima Nitisaroj, and Josie Li. 2017. CoNLL 2017 shared task: Multilingual parsing from raw text to universal dependencies. In *Proceedings of the CoNLL 2017 Shared Task: Multilingual Parsing from Raw Text to Universal Dependencies*, pages 1–19, Vancouver, Canada, August. Association for Computational Linguistics.

Marek Świdziński and Marcin Woliński. 2010. Towards a bank of constituent parse trees for Polish. In Petr Sojka, Aleš Horák, Ivan Kopeček, and Karel Pala, editors, *Text, Speech and Dialogue: 13th International Conference, TSD 2010, Brno, Czech Republic*, number 6231 in Lecture Notes in Artificial Intelligence, pages 197–204, Heidelberg. Springer-Verlag.

AlphaMWE: Construction of Multilingual Parallel Corpora with MWE Annotations

Lifeng Han[Π], **Gareth J. F. Jones**[Π], and **Alan Smeaton**[Ω]

[Π] ADAPT Research Centre
[Ω] Insight Centre for Data Analytics
School of Computing, Dublin City University, Dublin, Ireland
`lifeng.han@adaptcentre.ie {gareth.jones, alan.smeaton}@dcu.ie`

Abstract

In this work, we present the construction of multilingual parallel corpora with annotation of multiword expressions (MWEs). MWEs include verbal MWEs (vMWEs) defined in the PARSEME shared task that have a verb as the head of the studied terms. The annotated vMWEs are also bilingually and multilingually aligned manually. The languages covered include English, Chinese, Polish, and German. Our original English corpus is taken from the PARSEME shared task in 2018. We performed machine translation of this source corpus followed by human post editing and annotation of target MWEs. Strict quality control was applied for error limitation, i.e., each MT output sentence received first manual post editing and annotation plus second manual quality rechecking. One of our findings during corpora preparation is that accurate translation of MWEs presents challenges to MT systems. To facilitate further MT research, we present a categorisation of the error types encountered by MT systems in performing MWE related translation. To acquire a broader view of MT issues, we selected four popular state-of-the-art MT models for comparisons namely: Microsoft Bing Translator, GoogleMT, Baidu Fanyi and DeepL MT. Because of the noise removal, translation post editing and MWE annotation by human professionals, we believe our AlphaMWE dataset will be an asset for cross-lingual and multilingual research, such as MT and information extraction. Our multilingual corpora are available as open access at `github.com/poethan/AlphaMWE`.

1 Introduction

Multiword Expressions (MWEs) have long been of interest to both natural language processing (NLP) researchers and linguists (Sag et al., 2002; Constant et al., 2017; Pulcini, 2020). The automatic processing of MWEs has posed significant challenges for some fields in computational linguistics (CL), such as word sense disambiguation (WSD), parsing and (automated) translation (Lambert and Banchs, 2005; Bouamor et al., 2012; Skadina, 2016; Li et al., 2019; Han et al., 2020). This is caused by both the variety and the richness of MWEs as they are used in language.

Various definitions of MWEs have included both syntactic structure and semantic viewpoints from different researchers covering syntactic anomalies, non-compositionality, non-substitutability and ambiguity (Constant et al., 2017). For instance, Baldwin and Kim (2010) define MWEs as "lexical items that: (i) can be decomposed into multiple lexemes; and (ii) display lexical, syntactic, semantic, pragmatic and/or statistical idiomaticity". However, as noted by NLP researchers for example in (Constant et al., 2017), there are very few bilingual or even multilingual parallel corpora with MWE annotations available for cross-lingual NLP research and for downstream applications such as machine translation (MT) (Johnson et al., 2016).

With regard to MWE research, verbal MWEs are a mature category that has received attention from many researchers (Maldonado et al., 2017). Verbal MWEs have a verb as the head

Joint Workshop on Multiword Expressions and Electronic Lexicons, pages 44–57
Barcelona, Spain (Online), December 13, 2020.

of the studied term and function as verbal phrases, such as "*kick* the bucket", "*cutting* capers" and "*go* to one's head". In this work, we present the construction of a multilingual corpus with vMWEs annotation, including English-Chinese, English-German and English-Polish language pairs. The same source monolingual corpus is in English with its vMWE tags from the shared task affiliated with the SIGLEX-MWE workshop in 2018 (Walsh et al., 2018; Ramisch et al., 2018). Several state-of-the-art (SOTA) MT models were used to perform an automated translation, and then human post editing and annotation for the target languages was conducted with cross validation to ensure the quality, i.e., with each sentence receiving post-editing and rechecking by at least two people.

In order to get a deeper insight into the difficulties of processing MWEs we carried out a categorisation of the errors made by MT models when processing MWEs. From this we conclude that current state-of-the-art MT models are far from reaching parity with humans in terms of translation performance, especially on idiomatic MWEs, even for sentence level translation, although researchers sometimes claim otherwise (Wu et al., 2016; Hassan et al., 2018).

The rest of this paper is organised as follows. In the next section we present related work and then detail the corpus preparation stages including selection of MT models. We then look at the various kinds of issues that MT has with MWEs. This analysis, along with the public release of the corpora as a resource to the community, is the main contribution of the paper.

2 Related Work

There are a number of existing studies which focus on the creation of *monolingual* corpora with vMWE annotations, such as the PARSEME shared task corpora (Savary et al., 2017; Ramisch et al., 2018). The 2020 edition of this task covers 14 languages including Chinese, Hindi, and Turkish as non-European languages. Some work from monolingual English corpora includes the MWE aware "English Dependency Corpus" from the Linguistic Data Consortium (LDC2017T01) that covers *compound words* used to train parsing models. Also related to this are English MWEs from "web reviews data" by Schneider et al. (2014) that covers *noun, verb* and *preposition super-senses* and English verbal MWEs from Walsh et al. (2018) and Kato et al. (2018) that covers PARSEME shared task defined vMWE categories. However, all these works were performed in monolingual settings, independently by different language speakers without any bilingual alignment. These corpora are helpful for monolingual MWE research such as *discovery* or *identification*, however, it would be difficult to use these corpora for bilingual or multilingual research such as MT or cross-lingual information extraction.

The work most related to ours is from Vincze (2012), who created an English-Hungarian parallel corpus with annotations for light verb constructions (LVCs). As many as 703 LVCs for Hungarian and 727 for English were annotated in this work, and a comparison between English and Hungarian data was carried out. However, the work did not cover other types of vMWEs, for instance inherently adpositional verbs, verbal idioms, or verb-particle constructions, and it was not extended to any other language pairs. In our work, we annotate in a multilingual setting including far distance languages such as English, German, Polish and Chinese, in addition to the extension of vMWE categories. In other recent work Han et al. (2020), we performed an automatic construction of bilingual MWE terms based on a parallel corpus, in this case English-Chinese and English-German. We first conducted automated extraction of monolingual MWEs based on part-of-speech (POS) patterns and then aligned the two side monolingual MWEs into bilingual terms based on statistical lexical translation probability. However, due to the automated procedure, the extracted bilingual "MWE terms" contain not only MWEs but also normal phrases. Part of the reason for this is due to the POS pattern design which is a challenging task for each language and needs to be further refined (Skadina, 2016; Rikters and Bojar, 2017; Han et al., 2020).

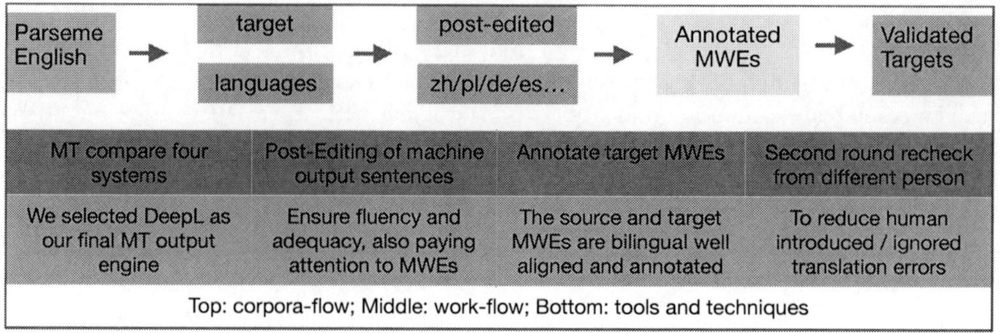

Figure 1: Workflows to prepare AlphaMWE.

3 Experimental Work

In this section we describe our corpus preparation method, selection of the MT models used in our investigation, and the resulting open-source corpora AlphaMWE.

3.1 Corpus Preparation

To construct a well aligned multilingual parallel corpus, our approach is to take a monolingual corpus from the PARSEME *vMWE discovery and identification shared task* as our root corpus. Our rationale here is that this shared task is well established and its process of tagging and categorisation is clear. Furthermore, as we plan to extend the MWE categories in the future, we enrich the PARSEME shared task corpus with potential for other downstream research and applications, including bilingual and multilingual NLP models. The English corpus (Walsh et al., 2018) we used from the PARSEME shared task follows the annotation guidelines having a broad range of vMWE categories tagged. These include inherently adpositional verbs, light verb constructions, multi-verb constructions, verbal idioms, and verb-particle constructions. The English corpus contains sentences from several different topics, such as news, literature, and IT documents. For the IT document domain, vMWEs are usually easier or more straightforward to translate, with a high chance of repetition, e.g. "apply filter" and "based on". For the literature annotations, the vMWEs include richer samples with many idiomatic or metaphor expressions, such as "cutting capers" and "gone slightly to someone's head" that cause MT issues.

Fig. 1 shows our workflow. This first used MT models to perform automated translation for the target language direction, then human post editing of the output hypotheses with annotation of the corresponding target side vMWEs which are aligned with the source English ones. Finally, to avoid human introduced errors, we apply a cross validation strategy, where each sentence receives at least a second person's quality checking after the first post-editing. Tagging errors are more likely to occur if only one human has seen each sentence (we discuss some error samples from English source corpus in later sections).

3.2 MT Model Selection

We tested a number of example sentences from the English testset to compare state-of-the-art MT from Microsoft Bing (Chowdhary and Greenwood, 2017), GoogleMT (Vaswani et al., 2017), Baidu Fanyi (Sun et al., 2019), and DeepL[1], as in Fig. 2. We illustrate the comparative performances with two worked example translations. As a first example sentence, GoogleMT and Bing Translator have very similar outputs, where the MT output sentences try to capture and produce as much information as possible, but make the sentences redundant or awkward to read, such as the phrase "验证... 是否验证了 (yàn zhèng ... Shì fǒu yàn zhèng le)" where they use a repeated word "验证" (yàn zhèng, *verify*). Although the DeepL Translator does not produce a

---

[1]https://www.deepl.com/en/translator (All testing was performed in 2020/07 from 4 MT models)

Two sample sentences' MT outputs comparison from head of test file	
Source	# text = SQL Server verifies that the account name and password were validated when the user logged on to the system and grants access to the database, without requiring a separate logon name or password.
DeepL	# text = SQL Server 会在用户登录系统时验证账户名和密码，并授予对数据库的访问权限，而不要求单独的登录名或密码。
Google	# text = SQL Server验证用户登录系统时是否验证了帐户名和密码，并授予对数据库的访问权限，而无需单独的登录名或密码。
Bing	[text] SQL Server 验证用户登录到系统时是否验证了帐户名称和密码，并授予对数据库的访问权限，而无需单独的登录名称或密码。
Baidu	#或者，在没有密码的情况下验证用户名和用户名是否被登录到数据库中，并且系统是否授予登录权限。
Ref.	# 文本 = SQL Server 会在用户登录系统时验证账户名和密码的有效性，并授予对数据库的访问权限，而不要求单独的登录名或密码。
Source	# text = See the http://officeupdate.microsoft.com/, Microsoft Developer Network Web site for more information on TSQL.
DeepL	# text = 有关 TSQL 的更多信息，请参见 http://officeupdate.microsoft.com/，Microsoft Developer Network Web 站点。
Google	# text =有关Microsoft 的更多信息，请参见http://officeupdate.microsoft.com/，Microsoft开发人员网络网站。
Bing	[文本] 有关 TSQL http://officeupdate.microsoft.com/了解有关 TSQL 的相关信息，请参阅 Microsoft 开发人员网络网站。
Baidu	#text= ，以获取有关TSQL的详细信息。
Ref.	# text = 有关 TSQL 的更多信息，请参见 http://officeupdate.microsoft.com/，微软开发人员网络互联网站点。
Blue: redundancy; green: adding error; pink: reordering error; : dropping error.	

Figure 2: Sample comparison of outputs from four MT models.

perfect translation since it drops the source word "validated" which should be translated as "有效性 (yǒu xiào xìng)"(as one candidate translation), the overall output is fluent and the source sentence meaning is mostly preserved. Baidu translator yields the worst output in this example. It produces some words that were not in the source sentence (或者, huò zhě, *or*), loses some important terms' translation from source sentence ("SQL Server", the subject of the sentence), and the reordering of the sentence fails resulting in an incorrect meaning ("在没有密码的情况下, zài méi yǒu mì mǎ de qíng kuàng xià" is moved from the end of the sentence to the front and made as a condition). So, for this case, DeepL performed best.

For a second example sentence, GoogleMT confused the original term TSQL as SQL. Bing MT had a similar issue with the last example, i.e. it produced redundant information "有关 (yǒu guān)" (*about/on*). In addition it concatenated the website address and normal phrase "了解有关 (liǎo jiě yǒu guān)" together with a hyperlink. GoogleMT and Bing both translate half of the source term/MWE "Microsoft Developer Network Web" as "Microsoft 开发人员网络网站" (kāi fā rén yuán wǎng luò wǎng zhàn) where they kept "Microsoft" but translated "Developer Network Web". Although this is one reasonable output since Microsoft is a general popular named entity while "Developer Network Web" consists of common words, we interpret "Microsoft Developer Network Web" as a named entity/MWE in the source sentence that consists of all capitalised words which would be better translated overall as "微软开发人员网络网站 (wēi ruǎn kāi fā rén yuán wǎng luò wǎng zhàn)" or be kept as the original capitalised words as a foreign term in the output, which is how DeepL outputs this expression. However, Baidu totally drops out this MWE translation and another word translation is not accurate, "more" into 详细 (xiáng xì). Based on these samples, we chose to use DeepL as the provider of our MT hypotheses.

3.3 Result: AlphaMWE

Regarding the size of the corpus, we extracted all 750 English sentences which have vMWE tags included. The target languages covered so far include Chinese, German and Polish with sample sentences in Appendix (Fig. 11). There are several situations and decisions that are worth noting: a) when the original English vMWEs are translated into a general phrase in the target language but not choosing sequence of MWEs, we tried to offer two different references, with

Source	At the corner of 72nd Street and Madison Avenue, he <u>waved down</u> a cab.
DeepL	在72街和麦迪逊大道的拐角处，他向一辆出租车招手。 Zài 72 jiē hé mài dí xùn dà dào de guǎi jiǎo chù, tā xiàng yī liàng chū zū chē <u>zhāo shǒu</u>.
Bing	在72街和麦迪逊大道的拐角处，他挥手示意一辆出租车。 zài 72 jiē hé mài dí xùn dà dào de guǎi jiǎo chù , tā <u>huī shǒu shì yì</u> yí liàng chū zū chē.
Google	在第72街和麦迪逊大街的拐角处，他挥舞着出租车。 Zài dì 72 jiē hé mài dí xùn dà jiē de guǎi jiǎo chù, tā <u>huī wǔ zhe</u> chū zū chē.
Baidu	在72街和麦迪逊大街的拐角处，他挥手叫了一辆出租车。 zài 72 jiē hé mài dí xùn dà jiē de guǎi jiǎo chù, tā <u>huī shǒu jiào le</u> yí liàng chū zū chē.
Ref.	在72街和麦迪逊大道的拐角处，他<u>招手示停了</u>一辆出租车。 Zài 72 jiē hé mài dí xùn dà dào de guǎi jiǎo chù, tā <u>zhāo shǒu shì tíng le</u> yī liàng chū zū chē.

Figure 3: MT issues with MWEs: common sense. Pinyin offered by GoogleMT with post-editing.

one of them being revised in a vMWE/MWE presentation in the target; b) when the original English sentence terms were translated into the correct target language but in a different register, e.g. the source language has low register (thx, for instance), we offer two reference sentences, with one of them using the same low register and the other with (formal) full word spelling; c) for the situations where a single English word or normal phrase is translated into a typical vMWE in the target language, or both source and target sentences include vMWEs but the source vMWE was not annotated in the original English corpus, we made some additions to include such vMWE (pairs) into AlphaMWE; d) for some wrong/incorrect annotation in the source English corpus, or some mis-spelling of words, we corrected them in AlphaMWE; e) we chose English as root/source corpus, since the post-editing and annotation of target languages requires the human annotators to be fluent/native in both-side languages, and all editors were fluent in English as well as being native speakers in the specific target languages respectively.

We examined the development and test data sets from the annual Workshop of MT (WMT) (Bojar et al., 2017) and also from the NIST MT challenges where they offered approximately 2,000 sentences for development/testing over some years. This means that our bilingual/multilingual corpora with 750 sentences is comparable to such standard shared task usage.

4 MT Issues with MWEs

We performed an analysis of the behaviour of various MT systems when required to translate MWEs or MWEs related context. Due to space limitations, in this paper we focus on the English→Chinese language pair. We also highlight some issues on English→German and English→Polish in the next section, but leave the detailed analysis of other language pairs for future work. When MT produces incorrect or awkward translations this can fall into many different categories, and from our analysis we classify them as: *common sense, super sense, abstract phrase, idiom, metaphor and ambiguity*, with ambiguity further sub-divided. These classifications are to be further refined in the future, e.g. the differences between metaphor and idiom are usually fuzzy. We now list each of these with examples to support future MT research on improving the quality of MT when handling MWEs.

4.1 Common Sense

The first error category is the *common sense* issue. For instance, the sentence in Fig. 3 includes the vMWE "waved down" which in general understanding indicates that "he succeeded in getting the cab" and not only "waved his hand". However, in the translation by DeepL and Bing this vMWE was wrongly translated as "he waved his hand to the cab" missing part of the original meaning; the MT output by GoogleMT is also incorrect, saying "he waves with the cab in hand";

Source	Each time he took a walk, he felt as though he were leaving himself behind, and by <u>giving</u> himself <u>up</u> to the movement of the streets, by reducing himself to a seeing eye, he was able to escape the obligation to think, and this, more than anything else, brought him a measure of peace, a <u>salutatory emptiness within</u>.
DeepL	每一次散步，他都觉得自己好像把自己抛在了脑后，把自己<u>交给</u>了街道的运动，把自己还原成了一只看得见的眼睛，他就能摆脱思考的义务，这比什么都重要，这给他带来了一定程度的平静，<u>内心的空虚让人敬佩</u>。(jiāo gěi; nèi xīn de kōng xū ràng rén jìng pèi)
Bing	每次散步时，他都觉得自己好像要把自己抛在脑后，通过向街道运动<u>自在</u>，通过把自己留眼，他能够逃避思考的义务，这比什么都重要，给他带来了一定程度的和平，一种<u>有益的空虚</u>。(zì zài; yǒu yì de kōng xū)
Google	每次散步时，他都会感觉自己好像在抛弃自己，<u>投身于大街小巷</u>，睁大了眼睛，这使他摆脱了思考的义务，而这，最重要的是，他带给他一种和平的感觉，一种<u>内在的称呼空虚</u>。(tóu shēn yú; nèi zài de chēng hu kōng xū)
Baidu	每次他散步，他都觉得自己好像是在离开自己，把自己<u>交给</u>街道的流动，把自己变成一个有眼光的人，他就可以逃避思考的义务，而这比其他任何事情都能给他带来某种程度的平和，一种<u>内在的致意的空虚</u>。(nèi zài de zhì yì de kōng xū)
Ref.	每一次散步，他都觉得自己好像把自己抛在了脑后，<u>投身于大街小巷</u>，把自己还原成了一只看得见的眼睛，他就能摆脱思考的义务，这给他带来了某种程度的平静和<u>内心悦纳的空无</u>，远胜于其他。(nèi xīn yuè nà de kōng wú)

Figure 4: MT issues with MWEs: super sense.

Source	Quinn had his doubts, but this was <u>all he had to **go on**</u>, his only bridge to the present.
DeepL	奎恩有他的疑虑，但这是他<u>唯一的依靠</u>，是他通往现在的唯一桥梁。(wéi yī de yī kào)
Bing	奎因有他的怀疑，但这就是他<u>必须**去**的</u>，他唯一的桥梁到现在。 (bì xū qù de)
Google	奎因有他的疑惑，但这就是他<u>所**要**做的</u>，是他通往现在的唯一桥梁。 (suǒ yào zuò de)
Baidu	奎因有他的疑虑，但这是他<u>所**要做**的</u>，是他通往现在的唯一桥梁。 (suǒ yào zuò de)
Ref.	奎恩曾有他的疑虑，但这是他<u>**开展工作**的所有依据</u>，是他通往现在的唯一桥梁。(**kāi zhǎn gōng zuò** de suǒ yǒu yī jù)

Figure 5: MT issues with MWEs: abstract phrase

the Baidu translation of this sentence is semantically correct that "he waved and got one cab" though it does not use a corresponding Chinese side vMWE " 招手示停 (zhāo shǒu shì tíng)"[2].

4.2 Super Sense

For this category of translation issue, it is related to *a form of state of mind* and we need to make a logical prediction to guess the *positiveness* or *negativeness* of some words, in the choice of Chinese characters. As in Fig. 4, the MT systems each have advantages for different parts of this long sentence. However, none of them is perfect. For instance, for the translation of vMWE "giving (himself) up (to)", the DeepL and Baidu outputs give very literal translation by saying "he gives himself to", the Bing translator drops the vMWE, while GoogleMT preserves the correct meaning in the translation "投身于 (tóu shēn yú)" from the reference indicating "he devoted himself". However, GoogleMT's output for the phrase "salutatory emptiness within" is very poor and makes no sense; the reference is "the emptiness that he welcomes" for which Baidu has a closer translation "内在的致意的空虚 (nèi zài de zhì yì de kōng xū)". All four MT outputs also use the same Chinese words "空虚 (kōng xū)" which is a term with negative meaning, however, the sentence indicates that he is welcoming this emptiness, which should be the corresponding Chinese words "空无 (kōng wú)", an unbiased or positive meaning.

4.3 Abstract Phrase

The *abstract phrases* can have different exact meanings and we usually need some background information from the sentence or paragraph to select the correct word choices in the target

---

[2]We give full sentence pronunciation (in Pinyin) of Chinese characters in this figure, for the following examples, we only present the Chinese Pinyin for MWEs and studied words of the sentences to save space.

Source	I was smoking my pipe quietly by my dismantled steamer, and saw them all <u>cutting capers</u> in the light, with their arms lifted high, when the stout man with mustaches came tearing down to the river, a tin pail in his hand, assured me that everybody was 'behaving splendidly, splendidly, dipped about a quart of water and <u>tore back</u> again.'
DeepL	我在拆开的汽船旁静静地抽着烟斗，看到他们都在灯光下高举双臂切着荠菜，这时，那个留着胡子的壮汉撕扯着来到河边，手里拿着一个铁皮桶，向我保证说，大家都'表现得很精彩，很精彩，浸了大约一夸脱的水，又撕扯回来了。(qiè zhe jì cài; sī chě huí lái)
Bing	我悄悄地用我拆除的蒸笼抽我的烟斗，看到他们所有的切割披肩在光中，他们的手臂抬起来高，当粗壮的人用胡子来到河中，一个锡桶在他的手中，向我保证，每个人都'表现辉煌，辉煌，浸约夸脱的水，并再次撕毁。(qiē gē pī jiān; zài cì sī huǐ)
Google	我正用拆卸的蒸锅安静地抽着烟斗，看到他们都在灯光下割下刺山柑，双臂高高举起，当时那留着小胡子的矮壮男人向河边撕下，手里拿着一个铁桶，向我保证 每个人都表现得非常出色，表现得非常出色，蘸了一夸脱的水，然后又撕了回来。(gē xià cì shān gān; sī le huí lái)
Baidu	我正静静地在我拆掉的汽船旁抽着烟斗，看见他们都高举着胳膊，在灯光下割着山柑，这时那个长着胡子的胖男人手里拿着一个锡桶，朝河里跑来，向我保证每个人都表现得很好，很漂亮，蘸了一夸脱水，然后又往回跑。(gē zhe shān gān; wǎng huí pǎo)
Ref.	我在拆开的汽船旁静静地抽着烟斗，看到他们都在灯光下欢呼雀跃，高举双臂，这时，那个留着胡子的大块头，手里拿着一个铁皮桶，快速来到河边，向我确保大家都"表现得很精彩，很精彩"，他浸了大约一夸脱的水，又快速回去了。(huān hū què yuè; kuài sù huí qù)

Figure 6: MT issues with MWEs: idioms

language[3]. With the example sentence in Fig. 5, from the context, we know that "go on" in this sentence means "to work from" using all the information he had. The phrase "this was all he had to go on" is then to be interpreted as "this is all the information he had to work from". At the end of the sentence, "the present" is the "present person" he needs to look for (with the picture of this person's younger age portrait). However, Bing translated it as "this is (where) he had to go" which is an incorrect interpretation of "had to go"; furthermore, Bing's translation of the second half of the sentence kept the English order, without any reordering between the words, which is grammatically incorrect in Chinese, i.e. "他唯一的桥梁到现在 (tā wéi yī de qiáo liáng dào xiàn zài)". GoogleMT and Baidu translated it as "what he need to do" which is also far from correct, while DeepL successfully translated the part "his only thing to relying on" but dropped the phrase "go on", i.e., *to do what*. *Abstract Phrase* can include *Super Sense* as its sub-category, however, it does not necessarily relate to a state of mind.

4.4 Idioms

The use of *idioms* often causes wrongly translated sentences, mostly resulting in humorous output due to literal translation. For example, in the sentence in Fig. 6, the vMWEs "*cutting capers*" and "tore back" are never translated correctly at the same time by any of the four MT models we used. The idiom "cutting capers" indicates frolic or romp, to "act in the manner of a young goat clumsily frolicking about" and here it means "they are in a happy mood, playful and lively movement" which should properly be translated as the corresponding Chinese idiom "欢呼雀跃 (huān hū què yuè, happily jumping around like sparrows)". However, all four MT models translated it literally into "cutting" actions just with different subjects, i.e., what they cut. The idiom (slang) "tore back" means the stout man *walked back rapidly*, which the Baidu translation gives the closest translation as "往回跑 (wǎng huí pǎo, run back)" but the other three models translated into an action "tear something (to be broken)" which is incorrect.

4.5 Metaphor

The first sentence vMWE "blown to bits" in Fig. 7 is a *metaphor* to indicate "everything is gone", instead of the physical "blowing action". However, the three MT models DeepL, GoogleMT and

---

[3]it sometimes belongs to the context-unaware ambiguity (CUA) that we will mention later, however, CUA not necessarily means "abstract phrase", and usually needs paragraph information, not only sentence level. Furthermore, in some situations, we just don't know how to interpret "abstract phrase", i.e. the candidate interpretations are unknown without context, and this is different from ambiguity.

Source	The what? Auster laughed, and in that laugh everything was suddenly <u>blown to bits</u>. The chair was comfortable, and the beer had <u>gone slightly to his head</u>.
DeepL	那个什么？奥斯特笑了，在这笑声中，一切突然<u>被炸得粉碎</u>。(bèi zhà dé fěn suì) 椅子很舒服，啤酒已经微微<u>到了他的头上</u>。(wēi wēi dào le tā de tóu shàng)
Bing	什么？奥斯特笑了，在笑，一切都突然<u>被吹成位</u>。(bèi chuī chéng wèi) 椅子很舒服，啤酒稍微<u>到他的头去了</u>。(shāo wēi dào tā de tóu qù le)
Google	什么啊 Auster笑了起来，在那笑声中，一切突然<u>被炸碎了</u>。(bèi zhà suì le) 椅子很舒服，啤酒微微<u>飘到他的头上</u>。(wēi wēi piāo dào tā de tóu shàng)
Baidu	什么？奥斯特笑了，在那笑声中，一切都突然<u>被炸成碎片</u>。(bèi zhà chéng suì piàn) 椅子很舒服，啤酒已经<u>稍稍流到他的头上了</u>。(shāo shāo liú dào tā de tóu shàng le)
Ref.	那个什么？奥斯特笑了，在这笑声中，一切突然<u>化为乌有</u>。(huà wéi wū yǒu) 椅子很舒服，啤酒已经微微<u>让他上了头</u>。(wēi wēi ràng tā shàng le tóu)

Figure 7: MT issues with MWEs: metaphor

Source	But it did not <u>give me the time of day</u>.
DeepL	但它并没有<u>给我时间</u>。(gěi wǒ shí jiān)
Bing	但它没有<u>给我一天的时间</u>。(gěi wǒ yī tiān de shí jiān)
Google	但这没有<u>给我一天的时间</u>。(gěi wǒ yī tiān de shí jiān)
Baidu	但它没有<u>给我一天中的时间</u>。(gěi wǒ yī tiān zhōng de shí jiān)
Ref.	但我没有<u>感到这个对于我特殊</u> / 但这不是<u>我的菜</u>。(gǎn dào zhè ge duì yú wǒ tè shū / ... wǒ de cài)
Context	An old Mormon missionary in Nauvoo once gripped my knee hard as we sat side by side, and he put his arm about me and called me "Brother." We'd only met ten minutes before. He took me to his good bosom. His eyes began to mist. I was a prospect, an exotic prospect in old tennis shoes and a sweatshirt. His heart opened to me. It opened like a cuckoo clock. But it did not ...

Figure 8: MT issues with MWEs: context-unaware ambiguity

Baidu translate it as "exploded into pieces (by bombs)", while BingMT translates it even more literally into "blown to (computer) bits". There is a corresponding Chinese vMWE "化为乌有 (huà wéi wū yǒu, vanish into nothing)" which would be a proper choice for this source vMWE translation. The second sentence vMWE "gone (slightly) to his head" is a metaphor to indicate "got slightly drunk". However, all four MT models translate it as physically "beer moved to his head" but by slightly different means such as *flow* or *flutter*. The corresponding translation as a MWE should be "微微让他上了头 (wéi wéi ràng tā **shàng le tóu**)", using the same characters, but the character order here makes so much difference, meaning "slightly drunk".

4.6 Ambiguity

We encountered different kinds of situation that cause ambiguity in the resulting translation when it meets MWEs or named entities, so we further divide ambiguity into three sub-classes.

4.6.1 Context-Unaware Ambiguity

In this case, the *context*, i.e. the background information, is needed for correct translation of the sentence. For instance, see Fig. 8. DeepL gives the translation "it did not give me time though", while Bing and GoogleMT give the same translation "it/this did not give me one day's time" and Baidu outputs a grammatically incorrect sentence. From the pre-context, we understand that it means the speaker "did not feel that is special to him" or "did not have affection of that" after *all the Mormon missionary's effort towards him*. Interestingly, there is a popular Chinese idiom (slang) that matches this meaning very well "不是我的菜 (bù shì wǒ

Source	The moment they know the <u>de-gnoming</u>'s going on they storm up to have a look. Then someone says that it can't be long now before the Russians <u>write Arafat off</u>.
DeepL	他们一知道去核的事，就会冲上去看一看。(qù hé) 然后有人说，现在用不了多久，俄罗斯人就会**把阿拉法特注销**。(**bǎ ā lā fǎ tè zhù xiāo**)
Bing	当他们知道去诺格明是怎么回事，他们冲了起来看看。(qù nuò gé míng) 然后有人说，现在俄罗斯人要不长了，就**把阿拉法特注销了**。(**bǎ ā lā fǎ tè zhù xiāo** le)
Google	当他们知道正在逐渐消失的那一刻，他们便冲上去看看。(zhèng zài zhú jiàn xiāo shī) 然后有人说，不久之后俄罗斯人**将阿拉法特注销**。(**jiāng ā lā fǎ tè zhù xiāo**)
Baidu	他们一知道德格诺明正在进行，就冲上去看一看。(dé gé nuò míng) 然后有人说，俄国人很快就会把阿拉法特**一笔勾销了**。(bǎ ā lā fǎ tè **yī bǐ gōu xiāo** le)
Ref.	一知道去地精的事在进行，他们就冲上去观看。(qù dì jīng) 然后有人说，现在用不了多久，俄罗斯人就会**把阿拉法特下課** / 让...下台。(**bǎ ā lā fǎ tè xià kè**; ràng...xià tái)

Figure 9: MT issues with MWEs: social/literature-unaware ambiguity

de cài, literally *not my dish*)". From this point of view, the context based MT model deserves some more attentions, instead of only focusing on sentence level. When we tried to put all background context information as shown in Fig.8 into the four MT models, they produce as the same output for this studied sentence, as for sentence level MT. This indicates that current MT models still focus on sentence-by-sentence translation when meeting paragraphs, instead of using context inference.

4.6.2 Social/Literature-Unaware Ambiguity

In this case, *social knowledge* of current affairs from news, or *literature knowledge* about some newly invented entities / phrases are required in order to get a correct translation output. For instance, Fig. 9 includes two sentences, one from politics and another from literature.

In the first sentence, "de-gnoming" is a literature word from Harry Potter, invented by its author, to refer to the process of ridding a garden of gnomes, *a small magical beast*. Without this literature knowledge it is not possible to translate the sentence correctly. For instance, even though this sentence is from a very popular novel that has been translated into most languages, DeepL translated it as "去核 (qù hé, de-nuclear)", Bing translated it as "去诺格明 (qù nuò gé míng, *de*-nuògémíng" where "nuògémíng" is a simulation of the pronunciation of "gnoming" in a Chinese way, Baidu translated it as "德格诺明 (dé gé nuò míng)" which is the simulation of the pronunciation of the overall term "de-gnoming".

In the second sentence, "write Arafat off" is to dismiss "Yasser Arafat", Chairman of the Palestine Liberation Organization, who is a historical person's name. However, all three models DeepL, Bing, and GoogleMT translated it into "把/将阿拉法特注销 (bǎ/jiāng ā lā fǎ tè zhù xiāo, *deregister Arafat*)" which treated "Arafat" as a tittle of certain policy/proceeding, not being able to recognize it as a personal named entity, while Baidu made the effort to use the Chinese idiom "一笔勾销 (yī bǐ gōu xiāo, *cancel everything*, or *never mention historical conflicts*)" for "write off" but it is not a correct translation. Interestingly, if we put these two sentences into a web search engine it retrieves the correct web pages as context in the top list of the search result. This may indicate that future MT models could consider to include web search results as part of their knowledge of background for translation purposes.

4.6.3 Coherence-Unaware Ambiguity

This kind of MWE ambiguity can be solved by the *coherence* of the sentence itself, for instance, the example in Fig. 10. The four MT models all translated the vMWE itself "have an operation" correctly in meaning preservation by "做/接受/动手术 (zuò/jiē shòu/dòng shǒu shù)" just with different Chinese word choices. However, none of the MT models translated the "reason of the operation", i.e., "complaint" correctly. The word complaint has two most commonly

Source	Two months ago I had to <u>have an operation</u> for a serious ***complaint***.
DeepL	两个月前，我因为一次严重的**投诉**不得不做<u>手术</u>。(**tóu sù** … zuò shŏu shu)
Bing	两个月前，我不得不做一个严重的**投诉**手术。(zuò … **tóu sù** shŏu shù)
Google	两个月前，我不得不接受一次手术以应对严重的**投诉**。(jiē shòu yī cì shŏu shù … **tóu sù**)
Baidu	两个月前，我因为严重的**投诉**不得不<u>动手术</u>。(**tóu sù** … dòng shŏu shù)
Ref.	两个月前，我因为一次严重的**症状**不得不<u>做手术</u>。(**zhèng zhuàng** … zuò shŏu shù)

Figure 10: MT issues with MWEs: coherence-unaware ambiguity

used meanings "a statement that something is unsatisfactory or unacceptable" or "an illness or medical condition" and all four models chose the first one. According to simple logic of social life, people do not need to "have an operation" due to "a statement", instead their "medical condition" should have been chosen to translate the word "complaint". Because of the incorrectly chosen candidate translation of the word "complaint", Bing's output even invented a new term in Chinese "投诉手术 (tóu sù shŏu shù, *a surgery of complaint statement kind*)" which makes no sense.

5 Conclusion and Future Work

In this paper, we presented the construction of multilingual parallel corpora, AlphaMWE, with vMWEs as pioneer annotations by native speakers of the corresponding languages. We described the procedure of MT model selection, human post editing and annotation, and compared different state-of-the-art MT models and classified the MT errors from vMWEs related sentence/context translations. We characterised the errors into different categories to help MT research to focus on one or more of them to improve the performance of MT.

We performed the same process as described here for English→Chinese, English→German and English→Polish and similarly categorised the MT issues when handling MWEs. The English→German issues can be categorized into: (1) there are cases where the corresponding German translation of English MWEs can be one word, which is partially because that German has separable verbs, (2) the automated translation to German is biased towards choosing the polite or formal form of the words, which is generally fine but depends on the context to decide which form is more suitable, and (3) English vMWEs are often not translated as vMWEs to German. In the main, English→Polish MT errors fall into the category of coherence-unaware errors, literal translation errors and context unaware situation errors.

We name our process as AlphaMWE to indicate that we will continue to maintain the developed corpora which are publicly available and extend them into other possible language pairs, e.g. Spanish, French and Italian (under-development). We also plan to extend the annotated MWE genres beyond the vMWEs defined in the PARSEME shared task.

Acknowledgements

The ADAPT Centre for Digital Content Technology is funded under the SFI Research Centres Programme (Grant 13/RC/2106) and is co-funded under the European Regional Development Fund. The input of Alan Smeaton is part-funded by SFI under grant number SFI/12/RC/2289 (Insight Centre). The authors are very grateful to their colleagues who helped to create the AlphaMWE corpora by post editing and annotation work across all language pairs, to Yi Lu and Dr. Paolo Bolzoni for helping with the experiments, to Lorin Sweeney, Roise McGagh, and Eoin Treacy for discussions about English MWEs and terms, Yandy Wong for discussion of Cantonese examples, and Hailin Hao and Yao Tong for joining the first discussion. The authors also thank the anonymous reviewers for their thorough reviews and insightful comments.

References

Timothy Baldwin and Su Nam Kim. 2010. Multiword expressions. In *Handbook of Natural Language Processing, Second Edition*, pages 267–292. Chapman and Hall.

Ondřej Bojar, Rajen Chatterjee, Christian Federmann, Yvette Graham, Barry Haddow, Shujian Huang, Matthias Huck, Philipp Koehn, Qun Liu, Varvara Logacheva, Christof Monz, Matteo Negri, Matt Post, Raphael Rubino, Lucia Specia, and Marco Turchi. 2017. Findings of the 2017 conference on machine translation (WMT17). In *Proceedings of the Second Conference on Machine Translation*, pages 169–214, Copenhagen, Denmark, September. Association for Computational Linguistics.

Dhouha Bouamor, Nasredine Semmar, and Pierre Zweigenbaum. 2012. Identifying bilingual multi-word expressions for statistical machine translation. In *Conference on Language Resources and Evaluation*.

Vishal Chowdhary and Scott Greenwood. 2017. Emt: End to end model training for msr machine translation. In *Proceedings of the 1st Workshop on Data Management for End-to-End Machine Learning*.

Mathieu Constant, Gülşen Eryiğit, Johanna Monti, Lonneke van der Plas, Carlos Ramisch, Michael Rosner, and Amalia Todirascu. 2017. Survey: Multiword expression processing: A Survey. *Computational Linguistics*, 43(4):837–892.

Lifeng Han, Gareth J. F. Jones, and Alan Smeaton. 2020. MultiMWE: Building a multi-lingual multi-word expression (MWE) parallel corpora. In *Proceedings of The 12th Language Resources and Evaluation Conference*, pages 2970–2979, Marseille, France. European Language Resources Association.

Hany Hassan, Anthony Aue, C. Chen, Vishal Chowdhary, J. Clark, C. Federmann, Xuedong Huang, Marcin Junczys-Dowmunt, W. Lewis, M. Li, Shujie Liu, T. Liu, Renqian Luo, Arul Menezes, Tao Qin, F. Seide, Xu Tan, Fei Tian, Lijun Wu, Shuangzhi Wu, Yingce Xia, Dongdong Zhang, Zhirui Zhang, and M. Zhou. 2018. Achieving human parity on automatic chinese to english news translation. *ArXiv*, abs/1803.05567.

Melvin Johnson, Mike Schuster, Quoc V. Le, Maxim Krikun, Yonghui Wu, Zhifeng Chen, Nikhil Thorat, Fernanda B. Viégas, Martin Wattenberg, Greg Corrado, Macduff Hughes, and Jeffrey Dean. 2016. Google's multilingual neural machine translation system: Enabling zero-shot translation. *CoRR*, abs/1611.04558.

Akihiko Kato, Hiroyuki Shindo, and Yuji Matsumoto. 2018. Construction of Large-scale English Verbal Multiword Expression Annotated Corpus. In *Proceedings of the Eleventh International Conference on Language Resources and Evaluation (LREC 2018)*, Miyazaki, Japan, May 7-12, 2018.

Patrik Lambert and Rafael E. Banchs. 2005. Data Inferred Multi-word Expressions for Statistical Machine Translation. In *Proceedings of Machine Translation Summit X*, pages 396–403, Thailand.

Xiaoqing Li, Jinghui Yan, Jiajun Zhang, and Chengqing Zong. 2019. Neural name translation improves neural machine translation. In Jiajun Chen and Jiajun Zhang, editors, *Machine Translation*, pages 93–100, Singapore. Springer Singapore.

Alfredo Maldonado, Lifeng Han, Erwan Moreau, Ashjan Alsulaimani, Koel Dutta Chowdhury, Carl Vogel, and Qun Liu. 2017. Detection of verbal multi-word expressions via conditional random fields with syntactic dependency features and semantic re-ranking. In *The 13th Workshop on Multiword Expressions @ EACL 2017*. ACL.

Virginia Pulcini. 2020. English-derived multi-word and phraseological units across languages in the global anglicism database. *Textus, English Studies in Italy*, (1/2020):127–143.

Carlos Ramisch, Silvio Ricardo Cordeiro, Agata Savary, Veronika Vincze, Verginica Barbu Mititelu, Archna Bhatia, Maja Buljan, Marie Candito, Polona Gantar, Voula Giouli, Tunga Güngör, Abdelati Hawwari, Uxoa Iñurrieta, Jolanta Kovalevskaitė, Simon Krek, Timm Lichte, Chaya Liebeskind, Johanna Monti, Carla Parra Escartín, Behrang QasemiZadeh, Renata Ramisch, Nathan Schneider, Ivelina Stoyanova, Ashwini Vaidya, and Abigail Walsh. 2018. Edition 1.1 of the PARSEME shared task on automatic identification of verbal multiword expressions. In *Proceedings of the Joint Workshop on Linguistic Annotation, Multiword Expressions and Constructions (LAW-MWE-CxG-2018)*, pages 222–240, Santa Fe, New Mexico, USA, August. Association for Computational Linguistics.

Matīss Rikters and Ondřej Bojar. 2017. Paying Attention to Multi-Word Expressions in Neural Machine Translation. In *Proceedings of the 16th Machine Translation Summit*, Nagoya, Japan.

Ivan A. Sag, Timothy Baldwin, Francis Bond, Ann Copestake, and Dan Flickinger. 2002. Multiword expressions: A pain in the neck for nlp. In Alexander Gelbukh, editor, *Computational Linguistics and Intelligent Text Processing*, pages 1–15, Berlin, Heidelberg. Springer Berlin Heidelberg.

Agata Savary, Carlos Ramisch, Silvio Cordeiro, Federico Sangati, Veronika Vincze, Behrang Qasemi-iZadeh, Marie Candito, Fabienne Cap, Voula Giouli, Ivelina Stoyanova, and Antoine Doucet. 2017. The PARSEME shared task on automatic identification of verbal multiword expressions. In *Proceedings of the 13th Workshop on Multiword Expressions (MWE 2017)*, pages 31–47, Valencia, Spain.

Nathan Schneider, Spencer Onuffer, Nora Kazour, Emily Danchik, Michael T. Mordowanec, Henrietta Conrad, and Noah A. Smith. 2014. Comprehensive annotation of multiword expressions in a social web corpus. In *Proceedings of the Ninth International Conference on Language Resources and Evaluation (LREC-2014)*, pages 455–461, Reykjavik, Iceland, May. European Languages Resources Association.

Inguna Skadina. 2016. Multi-word expressions in english-latvian machine translation. *Baltic J. Modern Computing*, 4:811–825.

Meng Sun, Bojian Jiang, Hao Xiong, Zhongjun He, Hua Wu, and Haifeng Wang. 2019. Baidu neural machine translation systems for WMT19. In *Proceedings of the Fourth Conference on Machine Translation (Volume 2: Shared Task Papers, Day 1)*, pages 374–381, Florence, Italy. Association for Computational Linguistics.

Ashish Vaswani, Noam Shazeer, Niki Parmar, Jakob Uszkoreit, Llion Jones, Aidan N. Gomez, Lukasz Kaiser, and Illia Polosukhin. 2017. Attention is all you need. In *Conference on Neural Information Processing System*, pages 6000–6010.

Veronika Vincze. 2012. Light verb constructions in the SzegedParalellFX English–Hungarian parallel corpus. In *Proceedings of the Eighth International Conference on Language Resources and Evaluation (LREC'12)*, pages 2381–2388, Istanbul, Turkey, May. European Language Resources Association.

Abigail Walsh, Claire Bonial, Kristina Geeraert, John P. McCrae, Nathan Schneider, and Clarissa Somers. 2018. Constructing an annotated corpus of verbal MWEs for English. In *Proceedings of the Joint Workshop on Linguistic Annotation, Multiword Expressions and Constructions (LAW-MWE-CxG-2018)*, pages 193–200, Santa Fe, New Mexico, USA, August. Association for Computational Linguistics.

Yonghui Wu, Mike Schuster, Zhifeng Chen, Quoc V. Le, Mohammad Norouzi, Wolfgang Macherey, Maxim Krikun, Yuan Cao, Qin Gao, Klaus Macherey, Jeff Klingner, Apurva Shah, Melvin Johnson, Xiaobing Liu, Lukasz Kaiser, Stephan Gouws, Yoshikiyo Kato, Taku Kudo, Hideto Kazawa, Keith Stevens, George Kurian, Nishant Patil, Wei Wang, Cliff Young, Jason Smith, Jason Riesa, Alex Rudnick, Oriol Vinyals, Greg Corrado, Macduff Hughes, and Jeffrey Dean. 2016. Google's neural machine translation system: Bridging the gap between human and machine translation. *CoRR*, abs/1609.08144.

Appendix A: AlphaMWE Corpus Presentation Examples.

As shown in the examples (Fig. 11) from Chinese, German and Polish, all involved languages are sentence by sentence aligned, including the vMWEs paired with order which are put behind the sentences into the bracket pairs. AlphaMWE also includes statistics of the annotated vMWEs, and a multilingual vMWEs glossary. The AlphaMWE corpora are divided evenly into five portions which were designed in the post-editing and annotation stage. As a result, it is convenient for researchers to use them for testing NLP models, choosing any subset portion or combination, or cross validation usage.

Error Examples from English Corpus Fixed in AlphaMWE

Some error annotations of vMWEs in source monolingual corpus surly have some impact on the accuracy level of the *vMWE discovery and identification* shared task, but also affect the bilingual usage of AlphaMWE, so we tried to address all these cases. For instance, the example sentence in Fig. 5, English corpus annotated wrongly the sequence "had to go on" as a verbal idioms (VIDs) which is not accurate. The verb "had" here is affiliated with "all he had" instead of "to go on". So either we shall annotate "go on" as vMWE in the sentence or the overall clause *"all he had to go on"* as a studied term.

Another example with a different type of vMWE is the sentence "He put them on in a kind of trance." where the source English corpus tagged "put" and "trance" as Light-verb construction

Plain English Corpus	The chair was comfortable, and the beer had <u>gone</u> slightly <u>to his head</u>. I was smoking my pipe quietly by my dismantled steamer, and saw them all <u>cutting capers</u> in the light, with their arms lifted high, when the stout man with mustaches came *tearing down* to the river, a tin pail in his hand, assured me that everybody was 'behaving splendidly, splendidly, dipped about a quart of water and *tore back* again. (*the italic was not annotated in source English*)
English MWEs	gone (slightly) to his head, cutting capers, tearing down, tore back
Target Chinese Corpus	椅子很舒服，啤酒已经微微<u>让他上了头</u>。[sourceVMWE: gone (slightly) to his head][targetVMWE: (微微)让他上了头] 我在拆开的汽船旁静静地抽着烟斗，看到他们都在灯光下<u>欢呼雀跃</u>，高举双臂，这时，那个留着胡子的大块头，手里拿着一个铁皮桶，<u>快速来到</u>河边，向我确保大家都"表现得很精彩，很精彩"，他浸了大约一夸脱的水，又<u>快速回去了</u>。[sourceVMWE: cutting capers; tearing down; tore back][targetVMWE: 欢呼雀跃; 快速到; 快速回去]
Target German Corpus	Der Stuhl war bequem, und das Bier war ihm leicht <u>zu Kopf gestiegen</u>. [sourceVMWE: gone (slightly) to his head][targetVMWE: (leicht) zu Kopf gestiegen] Ich rauchte leise meine Pfeife an meinem zerlegten Dampfer und sah, wie sie alle im Licht mit hoch erhobenen Armen <u>Luftsprünge machten</u>, als der stämmige Mann mit Schnurrbart mit einem Blecheimer in der Hand zum Fluss <u>hinunterkam</u> und mir versicherte, dass sich alle "prächtig, prächtig benahmen, etwa einen Liter Wasser eintauchte und wieder <u>zurückwankte</u>". [sourceVMWE: cutting capers; tearing down; tore back] [targetVMWE: Luftsprünge machten; hinunterkam; zurückwankte]
Target Polish Corpus	Krzesło było wygodne, a piwo lekko <u>uderzyło mu do głowy</u>. [sourceVMWE: gone (slightly) to his head] [targetVMWE: (lekko) uderzyło mu do głowy] Cicho paliłem swoją fajkę przy zdemontowanym parowcu i widziałem, jak wszyscy <u>pląsają</u> w świetle, z podniesionymi wysoko ramionami, gdy twardziel z wąsami <u>przyszedł szybkim krokiem</u> do rzeki, blaszany wiaderko w dłoni, zapewnił mnie, że wszyscy "zachowują się wspaniale, wspaniale, nabrał około ćwiartkę wody i <u>zawrócił szybkim krokiem</u>". [sourceVMWE: cutting capers; tearing down; tore back][targetVMWE: pląsają; przyszedł szybkim krokiem; zawrócił szybkim krokiem]
AlphaMWE corpora examples from multilingual parallel files. "cutting capers" was annotated as VID type of MWEs, while "tearing down" and "tore back" were not annotated in the source English corpus. We added them into AlphaMWE multilingual corpora since they do cause translation errors for most state-of-the-art MT models. The bilingual MWEs are aligned with their appearance order from sentence inside the afterwards attached bracket-pairs.	

Figure 11: AlphaMWE corpora samples with two sentences

(VLC.cause). However, the phrase is with "put...on" instead of "put...trance". "put someone into a trance" is a phrase to express "make someone into a half-conscious state". However, for this sentence, if we check back a bit further of the context, it means "he put on his cloth in a kind of trance". The word "trance" is affiliated with the phrase "*in a kind of trance*" instead of "put".

Appendix B: English→German/Polish MT Samples Reflecting Afore Mentioned MWE Related Issues.

English→German

Firstly, for the English vMWE translates into single German word, let's see the vMWE "woke up" the sentence "An old woman with crinkly grey hair woke up at her post outside the lavatory and opened the door, smiling and grasping a filthy cleaning rag." has corresponding German aligned word "erwachte" with a suitable translation "Eine alte Frau mit krausem, grauem Haar erwachte auf ihrem Posten vor der Toilette und öffnete die Tür, lächelte und griff nach einem schmutzigen Putzlappen.".

This also occurs in English to Chinese translation, such as an English verb+particle MWE getting aligned to one single Chinese character/word. For example, in this sentence "The fact that my name has been mixed up in this.", the vMWE (VPC) *mixed up* gets aligned to single character word "混 (hùn)" in a suitable translation "事实上，我的名字已经被混在这里面了。(Shì shí shàng, wǒ de míng zì yǐ jīng bèi hùn zài zhè lǐ miàn le)".

Secondly, for the automatic translation to German that is very *biased* towards choosing the polite or formal form, see the examples such as "Sie"instead of the second form singular "du"for "you", "auf Basis von" instead of "basierend auf" for "based on". To achieve a higher accuracy level of MT, it shall depend on the context of usage to decide which form is more suitable.

Thirdly, for the English verbal multiword expressions that are often not translated as verbal multiword expressions to German. This indicates some further work to explore by MT researchers to develop better models to have the machine producing corresponding German existing MWEs.

English→Polish

Regarding the MT output issues on English to Polish that fall into coherence-unaware error, for instance, the vMWE "write off" in sentence "Then someone says that it can't be long now before the Russians write Arafat off." was translated as "Wypiszą" (Potem ktoś mówi, że już niedługo Rosjanie wypiszą Arafata.) which means "prescribe", instead of correct one "spiszą na straty (Arafata)". This error shall be able to avoid by the coherence of the sentence itself in meaning preservation models.

For the literal translation, we can see the example vMWE "gave (him) a look" in the sentence "She ruffled her feathers and gave him a look of deep disgust." which was literally translated as "dała mu spojrzenie", however, in Polish, people use **throw** a look" as "rzuciła (mu) spojrzenie" instead of "gave (dała, a female form)"[4]. Another example of literal translation leading to errors is the vMWE "turn the tables" from sentence "Now Iran wants to turn the tables and is inviting cartoonists to do their best by depicting the Holocaust." which is translated as "odwrócić stoliki (turn tables)", however, it shall be "odwrócić sytuację (turn the situation)" or "odwrócić rolę (turn role)" with a proper translation "*Teraz Iran chce odwrócić sytuację i zachęca rysowników, by zrobili wszystko, co w ich mocy, przedstawiając Holocaust.*" These two examples present the localization issue in the target language.

For the context unaware issue, we can look back to the example sentence "But it did not give me the time of day." from Fig. 8. It was literally translated word by word into "Ale nie dało mi to pory dnia." which is in the sense of hour/time. However, it shall be "Nie sądzę aby to było coś wyjątkowo/szczególnie dla mnie. (I do not think this is special to me.)" based on the context, or "Ale to nie moja bajka" as an idiomatic expression which means "not my fairy tale" (indicating *not my cup of tea*).

Appendix C: Initial Post-editing and Annotation Contact List (Fig.12).

en->zh	Lifeng Han, <lifeng.han@adaptcentre.ie> ADAPT Research Centre, DCU, Dublin, Ireland
	Ning Jiang, <njiang@tcd.ie> School of Linguistic, Speech and Communication Sciences, TCD, Ireland
	Qinyuan Li, <liq3@tcd.ie> School of Education, Trinity College Dublin (TCD), Ireland
	Pan Pan, <panpan@m.scnu.edu.cn> School of Foreign Studies, South China Normal University, Guangzhou, China
en->de	Gültekin Cakir, <gueltekin.cakir@mu.ie> Innovation Value Institute, Maynooth University, Ireland
	Daniela Gierschek, <daniela.gierschek@uni.lu> Institute of Luxembourgish Linguistics and Literature, Université du Luxembourg, 2 Avenue de l'Université, 4365 Esch-sur-Alzette, Luxembourg
	Vanessa Smolik, <v.smolik@uni-bielefeld.de> Bielefeld University, Universitätsstraße 25, 33615 Bielefeld, Germany
en->pl	Teresa Flera, <t.flera@uw.edu.pl> Doctoral School of Humanities (Institute of English Studies), University of Warsaw, Poland
	Sonia Ramotowska, <s.ramotowska@uva.nl> Institute for Logic, Language and Computation, University of Amsterdam, Science Park 107, 1098 XG Amsterdam, The Netherlands

Figure 12: AlphaMWE corpora initial contact list (with alphabetical order)

---

[4]a proper translation: *Nastroszyła sobie pióra i rzuciła mu spojrzenie głębokiego obrzydzenia.* Also the MT output word for "Nastroszyła" was "Zdruzgotała" which is wrong meaning.

Annotating Verbal MWEs in Irish for the PARSEME Shared Task 1.2

Abigail Walsh   **Teresa Lynn**   **Jennifer Foster**

ADAPT Centre

School of Computing

Dublin City University

`{abigail.walsh,teresa.lynn}@adaptcentre.ie`

`jennifer.foster@dcu.ie`

Abstract

This paper describes the creation of two Irish corpora (labelled and unlabelled) for verbal MWEs for inclusion in the PARSEME Shared Task 1.2 on automatic identification of verbal MWEs, and the process of developing verbal MWE categories for Irish. A qualitative analysis on the two corpora is presented, along with discussion of Irish verbal MWEs.

1 Introduction

Multiword expressions (MWEs) present a well-documented challenge in the field of NLP, given that they appear in a variety of forms, are idiosyncratic in nature, and prevalent in our lexicon (Jackendoff, 1997; Sag et al., 2002; Baldwin and Kim, 2010). That said, their correct handling can aid in a number of NLP tasks, including word-sense disambiguation, parsing, and machine translation (Constant et al., 2017). This has given rise to a number of working groups dedicated to identifying and interpreting MWEs. PARSEME is one such group, with the aim of improving cross-lingual processing of MWEs. Their shared task on the automatic identification of verbal MWEs (Savary et al., 2017; Ramisch et al., 2018) is now in its third iteration, and their guidelines have expanded to include 27 languages. This year saw the addition of Irish, as the first of the Celtic languages to participate. Two corpora of Irish text were created for this shared task: a small corpus consisting of manually labelled verbal MWEs (VMWEs), and a much larger corpus for use in unsupervised VMWE identification.

Research on MWEs in Irish is still sparse, and much work remains to define the types of MWEs that exist. Most of the literature on Irish linguistics and syntax focuses on a theoretical analysis of the language, and any discussion of idiomatic constructions, which are frequently exceptional cases, tends to be brief. (Stenson, 1981; Christian Brothers, 1999; Uí Dhonnchadha, 2009). Some studies offer more in-depth analysis on particular types of MWEs, such as light-verb constructions (Bloch-Trojnar, 2009; Bayda, 2015), the idiomatic use of prepositions with verbs (Ó Domhnalláin and Ó Baoill, 1975) and idioms (Ní Loingsigh, 2016). Others have offered a preliminary categorisation of Irish MWEs (Veselinović, 2006; Walsh et al., 2019). The categorisation carried out in our previous work (Walsh et al., 2019) is largely based on the annotation guidelines developed for the PARSEME shared tasks[1], and as such can be used as a starting point for the development of a comprehensive set of VMWE categories for Irish.

2 Verbal MWE Categories in Irish

Given that the focus of PARSEME is on the identification of verbal MWEs, some categories of MWEs considered in our previous work, such as nominal compounds or fixed expressions, are excluded. The categories examined here include two universal categories (verbal idioms and light verb constructions) that are found in all participating languages of the PARSEME shared task: two quasi-universal categories

---

[1]`https://parsemefr.lis-lab.fr/parseme-st-guidelines/1.1/?page=home`

Joint Workshop on Multiword Expressions and Electronic Lexicons, pages 58–65

Barcelona, Spain (Online), December 13, 2020.

(verb-particle constructions and inherently reflexive verbs) that are valid in many but not all participating languages, and one experimental category (inherently adpositional verbs) which can be optionally annotated.

Light verb constructions (LVCs)   are described in the PARSEME guidelines as formed by a verb, v, and a (single or compound) noun, n, which either directly depends on v or is introduced by a preposition. Constructions where v's syntactic subject is n's semantic argument are full LVCs and annotated as `LVC.full`, while constructions where the subject of v is the cause or source of the event or state expressed by n are annotated as `LVC.cause`. Examples include the `LVC.full` *déan dearmad* (do negligence) 'forget' and the `LVC.cause` *cuir áthas* (put joy) 'make happy'.

Verb particle constructions (VPCs)   – sometimes called phrasal verbs – consist of a verb, and a dependent intransitive particle (usually a directional adverb in Irish), where the particle causes a significant shift in meaning in the verb. This change in meaning can be either fully non-compositional (annotated as `VPC.full`, e.g. *tabhair amach* (give out) 'scold') or semi-compositional (annotated as `VPC.semi`, e.g. *glan suas* (clean up) 'clean up').

Inherently adpositional verbs (IAVs)   are considered an experimental category in the PARSEME guidelines and language teams may optionally annotate for this category as a final step in the annotation process. The construction consists of a verb and a dependent prepositional phrase, where the preposition is considered integral to the construction, i.e. "it cannot be omitted without markedly altering the meaning of the verb". This construction occurs frequently in Irish (e.g. *buail le* (hit with) 'meet'), and as such it was decided to annotate this category in the current edition, to determine whether future versions of the corpus should contain this category. VMWEs can themselves form part of the IAV construction, as in the IAV *cuir suas le* (put up with) 'put up with', which contains the VPC *cuir suas* (put up) 'put up', which is why this category must be annotated last.

Verbal idioms (VIDs)   are idiomatic constructions with at least two lexicalised parts, including a head and at least one dependent. These dependents can be of several different categories (e.g. *tar an crú ar an tairne* (come the shoe on the nail) 'come to the test', *ag siúl le chéile* (at walking with each-other) 'courting'). Also included in VIDs are sentential expressions with no open slots, such as proverbs (e.g. *Ní neart go cur le chéile* (is-not strength without put with each-other) 'There's strength in unity').

2.1   Difficult Decisions

Annotating LVCs with IAV   Many LVCs select for a specific preposition, and the construction never occurs without that preposition (e.g. *déan iarracht ar* (make attempt **on**) 'make an attempt **at**', and *bain triail as* (take test **from**) 'try'). In analysis of the LVC, Irish scholars often include the preposition as an integral part of the construction (Stenson, 1981; Bloch-Trojnar, 2009; Bayda, 2015). There was some debate on whether to additionally annotate these LVC constructions with a selected preposition as IAV, as it was difficult to determine if the preposition was integral to the semantics of the construction, and whether omitting it caused a marked change in the meaning of the verb. It was decided not to extend these LVCs with the IAV label unless the preposition clearly caused a shift in meaning to the verb taken alone. This decision may be revisited in future versions of the corpus.

Terminology: VPC versus IAV   The term *verb particle construction* is rarely used in Irish linguistic discourse, however *phrasal verbs* are discussed by various authors (Veselinović, 2006; Uí Dhonnchadha, 2009), although there seems to be a difference in the usage of the term. In the PARSEME guidelines, as with many other authors, the term *phrasal verb* is used synonymously with verb particle constructions. In English, particles are often homonymous with prepositions (though not always: e.g. *back, through*), although their behaviour is markedly different (Jackendoff, 2002). Uí Dhonnchadha (2009) uses the term *phrasal verb* to refer specifically to verbs that can combine with prepositions to give rise to idiomatic readings, as in *éirigh le* (rise with) 'succeed', whereas there does not appear to be any discussion of verb + adverb constructions such as *éirigh amach* (rise out) 'revolt'. Furthermore, the preposition *le* 'with' in *éirigh le* does not appear to follow the specifications for a particle according to the PARSEME guidelines (i.e. it should not govern a complement), given that it forms a constituent with the noun phrase rather than the verb, as in *d'éirigh léi* (succeeded with-she) 'she succeeded'. In order to align with the categorisation of VPCs outlined by the PARSEME annotation guidelines, it was decided to annotate *éirigh le*, and similar constructions as IAV. To avoid confusion in the future, language-specific tests for identifying particles in Irish will be added to the guidelines.

Idiomatic constructions with the verb "be" There are two verbs for "be" in Irish: the substantive verb *bí* conjugates as a normal verb (past tense: *bhí*, present tense: *tá*) and is used to express state, including feelings and emotions, possession, location and existence; and the copula *is* that is used in many other constructions, such as classification, equivalency constructions, or comparisons (Christian Brothers, 1997).

The substantive *bí* can be combined with certain prepositions to express things like possession (*bí + ag/ar* (be at/on) 'have', *tá hata agam* (is hat at-me) 'I have a hat'), desire (*bí + ó* (be from) 'want', *tá cáca uaim* (is cake from-me) 'I want cake'), intention (*bí + faoi* (be under) 'intend to', *tá fúm é a dhéanamh* (is under-me it ⟨*part*⟩ doing) 'I intend to do it') and membership of a class (*bí + i +* ⟨*possessive_pronoun*⟩ (be in ⟨*possessive_pronoun*⟩) 'be of the class', *tá mé i mo chócaire* (is I in my chef) 'I am a chef'), among others. The latter construction was annotated as VID as it has two lexicalised dependents (the preposition *i* and the possessive pronoun[2]). The question of whether the prepositions were integral to the meaning of the other constructions was complicated by the fact that these prepositions could be applied to other verbs to give rise to a similar meaning (e.g. *teastaigh + ó* (be wanted from) = 'wanting from'), making it unclear whether the prepositions were truly causing a shift in the meaning of the verb. Ultimately, such constructions were not annotated.

The copula appears in certain idiomatic constructions such as copula + preposition combinations (e.g. *is + le* (be with) (possession), *an leatsa an cupán?* (interrogative-be with-you the cup) 'is the cup yours?'; *is + as* (be from) (origin), *is as Chiarraí mé* (is from Kerry me) 'I am from Kerry'), copula + adjective combinations (*is + maith + le* (is good with) 'like', *is maith liom tae* (is good with-me tea) 'I like tea') and other unique idiomatic constructions (Josie + *is + ainm + di* (Josie be name to-her) 'Josie is her name'). These cannot be categorised as VMWEs, given that the syntactic head of copular constructions is not a verb.

Inherently reflexive verbs (IRVs) are a quasi-universal category that occur rarely if at all in Irish. An IRV consists of a verb v and a reflexive clitic $RCLI$ where either v never occurs without $RCLI$, or the meaning changes significantly. In Irish, the reflexive pronoun is formed through the combination of *féin* + personal pronoun. Very few constructions appear to require the reflexive pronoun to give a different meaning (possibly: *iompair mé* 'I carry' vs. *iompair mé féin* (carry I self) 'I behave myself'). However, certain verb + inflected preposition constructions can imply reflexivity (e.g. *bailigh + leis* (gather with-him) 'remove himself/be off'). It was decided to annotate such constructions with IRV in this version of the corpus, but this decision may be changed in the future, due to their scarcity and lack of an explicit $RCLI$.

3   Creation of Corpora

Previous editions of the shared task were focused on supervised training of MWE identification, through a manually annotated corpus of VMWEs that was also annotated for POS information, morphological tags, and dependency trees. This edition, however, included a corpus for unsupervised training, which contained no VMWE information, but was automatically tokenised, lemmatised and parsed using UD-Pipe (Straka and Straková, 2017).[3]

---

[2]Possessive pronouns in VIDs have special lexicalization status and can be realised by different lexemes depending on number and person.

[3]Note that the unlabelled corpus include MWEs of the kind annotated by UD (i.e. flat, fixed, compound and compound:prt)

3.1 Labelled Corpus

The 1,700 sentences in the labelled corpus were taken from version 2.5 of the Irish Universal Dependency Treebank (Zeman et al., 2019). The sentences contain gold-standard annotations at the following levels: POS-information, morphological features and dependency syntax.

Three annotators helped with the manual VMWE annotation. Annotator A had prior experience with the annotation of Irish MWEs and verbal MWEs for other languages according to the PARSEME guidelines, while Annotator B and Annotator C were practised experts in Irish linguistics and syntactic annotation. 100 sentences were annotated by Annotator A as a pilot annotation task, during which the categories `LVC.full`, `LVC.cause`, `VPC.full`, `VPC.semi`, `VID`, `IAV`, `IRV` were fixed upon. 600 sentences were then selected and used by Annotators B and C to test the categorisation guidelines through annotation. Annotator A annotated the other 1000 sentences, and then performed a review on all 1700 sentences, including the 100 pilot sentences and the 600 test sentences.

A portion of the corpus (800 sentences) was doubly annotated at the beginning and the end of the annotation period by Annotator A in order to measure intra-annotator agreement. The first pass of annotation found 312 VMWEs, while the second pass found 270. The F_{measure} was 0.71, the κ score was 0.66 (i.e. substantial agreement), and the κ_{cat} score was 0.84 (i.e. almost perfect agreement) (Landis and Koch, 1977). F_{measure} is an optimistic measure that ignores agreement due to chance, κ is an estimated Cohen's κ that measures the rate of agreement of annotation for all verbs in the corpus, whereas κ_{cat} takes into account only those VMWEs where both passes agreed on the span.

In total, 662 MWEs were annotated. The most frequent category of VMWE was `LVC.full`, closely followed by `IAV`, while the least frequent category was `IRV`. When compared with the English corpus for edition 1.1 of the shared task (Walsh et al., 2018),[4] it is clear that the density of VMWEs is much higher for Irish (1 per 2.6 sentences, or 1 out of every 8 verb phrases) versus English (1 per 8.9 sentences, or 1 out of every 47.8 verb phrases).[5] Given that over a quarter of the VMWEs annotated were `IAV`, there is a strong argument for consistently annotating this category – in Irish if not for other languages.

Category	#Annotations	Category	#Annotations
LVC.full	201	VPC.full	28
IAV	183	VPC.semi	20
LVC.cause	119	IRV	6
VID	105	**Total**	**662**

Table 1: Number of annotations per category.

3.2 Unlabelled Corpus

The unlabelled corpus consists of 1,379,824 sentences compiled from the sources listed in Table 2.[6] UDPipe trained on v2.5 of the Irish UD treebank was used to perform the following steps automatically: tokenisation, POS-tagging, lemmatisation, morphological analysis, and dependency parsing. To aid correct splitting of sentences, a pre-processing step was included where a period was added at the end of each line where it did not already exist. Based on a manual inspection of a subsection of the data (100 sentences from each source), some issues were noticed with the lemmatisation (e.g. *dtagraíonn* lemmatised to *tagraigh* when it should be *tagair*; lemma *n-oibrítí* has both initial mutation and is in its plural form), tokenisation (*d'imir* should be tokenised into *d'* and *imir*) and POS-tagging (*is* tagged as `AUX Cop` when it should be `CCONJ Coord`), which we assume affect parsing.[7]

3.3 Performance of the Shared Task Systems

The task of identification incorporates two subtasks: identifying the span of candidate VMWEs, and labelling these candidates. This edition of the shared task focused on the handling of *unseen* VMWEs,

---

[4]As Irish is the only Celtic language in the PARSEME shared task, English can be considered the closest language neighbour.
[5]# verb phrases estimated using POS information from released cupt files
[6]Text from Vicipéid Irish Wikipedia accessed 1/11/2019 and text from OPUS accessed at `http://opus.nlpl.eu/`
[7]To give an upper bound on parsing accuracy, UDPipe achieves UAS 0.85 and LAS 0.78 on the v2.5 test set.

Source	Size	License
Citizen's Information website	10,297	CC BY 4.0
EU Bookshop (OPUS)	113,363	open-source
Paracrawl (OPUS)	782,769	Creative Commons CC0 Licence
Tatoeba (OPUS)	1,894	CC–BY 2.0 FR
Vicipéid	302,838	GNU Free Documentation License (GFDL)

Table 2: Sources of unlabelled data, size in # sentences, and licence of the source

i.e. identifying VMWEs that were not annotated in the training and development datasets. To that end, the annotated data was split so as to include at least 300 unseen VMWEs in the test set.

Of the 9 systems participating in the shared task, 6 were submitted for Irish, with 5 of them achieving $F1$ scores above 0. The highest achieved $F1$ score for unseen MWEs in Irish was 19.54, while the cross-lingual macro-average $F1$ score (based on unseen MWEs) for the same system was 38.53. The categories IAV and VPC.full appear the easiest to identify, while VID proved difficult. VPC.semi and IRV were not identified at all, possibly as the number of examples of each was too few (20 and 6 respectively).

In general, the systems performed more poorly on Irish when compared with other languages, particularly compared to Hindi, which had a similarly sized corpus, and the best unseen MWE-based $F1$ score was 53.11. The language that performed most similarly was Hebrew, where the best unseen MWE-based $F1$ score was 19.59. There are a number of reasons that could explain the poor performance on the Irish dataset. The dataset contained a relatively small number of VMWEs in the corpus (662), when compared to the second smallest number, which was 1034 in Hindi. In addition, as a result of including 301 unseen VMWEs in the Irish test set, the rate of unseen VMWEs with regards to the training and development set was 0.69, the highest for any language. Another possible reason for the high rate of unseen VMWEs occurring is the source of the annotated data; the sentences in the Irish UD treebank (Lynn and Foster, 2016) come from a balanced corpus with a mixture of domains and genres. This can result in MWEs of varying types occurring throughout the data. Given the proportionally higher rate of unseen VMWEs, coupled with the smaller amount of data overall, it is unsurprising that systems did not perform as well on the Irish data as on other languages.

4   Conclusion

This paper describes an initial attempt at the manual annotation of Irish verbal MWEs, including developing a categorisation scheme that aligns with the PARSEME annotation guidelines. It was found that seven of the categories were applicable to Irish language, and the experimental category of IAV occurred frequently.

The results of this annotation are explored, along with results from participating systems in the shared task. It appears that the submitted systems found the task of automatic identification particularly difficult for Irish; this is likely due to the small size of the corpus and number of VMWEs annotated, the high rate of unseen VMWEs in the test data when compared to other languages, and the relatively large number of potential categories that increases the complexity of the task.

In the future we plan to continue the work of manual annotation of these VMWEs, particularly in defining the categories more precisely, refining the Irish-specific guidelines and adding language-specific tests for certain categories such as VPCs, and expanding the size of the corpus.

Acknowledgements

The first author's work is funded by the Irish Government Department of Culture, Heritage and the Gaeltacht under the GaelTech Project, and is also supported by Science Foundation Ireland in the ADAPT Centre (Grant 13/RC/2106) (http://www.adaptcentre.ie) at Dublin City University.

References

Timothy Baldwin and Su Nam Kim. 2010. Multiword expressions. *Handbook of Natural Language Processing, Second Edition*, pages 267–292, 01.

Victor Bayda. 2015. Irish constructions with bain. *Yn llawen iawn, yn llawn iaith: Proceedings of the 6th International Colloquium of Societas Celto-Slavica. Vol. 7 of Studia Celto-Slavica. Johnston, D., Parina, E. and Fomin, M. (eds)*, 7:213–228, 01.

Maria Bloch-Trojnar. 2009. On the Nominal Status of VNs in Light Verb Constructions in Modern Irish. In *PASE Papers 2008. Vol. 1: Studies in Language and Methodology of Teaching Foreign Languages*, page 25–33, Wrocław: Oficyna Wydawnicza ATUT.

The Christian Brothers. 1997. *New Irish Grammar*. Dublin: Fallon.

The Christian Brothers. 1999. *Graiméar Gaeilge na mBráithre Críostaí*. An Gúm, Baile Átha Cliath.

Mathieu Constant, Gülşen Eryiğit, Johanna Monti, Lonneke van der Plas, Carlos Ramisch, Michael Rosner, and Amalia Todirascu. 2017. Multiword expression processing: A Survey. *Computational Linguistics*, 43(4):837–892, December.

Ray Jackendoff. 1997. *The Architecture of the Language Faculty*. Linguistic Inquiry Monographs volume 28. MIT Press.

Ray Jackendoff. 2002. English particle constructions, the lexicon, and the autonomy of syntax. *Verb-Particle Explorations*, pages 67–94.

J. Richard Landis and Gary G. Koch. 1977. The Measurement of Observer Agreement for Categorical Data. *Biometrics*, 33(1):159–174.

Teresa Lynn and Jennifer Foster. 2016. Universal Dependencies for Irish. In *Proceedings of the Second Celtic Language Technology Workshop*, Paris, France.

Katie Ní Loingsigh. 2016. *Tiomsú agus Rangú i mBunachar Sonraí ar Chnuasach Nathanna Gaeilge as Saothar Pheadair Uí Laoghaire*. Ph.D. thesis, Dublin City University.

Carlos Ramisch, Silvio Ricardo Cordeiro, Agata Savary, Veronika Vincze, Verginica Barbu Mititelu, Archna Bhatia, Maja Buljan, Marie Candito, Polona Gantar, Voula Giouli, Tunga Güngör, Abdelati Hawwari, Uxoa Iñurrieta, Jolanta Kovalevskaitė, Simon Krek, Timm Lichte, Chaya Liebeskind, Johanna Monti, Carla Parra Escartín, Behrang QasemiZadeh, Renata Ramisch, Nathan Schneider, Ivelina Stoyanova, Ashwini Vaidya, and Abigail Walsh. 2018. Edition 1.1 of the PARSEME shared task on automatic identification of verbal multiword expressions. In *Proceedings of the Joint Workshop on Linguistic Annotation, Multiword Expressions and Constructions (LAW-MWE-CxG-2018)*, pages 222–240. ACL.

Ivan A. Sag, Timothy Baldwin, Francis Bond, Ann A. Copestake, and Dan Flickinger. 2002. Multiword Expressions: A Pain in the Neck for NLP. In *Proceedings of Computational Linguistics and Intelligent Text Processing, Third International Conference*, pages 1–15, Mexico City, Mexico, 02.

Agata Savary, Carlos Ramisch, Silvio Cordeiro, Federico Sangati, Veronika Vincze, Behrang QasemiZadeh, Marie Candito, Fabienne Cap, Voula Giouli, Ivelina Stoyanova, and Antoine Doucet. 2017. The PARSEME shared task on automatic identification of verbal multiword expressions. In *Proceedings of the 13th Workshop on Multiword Expressions (MWE 2017)*, pages 31–47, Valencia, Spain, April. Association for Computational Linguistics.

Nancy Stenson. 1981. *Studies in Irish syntax*. Ars linguistica. Tübingen: Gunter Narr Verlag.

Milan Straka and Jana Straková. 2017. Tokenizing, POS Tagging, Lemmatizing and Parsing UD 2.0 with UDPipe. In *Proceedings of the CoNLL 2017 Shared Task: Multilingual Parsing from Raw Text to Universal Dependencies*, pages 88–99, Vancouver, Canada, August. Association for Computational Linguistics.

Elaine Uí Dhonnchadha. 2009. *Part-of-Speech Tagging and Partial Parsing for Irish using Finite-State Transducers and Constraint Grammar*. Ph.D. thesis, Dublin City University.

Elvira Veselinović. 2006. How to put up with cur suas le rud and the bidirectionality of contact. *The Celtic Englishes IV*, page 173–190.

Abigail Walsh, Claire Bonial, Kristina Geeraert, John P. McCrae, Nathan Schneider, and Clarissa Somers. 2018. Constructing an annotated corpus of verbal MWEs for English. In *Proceedings of the Joint Workshop on Linguistic Annotation, Multiword Expressions and Constructions (LAW-MWE-CxG-2018)*, pages 193–200, Santa Fe, New Mexico, USA, August. Association for Computational Linguistics.

Abigail Walsh, Teresa Lynn, and Jennifer Foster. 2019. Ilfhocail: A Lexicon of Irish MWEs. In *Joint Workshop on Multiword Expressions and WordNet (MWE-WN 2019)*, Florence, Italy, 08.

Daniel Zeman, Joakim Nivre, Mitchell Abrams, Noëmi Aepli, Željko Agić, Lars Ahrenberg, Gabrielė Aleksandravičiūtė, Lene Antonsen, Katya Aplonova, Maria Jesus Aranzabe, Gashaw Arutie, Masayuki Asahara, Luma Ateyah, Mohammed Attia, Aitziber Atutxa, Liesbeth Augustinus, Elena Badmaeva, Miguel Ballesteros, Esha Banerjee, Sebastian Bank, Verginica Barbu Mititelu, Victoria Basmov, Colin Batchelor, John Bauer, Sandra Bellato, Kepa Bengoetxea, Yevgeni Berzak, Irshad Ahmad Bhat, Riyaz Ahmad Bhat, Erica Biagetti, Eckhard Bick, Agnė Bielinskienė, Rogier Blokland, Victoria Bobicev, Loïc Boizou, Emanuel Borges Völker, Carl Börstell, Cristina Bosco, Gosse Bouma, Sam Bowman, Adriane Boyd, Kristina Brokaitė, Aljoscha Burchardt, Marie Candito, Bernard Caron, Gauthier Caron, Tatiana Cavalcanti, Gülşen Cebiroğlu Eryiğit, Flavio Massimiliano Cecchini, Giuseppe G. A. Celano, Slavomír Čéplö, Savas Cetin, Fabricio Chalub, Jinho Choi, Yongseok Cho, Jayeol Chun, Alessandra T. Cignarella, Silvie Cinková, Aurélie Collomb, Çağrı Çöltekin, Miriam Connor, Marine Courtin, Elizabeth Davidson, Marie-Catherine de Marneffe, Valeria de Paiva, Elvis de Souza, Arantza Diaz de Ilarraza, Carly Dickerson, Bamba Dione, Peter Dirix, Kaja Dobrovoljc, Timothy Dozat, Kira Droganova, Puneet Dwivedi, Hanne Eckhoff, Marhaba Eli, Ali Elkahky, Binyam Ephrem, Olga Erina, Tomaž Erjavec, Aline Etienne, Wograine Evelyn, Richárd Farkas, Hector Fernandez Alcalde, Jennifer Foster, Cláudia Freitas, Kazunori Fujita, Katarína Gajdošová, Daniel Galbraith, Marcos Garcia, Moa Gärdenfors, Sebastian Garza, Kim Gerdes, Filip Ginter, Iakes Goenaga, Koldo Gojenola, Memduh Gökırmak, Yoav Goldberg, Xavier Gómez Guinovart, Berta González Saavedra, Bernadeta Griciūtė, Matias Grioni, Normunds Grūzītis, Bruno Guillaume, Céline Guillot-Barbance, Nizar Habash, Jan Hajič, Jan Hajič jr., Mika Hämäläinen, Linh Hà Mỹ, Na-Rae Han, Kim Harris, Dag Haug, Johannes Heinecke, Felix Hennig, Barbora Hladká, Jaroslava Hlaváčová, Florinel Hociung, Petter Hohle, Jena Hwang, Takumi Ikeda, Radu Ion, Elena Irimia, Ọlájídé Ishola, Tomáš Jelínek, Anders Johannsen, Fredrik Jørgensen, Markus Juutinen, Hüner Kaşıkara, Andre Kaasen, Nadezhda Kabaeva, Sylvain Kahane, Hiroshi Kanayama, Jenna Kanerva, Boris Katz, Tolga Kayadelen, Jessica Kenney, Václava Kettnerová, Jesse Kirchner, Elena Klementieva, Arne Köhn, Kamil Kopacewicz, Natalia Kotsyba, Jolanta Kovalevskaitė, Simon Krek, Sookyoung Kwak, Veronika Laippala, Lorenzo Lambertino, Lucia Lam, Tatiana Lando, Septina Dian Larasati, Alexei Lavrentiev, John Lee, Phng Lê H`ông, Alessandro Lenci, Saran Lertpradit, Herman Leung, Cheuk Ying Li, Josie Li, Keying Li, KyungTae Lim, Maria Liovina, Yuan Li, Nikola Ljubešić, Olga Loginova, Olga Lyashevskaya, Teresa Lynn, Vivien Macketanz, Aibek Makazhanov, Michael Mandl, Christopher Manning, Ruli Manurung, Cătălina Mărănduc, David Mareček, Katrin Marheinecke, Héctor Martínez Alonso, André Martins, Jan Mašek, Yuji Matsumoto, Ryan McDonald, Sarah McGuinness, Gustavo Mendonça, Niko Miekka, Margarita Misirpashayeva, Anna Missilä, Cătălin Mititelu, Maria Mitrofan, Yusuke Miyao, Simonetta Montemagni, Amir More, Laura Moreno Romero, Keiko Sophie Mori, Tomohiko Morioka, Shinsuke Mori, Shigeki Moro, Bjartur Mortensen, Bohdan Moskalevskyi, Kadri Muischnek, Robert Munro, Yugo Murawaki, Kaili Müürisep, Pinkey Nainwani, Juan Ignacio Navarro Horñiacek, Anna Nedoluzhko, Gunta Nešpore-Bērzkalne, Lng Nguy˜ên Thị, Huy`ên Nguy˜ên Thị Minh, Yoshihiro Nikaido, Vitaly Nikolaev, Rattima Nitisaroj, Hanna Nurmi, Stina Ojala, Atul Kr. Ojha, Adédayọ Olúòkun, Mai Omura, Petya Osenova, Robert Östling, Lilja Øvrelid, Niko Partanen, Elena Pascual, Marco Passarotti, Agnieszka Patejuk, Guilherme Paulino-Passos, Angelika Peljak-Łapińska, Siyao Peng, Cenel-Augusto Perez, Guy Perrier, Daria Petrova, Slav Petrov, Jason Phelan, Jussi Piitulainen, Tommi A Pirinen, Emily Pitler, Barbara Plank, Thierry Poibeau, Larisa Ponomareva, Martin Popel, Lauma Pretkalniṇa, Sophie Prévost, Prokopis Prokopidis, Adam Przepiórkowski, Tiina Puolakainen, Sampo Pyysalo, Peng Qi, Andriela Rääbis, Alexandre Rademaker, Loganathan Ramasamy, Taraka Rama, Carlos Ramisch, Vinit Ravishankar, Livy Real, Siva Reddy, Georg Rehm, Ivan Riabov, Michael Rießler, Erika Rimkutė, Larissa Rinaldi, Laura Rituma, Luisa Rocha, Mykhailo Romanenko, Rudolf Rosa, Davide Rovati, Valentin Roșca, Olga Rudina, Jack Rueter, Shoval Sadde, Benoît Sagot, Shadi Saleh, Alessio Salomoni, Tanja Samardžić, Stephanie Samson, Manuela Sanguinetti, Dage Särg, Baiba Saulīte, Yanin Sawanakunanon, Nathan Schneider, Sebastian Schuster, Djamé Seddah, Wolfgang Seeker, Mojgan Seraji, Mo Shen, Atsuko Shimada, Hiroyuki Shirasu, Muh Shohibussirri, Dmitry Sichinava, Aline Silveira, Natalia Silveira, Maria Simi, Radu Simionescu, Katalin Simkó, Mária Šimková, Kiril Simov, Aaron Smith, Isabela Soares-Bastos, Carolyn Spadine, Antonio Stella, Milan Straka, Jana Strnadová, Alane Suhr, Umut Sulubacak, Shingo Suzuki, Zsolt Szántó, Dima Taji, Yuta Takahashi, Fabio Tamburini, Takaaki Tanaka, Isabelle Tellier, Guillaume Thomas, Liisi Torga, Trond Trosterud, Anna Trukhina, Reut Tsarfaty, Francis Tyers, Sumire Uematsu, Zdeňka Urešová, Larraitz Uria, Hans Uszkoreit, Andrius Utka, Sowmya Vajjala, Daniel van Niekerk, Gertjan van Noord, Viktor Varga, Eric Villemonte de la Clergerie, Veronika Vincze, Lars Wallin, Abigail Walsh, Jing Xian Wang, Jonathan North Washington, Maximilan Wendt, Seyi Williams, Mats Wirén, Christian Wittern, Tsegay Woldemariam, Tak-sum Wong, Alina Wróblewska, Mary Yako, Naoki Yamazaki, Chunxiao Yan, Koichi Yasuoka, Marat M. Yavrumyan, Zhuoran Yu, Zdeněk Žabokrtský, Amir Zeldes, Manying Zhang, and Hanzhi Zhu. 2019. Universal dependencies 2.5. LINDAT/CLARIAH-CZ digital library at the Institute of Formal and Applied Linguistics (ÚFAL), Faculty of Mathematics and Physics, Charles University.

Tomás Ó Domhnalláin and Dónall Ó Baoill. 1975. *Réamhfhocail le briathra na Gaeilge*. Tuarascáil taighde. Institiúid Teangeolaíochta Éireann.

VMWE discovery: a comparative analysis between Literature and Twitter Corpora

Vivian Stamou[1], Artemis Xylogianni[2], Marilena Malli[2],
Penny Takorou[2] and Stella Markantonatou[1]
Institute for Language and Speech Processing (ILSP / "Athena" R.C.)[1]
`{vivianstamou, stilianimarkantonatou}@gmail.com`
Department of French and Language Literature, University of Athens[2]
`{artemis.xylo, mallimariaeleni, pennytak07}@gmail.com`

Abstract

We evaluate manually five lexical association measurements as regards the discovery of Modern Greek verb multiword expressions with two or more lexicalised components using `mwetoolkit3` (Ramisch et al., 2010). We use Twitter corpora and compare our findings with previous work on fiction corpora. The results of LL, MLE and T-score were found to overlap significantly in both the fiction and the Twitter corpora, while the results of PMI and Dice do not. We find that MWEs with two lexicalised components are more frequent in Twitter than in fiction corpora and that lean syntactic patterns help retrieve them more efficiently than richer ones. Our work (i) supports the enrichment of the lexicographical database for Modern Greek MWEs 'IDION' (Markantonatou et al., 2019) and (ii) highlights aspects of the usage of five association measurements on specific text genres for best MWE discovery results.

1 Introduction

Most prior work on MWE discovery exploits lexical association measures (AMs). MWE discovery experiments on Twitter corpora has investigated alternatives to AMs. Daoud et al. (2015), who study Arabic tweets, generate candidate MWEs by storing bi-/tri-grams and their frequencies, filter them on the basis of the frequency of relevant query responses and ensure filtering validity with a confidence ratio measure that takes into account the number of distinct tweets in which a MWE appears. Londhe et al. (2016) propose a language agnostic, graph based method for multilingual MWE extraction (bigrams) from Twitter corpora, evaluate it on various datasets and yield promising results in a number of languages; in the case of English, however, AMs outperform their method.

Prior work on verb MWEs (VMWEs) has focused on expressions with two lexicalised components (Markantonatou et al., 2018) namely to particle verbs and light verb constructions (Stevenson et al., 2004; Constant et al., 2017). Reported work on Modern Greek VMWE discovery with the use of AMs includes Stripeli et al. (2020), who work with light verbs, and Stamou et al. (2020), who work with all types of VMWEs in fiction corpora. To the best of our knowledge, this is the first work on mining VMWEs with 2 or more lexicalised components in Modern Greek Twitter corpora (with lexicography as a goal).

AM performance has been found to be subject to corpus characteristics (size, type etc.) and to the type of target MWEs (see the AMs' evaluation literature with regards to VMWEs, e.g., German and English Verb+Preposition MWEs (Krenn et al., 2011; Baldwin et al., 2005), Verb particle MWEs (Hoang et al., 2009), English, Portuguese and Spanish Verb+Object MWEs (Garcia et al., 2019). Since different AMs seem to achieve best results on different corpora, MWE types and frequencies (Garcia et al., 2019), combinations of AMs have been found to be more efficient for discovery purposes (Pecina and Schlesinger, 2006). We use the `mwetoolkit3` (Ramisch et al., 2010), and discuss the application of five AMs, namely Dice, Log likelihood (LL)[1], MLE (Maximum Likelihood Estimation), PMI (Pointwise Mutual Information) and T-score, on Twitter corpora. The tool offers a complete pipeline for MWE extraction

---

[1]It should be noted that LL is implemented only for bigrams.

Joint Workshop on Multiword Expressions and Electronic Lexicons, pages 66–72
Barcelona, Spain (Online), December 13, 2020.

where candidate phrases are created with n-grams or predefined linguistic patterns applied on corpora annotated for lemma and PoS tags.

In Section 2 we present the details reported in Stamou et al. (2020) that are important to the work discussed in this paper. In Section 3 we present and evaluate three experiments. In Section 4, the differences observed between the two datasets, namely Twitter and fiction corpora, are discussed. In Section 5 we present our conclusions and comment on the use of the AMs for lexicographic purposes.

2 Experiments with fiction corpora of Modern Greek

Stamou et al. (2020) used `mwetoolkit3` (Ramisch et al., 2010) to discover VMWEs in fiction corpora tagged and lemmatised with the ILSP tools (Papageorgiou et al., 2000). A Gold Standard (GS) was defined from these corpora by three expert annotators. Two experiments were conducted, one with simple and one with enriched linguistic patters. In the first experiment, six syntactic patterns were applied comprising the most frequent PoS sequences in the GS. The results were evaluated both manually and automatically. Manual evaluation was applied to identify True and False positives in the first 3000 candidates returned by each of the following AMs: Dice, LL, MLE, PMI, T-score. In the second experiment, richer patterns were used featuring double prepositional phrases and conjunction structures, as shown in Table 1 (brackets denote optionality).

Table 1: Rich VMWE patterns used by Stamou et al. (2020)

Patterns
(Pn)+(Vb)+**Vb**+(Ad)+(At)+(Aj)+(At)+**No**+(Pn)+(Aj)
Vb+(At)+(No)+**Cj**+(Pn)+(At)+(No)
Vb+**Cj**+(Pt)+(Pt)+**Vb**
(Pn)+Pn+(Pt)+(Pt)+(Vb)+**Vb**+(Pn)+**No**+(Pt)+(Pn)+(Vb)+**Vb**
(Pn)+(Vb)+**Vb**+(At)+(No)+(Ad)+**AsPp**+(Aj)+(At)+**No**
(Pn)+(Vb)+**Vb**+(Cj)+(Ad)+(At)+(No)+**AsPp**+(Ad)+(At)+**No**+(At)+(No)
Vb+**AsPp**+(At)+**No**+ **AsPp**+(At)+No
(Pn)+(At)+(No)+(Pt)+**Pn**+(Vb)+**Vb**
(Pn)+(Vb)+**Vb**+**Ad**+(Ad)+(Pn)

The automatic evaluation of both experiments against the GS returned the following order of scores: T-score, MLE, LL, Dice, PMI while the manual evaluation showed Dice as the most reliable AM; PMI scored last in the first experiment and LL in the second. Reliability was expressed as interanotator agreement computed with Fleiss $\varkappa$ values. Similar observations can be found in Linardaki et al. (2010) and Gurrutxaga and Alegria (2011) for nominal Modern Greek MWEs and Basque VMWEs respectively.

In the first experiment, T-score, MLE and LL shared about 850 out of the first 3000 phrases returned by each one of these AMs. Dice and PMI promoted less frequent VMWEs not included in the other AM results. These facts suggested that annotators tended to select hapax legomena, in contrast to automatic evaluation that relies on an, inevitably, incomplete GS.

Summing up Stamou et al. (2020) work: (i) rich syntactic patterns enhanced VMWE discovery results (ii) manual evaluation supported the discovery of less frequent VMWEs (iii) Dice (the most reliable AM in both experiments) and PMI (it returned VMWEs not found by the other AMs) should be applied for a more efficient VMWE discovery procedure (Church and Hanks, 1989; Pereira and Mendes, 2002).

3 Experiments on a Twitter corpus of Modern Greek

1M tweets (13.531.036 tokens, 253.230 Types & 1.160.036 sentences) were preprocessed to remove mentions, https links, hashtags and emoticons and were tagged and lemmatised with the ILSP tagger. In these experiments, we paid special attention to food language; a subcorpus was created by querying dish names such as πατάτες τηγανητές 'french fries', πιπεριά Φλωρίνης 'Florinis pepper'. These tweets formed a 10-15% of our tweet corpus. Throughout our study we tried to see whether this subcoprus behaves differently from the remaining tweet corpora but in no step we found some remarkable difference. Therefore, the results reported here concern the whole corpus, including the tweets related to food.

3.1   First experiment: the Baseline

We used the enriched syntactic patterns of Stamou et al. (2020) (Table 1) to obtain a baseline and manually checked the top 3000 lemmatized phrases per AM. Only 310 unique lemmatised phrases were judged as True positives out of 15,000 candidates. The AM order by decreasing reliability in Fleiss $\varkappa$ scores was: MLE (0.82), T-score (0.79), LL (0.70), Dice (0.61), PMI (0.50). When the amount of discovered VMWEs by each AM is considered, PMI scores first (107 VMWEs) followed by LL (106 VMWEs), MLE (74 VMWEs), T-score (71 VMWEs) and Dice (60 VMWEs). As in the case of fiction corpora, we observe that the T-score, LL and MLE sets overlap significantly (Figure 1).

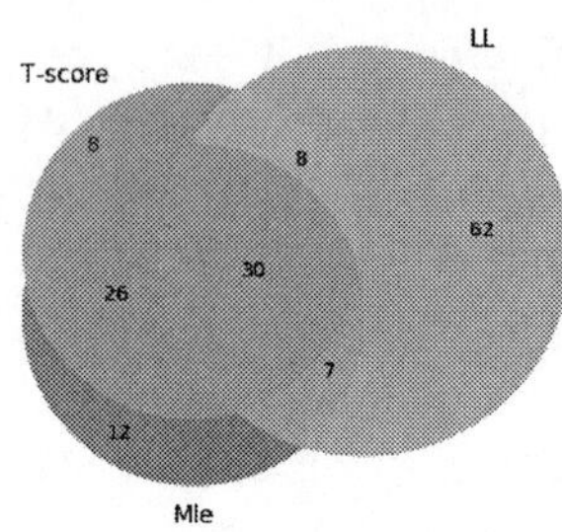

Figure 1: Intersection among T-score, LL and MLE True positives.

3.2   Second experiment: Leaner patterns

We used leaner patterns because the Twitter corpora returned VMWEs with few lexicalised components (Section 4). The leaner syntactic constructions contained at most four PoS tag sequences per pattern and were simplified versions of the rich patterns but not identical with the lean patterns used by Stamou et al. (2020). Again, the annotators checked the top 3000 phrases returned by each AM. Dice was found the most reliable AM and PMI the less reliable one. Dice returned 86 MWEs, T-score 83, MLE 72, LL 66 and PMI 60 (these results are an indication that PMI performs better with rich patterns). In total, 184 unique VMWEs were extracted. Again, the T-score, MLE and LL sets were found to share a considerable number of phrases (47 phrases), while Dice and PMI, the best and the worse scores respectively, had only one common phrase. The results of the two experiments (with rich and lean patterns) had only 25 phrases in common; the leaner patterns helped to discover 159 new phrases.

3.3   6000 candidates: Evaluation of the applied AMs

The Baseline returned results similar to those obtained from fiction corpora (first experiment): LL, MLE and T-score overlapped significantly but Dice and PMI did not intersect. These facts suggest that for VMWE discovery purposes the results of one of/the intersection of LL, MLE and T-score should be evaluated as well as the results of Dice and PMI. To test this idea, we evaluated more candidate phrases (+3000, total 6000 phrases per AM) because our Twitter corpora are twice in size as compared to the fiction corpora. The LL, MLE and T-score set received a high Fleiss $\varkappa$ value (0.79). In the additional 3000 phrases, Dice and PMI received low kappa values ($\varkappa$=0.58 and $\varkappa$=0.45 respectively) and returned 62 and 65 True positives respectively. Again it was observed that PMI retrieves low frequency VMWEs with more than two lexicalised components. If the 6000 candidates are considered, the set LL-MLE-T-score returned 137 True positives, PMI 65 + 107 = 172 and Dice 60+62=122. The total amount of identified VMWES was 431; the improvement is not impressive given the amount of annotation effort required. We estimate that we received per AM a 2% of True Positives (60 VMWEs) out of the 3000 candidates; this estimation illustrates the significant overlap among the LL, MLE and T-score (we obtained 137 MWEs when the "expected" ones were 180).

4 VMWEs in fiction and Twitter corpora

The plots of the number of lexicalised components in the VMWEs (Figure 2) reveal that VMWEs with two lexicalised components prevail in Twitter corpora and VMWEs with more than two lexicalised components in fiction corpora. This (not unexpected) fact may partly explain the results of our second experiment where lean patterns returned several new VMWEs.

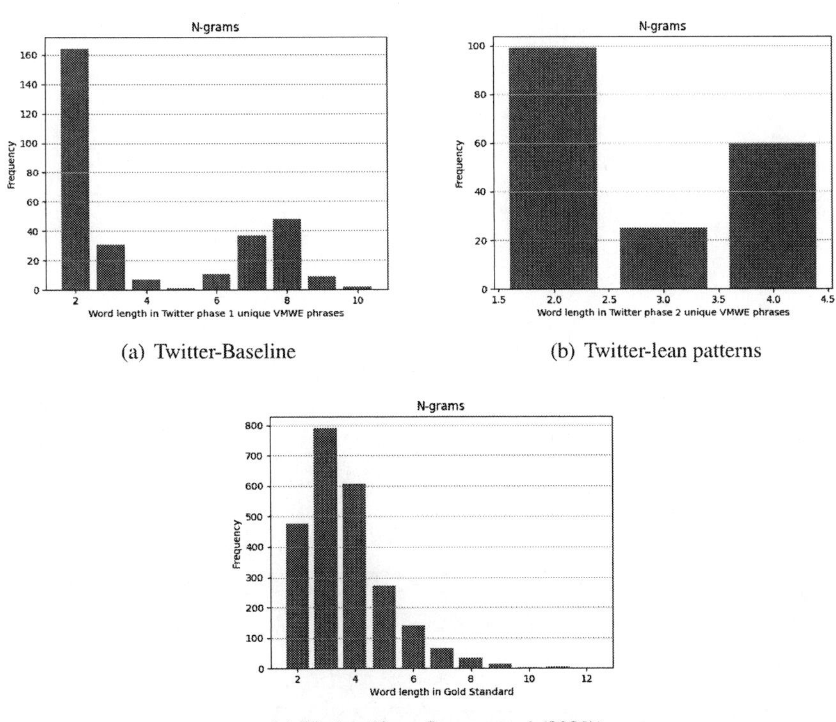

(a) Twitter-Baseline   (b) Twitter-lean patterns

(c) Fiction (from Stamou et al.(2020))

Figure 2: Number of lexicalised components in the retrieved VMWEs.

The first two phrases below were extracted from the fiction corpora and the next two from the Twitter corpus:

(1)   **μπαίνει**   αμέσως   **στο νόημα**
      get.PRES.3SG immediately to   the point.ACC
      'getting the hang of it'

(2)   **Ἔριξες**   *άδεια*   *για να*   *πιάσεις γεμάτα*
      throw.PAST.3SG. empty.ACC in   order to   catch.PAST.3SG. full.ACC
      'to fish for information'

(3)   **κατεβάζω ρολά**
      put.down.PRES.1SG shutters.ACC
      'to shutdown'

(4)   **τρώω**   ένα   ωραίο   **μπλοκ**
      eat.PRES.1SG one.ACC nice.ACC block
      'I was blocked in the social media'

Furthermore, the plots of the frequencies of the True positives per experiment with Twitter corpora (Figure 3), suggest that the VMWEs obtained with the leaner patterns were of higher frequency than the ones obtained with the Baseline (rich patterns). Again, this seems to be a reasonable result in the context of

Twitter corpora. At the same time it shows that patterns, frequency and number of lexicalised components of VMWEs may interact. Stamou et al. (2020) who also conducted separate experiments with lean and rich syntactic patterns on fiction corpora do not report a similar effect.

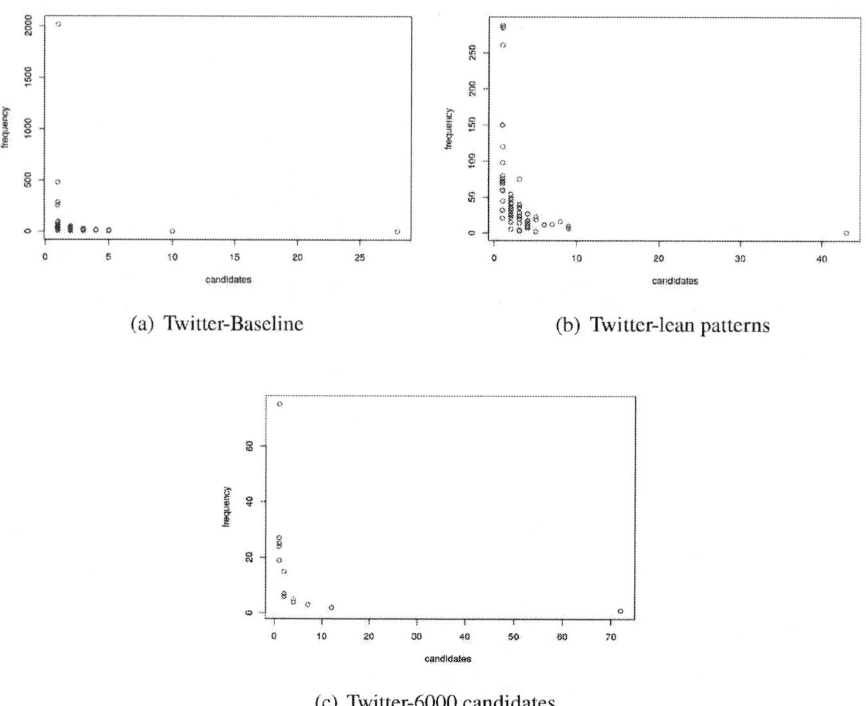

(a) Twitter-Baseline

(b) Twitter-lean patterns

(c) Twitter-6000 candidates

Figure 3: Frequencies of the retrieved VMWEs with the three experiments

5   Conclusions

Our experiments on Twitter corpora of Modern Greek, compared to experiments conducted by Stamou et al. (2020) on fiction corpora of this language, have shown that manual annotation of AM results better suits lexicographic purposes because it exploits more efficiently the output of PMI and Dice that tend to return hapax legomena and long VMWEs. Significant economy in evaluation effort can be achieved if the results of Dice and PMI are evaluated independently, because they hardly intersect, and only the intersection of LL, MLE and T-score results is evaluated. Furthermore, our experiments revealed that VMWEs with two lexicalised components prevail in Twitter corpora (but not in fiction corpora) and can be better identified with lean syntactic patterns rather than rich ones. This result could be of interest to lexicographers; it also indicates that there is an interaction among patterns used, number of lexicalised components and frequency of VMWEs in the corpus. We plan to accommodate the new VMWEs detected in the two corpora at the IDION database[2].

Acknowledgements

This work was supported by the project "GRE-Taste" (T1EDK-02015) that is funded by the action "RESEARCH-CREATE-INNOVATE" and co-financed by Greek National Funds and the European Union.

---

[2]The data can be reached at: http://idion.ilsp.gr/data.

References

Antton Gurrutxaga and Alegria, Inaki. 2011. Automatic extraction of NV expressions in basque: Basic issueson cooccurrence techniques. In *Proceedings of the Workshop on Multiword Expressions: from Parsing and Generation to the Real World*, pages 2-7. Portland, Oregon, USA. Association for Computational Linguistics.

Brigitte Krenn and Stefan Evert. 2011. Can we do better than frequency? a case study on extracting PP-verb collocations. In *39 the Annua lMeeting and 10th Conference of the European Chapter of the Association for Computational Linguistics (ACL39)* pages39–46,CNRS- Institut de Rechercheen Informatique de Toulouse, and Universite des Sciences Sociales,Toulouse,France,July.

Carlos Ramisch, Aline Villavicencio, and Christian Boitet. 2010. mwetoolkit: a Framework for Multiword Expression Identification. In Nicoletta Calzolari, Khalid Choukri, Bente Maegaard, Joseph Marian, Jan Odjik, Stelios Piperidis, Mike Rosner, and Daniel Tapias, editors, *Proceedings of LREC 2010*, Valetta, Malta. ELRA.

Draoud Draoud and Akram Alkooz, and Mohammad Daoud. 2015. Time-sensitive arabic multiword expressions extraction from social networks. *International Journal of Speech Technology* 19, 10.

Emilia Stripeli, Prokopis Prokopidis, and Haris Papageorgiou. 2020. Stella Markantonatou and Anastasia Christofidou (eds). 2020. Multiword expressions: Studies drawing on data from Modern Greek and other languages. Bulletin for Scientific Terminology and Neologisms (DEON), vol. 15. In *Academy of Athens*, pages 15(4):75-95, deltio epistimonikis orologias ke neologismon.

Evita Linardaki, Carlos Ramisch, Aline Villavicencio, and Angeliki/Aggeliki Fotopoulou. 2010. Towards the construction of language resources for greek multiword expressions: Extraction and evaluation. In Piperidis, S., Slavcheva, M., and Vertan, C., editors, *Proceedings of the LREC Workshop on Exploitation of multilingual resources and tools for Central and (South) Eastern European Languages*, pages 31–40, Valetta, Malta. May

Harris Papageorgiou, Prokopis Prokopidis, Voula Giouli, and Stelios Piperidis. 2000. A unified POS tagging architecture and its application to Greek. In *Proceedings of the Second International Conference on Languages Resources and Evalutation (LREC'00)*, Athens, Greece, May. European Language Resources Association (ELRA).

Hung Huu Hoang, Su Nam Kim, and Min-Yen Kan. 2009. A re-examination of lexical association measures. In *Proceedings of the Workshop on Multiword Expressions: Identification, Interpretation, Disambiguation and Applications (MWE 2009)*, pages 31-39, Singapore. Association for Computational Linguistics.

Kenneth W. Church and Patrick Hanks. 1989. Word association norms, mutual information, and lexicography. *In 27th Annual Meeting of the Association for Computational Linguistics*, pages 76-83. Vancouver, British Columbia, Canada, June. Association for Computational Linguistics.

Luisa Alice Santos Pereira and Amalia Mendes. 2002. A electronic dictionary of collocations for european portuguese: Methodology, results and applications. In Anna Braasch and Claus Povlsen, editors, *Proceedings of the 10th EURALEX International Congress,* pages 841-849, København, Denmark, Center for Sprogteknologi.

Marcos Garcia, Marcos Garcia Salido, and Margarita Alonso-Ramos. 2019. A comparison of statistical association measures for identifying dependency-based collocations in various languages. In *Proceedings of the Joint Workshop on Multiword Expressions and Wordnet (MWE-WN 2019*, pages 49-59, Florence, Italy, August, Association for Computational Linguistics.

Mathieu Constant, Gülşen Eryiğit and Johanna Monti and Lonneke van der Plas and Carlos Ramisch and Michael Rosner and Amalia Todirascu. 2017. Survey: Multiword Expression Processing: A Survey. *Computational Linguistics*, 43(4):837-892.

Nikhil Londhe, Rohini Srihari, and Vishrawas Gopalakrishnan. 2016. Time-independent and language-independent extraction of multiword expressions from twitter. In *Proceedings of COLING 2016, the 26th International Conference on Computational Linguistics: Technical Papers*, pages 2269-2278, Osaka, Japan, December. The COLING 2016 Organizing Commitee.

Pavel Pecina and Pavel Schlesinger. 2006. Combining association measures for collocation extraction. In *Proceedings of the COLING/ACL 2006 Main Conference Poster Sessions* pages 651-658, Sydney, Australia, July. Association for Computational Linguistics.

Stella Markantonatou, Panagiotis Minos, George Zakis, Vassiliki Moutzouri, Maria Chantou. 2019. IDION: A database for Modern Greek multiword expressions. *In Proceedings of Joint Workshop on Multiword Expressions and WordNet (MWE-WN 2019), Workshop at ACL 2019,* Florence, Italy.

Stella Markantonatou, Calros Ramisch, Agata Savary, and Veronica Vincze. 2018. *Multiword expressions at length and in depth: Extended papers from the MWE 2017 workshop.* Language Science Press.

Suzanne Stevenson, Afsaneh Fazly, and Ryan North. 2004. Statistical measures of the semi-productivity of light verb constructions. In *Proceedings of the Workshop on Multiword Expressions: Integrating Processing* pages 1-8, Barcelona, Spain. Association for Computational Linguistics.

Timothy Baldwin. 2005. Looking for prepositional verbs in corpus data. *In Proceedings of the 2nd ACL-SIGSEM Workshop on the Linguistic Dimensions of Prepositions and their use in computational linguistics formalisms and applications* Colchester, UK.

Vivian Stamou, Artemis Xylogianni, Marilena Malli, Penny Takorou, Stella Markantonatou. 2020. Evaluation of Verb Multiword Expressions discovery measurements in literature corpora of Modern Greek. *Proceedings of the Euralex XIX: Lexicography for Inclusion* Alexandroupolis, Greece (to appear).

Generationary or: "How We Went beyond Sense Inventories and Learned to Gloss"

Roberto Navigli
Sapienza University of Rome
Sapienza NLP Group
Italy
`navigli@di.uniroma1.it`

Abstract

In this talk I present Generationary, an approach that goes beyond the mainstream assumption that word senses can be represented as discrete items of a predefined inventory, and put forward a unified model which produces contextualized definitions for arbitrary lexical items, from words to phrases and even sentences. Generationary employs a novel span-based encoding scheme to fine-tune an English pre-trained Encoder-Decoder system and generate new definitions. Our model outperforms previous approaches in the generative task of Definition Modeling in many settings, but it also matches or surpasses the state of the art in discriminative tasks such as Word Sense Disambiguation and Word-in-Context. I also show that Generationary benefits from training on definitions from multiple inventories, with strong gains across benchmarks, including a novel dataset of definitions for free adjective-noun phrases, and discuss interesting examples of generated definitions.

Joint work with Michele Bevilacqua and Marco Maru.

Joint Workshop on Multiword Expressions and Electronic Lexicons, page 73
Barcelona, Spain (Online), December 13, 2020.

Multi-word Expressions for Abusive Speech Detection in Serbian

Ranka Stanković
University of Belgrade
ranka@rgf.bg.ac.rs

Jelena Mitrović
University of Passau
jelena.mitrovic@uni-passau.de

Danka Jokić
University of Belgrade
dankaiv@googlemail.com

Cvetana Krstev
University of Belgrade
cvetana@matf.bg.ac.rs

Abstract

This paper presents our work on the refinement and improvement of the Serbian language part of Hurtlex, a multilingual lexicon of words to hurt. We pay special attention to adding Multi-word expressions that can be seen as abusive, as such lexical entries are very important in obtaining good results in a plethora of abusive language detection tasks. We use Serbian morphological dictionaries as a basis for data cleaning and MWE dictionary creation. A connection to other lexical and semantic resources in Serbian is outlined and building of abusive language detection systems based on that connection is foreseen.

1 Introduction

This paper presents initial results in an on-going collaboration between University of Passau and University of Belgrade aimed at improving the lexical resources that will aid abusive speech detection in Serbian. Discriminatory messages and exhortation to violence are related to offensive and hate speech, which has been gaining more attention due to the extensive use of online media and the Internet in general. The concept of abusive speech, as an umbrella term for phenomena such as offensive and hate speech, its content and forms of expression are analysed, trying to define its vocabulary, collocations, colloquial expressions, and context.

Starting from the definition of hate speech as 'any communication that disparages a person or a group on the basis of some characteristic such as race, color, ethnicity, gender, sexual orientation, nationality, religion, or other characteristic' (Nockleby, 2000) it is clear that hate speech is a complex social and linguistic phenomenon. Abusive language and its detection have been gaining more attention recently. Caselli et al. (2020) define abusive language as 'hurtful language that a speaker uses to insult or offend another individual or a group of individuals based on their personal qualities, appearance, social status, opinions, statements, or actions. This might include hate speech, derogatory language, profanity, toxic comments, racist and sexist statements.' Computational processing of such language requires usage of finely-tuned, task specific language tools and resources, especially for morphologically rich and low-resource languages such as Serbian.

In the process of building a conceptual framework of abusive language, special attention is paid to Multi-word expressions (MWEs) which allow for better and more precise detection of this linguistic phenomenon. The development of the MWE lexicon also helps in reducing ambiguity. The lexical resource, consisting of words that could be used as a trigger for recognition of abusive language is built, with an idea that the Serbian system for recognition and normalization of abusive expressions will also take into consideration phrases and figurative speech as an indicator. Both explicit and implicit abusive language (hateful and offensive messages that are not apparent at first glance) will be analysed.

The remainder of the paper is structured as follows. Related work is given in Section 2 with a short overview of approaches for developing this type of resources in Subsection 2.1. One the existing,

Joint Workshop on Multiword Expressions and Electronic Lexicons, pages 74–84
Barcelona, Spain (Online), December 13, 2020.

publicly available resources, Hurtlex, that we base our work on, is introduced in Subsection 2.2. The analysis and improvement of Hurtlex for Serbian is given in Subsection 3.1. Overview of acquiring, describing and classifying the additional dataset is given in Section 4.1. Building of the morphological dictionary and its application in graphs is given in Subsection 4.2. In conclusion, our main research questions related to whether MWEs include trigger words and what is their role, and are the abusive MWEs mainly compositional or not, are presented at the end of the paper.

2 Related work

The use of offensive and hateful language has been a concern since the early days of the Internet. It has been estimated that the number of MWEs in the lexicon of a native speaker has the same order of magnitude as the number of single words (Moreno-Ortiz et al., 2013). Consequently, their detection is of great importance for abusive language identification. In our abusive language detection system, we are giving the same relevance to MWEs as to the individual words. Without MWE identification, an expression could be marked as not abusive since it does not contain abusive words e.g. *zapržiti nekome čorbu* (eng. to spice up someone's stew) with figurative meaning of meddling with someone's life in a negative way, deliberately making things difficult.

The majority of current hate speech, offensive and abusive language detection systems in social media are based on lexicons or blacklists (Chen et al., 2012; Colla et al., 2020; Pamungkas et al., 2020). The advantage of this approach relates to a vast number of swear words and offenses that can be detected solely using lexicons. The disadvantage of using lexicons is that swear words are used in everyday speech often without offensive intent, therefore their detection may lead to false-positive results. Another disadvantage of lexicons is due to the necessity of their maintenance since they evolve with natural language changes. While Pedersen (Pedersen, 2020) reported high accuracy of hate speech detection when using a lexicon only, lexicons are not sufficient as a resource for hate speech detection. They could be used as a baseline for comparison with more advanced methods since subtle hateful messages (Kwok and Wang, 2013), and language nuance cannot be detected accurately using this method. In addition, some insults which might be unacceptable to one group might be acceptable to another, thus taking context into account is very important (Nobata et al., 2016).

Several authors reported using a multilingual online lexicon of hate speech available at hatebase.org in their research. (Wiegand et al., 2018; Silva et al., 2016; Nobata et al., 2016). Wiegand et al. (2018) built a lexicon of abusive words using the subjectivity lexicon of Therese Wilson that is in essence a sentiment lexicon. They took words with negative polarity as a baseline for creating a basic lexicon of 551 words, which was further enriched via machine learning into a lexicon of 2898 abusive words. Several authors used the Wiegand lexicon as a blacklist in their hate speech and abusive language detection systems (Wiegand et al., 2018; Pedersen, 2020; Caselli et al., 2020). As noted by Wiegand et al. (2018), lexicons that contain different part of speech give better results than those containing just nouns, therefore we employed this approach in building our first abusive words lexicon.

An approach for racial, national, and religious hate speech detection adopted by Gitari et al. (2015) was based solely on the usage of lexicon and rules. They used semantics and subjectivity features – polarity, intensity, and subjectivity level of words, using the domain corpus of hateful content and Subjectivity lexicon of Therese Wilson in combination with the SentiWordNet (Esuli and Sebastiani, 2006).For classification, they leveraged rules and achieved a result of F1 = 0.783 for strongly hateful sentences on a manually annotated domain corpus.

Razavi et al. (2010) created one of the first systems for flame speech detection that used a 3-layer classifier, rules, and dictionary of abusive and derogatory terms. They noticed that offensive language was characterized by extreme subjectivity. Hence, they used a combination of term's offensiveness and subjectivity impact to calculate and assign a weight from 1 to 5 to each entry of their dictionary. Those weights were later corrected through adaptive learning on the training data set resulting in the Insulting or Abusive Language Dictionary (IALD). The dictionary contains terms such as "chew Somebody's ass out" that become a search template by replacing somebody with * or by adding suffixes or prefixes to verbs or nouns (e.g. suffix -ing for verbs and -es to nouns). They achieved an accuracy of 96,78% in

10-fold cross-validation on the binary classifier.

2.1 Resources for offensive and hate speech

When developing a lexicon of hateful, offensive or abusive words, researches usually start from the existing resources: (i) subjectivity lexicons, since it is assumed that hate speech contains elements of extreme subjectivity (Razavi et al., 2010; Wiegand et al., 2018), (2) a lexicon of sentimental words and expressions, and SentiWordNet (Gitari et al., 2015), where it is assumed that abusive language consists of words indicating negative polarity of feelings, (3) list of offensive words and expressions (Bassignana et al., 2018) and (Hatebase.org), whether made by experts and/or obtained using crowdsourcing.

In an abusive content detection system, a lexicon could be used in one of the following ways: (i) As a classification feature, either as a binary indicator of the abusive word occurrence in the examined text (Pamungkas and Patti, 2019), or a numerical value corresponding to the number of abusive words and its level of abusiveness (Razavi et al., 2010); (2) When applying rules for classification of offensive content, the authors may decide to classify the text in a certain category based on the number of abusive expressions above a certain threshold, e.g. if 2 or more notions of high abusiveness are found in text, it is marked as very abusive (Gitari et al., 2015; Pedersen, 2020); (3) Training of classifiers for recognizing abusive speech in text using the lexicon content as the training set (Wiegand et al., 2018).

On the other hand, high quality corpora of hate speech, offensive speech, and abusive language are just as important for tackling the detection of these phenomena online (Zampieri et al., 2019; Zampieri et al., 2020; Basile et al., 2019; Caselli et al., 2020). When it comes to Serbian abusive language resources and detection, the lexicon that we are working on is the first one of its kind. Still, some resources that will facilitate abusive language detection already exist. Serbian Morphological Dictionaries are certainly a staple in processing texts in Serbian (Krstev, 2008). In order to process implicitly abusive language, we need to take into account the usage of non-literal language, the rhetorical devices that are so often a part of such utterances, as shown in (Caselli et al., 2020; Mitrovic et al., 2020). The Ontology of Rhetorical Figures for Serbian (Mladenović and Mitrović, 2013) is a valuable resource for modelling and detection of rhetorical figures that play an important part in abusive language, e.g. irony, sarcasm, simile, hyperbole, litotes etc. Initial work on detecting some of these figures has been presented in (Mladenović et al., 2017; Krstev et al., 2020).

Using a corpus of newspaper articles from 2006, Krstev et al. (2007) presented the results of an information search experiment in search of attacks which are the result of national, racial, or religious hatred and intolerance. The aim was to develop a system which would recognize the news covering these topics, annotating certain components of the text, which, viewed individually or together, indicate the required information. The authors conclude that further development of the system could go in the direction of adding weight factors to the components (neutral, less neutral and offensive content and explicit content) which could be used to calculate the overall importance of a news item for the examined topic.

2.2 Multilingual HurtLex

HurtLex is a multilingual lexicon of hateful words in over 50 languages. The words are divided into 17 categories, plus a macrocategory indicating whether there is stereotype involved (Bassignana et al., 2018). Lemmas in this dictionary belong to one of these two levels: 1) conservative: obtained by translating offensive senses of the words in the original lexicon and 2) inclusive: obtained by translating all the potentially relevant senses of the words in the original lexicon.

The basis for HurtLex was a lexicon of offensive terms prepared by the Italian linguist Tullio De-Mauro, where offensive terms were split into 3 categories (negative stereotypes, derogatory words, and negative in context), and 17 subcategories. The creators of HurLex opted for a detailed categorization in order to have the possibility to search for a specific category or group of category types. This makes HurtLex amenable to automatic usage for tasks in many languages. Koufakou et al. (2020) used HurtLex in the TRAC-2 task for aggression and misogyny detection, to facilitate retrofitting of fastText word embeddings for English, Hindu, and Bengali. In Pamungkas et al. (2018), HurtLex was used to aid automatic identification of misogyny in English and Italian tweets, while in Colla et al. (2020) HurtLex was used in a system submission at OffensEval 2020, in the process of fine-tuning offensive language models for Danish, Turkish, and English. In the research presented in this paper, we are improving the Serbian part of HurtLex, as it can be a powerful resource for detecting abusive language in Serbian.

3 Serbian HurtLex revision

3.1 srHurtLex lexical cleaning

The initial version of HurtLex for Serbian[1] has been analysed, first from a lexical point of view, then from a grammatical point of view. The errors in srHurtLex were introduced due to the automatically generated translation. In the retrieved data set, consisting of 2518 entries, there were 1903 unique lemmas, written in both Latin and Cyrillic alphabet. After alphabet unification, 1819 unique lemmas were first analysed using the Serbian Morphological Dictionaries (Krstev, 2008). The manual check-up of unrecognised words followed, resulting in the removal of 803 entries (602 unique).

Our next task was to check each lemma and its assigned part of speech (POS): 1) in 1057 entries (678 unique) the correct lemma was used, for which 93 (64 unique) the incorrect POS was assigned; 2) 658 entries (467 unique after correction) had incorrect lemma, out of which 48 (41 unique after correction) with incorrect POS.

If we look at the percentages on unique lemmata, 34.5% were non words, 38.8% lemma forms were correct, 26.7% lemmata were wrong, but 6% had wrong POS in total. So, we had a correct lemma with a correct POS assigned in 35.1% of the cases. Statistical overview is given in Table 1. A small set of orthographic corrections, such as first upper case lemma, was also conducted. Several types of errors were detected: 1) transliteration of foreign words into Cyrillic: *diddlei, villainess, ferociousness, carcharodon*; 2) foreign (not-translated) words: *anguillidae, anguilliformes, animal*; 3) irrelevant named entities: *Istočni Goti, Abulija, Animalija, Drag kraljica*; 4) literal translations that are meaningless in Serbian: *jabuka poliranje, javni pogodnost, japanskih jedinica merenja, nevolja kafu, nestašluk odluka, novog krompira*; 5) lemma correction in order to respect agreement in gender and number: *ekstremne desničar* → *ekstremni desničar* 'extreme right-winger', or to put a lemma in its dictionary form *zaprljane* → *zaprljan* 'soiled', *zlostavljanja* → *zlostavljanje* 'abusing', *zlostavljao* → *zlostavljati* 'to abuse'.

	Entries	Unique lemma after correction	%	Entries wrong POS	Unique wrong POS	% wrong POS
Non words	803	602	34.5			
lemmaOK	1057	678	38.8	93	64	3.7
lemmaNOT	658	467	26.7	48	41	2.3
Total	2518	1747		141	105	6.0

Table 1: Statistic of lexical cleaning.

Bearing in mind that the initial version of HurLex for Serbian was mostly done automatically, without support of any tools and resources for Serbian language processing, such results were expected and certainly indicate that this phase is inevitable in the construction of similar lexicons.

After the removal of all the wrong entries, 1725 entries remained. After removing duplicates, 1402 entries remained with 1000 unique lemmata. A total of 90 candidate entries for removal were annotated as both inclusive and conservative.

3.2 srHurtLex reclassification

The focus of this research was on MWEs, where 265 entries with 198 unique lemma were retrieved. Out of 265 entries, agreement in assigned category is confirmed for 156 entries, with a few suggestions for better translation: *sveštenikov pomoćnik* 'priest's assistant' → *đakon* 'deacon', *svinjski mesar* 'pig butcher' → *kasapin* 'butcher', *ženski imitator* 'woman impersonator' → *travestit*'transvestite'. 109 entries were eliminated for various reasons: 34 entries were marked as inappropriate due to a bad translation, and 12 were marked both as inclusive and conservative, of which only one remained. Most of

---

[1]`https://github.com/valeriobasile/hurtlex/tree/master/lexica/SR/1.2`

Label	HurtLex category description	no	yes	total
ps	negative stereotypes ethnic slurs	5	14	19
pa	professions and occupations	3	5	8
ddf	physical disabilities and diversity		2	2
ddp	cognitive disabilities and diversity	7	7	14
dmc	moral and behavioral defects	4	11	15
is	words related to social and economic disadvantage		3	3
or	plants	1		1
an	animals	26	10	36
asm	male genitalia	2	1	3
asf	female genitalia	2	1	3
pr	words related to prostitution	5	5	10
om	words related to homosexuality		8	8
qas	with potential negative connotations	9	23	32
cds	derogatory words	38	45	83
re	felonies and words related to crime and immoral behavior	5	16	21
svp	words related to the seven deadly sins of the Christian tradition	2	5	7
	total	109	156	265

Table 2: Statistic of HurtLex MWE categories.

others candidate for elimination were literate translations e.g. *domaća svinja* 'domestic pig' → *krme* 'pig', *komunalni otpad* 'communal waste' → *đubre* 'trash', *životinjski svet* 'animal world' → *stoka* 'cattle'.

A few examples may further illustrate why some MWEs had to be deleted from the Serbian HurtLex. The MWE *meka na dodir* 'soft to touch' may have near synonyms with abusive meaning *mekana, ljigava, slabašna* 'soft, slimy, week' but not in categories that were assigned to this entry: animals, female genitalia, male genitalia, derogatory words, cognitive disabilities and diversity, ethnic slurs. Also, *nekompetentna osoba* 'incompetent person', *neobrazovana osoba* 'uneducated person' can not be in the category *animals*. Instead of *zmija u travi* 'snake in the grass' one would use in Serbian just *zmija* 'snake'. Table 2 shows number of MWEs that were rejected (no) and confirmed (yes) per each HurtLex category.

4 MWE - dictionary construction

4.1 Selection of new abusive MWE entris

In order to find a set of words that can be triggers for MWEs and generally for offensive speech, a set of trigger (single) words was created. The lexical database Leximirka (Stanković et al., 2018), which supports Serbian electronic dictionaries (Krstev, 2008) was analyzed and entries with one of the following semantic markers were selected: Aug (augmentative, 103), Pej (pejorative, 89), POG (derogatory, 41). The additional 602 items from srHurtLex were added to the list. The Dictionary of Serbian Language (DS) (Vujanić, 2007) was also analysed and following abbreviations from dictionary entries were used to select additional words: vulg. (vulgar, 68), ir. (ironic, 224), pej. (pejorative, 981), pogrd. (derogative, 3), podr. (elongated, 29), prezr. (scornful, 17). A set of threats and offensive chunks (tweets, posts) was processed and additional 694 words were obtained.

The final list with 2,851 trigger (single) words (lemma) was used to collect MWEs that contains at least one of selected trigger word. Various sources were used: dictionaries, collection of threats and results of online search. Finally, a list of 4,624 MWEs was compiled that were candidates for the detection of some kind of offensive or hate speech.

This list was manually checked and each MWE was put into on of three categories: YES - abusive speech (1260), MAYBE – could lead to abusive content (462), NO – not abusive (2902). The manual classification was supported by search over a Twitter corpus collected specifically for his research, Web

	A	ADV	N	PRO	V	(blank)	Total
maybe	93	12	152	0	168	37	462
no	432	142	978	17	1333		2902
yes	213	39	367	0	474	167	1260
Total	738	193	1497	17	1975	204	4624
	%	%	%	%	%	%	
maybe	12.6	6.2	10.2	0.0	8.5	18.1	10.0
no	58.5	73.6	65.3	100.0	67.5	0.0	62.8
yes	28.9	20.2	24.5	0.0	24.0	81.9	27.2

Table 3: MWEs classified as yes, no, maybe and part of speech of trigger words.

and other corpora previously compiled. The distribution of MWEs by part of speech categories of their trigger word is presented in Table 3.

Further analysis showed that 45% of trigger words yielded no MWE marked as abusive, 19% had less abusive than MWEs categorized as not abusive or potentially abusive (NO and MAYBE), 14% had more abusive MWEs, while for 22% trigger words all extracted MWE were marked as abusive. An example of a trigger word for which both abusive and not abusive MWE were extracted is *junak* 'hero'. MWEs marked as abusive are: *junak gradskih salona*, 'hero of city salon' and *junak na jeziku* 'hero on the tongue (scaramouch)', while non-abusive are *junak romana* 'a hero of the novel', *junak našeg naroda* 'hero of our people'.

Since the list has been acquired automatically, manual correction of lemmas was necessary for 285 lemmas in YES classes. For example, MWEs composed of adjectives *topovski* 'relating to a cannon' are described in the dictionary as: "~meso" (meat, gender n.), "~hrana" (food, gender f.), where ~stands for a lemma itself. The automatic substitution produces incorrect MWEs "topovski meso", "topovski hrana" that have to be corrected in order to conform to the gender agreement with a noun, obtaining finally *topovsko meso*, *topovska hrana* 'meat/food for cannons'.

The categories in the lexicon are based on hate targets similar to (Silva et al., 2016) that originated from Hatebase.org scheme, which are further enriched with additional categories: Immoral and criminal activities, slurs, curses, and offense. A certain term in the lexicon can be assigned to several categories, in case it appears in the context of several types of abusive speech. Table 4 presents examples of abusive words in each category.

4.2 Lexical Representation of Multi-Word Abusive Expressions

In order to enable the detection of abusive language in Serbian texts it is necessary to represent in a lexicon both simple- and multi-word abusive expressions. Lexical representation should address various aspects of these expressions: morphological, syntactic, semantic, and usage. Morpho-syntactic characteristics of simple abusive words are for most of them already described in the Serbian Morpho-syntactic Dictionary (SrpMD) due to its comprehensiveness (Krstev, 2008). Various classes of multi-word expressions are represented in SrpMD as well, primarily noun and adjective expressions. However, none of the dictionary entries were labeled specifically for hate speech and abusive language detection (except with general markers for derogatory or pejorative usage, as mentioned in Subsection 4.1). Our aim was to enrich SrpMD with new MWEs related to abusive language, and to provide all relevant entries, both already existing and new, with markers appropriate for its detection.

In the first step, we analysed the mopho-syntactic structure of MWEs marked as positively or potentially abusive (markers MAYBE or YES). This list, originally having 1772 items, contained after separating variations in MWEs (e.g. *neka te (mutna) voda nosi* 'let the (muddy) water carry you', *visiti o (koncu / dlaci)* 'to hang on a tread/hair') 1832 items. The most frequent were, as expected, MWEs with 2 components (893), followed by MWE with 3 components (464), 4 components (279), 5 components (119) and 77 MWEs with more than 5 components. MWEs were tagged using Serbian tagger (Stanković et al., 2020) and separated in two groups: nominal phrases (653) and verbal phrases (1179). Among nominal

Abusive category	Examples – single word	Example - MWE
Ethnicity and nationality (ABUS=racial)	*Ciganin*/Gipsy, *fašista*/ fashist, *Kinez*/Chinese, *jevrejski*/jewish	*praviti se Kinez*/pretending to be Chinese, *ciganska posla*/ gypsy business
Physical/mental disability (ABUS=disability)	*bogalj*/disabled, *budala*/ fool, *imbecil*/imbecile	*ptičiji mozak*/bird's brain
Physical/age discrimination (ABUS=appearance)	*kicoš*/dandy, *ćumez*/schack *debeljuca*/fatty, *baba*/grandma	*ružan k'o lopov*/ugly as a thief *matora devojka*/old maid
Sexual orientation (ABUS=sexual)	*guza*/butt, *gej*/gay *homoseksualac*/homosexual *travestit*/transvestite	*pederast izgled*/gay look
Behavior (ABUS=behavior)	*cepidlaka*/stickler *danguba*/dangler *drkadžija*/wanker	*pokondirena tikva*/ conceited pumpkin
Class (social, economic) (ABUS=seclass)	*bedan*/poor *ubog*/retched *buržoazija*/bourgeoisie	*go k'o crkveni miš*/ naked as a church mouse
Immoral/criminal activities (ABUS=law)	*bandit, bitanga*/rascal *lagati*/to lie, *izdajnik*/traitor	*ratni profiter*/war profiteer
Religion (ABUS=religion)	*nevernik*/infidel	*islamski fundamentalista*/ islamic fundamentalist
Race (ABUS=race)	*crnja, crnčuga*/Negro *Azijat*/Asian	*crn čovek*/black man
Gender (ABUS=gender)	*kurva*/whore, *drolja*/slut *krava*/cow, *žigolo*/gigolo	*ženski petko*/feminized man *laka žena*/easy woman

Table 4: Categories of abusive words and expressions with characteristic examples.

phrases the most frequent pattern is A N (448), a noun preceded by an adjective that agrees with it in the number, the case and the gender, for instance *belosvetska kurva* 'worldwide whore'. The other frequent patterns are: N N (50), usually a noun followed by a noun in the genitive or the instrumental case, e.g. *šaka jada* 'handful of misery', or two coordinated nous, e.g. *krava muzara* 'dairy cow'; N PREP N (25), a noun followed by a prepositional phrase, e.g. *govno od čoveka* 'shit of a man', *roba s greškom* 'damaged goods'; A ADV N (11), adjectives as simile figures, e.g. *glup kao noć* 'stupid as night', N CONJ N (9), two nouns connected with a conjunction, e.g. *bruka i sramota* 'shame and disgrace'. It should be noted that since MWEs were not syntactically parsed, some expressions were incorrectly grouped, e.g. *leglo opozicije* 'opposition's lair' was incorrectly recognized as V N pattern instead of N N due to the ambiguity of the form *leglo* (*leglo* is a noun 'lair' but also a form of a verb *leći* 'to lie down'); these cases were manually corrected. It should also be stressed that the assignment of POS tags to MWEs does not define the POS, or the role, an MWE itself does. For instance, *pukla bruka* 'scandal burst' has a common verbal phrase structure V N; however, it is a frozen expression mostly used as an interjection.

As already mentioned, prior to this task SrpMD contained 79 multi-word entries (noun phrases) from the compiled list of 653 nominal MWEs, however, without any marker pointing to their usage. After reallocating those that were incorrectly put into this group, and separating those that are not used as nominal but rather as frozen expressions, e.g. *duga kosa kratka pamet* 'long hair short wit' the list of 518 new MWE nominal entries was prepared, using semi-automatic procedure for MWE lemma construction (Krstev, 2008; Stanković et al., 2016) that relies on the information about its components already represented in SrpMD. The morpho-syntactic information is automatically assigned to all forms of multi-word expressions, while specific markers that point to their abusive usage were added according to the prior classification: HRT=yes and HRT=maybe. This is certainly a very rough classification, but a systematic annotation with more granulated classes is an ongoing activity.

In Table 5 we present some examples of produced MWEs lemmas, and some of their automatically produced forms. It should be noted that this way of representing MWEs in lexicon has a drawback

noun lemma	ženski(ženski.A2:adms1g) petko(petko.N68:ms1v),NC_AXN+Hum+HRT=yes
noun form	ženskog petka,ženskog petka.N+Hum+HRT=yes:ms2v
adj lemma	glup(glup.A15:akms1g) kao klada,AC_A4X+Simile+HRT=yes
adj form	glupog kao klada,glup kao klada.A+Simile+HRT=yes:adms2g kao klada glupog,glup kao klada.A+Simile+HRT=yes:adms2g

Table 5: Two examples of MWE lemmas and their forms in the genitive case singular: *ženski petko* (abusive for a man not manly enough) and *glup kao klada* 'stupid as a log'

because it does not cover any sort of insertions that may occur in an analysed text. Thus, a lexical description of *glup kao klada* will recognize different word orders *glup kao klada* and *kao klada glup* but not even the simplest insertions *glup je kao klada* 'lit. stupid is as a log'. For that reason we have started the more elaborate description of adjective expressions – simile figures – that relies on their joint tabular and finite-state description (Krstev et al., 2020).

We have started to apply the similar approach to verbal expressions. Among the group of verbal expressions the most frequent are those with a structure V N (289), followed by V PREP N (124), V PRO N (52), V N PREP N (40). Again, this is a rough analysis because each group may contain syntactically very different expressions. For instance, the V N group contains besides frozen expressions, e.g. *ode glava* 'head gone', expressions without complements, e.g. *sejati strah* 'sow fear', expressions with complements in the dative case, e.g. *prosuti creva* NEKOME 'to spill guts (to somebody)', expressions with complements in the accusative case, e.g. *lišiti* NEKOGA *slobode* 'deprive (somebody) of freedom', expressions with prepositional phrases as complements *zabadati nos* U NEŠTO 'pierce one's nose (into something)'. So far, a number of different structures were described in tables that cover lexical variants, e.g. Ekavian od Ijekavian word form (*pogaziti reč/riječ* 'trample the word', or synonyms (*lomiti/polomiti/slomiti vrat* 'break a neck'), complements, adjuncts etc. These tables are complemented with finite-state automata (FSA) that deal with word order, model complements, etc. and that are used to retrieve verbal expressions in texts. So far three classes of V N were modelled, covering 68 verbal MWEs.[2] This approach enables formulation of elaborate retrieal queries, similar to those proposed in (Razavi et al., 2010), but more precise since instead of a joker character * a more sophisticated patterns are used for complements and other insertions, e.g. a nominal phrase in the dative case.

We used our simple and MWE dictionary entries marked as (potentially) abusive to search our Twitter corpus containing approximately 8000 tweets and obtained around 800 hits, of which 80-90% indicated the abusive language. These are, however, just preliminary results that have to be confirmed on larger and more versatile corpora.

Figure 1 presents a Leximirka panel[3] for MWE editing: the syntactic class is assigned to a MWE, components and their morphological information are described which allows automatic production of all inflected forms that can be examined. Specific markers for abusive speech, that are proposed in this paper, can be assigned to a MWE entry through this panel.

5 Conclusion

In this paper we presented initial results on the analysis, improvement and creation of the lexical resources that will aid abusive speech detection tasks in Serbian, with a special focus given to MWEs, but there is still much to be done. Options of using a hybrid approach that would merge a dictionary with machine-learning will be explored. Finally, a user-friendly interface that will enable the usage of these resources on the Web is under development. We plan to use our lexicon of abusive speech to build a corpus of abusive content similar to (Rezvan et al., 2018) who firstly created an offensive word lexicon and then collected Twitter messages that contain at least one word from the lexicon. As authors noted, presence of a word in a tweet is just an indication of its offensiveness, thus subsequent manual annotation

---

[2]It should be noted that more MWEs from our list are described since in our model one expression groups variations.

[3]Leximirka is an online application based on lexicographic database, covering a wide range of users (http://leximirka.jerteh.rs//) (Lazić and Škorić,).

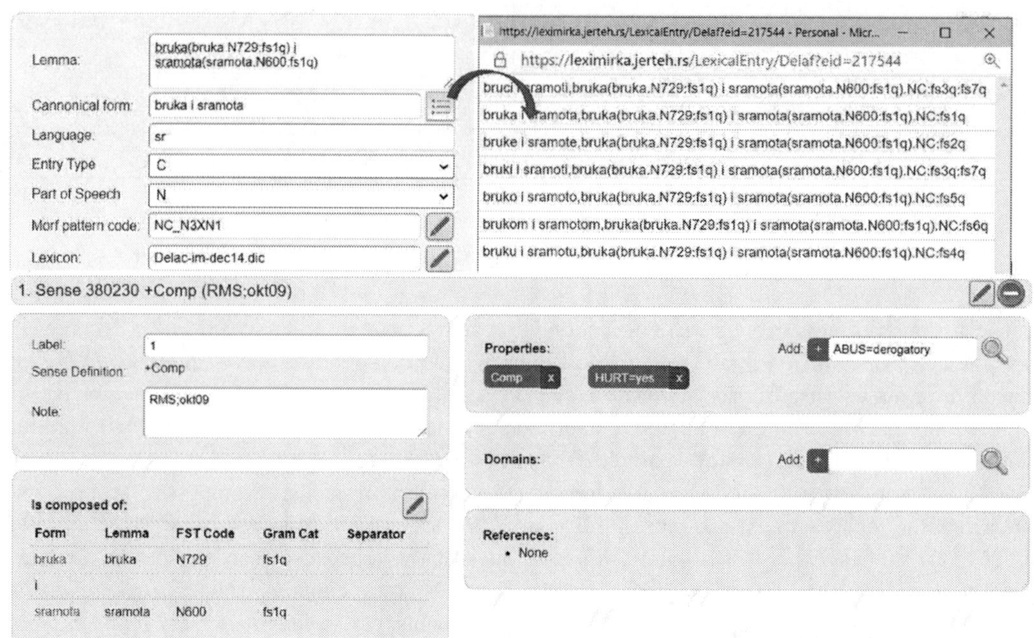

Figure 1: MWE editor in web portal Leximirka – description of a noun MWE *bruka i sramota* 'shame and disgrace'

is mandatory to assure correct classification of tweets.

In the next phases of the abusive words lexicon development, we plan to use: lists of slurs, abusive expressions, and courses built by conducting surveys and crowdsourcing (Mitrović et al., 2015), slang and dictionaries of synonyms, translation of existing lexicons in other languages, sentiment lexicon for Serbian language (Mladenović et al., 2016b), synsets from the Serbian WordNet (Mladenović et al., 2016a). We plan to use the lexicon for building a corpus of abusive content in social networks in Serbian as well as a classifier using rules and existing resources for Serbian language (Krstev et al., 2007). In addition, we plan to include the context rules and intensifiers following the approach presented in (Moreno-Ortiz et al., 2013) about the MWEs sentiment lexicon for Spanish. Additional attention will be given to the extension of the vocabulary with expressions that are not present in any existing lexicons, but evidenced in corpus as having offensive usage. The recognition of the different usages, that can be both offensive and non–offensive will be marked. The additional information about context or sense embeddings that will be useful for distinguishing between the two usages, could be added in the lexicon.

Acknowledgements

SPONSORED BY THE

The project on which this report is based was funded by the German Federal Ministry of Education and Research (BMBF) under the funding code 01IS20049. The author is responsible for the content of this publication. This research was partially supported by the Ministry of Education, Science and Technological Development of the Republic of Serbia and Deutcher Akademischer Austauschdienst - DAAD, Project years 2020-2021, Cross-Lingual Hate Speech Detection, and COST Action CA18209 - European network for Web-centred linguistic data science.

References

Valerio Basile, Cristina Bosco, Elisabetta Fersini, Debora Nozza, Viviana Patti, Francisco Manuel Rangel Pardo, Paolo Rosso, and Manuela Sanguinetti. 2019. Semeval-2019 task 5: Multilingual detection of hate speech against immigrants and women in twitter. In *Proceedings of the 13th International Workshop on Semantic Evaluation*, pages 54–63.

Elisa Bassignana, Valerio Basile, and Viviana Patti. 2018. Hurtlex: A multilingual lexicon of words to hurt. In *5th Italian Conference on Computational Linguistics, CLiC-it 2018*, volume 2253, pages 1–6. CEUR-WS.

Tommaso Caselli, Valerio Basile, Jelena Mitrović, Inga Kartoziya, and Michael Granitzer. 2020. I Feel Offended, Don't Be Abusive! Implicit/Explicit Messages in Offensive and Abusive Language. In *Proceedings of the Twelfth International Conference on Language Resources and Evaluation (LREC 2020)*, Marseille, France, May 11–16, 2020.

Ying Chen, Yilu Zhou, Sencun Zhu, and Heng Xu. 2012. Detecting offensive language in social media to protect adolescent online safety. In *2012 International Conference on Privacy, Security, Risk and Trust and 2012 International Confernece on Social Computing*, pages 71–80. IEEE.

Davide Colla, Caselli Tommaso, Valerio Basile, Jelena Mitrović, and Granitzer Michael. 2020. Grupato at semeval-2020 task 12: Retraining mbert on social media and fine-tuned offensive language models. In *Proceedings of the 14th International Workshop on Semantic Evaluation(SemEvaleval)*.

Andrea Esuli and Fabrizio Sebastiani. 2006. SENTIWORDNET: A publicly available lexical resource for opinion mining. In *Proceedings of the Fifth International Conference on Language Resources and Evaluation (LREC'06)*, Genoa, Italy, May. European Language Resources Association (ELRA).

Njagi Dennis Gitari, Zhang Zuping, Hanyurwimfura Damien, and Jun Long. 2015. A lexicon-based approach for hate speech detection. *International Journal of Multimedia and Ubiquitous Engineering*, 10(4):215–230.

Anna Koufakou, Valerio Basile, and Viviana Patti. 2020. Florunito@ trac-2: Retrofitting word embeddings on an abusive lexicon for aggressive language detection. In *Proceedings of the Second Workshop on Trolling, Aggression and Cyberbullying*, pages 106–112.

Cvetana Krstev, Sandra Gucul, Duško Vitas, and Vanja Radulović. 2007. Can we make the bell ring? In *Proceedings of the Workshop on a Common Natural Language Processing Paradigm for Balkan Languages*, pages 15–22.

Cvetana Krstev, Jelena Jaćimović, and Duško Vitas. 2020. Analysis of similes in serbian literary texts (1840-1920) using computational methods. In Svetla Koeva, editor, *Proceedings of the Fourth International Conference Computational Linguistics in Bulgaria (CLIB 2020)*. Institute for Bulgarian Language "Prof. Lyubomir Andreychin", Bulgarian Academy of Sciences, June.

Cvetana Krstev. 2008. *Processing of Serbian – Automata, Texts and Electronic Dictionaries*. University of Belgrade, Faculty of Philology, Belgrade.

Irene Kwok and Yuzhou Wang. 2013. Locate the hate: Detecting tweets against blacks. In *Proceedings of the twenty-seventh AAAI conference on artificial intelligence*, pages 1621–1622.

Biljana Lazić and Mihailo Škorić. From dela based dictionary to leximirka lexical database.

Jelena Mitrović, Miljana Mladenović, and Cvetana Krstev. 2015. Adding mwes to serbian lexical resources using crowdsourcing. In *poster presented at The 5th PARSEME general meeting. Iași, Romania*, pages 23–24.

Jelena Mitrovic, Cliff O'Reilly, Randy Allen Harris, and Michael Granitzer. 2020. Cognitive modeling in computational rhetoric: Litotes, containment and the unexcluded middle. In Ana Paula Rocha, Luc Steels, and H. Jaap van den Herik, editors, *Proceedings of the 12th International Conference on Agents and Artificial Intelligence, ICAART 2020, Volume 2, Valletta, Malta, February 22-24, 2020*, pages 806–813. SCITEPRESS.

Miljana Mladenović and Jelena Mitrović. 2013. Ontology of rhetorical figures for serbian. In Ivan Habernal and Václav Matoušek, editors, *Text, Speech, and Dialogue*, pages 386–393, Berlin, Heidelberg. Springer Berlin Heidelberg.

Miljana Mladenović, Mitrović Jelena, and Cvetana Krstev. 2016a. A language-independent model for introducing a new semantic relation between adjectives and nouns in a wordnet. In *Proceedings of Eighth Global WordNet Conference*, pages 218–225.

Miljana Mladenović, Jelena Mitrović, Cvetana Krstev, and Duško Vitas. 2016b. Hybrid sentiment analysis framework for a morphologically rich language. *Journal of Intelligent Information Systems*, 46(3):599–620.

Miljana Mladenović, Cvetana Krstev, Jelena Mitrović, and Ranka Stanković. 2017. Using lexical resources for irony and sarcasm classification. In *Proceedings of the 8th Balkan Conference in Informatics*, BCI '17, New York, NY, USA. Association for Computing Machinery.

Antonio Moreno-Ortiz, Chantal Pérez-Hernández, and Maria Del-Olmo. 2013. Managing multiword expressions in a lexicon-based sentiment analysis system for spanish. In *Proceedings of the 9th Workshop on Multiword Expressions*, pages 1–10.

Chikashi Nobata, Joel Tetreault, Achint Thomas, Yashar Mehdad, and Yi Chang. 2016. Abusive language detection in online user content. In *Proceedings of the 25th international conference on world wide web*, pages 145–153.

John T Nockleby. 2000. Hate speech. *Encyclopedia of the American constitution*, 3(2):1277–1279.

Endang Wahyu Pamungkas and Viviana Patti. 2019. Cross-domain and cross-lingual abusive language detection: A hybrid approach with deep learning and a multilingual lexicon. In *Proceedings of the 57th Annual Meeting of the Association for Computational Linguistics: Student Research Workshop*, pages 363–370.

Endang Wahyu Pamungkas, Alessandra Teresa Cignarella, Valerio Basile, and V. Patti. 2018. Automatic identification of misogyny in english and italian tweets at evalita 2018 with a multilingual hate lexicon. In *EVALITA@CLiC-it*.

Endang Wahyu Pamungkas, Valerio Basile, and Viviana Patti. 2020. Misogyny detection in twitter: a multilingual and cross-domain study.

Ted Pedersen. 2020. Duluth at semeval-2019 task 6: Lexical approaches to identify and categorize offensive tweets. *arXiv preprint arXiv:2007.12949*.

Amir H Razavi, Diana Inkpen, Sasha Uritsky, and Stan Matwin. 2010. Offensive language detection using multi-level classification. In *Canadian Conference on Artificial Intelligence*, pages 16–27. Springer.

Mohammadreza Rezvan, Saeedeh Shekarpour, Lakshika Balasuriya, Krishnaprasad Thirunarayan, Valerie L Shalin, and Amit Sheth. 2018. A quality type-aware annotated corpus and lexicon for harassment research. In *Proceedings of the 10th ACM Conference on Web Science*, pages 33–36.

Leandro Silva, Mainack Mondal, Denzil Correa, Fabrício Benevenuto, and Ingmar Weber. 2016. Analyzing the targets of hate in online social media. *arXiv preprint arXiv:1603.07709*.

Ranka Stanković, Cvetana Krstev, Ivan Obradović, Biljana Lazić, and Aleksandra Trtovac. 2016. Rule-based automatic multi-word term extraction and lemmatization. In *Proceedings of the 10th International Conference on Language Resources and Evaluation, LREC 2016, Portorož, Slovenia, 23–28 May 2016*, pages 507–514.

Ranka Stanković, Cvetana Krstev, Biljana Lazić, and Mihailo Škorić. 2018. Electronic dictionaries-from file system to lemon based lexical database. In *Proceedings of the 6th Workshop on Linked Data in Linguistics (LDL-2018) (clocated with LREC 2018), McCrae, JP, C. Chiarcos, T. Declerck, J. Gracia and B. Klimek*, pages 48–56.

Ranka Stanković, Branislava Šandrih, Cvetana Krstev, Miloš Utvić, and Mihailo Škorić. 2020. Machine Learning and Deep Neural Network-Based Lemmatization and Morphosyntactic Tagging for Serbian. In *Proceedings of The 12th Language Resources and Evaluation Conference*, pages 3947–3955, Marseille, France, May. European Language Resources Association.

Milica Vujanić, editor. 2007. *Rečnik srpskoga jezika*. Matica srpska.

Michael Wiegand, Josef Ruppenhofer, Anna Schmidt, and Clayton Greenberg. 2018. Inducing a lexicon of abusive words–a feature-based approach.

Marcos Zampieri, Shervin Malmasi, Preslav Nakov, Sara Rosenthal, Noura Farra, and Ritesh Kumar. 2019. Semeval-2019 task 6: Identifying and categorizing offensive language in social media (offenseval). In *Proceedings of the 13th International Workshop on Semantic Evaluation, SemEval@NAACL-HLT 2019, Minneapolis, MN, USA, June 6-7, 2019*, pages 75–86. Association for Computational Linguistics.

Marcos Zampieri, Preslav Nakov, Sara Rosenthal, Pepa Atanasova, Georgi Karadzhov, Hamdy Mubarak, Leon Derczynski, Zeses Pitenis, and Çağrı Çöltekin. 2020. SemEval-2020 Task 12: Multilingual Offensive Language Identification in Social Media (OffensEval 2020). In *Proceedings of SemEval*.

Disambiguation of Potentially Idiomatic Expressions
with Contextual Embeddings

Murathan Kurfalı, Robert Östling
Linguistics Department, Stockholm University
Stockholm, Sweden
`{murathan.kurfali,robert}@ling.su.se`

Abstract

The majority of multiword expressions can be interpreted as figuratively or literally in different contexts which pose challenges in a number of downstream tasks. Most previous work deals with this ambiguity following the observation that MWEs with different usages occur in distinctly different contexts. Following this insight, we explore the usefulness of contextual embeddings by means of both supervised and unsupervised classification. The results show that in the supervised setting, the state-of-the-art can be substantially improved for all expressions in the experiments. The unsupervised classification, similarly, yields very impressive results, comparing favorably to the supervised classifier for the majority of the expressions. We also show that multilingual contextual embeddings can also be employed for this task without leading to any significant loss in performance; hence, the proposed methodology has the potential to be extended to a number of languages.

1 Introduction

By definition, a multiword expression (MWE) is idiomatic in the sense that its meaning cannot be derived from the meanings of its components. However, whereas sometimes a sequence of words corresponding to an MWE only has the idiomatic interpretation (e.g., *by and large*), there is often also a literal interpretation of the same sequence, resulting in an ambiguity:

- And the final twenty minutes is a headlong adrenalin rush, frantically intercutting four separate battle sequences and never **dropping the ball** once.

- Now, **drop the ball** for a bounce, tap it softly up towards your hands but let it fall back to the pavement for another bounce. *(examples taken from Korkontzelos et al. (2013))*

Such multiword expressions are commonly referred as *potentially idiomatic expressions (henceforth, PIE)* and determining the correct meaning of a PIE in context is shown to be crucial for many downstream tasks including sentiment analysis (Williams et al., 2015), automatic spelling correction (Horbach et al., 2016) and machine translation (Isabelle et al., 2017). Most of the previous work capitalizes on the differences between the contexts where PIEs are used idiomatically and literally. Following that insight, we investigate the applicability of recent contextual embedding models to disambiguation of PIEs.

Contextual embeddings, e.g. ELMo (Peters et al., 2018) and BERT (Devlin et al., 2019), have emerged in the last few years and quickly become the standard in a variety of tasks. These are very deep neural language models which are pre-trained on large-scale corpora. Unlike the conventional static word embeddings, such as Word2Vec (Mikolov et al., 2013) where each word type is represented by a fixed vector, these models assign distinct representations for each input token dependent on their context. Hence, they are called *contextual word embeddings*, highlighting their sensitivity to the context. For example, in the sentence "Can you throw this can away?" the first and second occurrence of the token *can* are supposed to be assigned substantially different embeddings.

Joint Workshop on Multiword Expressions and Electronic Lexicons, pages 85–94
Barcelona, Spain (Online), December 13, 2020.

The extent of the contextuality of these embeddings, on the other hand, is still an open research topic (Ethayarajh, 2019). In this work, we specifically investigate whether such contextual embeddings provide sufficient contextual information to distinguish literal usages of PIEs from idiomatic ones. To this end, we represent the PIE tokens in a certain context by their corresponding BERT embeddings (Devlin et al., 2019) and perform both supervised and unsupervised PIE disambiguation. The results suggest that the plain BERT model, without any fine-tuning or further training, is able to encode the different usages of PIEs to the extent that, even a with simple linear classifier, we can substantially improve the state-of-the-art on common datasets in two different languages.

The unsupervised classification, on the other hand, is performed via hierarchical clustering, accompanied with a simple heuristic, that PIEs with literal interpretations are semantically closer to their context than the idiomatic ones. For the most of the time, the unsupervised classification also achieves unprecedented performance although not as consistently as its supervised counterpart, failing completely with some expressions.

Finally, we compare the performance of the monolingual BERT models with the multilingual-BERT (mBERT) to investigate the applicability of our approach to other low resource languages as well as to provide further insight regarding the cross-lingual capabilities of the multilingual contextual embeddings when they are employed directly; that is, without any fine-tuning in the target language. The results show that multilingual-BERT achieves comparable results to monolingual models across all datasets, suggesting that the proposed methodology can straightforwardly be extended to other languages.

2   Related Work

A number of models have been proposed in the literature to disambiguate PIEs, with a trend shifting from employing linguistic features to more neural approaches, similar to the rest of the field. Fazly et al. (2009) adopt an unsupervised approach relying on the hypothesis that multiword expressions are more likely to occur in different canonical forms when used literally. Sporleder and Li (2009) propose a generalized method (as opposed to "per-idiom classification") employing cohesion graphs which initially include all the words in the sentences. They hypothesize that a PIE is used figuratively if the removal of the PIE improves the cohesion. Li and Sporleder (2009) prepares a dataset consisting of high confidences instances found by (Sporleder and Li, 2009) and train a supervised classifier to classify the rest of the instances.

Rajani et al. (2014) use a variety of features including bag of all content words along with their concreteness measures and train a L2 regularized Logistic Regression (L2LR) classifier (Fan et al., 2008). Liu and Hwa (2017) also utilize the cues the context of the PIE provides and adopt an ensemble learning approach based on three different classifiers trained on different representations of the context. Liu and Hwa (2018) propose a "literal usage metric" which quantifies the literalness of PIE. This metric is computed as the average similarity between the words in the sentence and the "literal usage representation" which is the set of the words similar to the literal meanings of the PIE's main constituent words found in large corpus. Do Dinh et al. (2018) use a multi-task learning approach covering four different non-literal language using tasks including classification of idiomatic use of infinitive-verb compounds in German using recurrent Sluice networks (Ruder et al., 2019). Similar to (Sporleder and Li, 2009), (Liu and Hwa, 2019) adopt a generalized approach and propose a novel "semantic compatibility model" which is a modified version of CBOW, adapted specifically to the disambiguation of the PIEs task.

In a related line of research, contextual embeddings are successfully applied to the general problem of word sense disambiguation (WSD). Wiedemann et al. (2019) show that BERT embeddings form distinct clusters for different senses of a given word in line with its promise to be contextual. Huang et al. (2019) approach WSD as a sentence pair classification task and fine-tune BERT where the input consists of a sentence containing the target word and the one of its glosses and the objective is to classify if the gloss matches the sense of the target word in the sentence.

3 Method

The task here is to distinguish the compositional (literal) and non-compositional (idiomatic) usages of a *known* PIE in a certain context as opposed to MWE extraction which is the task of discovering MWEs in a corpus. Hence, the input to our method is a set of sentences containing a target PIE. We regard disambiguation of PIEs as a word sense disambiguation problem. Our basic assumption is that the context, in which PIEs occur literally and figuratively are distinct enough from each other to be assigned a fundamentally different contextual representations. Below, we briefly introduce the contextual language model we use in the experiments, BERT, followed by the descriptions of the supervised and the unsupervised classifiers.

3.1 BERT

BERT (*Bidirectional Encoder Representations for Transformers*) is a multi-layer Transformer encoder based language model (Devlin et al., 2019). As the transformer encoder reads its input at once, BERT learns words full context (both from left and from right), as opposed to directional models where the input is processed from one direction to another. BERT takes a pair of sentences padded with the special "[CLS]" token in the beginning of the first sentence and "[SEP]" token after the end of each sentence indicating sentence boundaries.

BERT is trained with two objective functions on large-scale unlabeled text: (i) Masked Language Modelling (MLM) and (ii) Next Sentence Prediction (NSP). In MLM, 15% of the input tokens are randomly replaced with a special "[MASK]" token and the task is to predict the masked token by looking at its context. Contrary to the traditional language modelling, where the task is to predict the next word given a sequence of words, the MLM objective forces BERT to consider the context in both sides hence increases its context sensitivity. The NSP objective is a binary classification task to determine if the second sentence in the input follows the first one in the original text. During training, BERT is fed with sentence pairs where half of the time the second sentence is randomly selected from the full corpus.

3.2 Supervised Classification

The supervised model consists of an encoder and a classifier. The task of encoder is to assign each token a representation in a way that every occurrence of each word is represented differently, reflecting their context. We use two different BERT models (Devlin et al., 2019) as encoders in our experiments:

- **Monolingual BERTs** We use bert-base-cased and German-bert[1] as the monolingual BERT models. Each model has the same architecture, consisting of 12 transformers layers and trained on huge monolingual corpus of the respective language.

- **multilingual BERT (mBERT):**[2] mBERT is trained on the concatenation of the 104 Wikipedia dumps with shared word-piece vocabulary. Since the training data does not contain any cross-lingual signal, the source and the extent of the cross-lingual capabilities of mBERT has been a topic of research on its own (Pires et al., 2019).

Since BERT's internal tokenizer splits some words into multiple tokens, e.g. 'microscope' becomes ['micro', '##scope'], we first compute a word-token map which keeps track of the word pieces PIEs are split into. Then, each PIE is represented by the average of their word piece embeddings,

$$V_{PIE_i} = \frac{1}{k} \sum_{j=1}^{k} v_{i,j}$$

where k is the number of word pieces that PIE is split into; $v_{i,j}$ is the representation of the jth word piece in the ith sentence in the dataset. We only count the lexicalised components in the canonical form

---

[1] https://deepset.ai/german-bert
[2] https://github.com/google-research/bert/blob/master/multilingual.md

of the PIEs as its constituents, e.g. we would leave out the embedding of any realization of *someone* from the embeddings of the MWE *break someone's heart*.

A typical characteristic of compositional PIEs is that their component words display larger variation of inflectional forms than idiomatic PIEs, which is a property that has previously been used as a feature for the purpose of disambiguation (Fazly et al., 2009) (e.g. "broke a leg" can be more likely to be used with the literal sense as opposed to "break a leg" which is almost always used figuratively). Yet, this correlation between the form and the meaning may obscure the results of our experiments as our main aim is to test the degree of contextuality captured by these contextual embeddings. Hence, in order to control for this variation, we lemmatize all the words in PIEs before feeding them to the encoder. In the case of German PIEs, where whether a PIE is written as one word or two words is a strong indicator of its sense, we always spell them as two words. We do not modify the sentence which we pass to encoder in any other way. As for classifier, we use a simple single-layer perceptron to predict the correct usage.s

3.3 Unsupervised Model

The unsupervised model uses the same representations that are used in the supervised setting. We use the hierarchical agglomerative clustering (HAC) algorithm (Day and Edelsbrunner, 1984). We experimented with various configurations and finally adopted Ward as the linkage criterion with Euclidean distances as the similarity metric. Additional experiments with k-means clustering algorithm also yielded similar results but we choose HAC over k-means as it is a deterministic algorithm so the results are more stable.[3]

The unsupervised model relies on the observation that the multiword expressions are semantically in sharp contrast with their surrounding context when used idiomatically, following the previous studies (Peng and Feldman, 2016; Liu and Hwa, 2018). We quantify these heuristics as the average of the cosine similarities between the words in the sentence and the PIE inspired by (Liu and Hwa, 2018):

$$score = \frac{1}{L} \sum_{j=1}^{L} \cos(V_{PIE}, w_j)$$

where w_j is the jth word in the sentence and $\cos(V_{PIE}, w_j)$ is the cosine similarity between the word embedding and the embedding of the PIE. Following our heuristics, we label all PIEs as "idioms" in the cluster, in which the average cosine similarity between PIEs and the sentence they occur in is the lowest.

4 Experiments

We conduct our experiments on the widely used datasets in two languages: the VNC dataset (Cook et al., 2008) and SemEval5b (Korkontzelos et al., 2013) for English and the Horbach dataset for German (Horbach et al., 2016).

Dataset	Language	# of MWEs	Idiom	Literal	Total
VNC	English	12	489 (66.4%)	248 (33.6%)	737
SemEval5b	English	10	1204 (50.7%)	1172 (49.3%)	2376
Horbach	German	6	3369 (64.2%)	1880 (35.8%)	5249

Table 1: Statistics of the datasets used in the experiments. Note that the statistics reflect the subset of the respective dataset used in experiments.

In order to have comparable results, we follow the the official train/test split of Semeval5b dataset whereas for VNC dataset, we used multiword expressions which have at least 10 instances with both literal and idiomatic usage following (Liu and Hwa, 2019). Since there is not any official train/test split for both VNC and Horbach datasets, we report the results of 5-fold cross-validation for the former[4] and 10-fold for the latter. We use Scikit-learn library (Pedregosa et al., 2011) to implement both perceptron

---

[3]All model selection experiments were performed with the VNC dataset only, thus leaving the larger SemEval5b and Horbach datasets untainted.

[4]Due to the limited size of the VNC dataset.

	Semeval5b		VNC		German Dataset	
Model	Acc	F-score	Acc	F-score	Acc	F-score
(Fazly et al., 2009)†	-	-	0.74	0.73	-	-
(Li and Sporleder, 2009)†	0.62	0.64	0.66	0.67	-	-
(Rajani et al., 2014)	0.75	0.71	0.7	0.69	-	-
(Liu and Hwa, 2017)	0.77	0.77	0.75	0.75	-	-
(Liu and Hwa, 2018)†	0.74	0.75	0.75	0.73	-	-
(Liu and Hwa, 2019)†	0.75	0.76	0.73	0.75	-	-
(Horbach et al., 2016)	-	-	-	-	0.86	-
(Do Dinh et al., 2018)	-	-	-	-	0.88	-
mBERT (Unsupervised)	0.81	0.81	0.69	0.69	0.50	0.55
mBERT (Supervised)	0.91	0.91	0.89	0.85	0.88	0.90
BERT-base (Unsupervised)	0.79	0.78	0.73	0.73	0.55	0.59
BERT-base (Supervised)	**0.94**	**0.93**	**0.91**	**0.90**	**0.94**	**0.94**

Table 2: Averaged results across all idioms in datasets. *BERT-base refers to the monolingual BERT trained on the language of the respective dataset. † indicates an unsupervised baseline.

and agglomerative clustering. The learning rate of the perceptron is set to 1×10^{-5}. The embeddings are normalized before they are fed into the classifiers. As the length of the available context differ for each dataset, we limit the context to the sentence containing the PIE. We use the embeddings from the last layer of the BERT models in the experiments; yet, we conduct a layer-wise analysis as well (see Section 6).

5   Results

Our average results with a detailed comparison with the previous studies are provided in Table 2 and per-idiom results in Figure 1 and in Appendix A. We report the overall accuracy and the F-score for the idiomatic ("figurative") class. The results indicate that contextual embeddings is clearly a better alternative to the previous approaches. The supervised classifier trained on monolingual BERT embeddings achieves the best performances, improving the current state-of-the-art models from 76+% to 91+% F-score on English and from 88% to 92% accuracy on German datasets. Similarly, the unsupervised classification outperforms or is on par with the previous state-of-the-art results on the English datasets but fails to perform equally well on German, which is further discussed in the next section.

Switching to the multilingual contextual embeddings does not lead to a significant decrease in performance, especially in the supervised setting where the results stay considerably above the previous state-of-the-art. It must be noted that the relatively lower performance of the multilingual embeddings in the unsupervised setting is because of a significant drop with certain PIEs, not due to a general failure of the classifier across all PIEs (Figure 1).

6   Discussion

In this section, we further discuss some implications of our results. Overall, we comprehensively evaluated our approach in three datasets. The performance of the supervised classification is pretty consistent across all the PIEs in two languages, ranging between 0.77 to 1.00 F-score with a mean of 0.92 ($\pm$0.06). Hence, the increase in the average results are not due to a significant increase in a subset of PIEs but constant improvement in all PIEs covered in the datasets.

As for unsupervised classification, in line with our hypothesis, most of the time BERT embeddings form distinct enough clusters corresponding the different usages of PIE, allowing high performing unsupervised classification. Yet, the unsupervised classifier is more prone to make errors as it completely fails with certain expressions which significantly lowers its overall performance (see Figure 1). We group the errors of the unsupervised classification under two categories:

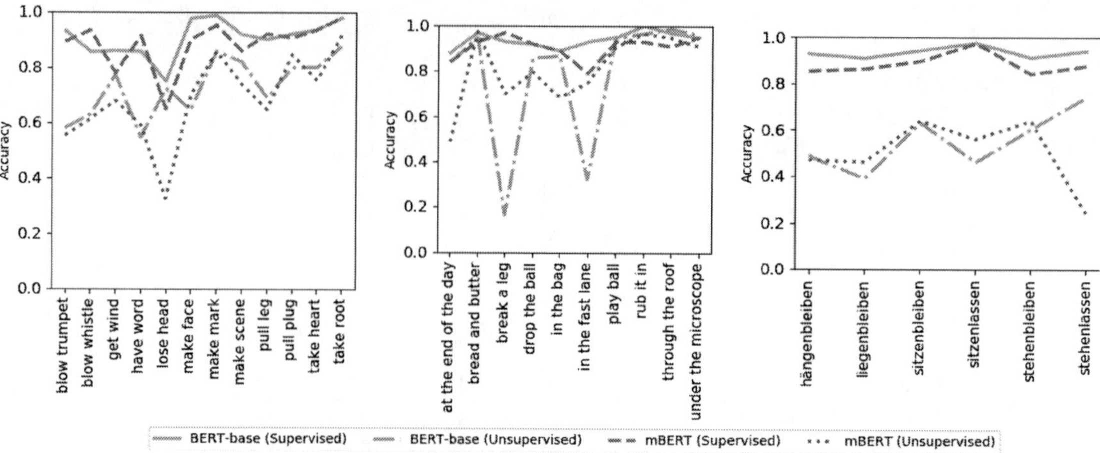

Figure 1: Idiom-wise performance (accuracy) of both classifiers with monolingual and multilingual contextual embeddings. The MWEs are represented in alphabetical order and the lines are added for visibility.

- **Clustering errors** occur due to the formation of poor clusters, consisting of PIEs with different usages. Clustering errors happen relatively rarely in English, where there are only four expressions ("blow whistle", "pull leg", "break a leg", "in the fast lane") with F-score < 0.6; as opposed to German where the unsupervised classifier achieves only 0.59 F-score on average. We suspect that behind the high error rate in German lies the fact that German MWEs exhibit a wider range of polysemy both in literal and figurative interpretation. Horbach et al. (2016) also discusses this point as one of the challenges during annotation, stating that there are not very clearly separated uses of the respective verbs in the dataset, as opposed to, e.g., "bread and butter" in English which has a dominant figurative interpretation. For example, according to (Horbach et al., 2016), stehen+bleiben (stand+still) has a large number of meanings, some of which are *(i) a person's heart may stand still; (ii) people may stand still in their mental development; (iii) you can claim that a statement cannot "remain standing" (remain uncontradicted)*. This point is also visible in the dendrograms of German PIEs where there are more distinct clusters on the lower levels (Figure 3). A preliminary analysis of these clusters show tendencies towards this direction, but a more systematic evaluation is left for future work.

- **Labeling errors** In this case, the lower performance of the unsupervised classifier is due to the failure of our heuristics to label the clusters correctly rather than the formation of poor clusters. The most representative example of this error is the expression "break a leg" where the supervised classification achieves the F-score of 0.89 whereas the unsupervised classifier completely fails as our heuristics fail to label the clusters correctly. We ran a further experiment with an updated heuristics where we directly measure the cosine similarity between the sentence and the PIE by

(a) BERT-base (b) Multilingual-BERT

Figure 2: The averaged results in accuracy over all layers.

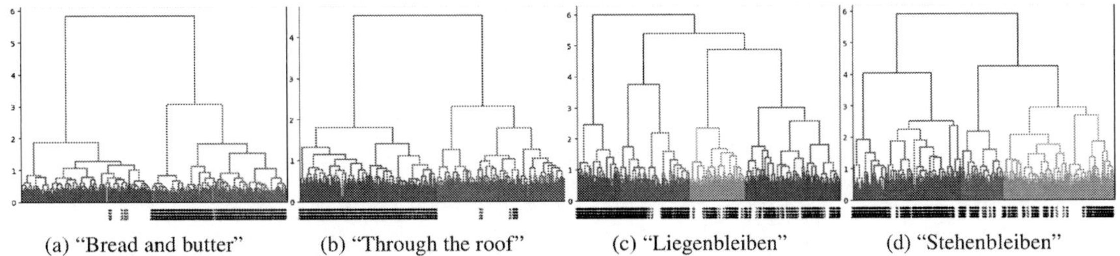

(a) "Bread and butter" (b) "Through the roof" (c) "Liegenbleiben" (d) "Stehenbleiben"

Figure 3: Hierarchical clustering of several cherry-picked English and German PIE embeddings obtained from the respective monolingual BERT model. The leaves corresponding to idiomatic examples are labeled whereas the rest are left empty in order to visualize how the idiomatic and literal instances are separated across clusters.

representing the former as the average of its constituents' embeddings (as opposed to average of the the pair-wise similarity between the PIE and the words in its context). However, the updated heuristics also yielded the same results, highlighting the need for more elaborate heuristics.

Furthermore, we ran all the experiments without performing lemmatization on the target expressions (see Section 3.2) to see if lemmatization had any adverse effect on BERT. Overall, lemmatization turned out to lead to mixed results (1 to 2 point change in F-score) but surprisingly mostly positive; the surface (*unlemmatized*) forms achieve slightly better performance (+1 F-score) only on VNC dataset in the supervised setting and on SemEval dataset in the unsupervised setting when multilingual embeddings are employed. However, as discussed in Section 3.2, without lemmatization it is not possible to know if the classifiers exploit the possible correlation between the surface forms and associated usages. Therefore, we believe lemmatization is a necessary pre-processing step as it allows us for that correlation, without harming the performance.

We, additionally, conducted a layer-wise analysis as different layers of BERT is shown to capture different properties of the language (Tenney et al., 2019). In addition to each layer, we experiment with the concatenation of the last four layers following the original BERT paper (Devlin et al., 2019) which claims that it yields the best contextualized embeddings. The results show that the sixth layer and upwards yield better performances where the concatenation of the last four layers leads mixed results, leading a slight drop on two datasets and increase in one (Figure 2).

Finally, as can be seen in Figure 1, the performance of the supervised classifier with mBERT embeddings are consistent across PIEs which suggests that disambiguation of PIEs can be performed with high accuracy in a large number of languages, requiring only a small set of annotated sentences, e.g. the portion of the VNC dataset used in the experiments contains only 61 sentences annotated per MWE on average (see Table 1).

7 Conclusion

In the current paper, we have proposed two methods, one supervised and one unsupervised, for disambiguation of potentially idiomatic expressions in running text. Our models utilize contextual embeddings which are able to recognize the different usages of the same lexical units and assign representations accordingly. Experimental results in two languages show both of our classifiers substantially outperform the previous state-of-the-art; yet, there is much room for improvement, especially with unsupervised classification which is less stable. The proposed methodology, furthermore, is shown to have a high potential to be extended into a large number of languages thanks to the multilingual contextual embeddings.

Acknowledgements

We would like to thank Mats Wirén for his useful comments and NVIDIA for their GPU grant.

References

Paul Cook, Afsaneh Fazly, and Suzanne Stevenson. 2008. The vnc-tokens dataset. In *Proceedings of the LREC Workshop Towards a Shared Task for Multiword Expressions (MWE 2008)*, pages 19–22.

William HE Day and Herbert Edelsbrunner. 1984. Efficient algorithms for agglomerative hierarchical clustering methods. *Journal of classification*, 1(1):7–24.

Jacob Devlin, Ming-Wei Chang, Kenton Lee, and Kristina Toutanova. 2019. BERT: Pre-training of deep bidirectional transformers for language understanding. In *Proceedings of the 2019 Conference of the North American Chapter of the Association for Computational Linguistics: Human Language Technologies, Volume 1 (Long and Short Papers)*, pages 4171–4186, Minneapolis, Minnesota, June. Association for Computational Linguistics.

Erik-Lân Do Dinh, Steffen Eger, and Iryna Gurevych. 2018. Killing four birds with two stones: Multi-task learning for non-literal language detection. In *Proceedings of the 27th International Conference on Computational Linguistics*, pages 1558–1569.

Kawin Ethayarajh. 2019. How contextual are contextualized word representations? comparing the geometry of bert, elmo, and gpt-2 embeddings. In *Proceedings of the 2019 Conference on Empirical Methods in Natural Language Processing and the 9th International Joint Conference on Natural Language Processing (EMNLP-IJCNLP)*, pages 55–65.

Rong-En Fan, Kai-Wei Chang, Cho-Jui Hsieh, Xiang-Rui Wang, and Chih-Jen Lin. 2008. Liblinear: A library for large linear classification. *Journal of machine learning research*, 9(Aug):1871–1874.

Afsaneh Fazly, Paul Cook, and Suzanne Stevenson. 2009. Unsupervised type and token identification of idiomatic expressions. *Computational Linguistics*, 35(1):61–103.

Andrea Horbach, Andrea Hensler, Sabine Krome, Jakob Prange, Werner Scholze-Stubenrecht, Diana Steffen, Stefan Thater, Christian Wellner, and Manfred Pinkal. 2016. A corpus of literal and idiomatic uses of german infinitive-verb compounds. In *Proceedings of the Tenth International Conference on Language Resources and Evaluation (LREC'16)*, pages 836–841.

Luyao Huang, Chi Sun, Xipeng Qiu, and Xuan-Jing Huang. 2019. Glossbert: Bert for word sense disambiguation with gloss knowledge. In *Proceedings of the 2019 Conference on Empirical Methods in Natural Language Processing and the 9th International Joint Conference on Natural Language Processing (EMNLP-IJCNLP)*, pages 3500–3505.

Pierre Isabelle, Colin Cherry, and George Foster. 2017. A challenge set approach to evaluating machine translation. In *Proceedings of the 2017 Conference on Empirical Methods in Natural Language Processing*, pages 2486–2496.

Ioannis Korkontzelos, Torsten Zesch, Fabio Massimo Zanzotto, and Chris Biemann. 2013. Semeval-2013 task 5: Evaluating phrasal semantics. In *Second Joint Conference on Lexical and Computational Semantics (* SEM)*, pages 39–47.

Linlin Li and Caroline Sporleder. 2009. Classifier combination for contextual idiom detection without labelled data. In *Proceedings of the 2009 Conference on Empirical Methods in Natural Language Processing: Volume 1-Volume 1*, pages 315–323. Association for Computational Linguistics.

Changsheng Liu and Rebecca Hwa. 2017. Representations of context in recognizing the figurative and literal usages of idioms. In *Thirty-First AAAI Conference on Artificial Intelligence*.

Changsheng Liu and Rebecca Hwa. 2018. Heuristically informed unsupervised idiom usage recognition. In *Proceedings of the 2018 Conference on Empirical Methods in Natural Language Processing*, pages 1723–1731.

Changsheng Liu and Rebecca Hwa. 2019. A generalized idiom usage recognition model based on semantic compatibility. In *Proceedings of the AAAI Conference on Artificial Intelligence*, volume 33, pages 6738–6745.

Tomas Mikolov, Ilya Sutskever, Kai Chen, Greg S Corrado, and Jeff Dean. 2013. Distributed representations of words and phrases and their compositionality. In *Advances in neural information processing systems*, pages 3111–3119.

Fabian Pedregosa, Gaël Varoquaux, Alexandre Gramfort, Vincent Michel, Bertrand Thirion, Olivier Grisel, Mathieu Blondel, Peter Prettenhofer, Ron Weiss, Vincent Dubourg, et al. 2011. Scikit-learn: Machine learning in python. *the Journal of machine Learning research*, 12:2825–2830.

Jing Peng and Anna Feldman. 2016. Experiments in idiom recognition. In *Proceedings of COLING 2016, the 26th International Conference on Computational Linguistics: Technical Papers*, pages 2752–2761.

Matthew E Peters, Mark Neumann, Mohit Iyyer, Matt Gardner, Christopher Clark, Kenton Lee, and Luke Zettlemoyer. 2018. Deep contextualized word representations. In *Proceedings of NAACL-HLT*, pages 2227–2237.

Telmo Pires, Eva Schlinger, and Dan Garrette. 2019. How multilingual is multilingual BERT? In *Proceedings of the 57th Annual Meeting of the Association for Computational Linguistics*, pages 4996–5001, Florence, Italy, July. Association for Computational Linguistics.

Nazneen Fatema Rajani, Edaena Salinas, and Raymond Mooney. 2014. Using abstract context to detect figurative language.

Sebastian Ruder, Joachim Bingel, Isabelle Augenstein, and Anders Søgaard. 2019. Latent multi-task architecture learning. In *Proceedings of the AAAI Conference on Artificial Intelligence*, volume 33, pages 4822–4829.

Caroline Sporleder and Linlin Li. 2009. Unsupervised recognition of literal and non-literal use of idiomatic expressions. In *Proceedings of the 12th Conference of the European Chapter of the ACL (EACL 2009)*, pages 754–762.

Ian Tenney, Dipanjan Das, and Ellie Pavlick. 2019. Bert rediscovers the classical nlp pipeline. In *Proceedings of the 57th Annual Meeting of the Association for Computational Linguistics*, pages 4593–4601.

Gregor Wiedemann, Steffen Remus, Avi Chawla, and Chris Biemann. 2019. Does bert make any sense? interpretable word sense disambiguation with contextualized embeddings. *arXiv preprint arXiv:1909.10430*.

Lowri Williams, Christian Bannister, Michael Arribas-Ayllon, Alun Preece, and Irena Spasić. 2015. The role of idioms in sentiment analysis. *Expert Systems with Applications*, 42(21):7375–7385.

Appendix A   Per-Idiom Results

(a) VNC dataset

MWE	Supervised Acc	Supervised F1	Unsupervised Acc	Unsupervised F1
blow trumpet	0.93	0.95	0.58	0.66
blow whistle	0.86	0.82	0.63	0.53
get wind	0.86	0.77	0.77	0.77
have word	0.86	0.92	0.55	0.66
lose head	0.75	0.78	0.72	0.72
make face	0.98	0.98	0.65	0.60
make mark	0.99	0.99	0.86	0.91
make scene	0.92	0.94	0.82	0.82
pull leg	0.90	0.79	0.69	0.55
pull plug	0.92	0.95	0.80	0.81
take heart	0.94	0.96	0.80	0.84
take root	0.98	0.99	0.88	0.92
Average	0.91	0.90	0.73	0.73

(b) SemEval5b dataset

MWE	Supervised Acc	Supervised F1	Unsupervised Acc	Unsupervised F1
at the end of the day	0.88	0.91	0.84	0.86
bread and butter	0.97	0.97	0.95	0.95
break a leg	0.93	0.89	0.17	0.00
drop the ball	0.92	0.86	0.86	0.77
in the bag	0.89	0.90	0.87	0.88
in the fast lane	0.93	0.95	0.32	0.46
play ball	0.95	0.95	0.95	0.95
rub it in	1.00	1.00	0.97	0.98
through the roof	0.97	0.98	0.99	0.99
under the microscope	0.95	0.93	0.96	0.95
Average	0.94	0.93	0.79	0.78

(c) German dataset

MWE	Supervised Acc	Supervised F1	Unsupervised Acc	Unsupervised F1
hängenbleiben	0.93	0.95	0.49	0.57
liegenbleiben	0.91	0.91	0.39	0.49
sitzenbleiben	0.94	0.96	0.63	0.67
sitzenlassen	0.98	0.99	0.46	0.60
stehenbleiben	0.91	0.91	0.60	0.59
stehenlassen	0.94	0.93	0.74	0.60
Average	0.94	0.94	0.55	0.59

Table 3: Per-idiom results of our supervised and unsupervised classifiers across datasets using monolingual BERT models

Appendix B   Visualization of MWE Embeddings

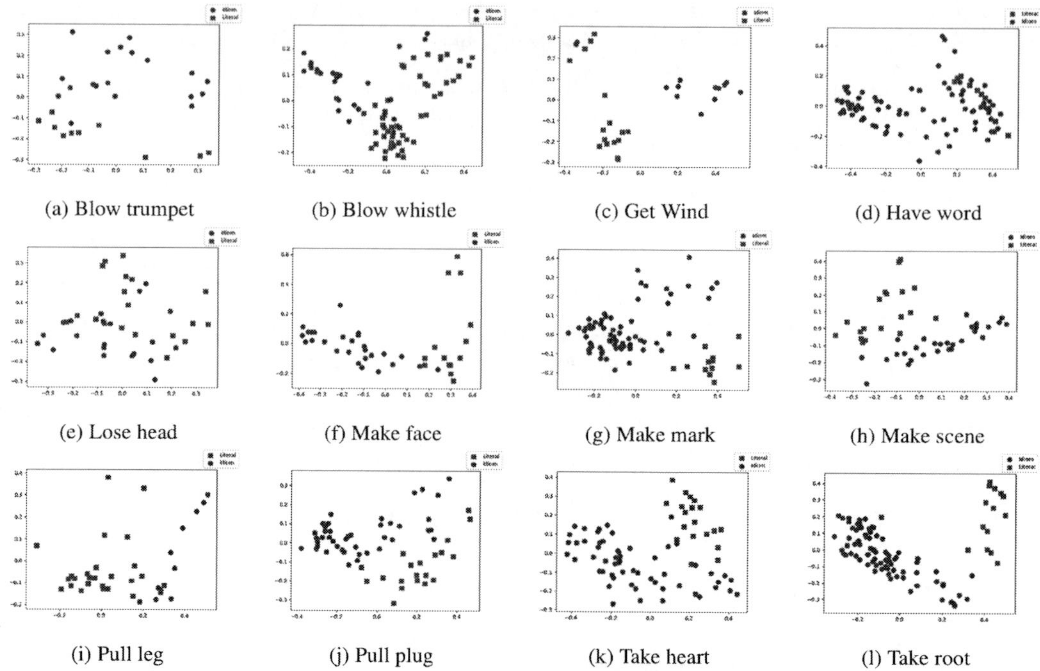

(a) Blow trumpet   (b) Blow whistle   (c) Get Wind   (d) Have word

(e) Lose head   (f) Make face   (g) Make mark   (h) Make scene

(i) Pull leg   (j) Pull plug   (k) Take heart   (l) Take root

Figure 4: PCA plots of the BERT-base embeddings for the VNC dataset

Comparing `word2vec` and `GloVe` for Automatic Measurement of MWE Compositionality

Thomas Pickard
University of Leeds
Leeds LS2 9JT, UK
`mat2tmrp@leeds.ac.uk` , `tom@tompickard.co.uk`

Abstract

This paper explores the use of `word2vec` and `GloVe` embeddings for unsupervised measurement of the semantic compositionality of MWE candidates. Through comparison with several human-annotated reference sets, we find `word2vec` to be substantively superior to `GloVe` for this task. We also find Simple English Wikipedia to be a poor-quality resource for compositionality assessment, but demonstrate that a sample of 10% of sentences in the English Wikipedia can provide a conveniently tractable corpus with only moderate reduction in the quality of outputs.

1 Introduction

Multiword expressions (MWEs) are word combinations exhibiting one or more idiosyncrasies—lexical, syntactic, semantic, pragmatic or statistical (Sag et al., 2002). This paper is concerned specifically with **semantic compositionality**: the extent to which the meaning of an MWE can be understood from those of its component words. The semantics of compositional expressions such as *picnic basket* are clear to anyone familiar with the constituents *picnic* and *basket*, but a non-compositional phrase like *iron curtain* is opaque without further context.

Word embedding models such as `GloVe` (Pennington et al., 2014), `word2vec` (Mikolov et al., 2013a) and `doc2vec` (Le and Mikolov, 2014) are widely used in the Natural Language Processing (NLP) sphere, and are capable of capturing syntactic and semantic relationships between words through their representations in multi-dimensional vector space (Mikolov et al., 2013c). These models therefore offer an opportunity to automatically evaluate the compositionality of an MWE candidate by comparing the embedded representation of the complete expression with those of its component words; we may expect that the vectors of more decomposable phrases will be more similar to those of their constituents. Embedding models themselves also benefit from MWE discovery; by treating multi-word expressions as single units, one may obtain higher-quality representations of simplex words (Mikolov et al., 2013b).

Our main aim in this paper is to evaluate the performance of `GloVe` models for this purpose, in comparison with `word2vec`. Given that many state-of-the-art NLP applications have adopted BERT embeddings (Devlin et al., 2019), these were also considered. However, BERT's embeddings differ according to the sentence in which a given word appears. Since our methodology requires comparison between the vector representation of MWE candidates and their constituent words, the use of context-dependent embeddings seems inappropriate.

Section 2 outlines relevant past work in this area, in particular that of Roberts and Egg (2018), whose methodology we adapt and whose results provide us with a valuable point of comparison. Our method and resources are described in section 3, including the human-annotated reference sets used to evaluate our scores. Finally, we discuss our findings in section 4.

2 Past Research

Lin (1999) employs a substitution-based method to detect non-compositionality. However, while non-compositional phrases also exhibit **institutionalisation** (resistance to substitution of synonyms), the re-

Joint Workshop on Multiword Expressions and Electronic Lexicons, pages 95–100
Barcelona, Spain (Online), December 13, 2020.

verse implication does not hold: institutionalised phrases are not inherently non-compositional (Farahmand et al., 2015). Approaches based on substitution therefore seem better suited to discovery of institutionalised MWEs than to semantically non-compositional ones.

Schone and Jurafsky (2001) and Baldwin et al. (2003) adopt Latent Semantic Analysis (LSA) models based on co-occurrence with 1,000 frequent content words, but more promising results have been obtained through the application of predictive vector embeddings. In particular, the work of Salehi et al. (2015) demonstrated that word embeddings were superior to count-based distribution models when measuring the compositionality of MWEs. Interestingly, they did not find any benefit to using a more complex multi-sense skip-gram (MSSG) model to allow for polysemy of words and expressions . However, their approach was driven by (small) pre-existing lists of MWEs prouced by human annotators.

More recently, Roberts and Egg (2018) generated a large list (over 900k entries) of multi-word phrases, which they extracted from English Wikipedia and automatically scored for compositionality using an approach inspired by Salehi et al. (2015). Our methodology (described in section 3.3) is based on theirs, with alterations to the source corpora and reference sets as well as to the embedding models used.

3 Resources and Methodology

3.1 Corpora

Two training corpora were used, both derived from Wikipedia extracts. In both cases, the XML dumps were processed with a modified corpus reader from the `gensim` Python package (Řehůřek and Sojka, 2010), dividing content articles into sentences and tokens with `punkt` (Kiss and Strunk, 2006) and applying cleansing steps to remove much of the Wiki formatting markup. Note that no case normalisation or lemmatisation was applied.

SIMP20 Complete Simple English Wikipedia content from 2020-06-01. 31,796,513 tokens.

EN20_10P 10% sample of sentences from the 2020-05-20 English Wikipedia. 305,657,697 tokens.

3.2 Reference Sets

Five 'gold standard' lists of MWEs accompanied by compositionality rankings provided by human annotators were employed, providing reference points for intrinsic evaluation of our results. The same reference sets were used by Roberts and Egg (2018), and we also adopt their abbreviated names.

F_ENC (Farahmand et al., 2015). 1,042 nominal compounds (e.g. *greenhouse gas*, *machine language*), with four binary compositionality judgements made by fluent speakers with backgrounds in linguistics. Summing across the judgements produces a four-point scale.

R_ENC (Reddy et al., 2011). 90 noun compounds (e.g. *ivory tower*, *graduate student*), with mean compositionality scores derived from judgements (on a scale from 0 to 5) made by participants recruited through Amazon Mechanical Turk.

MC_VPC (McCarthy et al., 2003). 116 verb-particle pairs (e.g. *space out*, *lie down*), with judgements on a scale from 0-10 made by three judges. The mean of these scores is used, discounting any "don't know" responses. NB: Roberts and Egg (2018) report 117 instances in this dataset, likely due to the presence of a duplicate record which we have removed.

D_ADJN (Biemann and Giesbrecht, 2011). 135 adjective-noun compounds (*blue chip*, *smart card*), taken from the training and test data for the DiSCo 2011 Shared Task. Judgements were made by workers on Amazon Mechanical Turk, averaged and supplied in the range (0,100).

NB: Roberts and Egg (2018) report only 68 instances here. The reason for this is unclear; it may be that additional data were made available by the conference organisers since their work was undertaken. The coverage and correlation measured between their output and this dataset is very similar to that reported in their original paper[1]; we have no reason to believe that this discrepancy has had any negative impact on our findings.

---

[1] Roberts and Egg (2018) report $\rho = 0.525$, $r = 0.581$ with 64/68 MWEs matching. We obtain, using their published data and matching 118/135 MWEs, $\rho = 0.528$, $r = 0.605$.

MC_VN (McCarthy et al., 2007). 638 verb-object pairs (e.g. *take root*), taken from the list of Venkatapathy and Joshi (2005) and annotated by two judges on a scale from 1 to 6. These two scores are averaged. As Roberts and Egg (2018) point out, many of the pairs are discontiguous (*catch eye*); since our methodology examines only contiguous n-grams, the overlap with this set is restricted.

We also import the automatically-scored list produced by Roberts and Egg (2018), filtering out items which meet the authors' exclusion criteria. This leaves 917,647 items, which we denote by **RE_WIKI15** (since it was derived from the full April 2015 text of English Wikipedia, ca. 2.8 billion words).

3.3 Methodology

We collate corpus frequency counts for contiguous n-grams ($n \leq 3$) and identify MWE candidates by computing the Poisson association measure of Quasthoff and Wolff (2002), adjusting where appropriate to balance it for trigrams. A minimum frequency of 20 occurrences is applied. From the **SIMP20** corpus, we retain the 150,000 most strongly-associated candidate n-grams. For **EN20_10P**, we keep 500,000 items.

In order to enable retokenisation of MWE candidates in the corpora, the n-grams are sorted into distinct batches such that no overlaps are present: the first k words of any n-gram must not be the same as the last k words of any other n-gram in the same batch. A limit of 15 batches is set for **SIMP20** and 10 batches for **EN20_10P**. n-grams consisting entirely of stopwords (the 50 most frequent individual tokens in the corpus) and those which cannot be assigned to a batch are excluded. A total of 148,868 candidates from **SIMP20** and 469,587 from **EN20_10P** were evaluated for compositionality.

For each batch, we replace all instances of the candidate n-grams with a single token and construct `word2vec` (Mikolov et al., 2013a) and `GloVe` (Pennington et al., 2014) word embedding vectors for every simplex word exceeding the minimum frequency of 20, and for all MWE candidates in the batch.

The `word2vec` parameters were those found to be effective by Baroni et al. (2014)[2].

`GloVe` co-occurrence statistics were constructed using a symmetrical window of size 10 without crossing sentence boundaries, and weighted inversely by distance. To maintain tractability, the size of the co-occurrence matrices were restricted by limiting the vocabulary used to the most frequent N simplex words, plus the batch MWE candidates. N was taken to be 300,000, yielding a maximum total vocabulary of size $V = 394,012$ for batch 1 of the EN20_10P corpus. `GloVe` embedding vectors of 300 dimensions were trained with hyperparameters $x_{max} = 100$, $\alpha = 0.75$ and 10 negative samples, as was found to be effective by Pennington et al. (2014). The models were trained for 25 epochs with learning rate 0.05.

Compositionality scores were calculated as the mean cosine similarity between the vector representation of the MWE candidate and each of its component simplex words, ignoring stopwords (we make the assumption that very high-frequency terms are semantically uninformative). The greater the similarity between an MWE and its components, the more semantically transparent the expression.

4 Results

The correlation (Spearman ρ and Pearson's r) between our mean cosine distance measure and human annotations is reported for n-grams appearing on both our list and the reference sets, together with the size of this overlap, in Table 1. We also report the results of Roberts and Egg (2018), using `word2vec` on the full April 2015 English Wikipedia. As there are variances in the **MC_VPC** and **D_ADJN** reference sets, these statistics are recalculated using the authors' published data.

In order to explore the impact of restricting the vocabulary used for training the `GloVe` models, a further experiment was carried out on the **SIMP20** corpus, using an unrestricted vocabulary of 1,014,614 simplex words, together with the MWE candidates assigned to each batch. Table 2 shows the results of this experiment, with the correlations with the reference sets obtained being comparable to those achieved with the `word2vec` embeddings.

---

[2]Continuous bag-of-words, symmetrical window of size 5. Vectors of length 400 trained over 5 epochs with initial learning rate 0.025, dropping to 0.0001. Negative sampling with 10 samples, subsampling with threshold $t = 10^{-5}$.

Corpus	Model		F_ENC	R_ENC	MC_VPC	D_ADJN	MC_VN
SIMP20	`word2vec`	**Overlap**	179 / 1042	14 / 90	15 / 116	35 / 135	39 / 638
		Spearman ρ	0.169	0.257	0.317	0.316	0.354
		Pearson's r	0.227	0.323	0.398	0.326	0.381
SIMP20	`GloVe`	**Overlap**	183 / 1042	15 / 90	15 / 116	37 / 135	39 / 638
		Spearman ρ	-0.029	-0.061	-0.014	0.234	-0.008
		Pearson's r	-0.135	0.074	0.178	0.231	-0.257
EN20_10P	`word2vec`	**Overlap**	485 / 1042	39 / 90	27 / 116	96 / 135	71 / 638
		Spearman ρ	0.404	0.624	0.536	0.595	0.389
		Pearson's r	0.401	0.632	0.476	0.624	0.366
EN20_10P	`GloVe`	**Overlap**	486 / 1042	39 / 90	27 / 116	96 / 135	71 / 638
		Spearman ρ	-0.043	0.473	-0.122	0.078	-0.188
		Pearson's r	-0.075	0.415	-0.229	0.037	-0.219
WIKI15	`word2vec`	**Overlap**	631 / 1042	61 / 90	47 / 116	118 / 135	132 / 638
		Spearman ρ	0.458	0.615	0.424	0.528	0.392
		Pearson's r	0.473	0.603	0.372	0.605	0.395

Table 1: Correlations between automatically-generated compositionality scores and human-annotated "gold standard" reference lists. The **WIKI15** output is that of Roberts and Egg (2018).

Corpus	Model		F_ENC	R_ENC	MC_VPC	D_ADJN	MC_VN
SIMP20	`GloVe`, full vocab	**Overlap**	183 / 1042	15 / 90	15 / 116	37 / 135	39 / 638
		Spearman ρ	0.200	0.269	0.494	0.101	0.120
		Pearson's r	0.208	0.272	0.492	0.118	0.142

Table 2: `GloVe` model with unrestricted vocabulary on **SIMP20** corpus.

We find substantially lower correlation with the `GloVe`-derived compositionality scores than those obtained using `word2vec`, across both corpora. The `GloVe` model with unrestricted vocabulary appears comparable to `word2vec`, but required greater computational resources to train. Both practical and performance factors lead us to prefer `word2vec` for future work in this area. This aligns with the findings of Baroni et al. (2014) if we regard `GloVe` as an evolution of the 'count-based' vector paradigm, despite its reported success elsewhere (Pennington et al., 2014).

The Simple English Wikipedia corpus produces fewer matches with the reference lists of MWEs as well as weaker correlation with human compositionality judgements; the smaller size of this corpus and the nature of its content make it a poor hunting ground for multi-word expressions. However, our 10% sample of English Wikipedia yielded reasonable results while remaining tractable[3].

Our output lists and code resources are available at `https://github.com/Oddtwang/MWEs` .

Future work includes exploration of context-dependent embeddings such as `doc2vec` (Le and Mikolov, 2014) and BERT (Devlin et al., 2019) for compositionality assessment, particularly for n-grams which may not always form MWEs. Application of the technique to other corpora and languages with suitable MWE resources, e.g. Arabic (Alghamdi and Atwell, 2019) would also be valuable.

Acknowledgements

We are grateful to Dr Eric Atwell of the University of Leeds for his supervision of this work as part of an MSc dissertation project, and for bringing the topic of multi-word expressions to our attention.
Our `GloVe` models used an implementation by Maciej Kula, available from `https://github.com/maciejkula/glove-python`.

---

[3]Training the `word2vec` models took approximately 2.5 days for 10 batches on the 10% sample of English Wikipedia, using a single Windows desktop PC with an 8-core Intel i7 CPU @ 3.60GHz and 32GB RAM.

References

Ayman Alghamdi and Eric Atwell. 2019. Constructing a corpus-informed list of Arabic formulaic sequences (ArFSs) for language pedagogy and technology. *International Journal of Corpus Linguistics*, 24(2):202–228, August.

Timothy Baldwin, Colin Bannard, Takaaki Tanaka, and Dominic Widdows. 2003. An empirical model of multiword expression decomposability. In *Proceedings of the ACL 2003 Workshop on Multiword Expressions: Analysis, Acquisition and Treatment - Volume 18*, MWE '03, pages 89–96, Sapporo, Japan, July. Association for Computational Linguistics.

Marco Baroni, Georgiana Dinu, and Germán Kruszewski. 2014. Don't count, predict! A systematic comparison of context-counting vs. context-predicting semantic vectors. In *Proceedings of the 52nd Annual Meeting of the Association for Computational Linguistics (Volume 1: Long Papers)*, pages 238–247, Baltimore, Maryland, June. Association for Computational Linguistics.

Chris Biemann and Eugenie Giesbrecht. 2011. Distributional Semantics and Compositionality 2011: Shared Task Description and Results. In *Proceedings of the Workshop on Distributional Semantics and Compositionality*, pages 21–28, Portland, Oregon, USA, June. Association for Computational Linguistics.

Jacob Devlin, Ming-Wei Chang, Kenton Lee, and Kristina Toutanova. 2019. BERT: Pre-training of Deep Bidirectional Transformers for Language Understanding. *arXiv:1810.04805 [cs]*, May.

Meghdad Farahmand, Aaron Smith, and Joakim Nivre. 2015. A Multiword Expression Data Set: Annotating Non-Compositionality and Conventionalization for English Noun Compounds. In *Proceedings of the 11th Workshop on Multiword Expressions*, pages 29–33, Denver, Colorado, June. Association for Computational Linguistics.

Tibor Kiss and Jan Strunk. 2006. Unsupervised Multilingual Sentence Boundary Detection. *Computational Linguistics*, 32(4):485–525, November.

Quoc Le and Tomas Mikolov. 2014. Distributed representations of sentences and documents. In *Proceedings of the 31st International Conference on International Conference on Machine Learning - Volume 32*, ICML'14, pages II–1188–II–1196, Beijing, China, June. JMLR.org.

Dekang Lin. 1999. Automatic Identification of Non-compositional Phrases. In *Proceedings of the 37th Annual Meeting of the Association for Computational Linguistics*, pages 317–324, College Park, Maryland, USA, June. Association for Computational Linguistics.

Diana McCarthy, Bill Keller, and John Carroll. 2003. Detecting a Continuum of Compositionality in Phrasal Verbs. In *Proceedings of the ACL 2003 Workshop on Multiword Expressions: Analysis, Acquisition and Treatment*, pages 73–80, Sapporo, Japan, July. Association for Computational Linguistics.

Diana McCarthy, Sriram Venkatapathy, and Aravind Joshi. 2007. Detecting Compositionality of Verb-Object Combinations using Selectional Preferences. In *Proceedings of the 2007 Joint Conference on Empirical Methods in Natural Language Processing and Computational Natural Language Learning (EMNLP-CoNLL)*, pages 369–379, Prague, Czech Republic, June. Association for Computational Linguistics.

Tomas Mikolov, Kai Chen, Greg Corrado, and Jeffrey Dean. 2013a. Efficient Estimation of Word Representations in Vector Space. *arXiv:1301.3781 [cs]*, September.

Tomas Mikolov, Ilya Sutskever, Kai Chen, Greg Corrado, and Jeffrey Dean. 2013b. Distributed Representations of Words and Phrases and their Compositionality. *arXiv:1310.4546 [cs, stat]*, October.

Tomas Mikolov, Wen-tau Yih, and Geoffrey Zweig. 2013c. Linguistic Regularities in Continuous Space Word Representations. In *Proceedings of the 2013 Conference of the North American Chapter of the Association for Computational Linguistics: Human Language Technologies*, pages 746–751, Atlanta, Georgia, June. Association for Computational Linguistics.

Jeffrey Pennington, Richard Socher, and Christopher Manning. 2014. GloVe: Global Vectors for Word Representation. In *Proceedings of the 2014 Conference on Empirical Methods in Natural Language Processing (EMNLP)*, pages 1532–1543, Doha, Qatar, October. Association for Computational Linguistics.

Uwe Quasthoff and Christian Wolff. 2002. The Poisson Collocation Measure and its Applications. In *Second International Workshop on Computational Approaches to Collocations*, Wien. IEEE.

Siva Reddy, Diana McCarthy, and Suresh Manandhar. 2011. An Empirical Study on Compositionality in Compound Nouns. In *Proceedings of 5th International Joint Conference on Natural Language Processing*, pages 210–218, Chiang Mai, Thailand, November. Asian Federation of Natural Language Processing.

Radim Řehůřek and Petr Sojka. 2010. Software Framework for Topic Modelling with Large Corpora. In *Proceedings of the LREC 2010 Workshop on New Challenges for NLP Frameworks*, pages 45–50, Valetta, Malta, May. ELRA.

Will Roberts and Markus Egg. 2018. A Large Automatically-Acquired All-Words List of Multiword Expressions Scored for Compositionality. In *Proceedings of LREC 2018*. European Language Resources Association (ELRA), May.

Ivan A. Sag, Timothy Baldwin, Francis Bond, Ann Copestake, and Dan Flickinger. 2002. Multiword Expressions: A Pain in the Neck for NLP. In Alexander Gelbukh, editor, *Computational Linguistics and Intelligent Text Processing*, Lecture Notes in Computer Science, pages 1–15, Berlin, Heidelberg. Springer.

Bahar Salehi, Paul Cook, and Timothy Baldwin. 2015. A Word Embedding Approach to Predicting the Compositionality of Multiword Expressions. In *Proceedings of the 2015 Conference of the North American Chapter of the Association for Computational Linguistics: Human Language Technologies*, pages 977–983, Denver, Colorado, May. Association for Computational Linguistics.

Patrick Schone and Daniel Jurafsky. 2001. Is Knowledge-Free Induction of Multiword Unit Dictionary Headwords a Solved Problem? In *Proceedings of the 2001 Conference on Empirical Methods in Natural Language Processing*.

Sriram Venkatapathy and Aravind K. Joshi. 2005. Relative Compositionality of Multi-word Expressions: A Study of Verb-Noun (V-N) Collocations. In *Second International Joint Conference on Natural Language Processing: Full Papers*.

Automatic detection of unexpected/erroneous collocations in learner corpus

Jen-Yu Li and Thomas Gaillat
Linguistique Ingénierie et Didactique
des Langues (LIDILE),
Université Rennes 2
Place du recteur Henri Le Moal,
CS 24307 - 35043 Rennes cedex,
France
jenyuli@gmail.com

Abstract

This research investigates the collocational errors made by English learners in a learner corpus. It focuses on the extraction of unexpected collocations. A system was proposed and implemented with open source toolkit. Firstly, the collocation extraction module was evaluated by a corpus with manually annotated collocations. Secondly, a standard collocation list was collected from a corpus of native speaker. Thirdly, a list of unexpected collocations was generated by extracting candidates from a learner corpus and discarding the standard collocations on the list. The overall performance was evaluated, and possible sources of error were pointed out for future improvement.

1   Introduction

Multiword expressions (MWEs) are word combinations which present lexical, syntactic, semantic, pragmatic or statistical idiosyncrasies. The boundary between MWEs and collocations is subtle. In Ramisch et al. (2018), they defined collocations as combinations of words whose idiosyncrasy is purely statistical and show no substantial semantic idiosyncrasy. In this way they oppose MWEs to collocations. Some researchers (Sag et al., 2002) regard collocations as any statistically significant cooccurrences, which include all kinds of MWEs. Some other researchers (Garcia et al., 2019; Baldwin and Kim, 2010) consider collocations as a subset of MWEs. For Tutin (2013), collocation is a category of semantic phraseme. As defined by Mel'čuk (1998), a phraseme is a set of phrase which is not free (without freedom of selection of its signified and without freedom of combination of its components). In this sense, the meaning of phraseme is quite similar to MWE. In this research, we considered collocation as a subset of semantic phraseme and a subset of MWEs as well. To constrain the set of collocation candidates, we focus on the Verb-Noun (VN) construction.

Second language learners usually have problems with collocations. Some researchers have reported that the errors are related to the learners' L1 (Nesselhauf, 2003; Hong et al., 2011). The correction of wrong collocations[1], such as *to *create [construct] a taller and safer building*, in written essays can help learners increase their competence and thus their proficiency in English writing (Meunier and Granger, 2008). Therefore, the automatic detection and correction of erroneous collocations would be helpful for

---

[1] In this research, the terms *wrong collocations, erroneous collocations, unexpected collocations*, and *collocational errors* are interchangeable.

Joint Workshop on Multiword Expressions and Electronic Lexicons, pages 101–106
Barcelona, Spain (Online), December 13, 2020.

learners. Designing such a system would support specific feedback messages that could be employed to guide learners in their meta-cognitive learning processes (Shute 2008).

Such a system may be based on two kinds of corpora: a learner corpus which is used to extract known collocational errors, and a reference corpus to extract standard English collocations (Shei and Pain, 2000). Chang et al. (2008) proposed a method of bilingual collocation extraction from a parallel corpus to provide phrasal translation memory. Their system performance was exceptionally good (precision=0.98, recall=0.91). However, this approach required a bilingual dictionary, a parallel corpus for a specific L1 and English, as well as word-alignment matching of translations.

This paper presents a preliminary research on a learner corpus. In the following sections, we will briefly explain the method, present the results, and give some discussions.

2 Method

We propose a system to extract unexpected collocations in three stages: (a) implementation and evaluation of a collocation extraction module; (b) collection of standard collocations from a native corpus; (c) extraction of wrong collocations from a learner corpus. The main principle is, firstly, to extract all possible collocations in the learner corpus, and then identify standard collocations by the reference (collocations extracted from native corpus); the remainder of the items are considered as wrong collocations. Three evaluation points were made, aiming at the collocation extraction module, the reference of standard collocations, and the extraction of wrong collocations, respectively. The system diagram and the three stages are shown in Figure 1.

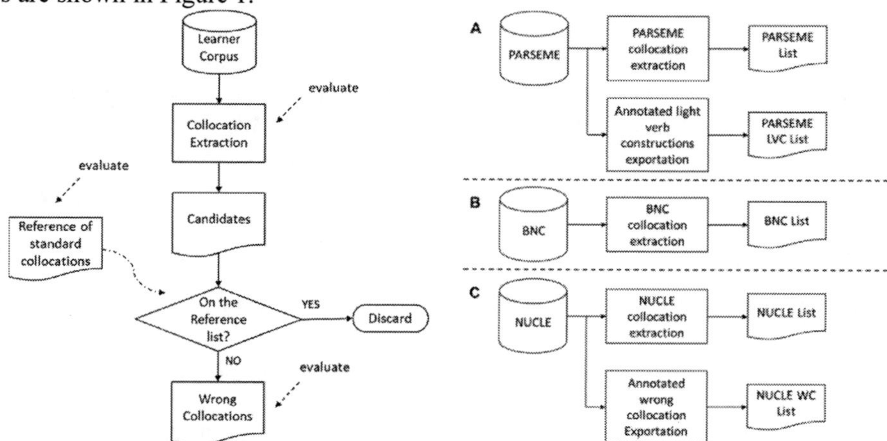

Figure 1. The system diagram and the three stages.

Stage A. Implementation and evaluation of the collocation extraction module: collocations were extracted from the PARSing and Multi-word Expressions (PARSEME[2]) corpus (Savary et al., 2015) with the implemented module. The results were saved as the PARSEME List. According to Garcia et al. (2019), light verb constructions (LVCs) can be regarded as collocations in VN form. The manually annotated LVCs were therefore retrieved and saved as the PARSEME LVC List. It is the gold standard (i.e. the ground truth) to evaluate the extraction module and to fine tune the parameters in the scripts.

Stage B. Collection of standard collocations: to have a large list of standard collocations, we used the implemented module to extract collocations from the British National Corpus (BNC[3]) (BNC Consortium, 2007) to form a list of standard collocations (the BNC List). The reference of standard collocations was built by merging the BNC List and the PARSEME LVC List. It was evaluated by manual verification. The errors in the reference list would degrade the credibility of our gold standard and thus might have a negative influence on the overall performance.

Stage C. Extraction of wrong collocations: we used the implemented module to extract candidate collocations (named as the NUCLE List) from the National University of Singapore Corpus of Learner

[2] https://lindat.mff.cuni.cz/repository/xmlui/handle/11372/LRT-2842
[3] https://ota.bodleian.ox.ac.uk/repository/xmlui/

English (NUCLE[4]) (Dahlmeier et al., 2013). The sentences manually annotated with erroneous collocations (*Wci* tag) were also exported, and the VN terms in these sentences were detected and saved in the NUCLE WC List. It was used to evaluate the overall performance of our system.

The scripts[5] were written in Python with Natural Language Toolkit (NLTK)[6] (Bird and Loper, 2004). Five lexical association measures were used in collocation extraction tasks, namely the raw frequency counting, t-test, chi-square test, log likelihood ratio, and pointwise mutual information. The formulas as well as an evaluation of 84 measures can be found in Pecina (2010).

3 Results

3.1 Evaluation of the collocation extraction module

To evaluate the module, we extracted the collocations from PARSEME and compared them with the PARSEME LVC List. The precision, recall, F_1 and $F_{0.5}$ scores were used as the accuracy metric. The best precision rate is 0.11 for the bigram detection with minimal frequency of 2, using raw frequency measure, and with the top 200 collocations. Meanwhile, the best recall rate is 0.11 when both bigram and trigram detection are used, and with minimal frequency equals 2 for top 300 collocations, with the log likelihood ratio or with the raw frequency measure. the best F_1 and $F_{0.5}$ are both 0.08 for the bigram detection using raw frequency measure with a minimal frequency of 2 and with top 300 collocations. Pointwise mutual information and chi-square methods cannot give good results even without applying filters. The results obtained by t-test methods are similar to raw frequency method. The window size was set to four. Shorter or longer window lengths were tried but did not have good results, which means the words of a collocation tends to co-occur in the span of four words.

3.2 Evaluation of the BNC list

For manual verification, 200 candidates were randomly sampled from the BNC list and given to an experienced English teacher. He validated firstly obvious collocations like *take place*. For the candidates that he was not sure about, he consulted the Corpus of Contemporary American English (COCA) collocate search tool[7]. If he found the candidate in the COCA corpus, it was validated; if not, the candidate was discarded. The final precision rate is 0.57.

3.3 Intersections between lists

Ideally the union of the BNC List and the PARSEME LVC List (noted as **BNC ∪ PARSEME LVC**) gives us the standard collocations, and NUCLE WC List gives the wrong collocations. Ideally there should be no overlapping in standard and wrong collocations. However, we found that there are intersections between the NUCLE WC List and the PARSEME LVC (11 collocations), between the NUCLE WC List and the BNC List (20 collocations), and between all three lists (4 collocations). The amount of this overlapping is therefore 27 (20+11-4=27), noted as **NUCLE WC ∩ (BNC ∪ PARSEME LVC)**; it is about 1.8% of the NUCLE WC List.

3.4 Optimization by selecting a threshold of Log Likelihood Ratio

Candidates were extracted from NUCLE and compared with the gold standard, i.e. the NUCLE WC List (1,471 erroneous VN collocations). Various thresholds of log likelihood ratio were tested for optimization. Figure 2(a) shows the global view of precision and recall versus different thresholds, and Figure 2(b) gives a zoom-in of threshold from zero to twelve. The highest precision is 0.5 when the threshold value is set to 430, where only two candidates are extracted. The precision and recall meet at the same level about 0.04 when the threshold is set to eight, and 1,408 candidates are extracted. The maximal

---

[4] NUCLE is a collection of 1,414 essays (in a total of 1.2 million words) written by students who are non-native English speakers. It is available by submitting a license agreement via https://www.comp.nus.edu.sg/~nlp/corpora.html
[5] Source codes are available online: https://github.com/jenyuli/wrong_collocation_extraction
[6] https://www.nltk.org/
[7] https://www.english-corpora.org/coca/

recall (0.83) is obtained by extracting all possible candidates (54,471), and the precision becomes extremely low (0.02).

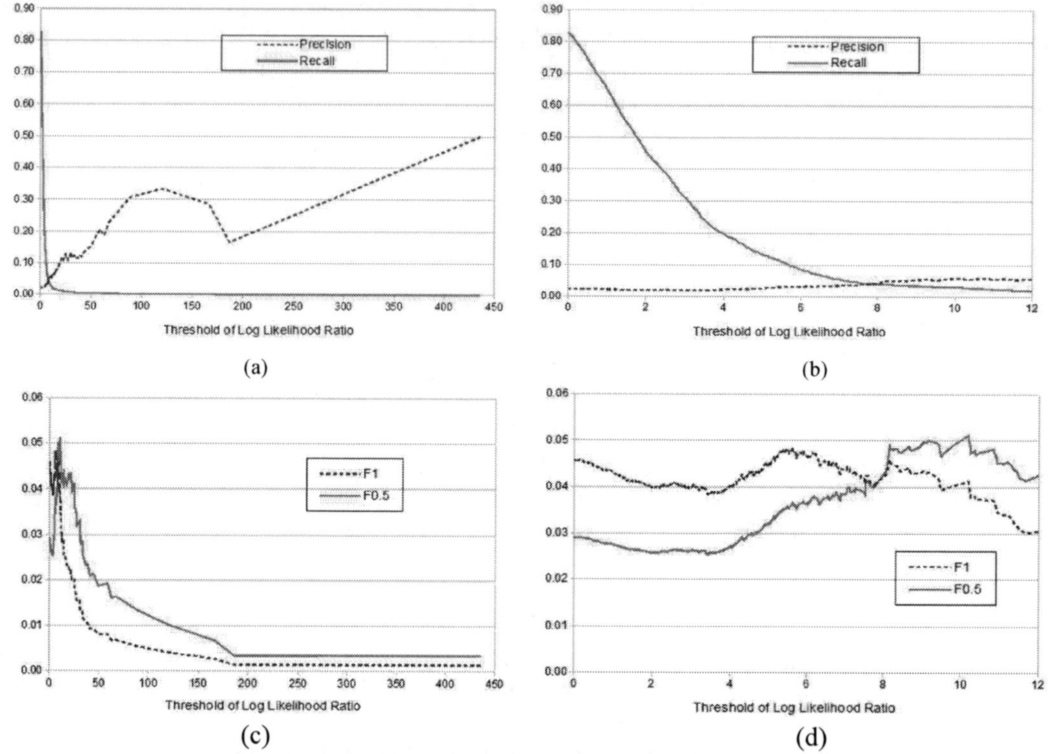

Figure 2. Precision, Recall, F_1 and $F_{0.5}$ scores versus log likelihood ratio.

Figure 2(c) and 2(d) demonstrate the global view and zoom-in of the F_1 and $F_{0.5}$ trends. We can see that the $F_{0.5}$ reaches its peaks (0.05) when the threshold is set to eight or ten; while the F_1 fluctuates around 0.04 to 0.05 when threshold is set lower than eight. Considering all four indices, the optimal value of the threshold can be set about eight.

4   Discussions and conclusion

As our experiment configuration is capable to extract wrong collocations from the leaner corpus, the overall performance is not satisfactory. Hence, we reviewed the results and point out some possible sources of errors for future studies.

First, regarding the PARSEME corpus, the gold standard was built based on the *LVC* tag, so it may be that the verbs of the collocations were biased. In fact, 44 out of 85 collocations on the list were constructed only by five verbs, namely *do, get, give, have,* and *take.* Therefore, the evaluation of the module was also biased. Regarding the BNC List, we have reached a precision of 0.57 due to the large size of corpus (100 million words) and a strict selection (top 10 for each sub-directory of the BNC). However, comparing with a previous study (Jian et al., 2004) which extracted 631,638 VN collocations from the BNC, we found that our standard collocation reference list (BNC U PARSEME LVC) was much smaller (n=942) and may have a negative influence on the performance. Regarding the NUCLE, because the Part-Of-Speech (POS) and the lemma are not available, we used a POS tagger and a Lemmatizer. Yet, their performances were not evaluated, so the gold standard NUCLE WC List was not perfectly accurate. As for the whole system, it may be helpful to incorporate a word dependency parser module to identify the object noun which received the action of the verb.

Our approach has shown a method to detect erroneous collocations in learner English. As it relies on the accurate extraction of a reference list, our next step will consist in exploring larger corpora for extraction. Such an extraction module would be of great benefit as part of a Computer Aided Language Learning System dedicated to the analysis of phraseology in learner texts.

Reference

Timothy Baldwin and Su Nam Kim. 2010. Multiword Expressions. In Nitin Indurkhya and Fred J. Damerau, editors, *Handbook of Natural Language Processing*, pages 267–292. Chapman and Hall/CRC, Boca Raton, FL, USA, Second edition.

Steven Bird and Edward Loper. 2004. NLTK: The Natural Language Toolkit. In *The Companion Volume to the Proceedings of 42st Annual Meeting of the Association for Computational Linguistics*, pages 214–217, Barcelona, Spain, July. Association for Computational Linguistics.

BNC Consortium, 2007, *The British National Corpus*. Distributed by Bodleian Libraries, University of Oxford.

Yu-Chia Chang, Jason S. Chang, Hao-Jan Chen, and Hsien-Chin Liou. 2008. An automatic collocation writing assistant for Taiwanese EFL learners: A case of corpus-based NLP technology. *Computer Assisted Language Learning*, 21(3):283–299, July.

Daniel Dahlmeier, Hwee Tou Ng, and Siew Mei Wu. 2013. Building a Large Annotated Corpus of Learner English: The NUS Corpus of Learner English. In *Proceedings of the Eighth Workshop on Innovative Use of NLP for Building Educational Applications*, pages 22–31, Atlanta, Georgia, June. Association for Computational Linguistics.

Dana Gablasova, Vaclav Brezina, and Tony McEnery. 2017. Collocations in Corpus-Based Language Learning Research: Identifying, Comparing, and Interpreting the Evidence. *Language Learning*, 67(S1):155–179.

Marcos Garcia, Marcos García Salido, Susana Sotelo, Estela Mosqueira, and Margarita Alonso-Ramos. 2019. Pay Attention when you Pay the Bills. A Multilingual Corpus with Dependency-based and Semantic Annotation of Collocations. In *Proceedings of the 57th Annual Meeting of the Association for Computational Linguistics*, pages 4012–4019, Florence, Italy, July. Association for Computational Linguistics.

Ang Leng Hong, Hajar Abdul Rahim, Tan Kim Hua, and Khazriyati Salehuddin. 2011. Collocations in Malaysian English learners' writing: A corpus-based error analysis. *3L: The Southeast Asian Journal of English Language Studies*, 17(Special Issue):31–44.

Jia-Yan Jian, Yu-Chia Chang, and Jason S. Chang. 2004. Collocational Translation Memory Extraction Based on Statistical and Linguistic Information. In *Proceedings of the 16th Conference on Computational Linguistics and Speech Processing*, pages 257–264, Taipei, Taiwan, September. The Association for Computational Linguistics and Chinese Language Processing (ACLCLP).

Batia Laufer and Tina Waldman. 2011. Verb-Noun Collocations in Second Language Writing: A Corpus Analysis of Learners' English. *Language Learning*, 61(2):647–672.

Claudia Leacock. 2010. Collocation Errors. In *Automated grammatical error detection for language learners*, pages 63–71. Morgan & Claypool Publishers, California.

Igor Mel'čuk. 1998. Collocations and Lexical Functions. In Anthony P. Cowie, editor, *Phraseology: theory, analysis, and applications*, Oxford linguistics, pages 23–53. Oxford Univ. Press, Oxford.

Fanny Meunier and Sylviane Granger, editors. 2008. *Phraseology in foreign language learning and teaching*. John Benjamins Pub. Co, Amsterdam ; Philadelphia.

Nadja Nesselhauf. 2003. The Use of Collocations by Advanced Learners of English and Some Implications for Teaching. *Applied Linguistics*, 24(2):223–242, June.

Pavel Pecina. 2010. Lexical association measures and collocation extraction. *Language Resources and Evaluation*, 44(1/2):137–158.

Carlos Ramisch, Silvio Cordeiro, Agata Savary, Veronika Vincze, Verginica Barbu Mititelu, Archna Bhatia, Maja Buljan, Marie Candito, Polona Gantar, Voula Giouli, Tunga Güngör, Abdelati Hawwari, Uxoa Iñurrieta, Jolanta Kovalevskaitė, Simon Krek, Timm Lichte, Chaya Liebeskind, Johanna Monti, Carla Parra Escartín, et al. 2018. Edition 1.1 of the PARSEME Shared Task on Automatic Identification of Verbal Multiword Expressions. In *Proceedings of the Joint Workshop on Linguistic Annotation, Multiword Expressions and Constructions (LAW-MWE-CxG-2018)*, pages 222–240, Santa Fe, United States, August. Association for Computational Linguistics.

Ute Römer. 2005. Section 4.5.4 Verbs and objects [BNC/BoE]. In *Progressives, patterns. pedagogy: a corpus-driven approach to English progressive forms, functions, contexts, and didactics*, pages 130–135. J. Benjamins Pub. Co, Amsterdam ; Philadelphia.

Ivan Sag, Timothy Baldwin, Francis Bond, Ann Copestake, and Dan Flickinger. 2002. Multiword Expressions: A Pain in the Neck for NLP. In *Proceedings of the 3rd International Conference on Computational Linguistics and Intelligent Text Processing*, number 2276, pages 1–15. Springer.

Agata Savary, Manfred Sailer, Yannick Parmentier, Michael Rosner, Victoria Rosén, Adam Przepiórkowski, Cvetana Krstev, Veronika Vincze, Beata Wójtowicz, Gyri Smørdal Losnegaard, Carla Parra Escartín, Jakub Waszczuk, Mathieu Constant, Petya Osenova, and Federico Sangati. 2015. PARSEME – PARSing and Multiword Expressions within a European multilingual network. In *7th Language & Technology Conference: Human Language Technologies as a Challenge for Computer Science and Linguistics (LTC 2015)*, Poznań, Poland, November.

Chi-Chiang Shei and Helen Pain. 2000. An ESL Writer's Collocational Aid. *Computer Assisted Language Learning*, 13(2):167–182, April.

Livnat Herzig Sheinfux, Tali Arad Greshler, Nurit Melnik, and Shuly Wintner. 2019. Verbal Multiword Expressions: Idiomaticity and flexibility. In Yannick Parmentier and Jakub Waszczuk, editors, *Representation and parsing of multiword expressions: Current trends*, pages 35–68. Language Science Press, Berlin.

Valerie J. Shute. 2008. Focus on Formative Feedback. *Review of Educational Research* 78(1):153–89, March.

Agnès Tutin. 2013. Les collocations lexicales : une relation essentiellement binaire définie par la relation prédicat-argument. *Langages*, n° 189(1):47–63, April.

Edition 1.2 of the PARSEME Shared Task on Semi-supervised Identification of Verbal Multiword Expressions

Carlos Ramisch
Aix Marseille Univ,
CNRS, LIS, France

Agata Savary
University of Tours,
France

Bruno Guillaume
LORIA/Inria Nancy
Grand-Est, France

Jakub Waszczuk
University of
Duesseldorf, Germany

Marie Candito
Paris Diderot
University, France

Ashwini Vaidya
IIT Delhi,
India

Verginica Barbu Mititelu
Romanian Academy,
Romania

Archna Bhatia
Florida IHMC,
USA

Uxoa Iñurrieta
Univ. of the Basque
Country, Spain

Voula Giouli
Athena Research
Center, Greece

Tunga Güngör
Boğaziçi University
Turkey

Menghan Jiang
PolyU, Hong Kong
China

Timm Lichte
University of
Tübingen, Germany

Chaya Liebeskind
Jerusalem College
of Technology, Israel

Johanna Monti
"L'Orientale" University
of Naples, Italy

Renata Ramisch
NILC, UFSCar,
Brazil

Sara Stymne
Uppsala University,
Sweden

Abigail Walsh
Dublin City University,
Ireland

Hongzhi Xu
Shanghai International
Studies Univ., China

Abstract

We present edition 1.2 of the PARSEME shared task on identification of verbal multiword expressions (VMWEs). Lessons learned from previous editions indicate that VMWEs have low ambiguity, and that the major challenge lies in identifying test instances never seen in the training data. Therefore, this edition focuses on unseen VMWEs. We have split annotated corpora so that the test corpora contain around 300 unseen VMWEs, and we provide non-annotated raw corpora to be used by complementary discovery methods. We released annotated and raw corpora in 14 languages, and this semi-supervised challenge attracted 7 teams who submitted 9 system results. This paper describes the effort of corpus creation, the task design, and the results obtained by the participating systems, especially their performance on unseen expressions.

1 Introduction

Multiword expressions (MWEs) such as *to **throw** someone **under the bus*** 'to cause one's suffering to gain personal advantage' are idiosyncratic word combinations which need to be identified prior to further semantic processing (Baldwin and Kim, 2010; Calzolari et al., 2002). The task of MWE identification, that is, automatically locating instances of MWEs in running text (Constant et al., 2017) has received growing attention in the last 4 years. Progress on this task was especially motivated by shared tasks such as DiMSUM (Schneider et al., 2016), and two editions of the PARSEME shared tasks, edition 1.0 in 2017 (Savary et al., 2017), and edition 1.1 in 2018 (Ramisch et al., 2018).

Previous editions of the PARSEME shared task focused on the identification of verbal MWEs (VMWEs), because of their challenging traits: complex structure, discontinuities, variability, ambiguity, etc. (Savary et al., 2017). The problem is addressed from a multilingual perspective: editions 1.0 and 1.1 covered 18 and 20 languages, respectively. The annotation guidelines and methodology are unified across languages, offering a rich playground for system developers.

The framework proposed by the (closed track of) previous shared tasks was tailored for supervised learning. An annotated training corpus for each language was made available for system developers. The

Joint Workshop on Multiword Expressions and Electronic Lexicons, pages 107–118
Barcelona, Spain (Online), December 13, 2020.

systems, building mostly on statistical and deep learning techniques, were then able to identify MWEs in the test data based on regularities learned from the training corpora. The strength of supervised machine learning approaches lies in (a) contextual disambiguation and (b) generalisation power. In other words, the identification of ambiguous expressions should be conditioned on their contexts, and new expressions or variants should be identified even if they were not observed in the training corpus.

However, corpus studies show that supervised methods can take limited advantage of these strengths for VMWE identification. Firstly, even if a number of studies have been dedicated to contextual disambiguation (between idiomatic and literal occurrences of MWEs), recent work shows that this task is quantitatively of minor importance, because literal readings occur surprisingly rarely in corpora. Namely, based on manual annotation in German, Greek, Basque, Polish, and Brazilian Portuguese, Savary et al. (2019b) discovered that most expressions are potentially ambiguous, but the vast majority of them never occur literally nor accidentally.

Secondly, MWE idiosyncrasies manifest at the level of types (sets of occurrences of the same expression) and not at the level of tokens (single occurrences). This fact, in addition to MWE's Zipfian distribution and low proliferation rate, makes it unlikely to detect new MWEs based on a few instances of known ones (Savary et al., 2019a). Thus, the generalisation power of supervised learning only applies to variants of expressions already observed in the training data.

These two findings motivated the current edition of the PARSEME shared task focusing on the identification of *unseen VMWEs*. A VMWE annotated in the test set is considered unseen if the multi-set of lemmas of its lexicalised components was never annotated in the training data.[1] Differently from edition 1.1, by training data we understand all the gold data released before the training stage, i.e. both the subset meant for training proper (train) and the one meant for development/fine-tuning (dev). Therefore, the main novelties in this edition are:

1. Evaluation is not only based on overall F1, but emphasises performance on unseen VMWEs;
2. Corpora are split so that test sets contain at least 300 VMWEs unseen in training sets;
3. Raw corpora are provided to foster the development of semi-supervised VMWE discovery;
4. Unseen VMWEs are now defined with respect to train and dev sets, rather than train alone.

Moreover, we extended and enhanced the corpus annotation effort, both in terms of languages covered and of methods to increase the quality of existing corpora. This included a stronger integration with the Universal Dependencies (UD) framework.[2] The remainder of this paper describes the design of edition 1.2 of the PARSEME shared task, and summarises its outcomes.[3]

2 Manually Annotated Corpora

The corpus used in the shared task and the underlying cross-lingually unified and validated annotation guidelines result from continuous efforts of a multilingual community since 2015.[4] The 1.2 guidelines mostly follow those from edition 1.1, with decision flowcharts based on linguistic tests, allowing annotators to identify and categorise candidates into the following categories:[5]

- inherently reflexive verbs (IRVs), e.g. ⌐FR¬ *se rendre* (lit. 'return oneself') 'go'
- light verb constructions (LVCs), with 2 subcategories:
    - LVC.full, e.g. ⌐HE¬ לתת הסכמה (lit. 'give consent') 'approve'
    - LVC.cause, e.g. ⌐RO¬ *pune la dispoziţie* (lit. 'put at disposal') 'make available'
- verbal idioms (VIDs), e.g. ⌐TR¬ *ileri sürmek* (lit. 'lead forward') 'assert'
- verb-particle constructions (VPCs), with 2 subcategories:

---

[1]Instances whose lemmas match, but with different *forms* in training and test data, are considered seen VMWEs. We also distinguish seen-variant from seen-identical occurrences, to account for form mismatches.

[2]`http://universaledependencies.org`

[3]Although this paper was submitted anonymously and peer reviewed, the process may have been biased by public information about the shared task published online, including the names of organizers and language leaders who author this paper.

[4]`https://gitlab.com/parseme/corpora/-/wikis/home`

[5]`https://parsemefr.lis-lab.fr/parseme-st-guidelines/1.2/`

- VPC.full, e.g. ⃞DE *stellt her* (lit. 'puts here') 'produces'
- VPC.semi, e.g. ⃞ZH 获取到 (lit. 'capture arrive/to') 'capture'

- multi-verb constructions (MVCs), e.g. ⃞HI बैठ गया (lit. 'sit went') 'sat down'
- inherently adpositional verbs (IAVs), annotated non-systematically on an experimental basis, e.g. ⃞IT *intendersi di* (lit. 'understand of') 'to know about'

The only changes to these guidelines are language-specific additions: (i) a Chinese-specific decision tree for MVCs, (ii) two Swedish-specific sections about identifying multiword tokens and distinguishing particles from prepositions and prefixes.

The manually annotated corpus for edition 1.2 covers 14 languages: German (DE), Basque (EU), Greek (EL), French (FR), Irish (GA), Hebrew (HE), Hindi (HI), Italian (IT), Polish (PL), Brazilian Portuguese (PT), Romanian (RO), Swedish (SV), Turkish (TR) and Chinese (ZH).[6]

New Languages   The underlined languages in the list above are those whose corpora are new or substantially increased with respect to editions 1.0 and 1.1.[7]

Chinese is the first language in the PARSEME collection in which word boundaries are not spelled out in running text. Thus, tokenisation constitutes a major challenge. We used previously tokenised texts from the Chinese UD treebank and some raw texts from the CoNLL 2017 parsing shared task corpus.[8] The latter was tokenised automatically and manually corrected when segmentation errors affected the right scope of a VMWE. About 48% of the annotated VMWEs consist in a single (multiword) token.

Irish is our first language of the Celtic genus, with new VMWE-related challenges. Firstly, frequent contractions of prepositions with personal pronouns make it hard to annotate IAVs. The preposition is usually lexicalised while the pronoun is not, as in ⃞GA *chuir sé orm* (lit. 'put he on-me') 'he bothered me'. However, since these contractions are seen in UD as inflected prepositions, they are represented as single words and lemmatised into the preposition alone.[9] Therefore, the only possible VMWE annotation is to consider the pronoun as an inflectional ending, i.e. part of the lexicalised preposition (*chuir sé orm*). Secondly, some copula constructions, like ⃞GA *X is ainm dom* (lit. 'X is name to-me') 'my name is X', are idiomatic and would normally find their place among the VIDs. This is, however, currently not possible because, according to our guidelines, a VMWE (in its syntactically least marked form) has to be headed by a verb. However, following the UD lexicalist morphosyntactic annotation principles, the head of a copula construction is the predicative noun (*ainm* 'name') rather than the copula (*is* 'is').

Swedish had a small annotated corpus in edition 1.0, but the new corpus was annotated from scratch. The main challenge was related to particle-verb combinations occurring as single tokens. Some of them can be seen either as unique words, i.e. no VMWE candidates, or as multiword tokens (MWTs), i.e. potential VPCs. This depends on whether they can occur both in the joint (one-token) and in the split (two-token) configuration, with the same or a different meaning. For instance, ⃞SV *pågå* (lit. 'on-go') 'be in progress' can be split but only with a changed meaning ⃞SV *gå på* (lit. 'go on') 'keep bringing the same issue up'. In ⃞SV *överleva* (lit. 'over-live') 'survive' the particle (*över*) is easily distinguished from the verb but the split configuration never occurs. Other compound verbs, like ⃞SV *sysselsätta* (lit. 'activity-put') 'put into work', cannot be split either. Currently, all such cases are considered MWTs and annotated as VPCs or VIDs. About 49% of the annotated VMWEs contain a single (multiword) token.

Enhancements in Previous Languages   For all other 11 languages, the current corpus builds upon edition 1.1, with some extensions and enhancements. In Greek, Hebrew, Polish and Brazilian Portuguese, new texts were annotated (mostly in the centralised FLAT platform)[10], which increased the pre-existing

---

[6] The annotated corpus for the 1.2 edition is available at `http://hdl.handle.net/11234/1-3367`

[7] Some languages present in editions 1.0 and 1.1 are not covered because the corpora were not upgraded: Arabic, Bulgarian, Croatian, Czech, English, Farsi, Hungarian, Lithuanian, Maltese, Slovene and Spanish.

[8] `http://hdl.handle.net/11234/1-2184`

[9] Note that other languages also have inflected (reflexive) pronouns, e.g. in IRVs: ⃞FR *je me rends* (lit. 'I return myself') 'I go', *il se rend* (lit. 'he returns himself') 'he goes', etc. The difference is that, in the Irish examples, the pronoun is not lexicalized and should normally not be annotated as a VMWE component.

[10] `https://proycon.anaproy.nl/software/flat/`

	S	A_1	A_2	F_{span}	κ_{span}	κ_{cat}
Greek (EL)	$874_{(1617)}$	$293_{(428)}$	$394_{(462)}$	$0.652_{(0.694)}$	$0.608_{(0.665)}$	$\mathbf{0.715}_{(0.673)}$
Irish (GA)	800	312	270	0.715	0.663	0.835
Polish (PL)	$900_{(2079)}$	$252_{(759)}$	$296_{(707)}$	$\mathbf{0.774}_{(0.619)}$	$\mathbf{0.732}_{(0.568)}$	$\mathbf{0.907}_{(0.882)}$
Br. Portuguese (PT)	$1251_{(1000)}$	$253_{(275)}$	$232_{(241)}$	$0.672_{(0.713)}$	$0.640_{(0.684)}$	$\mathbf{0.928}_{(0.837)}$
Swedish (SV)	700	364	257	0.734	0.671	0.847
Chinese (ZH)	3953	883	840	0.584	0.544	0.833

Table 1: Inter-annotator agreement on S sentences with A_1 and A_2 VMWEs per annotator. F_{span} shows inter-annotator F-measure, κ_{span} shows chance-corrected agreement on annotation span, and κ_{cat} on category. Subscripts indicate agreement in edition 1.1 (on different samples).

corpora by 13%-209% in terms of the annotated VMWEs. In other languages, previous annotations were corrected in the layers of tokenisation, lemmatisation, morphosyntax or VMWEs.

Quality All 14 languages now benefit from morphosyntactic tagsets compatible with UD version 2. The tokenisation, lemmatisation, and morphosyntactic layers contain manual annotations for some languages (Chinese, French, Irish, Italian, Swedish, partly German, Greek, Polish and Portuguese) and automatic ones for the others (mostly with UDPipe[11] trained on UD version 2.5). The homogenisation of the morphosyntactic layer via a widely adopted framework such as UD facilitates the development of tools for corpus processing as well as for MWE identification by shared task participants.

In each language, most of the VMWE annotations were performed by a single annotator per file, except for Chinese and Turkish, where double annotation and adjudication was systematic. In most languages the post-annotation use of a custom consistency checking tool helped to reduce silence and noise (Savary et al., 2018, section 5.4). For the data annotated from scratch in edition 1.2 (Chinese, Greek, Irish, Polish and Portuguese)[12] we performed double annotation of a sample to estimate inter-annotator agreement (Savary et al., 2017; Ramisch et al., 2018). Compared to edition 1.1 (where roughly the same guidelines and methodology were used), the scores presented in Tab. 1 for Greek, Polish and Portuguese are clearly higher for categorisation.[13] For span, they are slightly lower in Greek and Portuguese but significantly higher in Polish. For all 6 languages, the contrast between the last two columns confirms the observation of previous editions that, once a VMWE has been correctly identified by an annotator, assigning it to the correct category is significantly easier.

Finally, we applied a set of validation scripts to ensure that all files respect the CUPT format (see below); each VMWE has a single category label among those specified in the guidelines; all dependency trees are acyclic; the mandatory metadata `text` and `source_sent_id` are present and the latter is well formatted; and that the same set of tokens is never annotated twice.

Corpus Release The annotated corpora were split into training, development and test set (see Section 5). They were released to participants in an instance of the CoNLL-U Plus format[14] called CUPT.[15] As described in more detail by Ramisch et al. (2018), it is a TAB-separated textual format with one token per line and 11 columns: the first 10 correspond to morpho-syntactic information identical to CoNLL-U such as the token's LEMMA and UPOS tags, and the 11th column contains the VMWE annotations in the form of numerical indices and a category label. Appendix B presents some corpus statistics, including the number of annotated VMWEs per category. Virtually all corpora are released

---

[11]`http://ufal.mff.cuni.cz/udpipe`

[12]Hebrew was excluded due to insufficient quantity of newly annotated data.

[13]Chinese had 17 annotators. They were numbered and assigned corpus sentences so that annotator n shared sentences with annotators n-1 and n+1. The outcomes of all annotators with even numbers were grouped into one cluster, and of those with odd numbers into another cluster, as if they were produced by two pseudo-annotators. For Irish, with only one active annotator, self-agreement was measured between the beginning and the end of the annotation process. For Greek, Polish and Portuguese, a subcorpus was annotated by 2 independent annotators.

[14]`http://universaldependencies.org/ext-format.html`

[15]`http://multiword.sourceforge.net/cupt-format`

Language	DE	EL	EU	FR	GA	HE	HI	IT	PL	PT	RO	SV	TR	ZH
tokens ($\times 10^6$)	185	25.6	21.3	915	34.2	12.9	78	281	1,902	307	12.7	2,474	19.8	67.2
sentences ($\times 10^6$)	10	1.04	1.33	34	1.38	0.45	3.6	12.3	159	26	0.48	164	1.39	4.11
tokens/sentence	18.5	24.5	16.0	26.9	24.8	38.5	21.7	22.9	12.0	11.8	26.6	15.1	14.5	16.3

Table 2: Number of tokens, sentences and average tokens/sentence ratio in the raw corpora

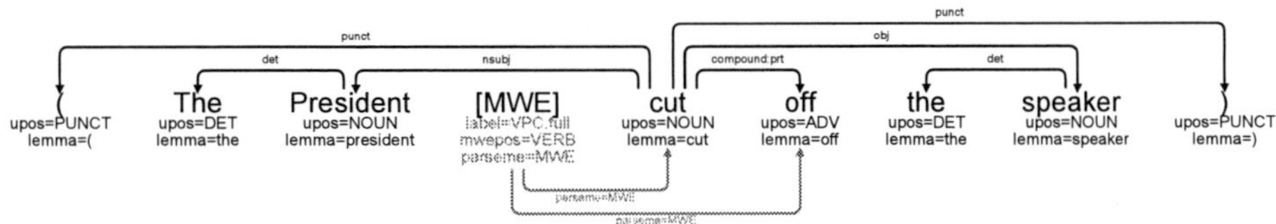

Figure 1: Example of Grew-match visualisation of a MWE annotation.

under various flavours of Creative Commons.[16]

3 Raw Corpora

In addition to the VMWE-annotated data, each language team prepared a large "raw" corpus, i.e., a corpus annotated for morphosyntax but not for VMWEs.[17] Raw corpora, uniformly released in the UD format, were meant for discovering unseen VMWEs. They have very different sizes (cf. Tab. 2) ranging from 12.7 to 2,474 millions of tokens. The genre of the data depends on the language, but efforts were put into making it consistent with the annotated data. The most frequent sources are CoNLL 2017 shared-task data, Wikipedia and newspapers.

For all languages except Italian, the raw corpus was parsed with UDPipe (Straka and Straková, 2017) using models trained on UD treebanks (2.0, 2.4 or 2.5). The Italian corpus was converted into UD from the existing annotated PAISÀ Corpus.[18] To ease their use by participants, each raw corpus was split into smaller files. We checked with a UD tool[19] that in the first 1,000 sentences of each file: (1) each sentence contains the required metadata, (2) the POS and dependency tags comply with the UD 2 tagsets, (3) the syntactic annotation forms a tree.

4 New Tools and Resources

Documentation Up to now, the release of data was coordinated with the organisation of shared tasks. This time, effort has been put into dissociating corpus annotation from shared tasks. Each language team was given a git repository containing development versions of the corpora. We have created a wiki containing instructions for language leaders to prepare data, recruit and train annotators, use common tools to create and manipulate data (e.g. the centralised annotation platform FLAT), etc. This documentation should evolve as the initiative moves towards more frequent releases of the data. We hope that this will allow more flexible resource creation, in accordance with each team's needs and resources. Moreover, extensions and enhancements in the corpora will be integrated into MWE identification tools faster.

Grew-match All along the annotation phase, the latest version of the annotated corpora (on a git repository) was searchable online via the Grew-match querying tool.[20] Grew-match is a generic graph-matching tool which was adapted to take into account the MWE annotations, by adding MWE-specific graph nodes and arcs, as shown in Figure 1: each MWE gives rise to a fake "token" node, heading arcs to all the components of the MWE. Language teams thus used Grew-match to identify potential errors

---

[16]Except parts of the CoNLL-U data, under other open (French, Polish, Irish) or unknown (Irish) licenses.

[17]The raw corpus for edition 1.2 is available at `http://hdl.handle.net/11234/1-3416` and described at `http://gitlab.com/parseme/corpora/wikis/Raw-corpora-for-the-PARSEME-1.2-shared-task`

[18]`http://www.corpusitaliano.it`

[19]`https://github.com/universalDependencies/tools`

[20]`http://match.grew.fr/` – tab "PARSEME".

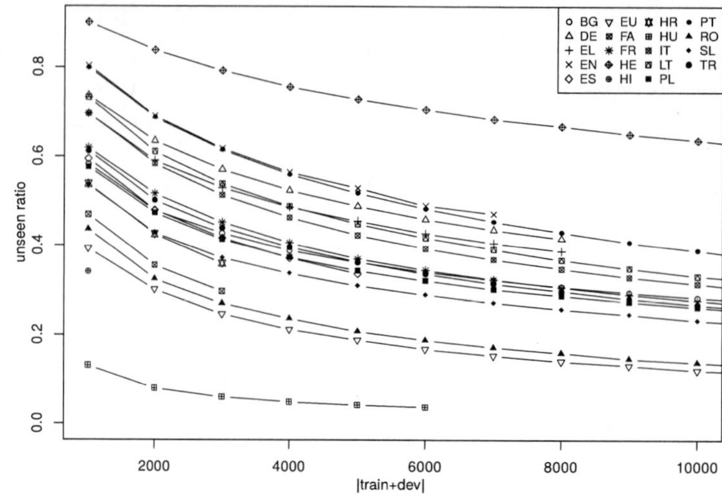

Figure 2: Per-language unseen ratios as a function of train+dev size (data from edition 1.1).

and inconsistencies, e.g., the VMWE in Figure 1 would be retrieved by searching for VMWEs lacking a verbal component (in this case, the MWE annotation is correct whereas the POS of *cut* is incorrect).

Evaluation Tools We adopt the script and metrics developed in edition 1.1 and described in detail by Ramisch et al. (2018). In addition to global and token-based precision (P), recall (R) and F-measure (F1), per language and macro-averaged, we evaluate participating systems on specific VMWE phenomena (e.g. continuous vs. discontinuous) and categories (e.g. VID, IRV, LVC.full). Especially relevant for this edition are the scores on unseen VMWEs, that is, those whose multi-set of lemmas never occur in the training data. In edition 1.1, by training data we meant the train subset only. Recently, we found that this introduced bias from those VMWEs which occurred in dev but not in train: they were still known in the gold data during the system development and tuning. Therefore, in edition 1.2, we redefined an unseen VMWE as a multiset of lemmas annotated in test but not in train+dev. Also differently from edition 1.1, the final macro-averaged and language-specific rankings emphasise results on unseen VMWEs.

5   Corpus Splits

Some datasets in edition 1.1 contained very few unseen VMWEs.[21] Using them as is would lead to statistically unreliable assessment of systems' performance on unseen VMWEs. Thus, we had to design a strategy to re-split the corpora controlling for the distribution of unseen VMWEs. Our two prerequisites were to: (i) ensure a sufficient absolute number of unseen VMWEs for each language (ii) adapt the strategy to the (7 out of 14) languages with no new annotated data compared to previous editions. Hence we could not use the strategy of the WNUT2017 shared task on novel and emerging entity recognition, which would consist in annotating new texts, pre-filtered so as not to contain the VMWEs already present in the existing data (Derczynski et al., 2017). Therefore, we decided to split the whole annotated data for each language by randomly placing sentences in the training (train), development (dev) or test sets.

We considered several splitting methods differing in the parameters that were controlled. Apart from the absolute *number* of unseen VMWEs, the unseen/all VMWE *ratio*, as well as the test/whole corpus size ratio, seemed like desirable parameters of the splitting method. However, these three parameters interact. Figure 2, which plots the average unseen ratio as a function of the train+dev size (in terms of the number of sentences), shows that unseen ratios greatly vary across languages, *even when controlling for train+dev size*. Furthermore, we can see that this ratio depends on the relative size of the train+dev/test sets. So while the unseen ratio may well depend on some traits intrinsic to the language, it clearly depends on other, external, factors (e.g. the chosen text genres and the particular split).

---

[21]E.g. Romanian, Basque, and Hungarian contain 26, 57, and 62 unseen VMWEs in test w.r.t. train+dev.

Language		DE	EL	EU	FR	GA	HE	HI	IT	PL	PT	RO	SV	TR	ZH
Dev w.r.t. train	Nb.	100	100	100	101	100	101	100	101	100	100	100	100	100	100
	Rate	0.37	0.32	0.19	0.24	0.79	0.61	0.54	0.31	0.23	0.25	0.12	0.37	0.27	0.38
Test w.r.t. train+dev	Nb.	301	300	300	300	301	302	300	300	301	300	299	300	300	300
	Rate	0.37	0.31	0.15	0.22	0.69	0.60	0.45	0.29	0.22	0.24	0.07	0.31	0.26	0.38

Table 3: Number and rate of unseen VMWEs in dev w.r.t. train and in test w.r.t. train+dev.

On the other hand, the unseen VMWE ratio was proved to better (inversely) correlate with MWE identification performance than with the training set size alone (Al Saied et al., 2018). The analysis above dissuaded us from controlling for a "natural" (i.e. close to the average across random splits) unseen ratio. Therefore two options were considered: (1) perform random splits using predetermined proportions for train/dev/test sets and pick a split that best approaches the "natural" unseen ratio for that language, while reaching a sufficient absolute number of unseen VMWEs in the test set; (2) target roughly the same absolute number of unseen VMWEs per language, while the test size and unseen ratio follow from it naturally. Both options restrict the unseen ratio (which still varies depending on the specific split). We preferred the second one because it gives equal weights to each language in system evaluation.

Implemented Splitting Method The splitting method relies on two parameters: the number of unseen VMWEs in test with respect to train+dev, and the number of unseen VMWEs in dev with respect to train. The latter ensures that dev is similar to test, so that systems tuned on dev have similar performances on test. The method strives to find a three-way train/dev/test split satisfying the input specification while preserving the "natural" data distribution (in particular, the unseen/all VMWEs ratios).

The same procedure is applied to split the full data into test and train+dev, and then to split train+dev into train and dev, so only the former is detailed below. The procedure takes as input a set of sentences, a target number of unseen VMWEs u_t, and a number N of random splits:

- We estimate s_t, the size (number of sentences) of the target test set leading to the desired value of u_t. As the average number of unseen VMWEs grows with the size of the test set,[22] we can use binary search to determine s_t.[23] In the course of the search, for a given test size, the average number of unseen VMWEs is estimated based on N random splits.
- For the resulting test size s_t, we compute the average unseen ratio r_t over the same N splits.
- N random splits with test size s_t are performed, and the one that best fits u_t and r_t is selected. More precisely, best fit means here the split, with u unseen and unseen ratio r, that minimises the cost function $c(u, r, u_t, r_t) = \frac{|u_t - u|}{u_t} + |r_t - r|$.

Splitting Results Table 3 shows the statistics of the splits obtained for all languages of the shared task using the above method, with N=100, u_t=300 (in test) and then u_t=100 (in dev). Due to different sizes and characteristics of the individual datasets and languages, the obtained test/train+dev and dev/train unseen ratios vary considerably, the former varying from 0.07 for Romanian to 0.69 for Irish.[24]

6 Systems and Results

Seven teams submitted 9 results to edition 1.2, summarised in Table 4. They use a variety of techniques including recurrent neural networks (ERMI, MultiVitamin, MTLB-STRUCT and TRAVIS), syntax-based candidate extraction and filtering including association measures (HMSid, Seen2Seen), and rule-based joint parsing and MWE identification (FipsCo). The VMWE-annotated corpora are used for model training or fine-tuning, as well as for tuning patterns and filters. Surprisingly, the provided raw corpora

---

[22]The input dataset is fixed, hence a larger test set means a smaller train set, therefore more unseen VMWEs.

[23]If the input set has T sentences, we iterate using a binary search for the test set size in the $[1, T - 1]$ interval. For instance, the first iteration picks $s = \lfloor T/2 \rfloor$, the interval considered next ($[1, s - 1]$ or $[s + 1, T - 1]$) depends on $U(s)$, the average number of unseen VMWEs in N random splits with test set of size s: if the current value is higher than $U(s)$, then the next binary search will operate on $[1, s - 1]$, and so on. The final value of s is assigned to s_t.

[24]Romanian's unseen ratio results from sentence pre-selection and leads to outstanding identification results.

System	Architecture	Use of corpora/resources		
		Annotated	Raw	External resources
ERMI	bidirectional LSTM + CRF	train model	train embed.	–
FipsCo	rule-based joint parsing+identification			VMWE lexicon
HMSid	syntactic patterns, association measures (AMs)	tune patterns and AMs		idiom dataset, FrWac corpus
MTLB-STRUCT	neural language model, fine-tuned for joint parsing+identification	tune BERT		multilingual BERT
MultiVitamin	neural binary ensemble classifier	train classifier		XLM-RoBERTa
Seen2Seen	rule-based extraction + filtering	tune filters		–
Seen2Unseen	+ lexical replacement, translation, AMs			Google Trans., Wiktionary, CoNLL 2017 corpus/embed.
TRAVIS-mono	neural language model, fine-tuned for MWE identification	tune BERT		monolingual BERT
TRAVIS-multi				multilingual BERT

Table 4: Architecture of the systems, and their use of provided and external resources.

System	#Lang	Unseen MWE-based				Global MWE-based				Global Token-based			
		P	R	F1	#	P	R	F1	#	P	R	F1	#
ERMI	14/14	25.3	27.2	26.2	1	64.8	52.9	58.2	2	73.7	54.5	62.6	2
Seen2Seen	14/14	36.5	00.6	01.1	2	76.2	58.6	66.2	1	78.6	57.0	66.1	1
MTLB-STRUCT	14/14	36.2	41.1	38.5	1	71.3	69.1	70.1	1	77.7	70.9	74.1	1
TRAVIS-multi	13/14	28.1	33.3	30.5	2	60.7	57.6	59.1	3	70.4	60.1	64.8	2
TRAVIS-mono	10/14	24.3	28.0	26.0	3	49.5	43.5	46.3	4	55.9	45.0	49.9	4
Seen2Unseen	14/14	16.1	12.0	13.7	4	63.4	62.7	63.0	2	66.3	61.6	63.9	3
FipsCo	3/14	04.3	05.2	05.7	5	11.7	8.8	10.0	5	13.3	8.5	10.4	5
HMSid	1/14	02.0	03.8	02.6	6	04.6	04.9	04.7	6	04.7	04.8	04.8	6
MultiVitamin	7/14	00.1	00.1	00.1	7	00.2	00.1	00.1	7	03.5	01.3	01.9	7

Table 5: Unseen MWE-based (w.r.t. train+dev), global MWE-based, and global token-based Precision (P), Recall (R), F-measure (F1) and F1 ranking (#). Closed track above separator, open track below.

seem to have been used by one system only, for training word embeddings (ERMI). We expected that the teams would use the raw corpus to apply MWE discovery methods such as those described in Constant et al. (2017, Sec. 2), but they may have lacked time to do so. The external resources used include morphological and VMWE lexicons, external raw corpora, translation software, pre-trained non-contextual and contextual word embeddings, notably including pre-trained mono- and multi-lingual BERT.

Table 5 shows the participation of the systems in the two tracks, the number of languages they covered, and their macro-average F1 score ranking across 14 languages.[25] Two system results were submitted to the closed track and 7 to the open track. Four results covered all 14 languages.[26] As this edition focuses on performances on unseen VMWEs, these scores are presented first.[27] In the open track, the best F1 obtained by MTLB-STRUCT (38.53) is by over 10 points higher the corresponding best score in the edition 1.1 (28.46, by SHOMA). These figures are, however, not directly comparable, due to differences in the languages covered in the two editions, the size and quality of the corpora. The closed-track system ERMI achieves promising results, likely thanks to word embeddings trained on the raw corpus.

The global MWE-based F1 scores for all, both seen and unseen, VMWEs exceed 66 and 70 for the closed and open track, respectively, against 54 and 58 in edition 1.1. Like for the unseen score, it remains to be seen how much this significant difference owes to new/enhanced resources, different language sets, and novel system architectures. The second best score across the two tracks is achieved by a closed-track system (Seen2Seen) using non-neural rule-based candidate extraction and filtering. Global token-based

[25]Full results: `http://multiword.sourceforge.net/sharedtaskresults2020/`

[26]Macro-averages are meaningless for systems not covering some languages, for which P=R=F1=0.

[27]When we first published the results, we wrongly considered the unseen in test with respect to train only. Here we provide the results with unseen with respect to train+dev, as explained in Section 4. Results will be updated on the website and in the final versions of system description papers.

System	Unseen MWE-based F1 score										
	DE	EL	EU	FR	HE	HI	IT	PL	PT	RO	TR
ERMI	21.98	29.81	26.99	24.40	08.40	39.25	12.71	25.92	28.33	21.28	36.46
MTLB-STRUCT	**49.34**	**42.47**	**34.41**	42.33	**19.59**	**53.11**	20.81	39.94	**35.13**	34.02	43.66
TRAVIS-mono	46.89	7.25	–	**48.01**	–	0.64	**26.16**	**43.44**	–	**40.26**	48.40
TRAVIS-multi	37.25	37.86	30.38	37.27	15.51	34.90	21.48	38.95	–	28.34	41.74
SHOMA (1.1)	18.40	29.67	18.57	44.66	14.42	47.74	11.83	17.67	29.36	17.95	**50.27**
Nb. VMWE (1.2)	3,217	6,470	2,226	4,295	2,030	361	3,178	5,841	5,174	2,036	6,579
Nb. VMWE (1.1)	3,323	1,904	3,323	5,179	1,737	534	3,754	4,637	4,983	5,302	6,635
Nb. unseen (1.2)	301	300	300	300	302	300	300	301	300	299	300
Nb. unseen (1.1)	232	192	57	240	307	214	179	137	141	26	378

Table 6: F1 scores on unseen VMWEs (in train+dev) of the 4 best systems in ed. 1.2, of the best open system in ed. 1.1 (SHOMA), nb. of VMWEs (train+dev), and nb. of unseen VMWEs (train+dev).

F1 scores are often slightly higher than corresponding MWE-based scores. An interesting opposition appears when comparing the global scores with those for unseen VMWEs. In the former, precision is usually higher than recall, whereas in the latter, recall exceeds precision, except for 2 systems.

As macro-averages hide inter-language variability, Table 6 shows unseen F1 scores for 11 languages present in editions 1.1 and 1.2. Results are not comparable across editions due to different corpora, but for languages with similar number of annotated total and unseen VMWEs, some systems reach higher unseen F1 scores than the best 1.1 system SHOMA (e.g. in German, French, and Hindi). However, this is not systematic (see Turkish) and the best scores are not always obtained by the same systems, preventing us from drawing strong conclusions. Performances for Chinese (not shown in Table 6) are surprisingly high, reaching unseen F1=60.19 (TRAVIS-mono). In Chinese, a many VMWEs are syntactically and lexically regular. A simple system with two rules would reach unseen MWE-based F1=27.33.[28]

One finding from the previous shared task editions (Section 5), is that performance for a given language is better explained by the unseen ratio for this language than by the size of the training set. This is even truer for the 1.2 edition, as we could measure a very high negative linear correlation between the highest MWE-based F1 score for a given language and the unseen ratio for that language (Pearson coefficient = -0.90). In contrast, the correlation between the best F1 and the size of the number of annotated VMWEs in the training set is quite poor (Pearson coefficient = 0.23). Appendix C plots these correlations graphically.

7 Conclusions and Future Work

The contributions of the PARSEME shared task 1.2 can be summarised as: (1) the creation and enhancement of VMWE-annotated corpora including three new languages, (2) an evaluation methodology to split the corpora ensuring the representativity of the target phenomenon, and (3) encouraging results hinting at improvements on the identification of unseen VMWEs. In the future, we would like to implement continuous corpus development, with frequent releases independent of shared tasks, so that new languages can join at any time and system developers benefit from latest corpus versions. Additionally, our long-term aim is to increase the coverage of MWE categories, including nominal expressions, adverbials, etc. Finally, we would like to pursue our efforts to design innovative setups for combining (unsupervised) MWE discovery, automatic and manual lexicon creation, and supervised MWE identification.

Acknowledgments

This work was supported by the IC1207 PARSEME COST action and project PARSEME-FR (ANR-14-CERA-0001). Thanks to Maarten van Gompel for his help with FLAT and to the University of Düsseldorf for hosting the server. Thanks to language leaders and annotators (Appendix A) for their hard work.

---

[28]R1: verbs ending with 入 are single-token VMWEs; R2: pairs of consecutive verbs linked with `mark` and such that the dependant's lemma belongs to a list of 7 lemmas: 到, 为, 出, 在, 成, 至 and 出 are VMWEs.

References

Hazem Al Saied, Marie Candito, and Mathieu Constant. 2018. A transition-based verbal multiword expression analyzer. In Stella Markantonatou, Carlos Ramisch, Agata Savary, and Veronika Vincze, editors, *Multiword expressions at length and in depth*. Language Science Press.

Timothy Baldwin and Su Nam Kim. 2010. Multiword expressions. In Nitin Indurkhya and Fred J. Damerau, editors, *Handbook of Natural Language Processing, Second Edition*, pages 267–292. CRC Press, Taylor and Francis Group, Boca Raton, FL. ISBN 978-1420085921.

Nicoletta Calzolari, Charles Fillmore, Ralph Grishman, Nancy Ide, Alessandro Lenci, Catherine MacLeod, and Antonio Zampolli. 2002. Towards best practice for multiword expressions in computational lexicons. In *Proceedings of the 3rd International Conference on Language Resources and Evaluation (LREC-2002)*, pages 1934–1940, Las Palmas.

Mathieu Constant, Gülşen Eryiğit, Johanna Monti, Lonneke van der Plas, Carlos Ramisch, Michael Rosner, and Amalia Todirascu. 2017. Multiword expression processing: A survey. *Computational Linguistics*, 43(4):837–892.

Leon Derczynski, Eric Nichols, Marieke van Erp, and Nut Limsopatham. 2017. Results of the WNUT2017 shared task on novel and emerging entity recognition. In *Proceedings of the 3rd Workshop on Noisy User-generated Text*, pages 140–147, Copenhagen, Denmark, September. Association for Computational Linguistics.

Carlos Ramisch, Silvio Ricardo Cordeiro, Agata Savary, Veronika Vincze, Verginica Barbu Mititelu, Archna Bhatia, Maja Buljan, Marie Candito, Polona Gantar, Voula Giouli, Tunga Güngör, Abdelati Hawwari, Uxoa Iñurrieta, Jolanta Kovalevskaitė, Simon Krek, Timm Lichte, Chaya Liebeskind, Johanna Monti, Carla Parra Escartín, Behrang QasemiZadeh, Renata Ramisch, Nathan Schneider, Ivelina Stoyanova, Ashwini Vaidya, and Abigail Walsh. 2018. Edition 1.1 of the PARSEME Shared Task on Automatic Identification of Verbal Multiword Expressions. In *Proceedings of the Joint Workshop on Linguistic Annotation, Multiword Expressions and Constructions (LAW-MWE-CxG-2018)*, pages 222–240. ACL.

Agata Savary, Carlos Ramisch, Silvio Cordeiro, Federico Sangati, Veronika Vincze, Behrang QasemiZadeh, Marie Candito, Fabienne Cap, Voula Giouli, Ivelina Stoyanova, and Antoine Doucet. 2017. The PARSEME shared task on automatic identification of verbal multiword expressions. In *Proceedings of the 13th Workshop on Multiword Expressions (MWE 2017)*, pages 31–47, Valencia, Spain, April. Association for Computational Linguistics.

Agata Savary, Marie Candito, Verginica Barbu Mititelu, Eduard Bejček, Fabienne Cap, Slavomír Čéplö, Silvio Ricardo Cordeiro, Gülşen Eryiğit, Voula Giouli, Maarten van Gompel, Yaakov HaCohen-Kerner, Jolanta Kovalevskaitė, Simon Krek, Chaya Liebeskind, Johanna Monti, Carla Parra Escartín, Lonneke van der Plas, Behrang QasemiZadeh, Carlos Ramisch, Federico Sangati, Ivelina Stoyanova, and Veronika Vincze. 2018. PARSEME multilingual corpus of verbal multiword expressions. In Stella Markantonatou, Carlos Ramisch, Agata Savary, and Veronika Vincze, editors, *Multiword expressions at length and in depth: Extended papers from the MWE 2017 workshop*, pages 87–147. Language Science Press., Berlin.

Agata Savary, Silvio Cordeiro, and Carlos Ramisch. 2019a. Without lexicons, multiword expression identification will never fly: A position statement. In *MWE-WN 2019*, pages 79–91, Florence, Italy. ACL.

Agata Savary, Silvio Ricardo Cordeiro, Timm Lichte, Carlos Ramisch, Uxoa Iñurrieta, and Voula Giouli. 2019b. Literal occurrences of multiword expressions: Rare birds that cause a stir. *The Prague Bulletin of Mathematical Linguistics*, 112:5–54, apr.

Nathan Schneider, Dirk Hovy, Anders Johannsen, and Marine Carpuat. 2016. SemEval-2016 Task 10: Detecting Minimal Semantic Units and their Meanings (DiMSUM). In *Proceedings of the 10th International Workshop on Semantic Evaluation (SemEval-2016)*, pages 546–559, San Diego, California, June. Association for Computational Linguistics.

Milan Straka and Jana Straková. 2017. Tokenizing, pos tagging, lemmatizing and parsing ud 2.0 with udpipe. In *Proceedings of the CoNLL 2017 Shared Task: Multilingual Parsing from Raw Text to Universal Dependencies*, pages 88–99, Vancouver, Canada, August. Association for Computational Linguistics.

A Composition of the Corpus Annotation Teams

DE: Timm Lichte (LL[29]), Rafael Ehren; **EL**: Voula Giouli (LL), Vassiliki Foufi, Aggeliki Fotopoulou, Stella Markantonatou, Stella Papadelli, Sevasti Louizou **EU**: Uxoa Iñurrieta (LL), Itziar Aduriz, Ainara Estarrona, Itziar Gonzalez, Antton Gurrutxaga, Larraitz Uria, Ruben Urizar; **FR**: Marie Candito (LL), Matthieu Constant, Bruno Guillaume, Carlos Ramisch, Caroline Pasquer, Yannick Parmentier, Jean-Yves Antoine, Agata Savary; **GA**: Abigail Walsh (LL), Jennifer Foster, Teresa Lynn; **HE**: Chaya Liebeskind (LL), Hevi Elyovich, Yaakov Ha-Cohen Kerner, Ruth Malka; **HI**: Archna Bhatia (LL), Ashwini Vaidya (LL), Kanishka Jain, Vandana Puri, Shraddha Ratori, Vishakha Shukla, Shubham Srivastava; **IT**: Johanna Monti (LL), Carola Carlino, Valeria Caruso, Maria Pia di Buono, Antonio Pascucci, Annalisa Raffone, Anna Riccio, Federico Sangati, Giulia Speranza; **PL**: Agata Savary (LL), Jakub Waszczuk (LL), Emilia Palka-Binkiewicz; **PT**: Carlos Ramisch (LL), Renata Ramisch (LL), Silvio Ricardo Cordeiro, Helena de Medeiros Caseli, Isaac Miranda, Alexandre Rademaker, Oto Vale, Aline Villavicencio, Gabriela Wick Pedro, Rodrigo Wilkens, Leonardo Zilio; **RO**: Verginica Barbu Mititelu (LL), Mihaela Ionescu, Mihaela Onofrei, Monica-Mihaela Rizea; **SV**: Sara Stymne (LL), Elsa Erenmalm, Gustav Finnveden, Bernadeta Griciūtė, Ellinor Lindqvist, Eva Pettersson; **TR**: Tunga Güngör (LL), Zeynep Yirmibeşoğlu, Gozde Berk, Berna Erden; **ZH**: Menghan Jiang (LL), Hongzhi Xu (LL), Jia Chen, Xiaomin Ge, Fangyuan Hu, Sha Hu, Minli Li, Siyuan Liu, Zhenzhen Qin, Ruilong Sun, Chengwen Wang, Huangyang Xiao, Peiyi Yan, Tsy Yih, Ke Yu, Songping Yu, Si Zeng, Yongchen Zhang, Yun Zhao.

B Statistics of the Corpora

Lang-part	Sent.	Tokens	Avg. length	VMWE	VID	IRV	LVC full	LVC cause	VPC full	VPC semi	IAV	MVC	LS ICV
DE-train	6568	126830	19.3	2950	1039	249	212	24	1286	140	0	0	0
DE-dev	602	11756	19.5	267	95	14	26	2	122	8	0	0	0
DE-test	1826	34976	19.1	824	303	59	73	7	336	46	0	0	0
DE-Total	8996	173562	19.2	4041	1437	322	311	33	1744	194	0	0	0
EL-train	17733	479679	27	6155	1933	0	3982	101	96	0	0	43	0
EL-dev	909	23911	26.3	315	98	0	203	5	4	0	0	5	0
EL-test	2805	75442	26.8	974	323	0	612	19	17	0	0	3	0
EL-Total	21447	579032	26.9	7444	2354	0	4797	125	117	0	0	51	0
EU-train	4440	61867	13.9	1690	347	0	1261	82	0	0	0	0	0
EU-dev	1418	20509	14.4	536	127	0	383	26	0	0	0	0	0
EU-test	5300	75431	14.2	2020	406	0	1508	106	0	0	0	0	0
EU-Total	11158	157807	14.1	4246	880	0	3152	214	0	0	0	0	0
FR-train	14377	360070	25	3870	1494	1037	1253	70	0	0	0	16	0
FR-dev	1573	39502	25.1	425	157	117	144	5	0	0	0	2	0
FR-test	5011	126420	25.2	1359	505	347	481	22	0	0	0	4	0
FR-Total	20961	525992	25	5654	2156	1501	1878	97	0	0	0	22	0
GA-train	257	6242	24.2	100	14	0	35	23	2	2	24	0	0
GA-dev	322	7020	21.8	126	22	0	29	22	6	5	42	0	0
GA-test	1121	25954	23.1	436	69	6	137	74	20	13	117	0	0
GA-Total	1700	39216	23	662	105	6	201	119	28	20	183	0	0
HE-train	14152	286262	20.2	1864	825	0	765	166	108	0	0	0	0
HE-dev	1254	25392	20.2	166	64	0	80	13	9	0	0	0	0
HE-test	3794	76827	20.2	503	219	0	204	44	36	0	0	0	0
HE-Total	19200	388481	20.2	2533	1108	0	1049	223	153	0	0	0	0
HI-train	282	5764	20.4	175	11	0	109	3	0	0	0	52	0
HI-dev	289	6272	21.7	186	11	0	126	0	0	0	0	49	0
HI-test	1113	23394	21	673	39	0	406	23	0	0	0	205	0
HI-Total	1684	35430	21	1034	61	0	641	26	0	0	0	306	0
IT-train	10641	292065	27.4	2854	999	783	502	112	74	2	343	19	20
IT-dev	1202	32652	27.1	324	109	81	52	18	11	0	44	4	5
IT-test	3885	106072	27.3	1032	376	280	180	44	20	0	110	10	12
IT-Total	15728	430789	27.3	4210	1484	1144	734	174	105	2	497	33	37
PL-train	17731	298437	16.8	5398	629	2723	1807	239	0	0	0	0	0
PL-dev	1425	23950	16.8	443	49	219	162	13	0	0	0	0	0

---

[29]LL stands for language leader.

Lang-part	Sent.	Tokens	Avg. length	VMWE	VID	IRV	LVC full	LVC cause	VPC full	VPC semi	IAV	MVC	LS ICV
PL-test	4391	73753	16.7	1345	148	687	451	59	0	0	0	0	0
PL-Total	23547	396140	16.8	7186	826	3629	2420	311	0	0	0	0	0
PT-train	23905	542497	22.6	4777	945	763	2960	98	0	0	0	11	0
PT-dev	1976	43676	22.1	397	80	73	236	6	0	0	0	2	0
PT-test	6236	142377	22.8	1263	281	191	763	23	0	0	0	5	0
PT-Total	32117	728550	22.6	6437	1306	1027	3959	127	0	0	0	18	0
RO-train	10920	195718	17.9	1218	304	771	108	35	0	0	0	0	0
RO-dev	7714	134340	17.4	818	228	504	56	30	0	0	0	0	0
RO-test	38069	685566	18	4135	1114	2552	352	117	0	0	0	0	0
RO-Total	56703	1015624	17.9	6171	1646	3827	516	182	0	0	0	0	0
SV-train	1605	24970	15.5	752	105	41	95	6	345	160	0	0	0
SV-dev	596	8889	14.9	270	40	24	42	0	108	56	0	0	0
SV-test	2103	31623	15	969	146	50	142	5	418	208	0	0	0
SV-Total	4304	65482	15.2	1991	291	115	279	11	871	424	0	0	0
TR-train	17945	267503	14.9	6212	3351	0	2858	0	0	0	0	3	0
TR-dev	1062	15935	15	367	187	0	179	0	0	0	0	1	0
TR-test	3304	48791	14.7	1151	604	0	546	0	0	0	0	1	0
TR-Total	22311	332229	14.8	7730	4142	0	3583	0	0	0	0	5	0
ZH-train	35326	575590	16.2	8113	676	0	927	148	0	3156	0	3206	0
ZH-dev	1141	18258	16	265	18	0	33	6	0	108	0	100	0
ZH-test	3462	55728	16	786	63	0	94	13	0	300	0	316	0
ZH-Total	39929	649576	16.2	9164	757	0	1054	167	0	3564	0	3622	0
Total	279785	5517910	19.7	68503	18553	11571	24574	1809	3018	4204	680	4057	37

C Correlation of Performance and Unseen Ratio/Training Set Size

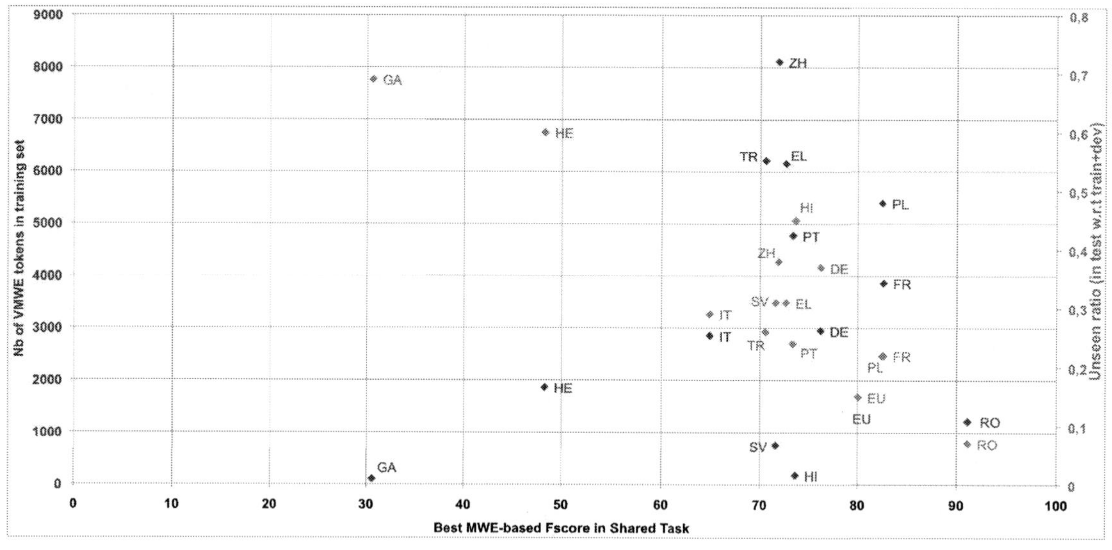

Figure 3: Relation between the performance of each language and its unseen ratio (red) and number of VMWEs tokens in the training set (blue). X axis: best MWE-based F1 score. Blue Y axis: Number of VMWEs in training set. Red Y axis: Unseen ratio.

HMSid and HMSid2 at PARSEME Shared Task 2020: Computational Corpus Linguistics and *unseen-in-training* MWEs

Jean-Pierre Colson
University of Louvain
Louvain-la-Neuve, Belgium
jean-pierre.colson@uclouvain.be

Abstract

This paper is a system description of HMSid, officially sent to the PARSEME Shared Task 2020 for one language (French), in the open track. It also describes HMSid2, sent to the organizers of the workshop after the deadline and using the same methodology but in the closed track. Both systems do not rely on machine learning, but on computational corpus linguistics. Their score for unseen MWEs is very promising, especially in the case of HMSid2, which would have received the best score for unseen MWEs in the French closed track.

1   Introduction

Although the PARSEME Shared Task 2018 (Savary et al., 2018) produced very interesting results for the extraction of verbal multiword expressions, one important note of caution has to be made: the participating systems produced poor results for unseen MWEs, i.e. expressions that were absent from the training data. As pointed out by the organizers of the new Parseme Shared Task 2020[1], a possible solution to this issue is the recourse to large MWE lexicons.

In this paper, however, we report the results of two systems offering promising results for *unseen* MWEs with no recourse to MWE lexicons: HMSid (*Hybrid Multi-layer System for the extraction of Idioms*) and HMSid2. Both systems are based on computational corpus linguistics: they just used the training data and an additional general linguistic corpus. As the models require a fine-tuned adaptation to each language under study, they were only applied to the French dataset of the PARSEME Shared Task 2020.

HMSid used as an external corpus the French WaCky corpus (Baroni et al., 2009) and was submitted to the PARSEME Shared Task 2020. As there was a recourse to an external corpus, it was logically put in the open track. Thanks to the feedback from the organizers of PARSEME 2020, however, we adapted the system in order to propose it in the closed track: the corpus used was the Wikipedia corpus included in the training data. The new version, HMSid2, was sent to the organizers after the official deadline. In this paper, both the official results of HMSid and the new results from HMSid2 are discussed.

Our theoretical starting point for both systems is that, while Deep Learning will surpass most techniques for reproducing elements that are somehow present in training sets, it will need additional corpus-

---

[1] Introduction to the PARSEME Shared Task 2020,
http://multiword.sourceforge.net/PHITE.php?sitesig=CONF&page=CONF_02_MWE-LEX_2020___lb__COL-ING__rb__&subpage=CONF_40_Shared_Task

Joint Workshop on Multiword Expressions and Electronic Lexicons, pages 119–123
Barcelona, Spain (Online), December 13, 2020.

based information for unseen-in-training MWEs. It should also be pointed out that MWE extraction is a daunting practical task, but that the theoretical background is also very complex, as it is related to grammatical and semantic structure. Information retrieval (Baeza-Yates and Ribeiro-Neto, 1999) has shown that semantic relations may be analyzed by very diverse methods, including vector space models and clustering methods. Many of its findings are compatible with the Distributional Hypothesis (Harris 1954): differences in meaning will be reflected by differences in distribution. However, the distribution of words is also affected by existing MWEs, as at least 50 percent of the words from any text will actually be included in MWEs, collocations or phraseological units (Sinclair, 1991). In addition, a wide array of studies in construction grammar (Hoffmann and Trousdale, 2013) strongly suggest that language structure consists of a very complex and probabilistic network of constructions at various levels of abstraction and schematicity.

It is no wonder then that very complex techniques are necessary for extracting MWEs, in much the same way as for the extraction of semantic links. In particular, the complex interplay between 1st-order co-occurrence (words appear together) and 2nd-order co-occurrence (words appear in similar contexts, Lapesa and Evert, 2014) probably requires a hybrid methodology. While deep learning and in particular neural networks are very efficient ways of gaining information from a training set, it may be complemented by a more traditional, corpus-based approach in the case of the extraction of data that are unseen in the training set.

The technical background for HMSid and HMSid2 is a combination of techniques inherited from Information Retrieval, such as *metric clusters* (Baeza-Yates and Berthier Ribeiro-Neto, 1999) and a query likelihood model, with a big data approach, in this case a large (unparsed and untagged) linguistic corpus: the French WaCky for HMSid and the Parseme French training corpus (Wikipedia) for HMSid2. As described in Colson (2017; 2018), a clustering algorithm based on the average distance between the component parts of the MWEs is measured, the *cpr-score (Corpus Proximity Ratio)*:

$$cpr = \frac{n(w_1, w_2, \dots, w_n)}{n\left(x_{t_1} = w_1, x_{t_2} = w_2, \dots, x_{t_n} = w_n \mid \max(t_{i+1} - t_i) \leq W; \ i = 1, \dots, n - 1\right)}$$

Figure 1. The *cpr-score*

This approach, as opposed to vector models, is a 1st-order model, as it is based on the co-occurrence of words and not on similar contexts. Given a window W of x tokens (depending on the language and the corpus, typically set at 20 for MWEs), the score simply measures the ratio between the number of exact occurrences of an n-gram, divided by the number of occurrences with a window between each gram. The main advantages of this metric are that it is not limited to bigrams, and that semantic links may be captured as well by enlarging the window, a point that has also been made by Lapesa and Evert (2014): larger windows may enable 1st-order models to capture semantic associations.

Experiments with large datasets of idiomatic MWEs have shown (Colson, 2018) that most formulaic and idiomatic constructions can be captured by co-occurrence clusters, provided that the corpus used is sufficiently large (at least 1 billion tokens). In order to reach a good compromise between results that could be extracted from co-occurrence in large corpora and recurrent patterns with specific categories of MWEs, a hybrid methodology was used, as detailed in the following section.

2   Methodology used for HMSid and HMSid2

In the PARSEME Shared Task 2020 for French, the following categories of verbal MWEs had to be extracted from the test set: IRV (inherently reflexive verbs, as in the English example *to help oneself*), LVC.cause (light-verb constructions in which the verb adds a causative meaning to the noun, as in the English *to grant rights*), LVC.full (light-verb constructions in which the verb only adds meaning expressed as morphological features, as in *to give a lecture*), MVC (multi-verb constructions, as in *to make do*) and VID (verbal idioms, e.g. *to spill the beans*).

After a number of preliminary tests, we decided to extract French MWEs from the test set in a two-step process. The first step concerned all categories of verbal MWEs, as described above, except the last one (VID, verbal idioms). The second step was just devoted to verbal idioms.

This two-step approach was motivated by the unpredictable character of verbal idioms: contrary to the other categories of MWEs used for the PARSEME Shared Task, idioms display a very irregular number of elements, of which the syntactic structure is also diverse.

During the first step, we used a Perl script and the Data::Table module[2] for storing each sentence at a time in RAM memory. For the categories IRV, LVC.cause, LVC.full and MVC, the specific syntactic features of these categories were taken into account by the algorithm: in the case of IRV, for instance, the parsed sentences provided by the PARSEME dataset made it easy to extract all pronouns preceding or following the verbs, and an additional check was performed in order to determine whether those pronouns were indeed French reflexive pronouns, including elision (e.g. the pronominal form *s'* instead of *se*). For LVC.cause, a list of French causative verbs was extracted from the training data (for instance *apporter, causer, créer, entraîner*). In the extraction phase, all objects depending on such causative verbs were measured by our co-occurrence score, the *cpr-score* (Colson, 2017; 2018) and the highest values were considered as cases of LVC.cause constructions. For LVC.full, a similar methodology was used, taking into account all subjects (for passive constructions) and objects (for direct object constructions) depending on verbs, excluding causative verbs, with a medium-range association between the subject/object and the verb (computed by the *cpr-score*). In the same way, the MVC category was extracted on the basis of the degree of association between two successive verbs, as in *faire remarquer* (to point out).

In the second step of our extraction methodology, verbal idioms were extracted and added to the results. This made it possible to add the category of verbal idioms in the labels of the final results if and only if the results had not yet received another category label, for instance LVC.full. Preliminary tests on the basis of the training data indeed revealed that our algorithm tended to assign the VID category quite often, whereas the annotators of the gold set had been rather strict as to the idiomatic character of verbal MWEs. Using two separate scripts was a simple way of avoiding interference in the results.

In the Perl script devoted to the extraction of VIDs, we also used the Data::Table module and selected in the parsed data all verbs, all their complements, and all complements of each complement. Extensive testing with the training data showed that this approach yielded higher scores than an n-gram based approach, in which the successive grams of each verb were analyzed left and right.

3   Results and discussion

Table 1 below displays the results obtained for HMSid, our system that was officially sent to the PARSEME Shared Task 2020. As explained in section 2, HMSid relied on an external corpus and was therefore placed in the open track.

Table 2 shows the results obtained with HMSid2, using the same methodology but relying solely on the training data and the training corpus, and therefore belonging to the closed track. The results with HMSid2 were sent to the organizers of the Shared Task after the deadline.

System	Track	Unseen MWE-based				Global MWE-based				Global Token-based			
		P	R	F1	Rank	P	R	F1	Rank	P	R	F1	Rank
HMSid	open	27.73	53.33	**36.49**	4	63.85	67.84	**65.79**	5	66.4	67.81	**67.1**	5

Table 1: Global results obtained with HMSid at the PARSEME 2020 Shared Task (French).

---

[2] https://metacpan.org/pod/Data::Table

System	Track	Unseen MWE-based				Global MWE-based				Global Token-based			
		P	R	F1	Rank	P	R	F1	Rank	P	R	F1	Rank
HMSid2	closed	32.53	49.33	**39.21**	1	68.90	72.04	**70.43**	2	71.10	72.63	**71.86**	2

Table 2: Global results obtained with HMSid2 at the PARSEME 2020 Shared Task (French).

As shown in Table 1, HMSid obtained a global F1 (Token-based) of 67.1, which puts it in 5th position in the open track. It should be noted, however, that its F1-score on unseen MWEs (36.49) puts it in 4th position (and very close to the 3d one), while its recall for unseen French MWEs is the best of all systems, open or closed track (53.33). This is noteworthy, because HMSid (and HMSid2) do not try to reproduce recurrent patterns from the training set, but rely on statistical extraction from a large linguistic corpus. In other words, both systems do not try to reproduce decisions made by annotators, as reflected in the training set, but are looking for statistical patterns in a large linguistic corpus, regardless of the training set. Of course, the training set was used for fine-tuning the statistical thresholds and deciding whether a combination was a MWE or not, and the different categories (which are in itself debatable, such as the distinction between LVC.full and LVC.cause) were integrated into the statistical extraction. The recall score on unseen MWEs also provides additional evidence of the statistical nature of recurrent MWEs in large linguistic corpora.

This is even more obvious with HMSid2, which used exactly the same methodology, as explained in the above section, but relied on the training corpus provided by the Shared Task (part of the Wikipedia corpus), and would therefore be placed in the closed track. Among the 3 systems submitted to the closed track for French, HMSid2 would receive rank 2 for the global F1-score (MWE-based or Token-Based), and rank 1 for unseen MWEs, with an F1-score (39.21) far better than those obtained by the other systems in the closed track (with respectively 24.4 and 3.67). The best overall system officially submitted to the French closed track (Seen2Seen) has an F1-score of 3.67 for unseen MWEs.

The difference between precision and recall, especially for unseen MWEs, should also be relativized by the choices made in the training and gold set. In spite of the excellent quality of the PARSEME annotated dataset, decisions as to the idiomatic character of a MWE will never be unanimous. In the case of the French dataset, for instance, the notion of verbal idiom (VID) was taken strictly by the annotators, but there are a few notable exceptions. A number of less idiomatic constructions were also labeled as VIDs. For instance, *avoir lieu* (to take place), *il y a* (there is / there are), *mettre en pratique* (to put into practice), *tenir compte de* (take into account), are all considered French verbal idioms in the training data, a choice that may be respected but has consequences on the statistical extraction. The statistical metric indeed had to be more tolerant for weaker associations when assigning the label 'VID', which contributed to a fairly good recall but a slightly lower precision. This appears clearly in all results from Tables 1 and 2, and in particular for unseen MWEs. In this case, one should bear in mind that the algorithm is looking for recurrent patterns in the linguistic system itself, as there are no similar examples in the training set.

Many cases of verbal idioms from the gold set are quite obvious, such as *tourner le dos à* (turn one's back on, lines 5817-19 of the gold set), *il pleuvait des cordes* (it was raining cats and dogs, lines 7415-17) or *sortir le grand jeu* (pull out all the stop, lines 12129-32), all three labelled as VID and also recognized by the algorithm because of the very strong association between the grams: a *cpr-score* of resp. 0.92 / 0.88 / 0.94. In other cases, however, the algorithm and the annotators are at odds. In lines 5868-9, for instance, *rester silencieux* (remain silent, keep quiet) is not considered as MWE by the annotators, but the *cpr-score* contradicts this view: 0.81. The same holds true of many other examples, such as *trouver un compromis* (lines 14387-89), not considered as a MWE in the gold set, but displaying a *cpr-score* of 0.80. In this specific case, it should be reminded that native speakers are not always the best judges of the idiomaticity of their own language. It may be pretty obvious for speakers or French and of English that a compromise may be *found* but a quick look at other European languages reveals that this is far from being the case: in Spanish, for instance, the common construction is *llegar a un compromiso*.

It should also be pointed out that the methodology used for HMSid and HMSid2 is easily applicable to other languages. As a matter of fact, we have already implemented it as an experimental web tool[3], *IdiomSearch* for English, German, Spanish, French, Dutch and Chinese. Measuring associations based on the *cpr-score* is indeed possible for any language, provided that the necessary web corpus is compiled. The only caveat is the goal of the classification. The Parseme Shared Task 2020, as the previous editions, wanted the systems to target very specific categories of verbal expressions, whereas our experimental tool *IdiomSearch* looks for recurrent statistical associations, whatever the precise category may be. Fine-tuning the algorithm to specific categories expected by the gold set, and annotated as such by native speakers of the language requires sophisticated training algorithms such as those used in deep learning.

In conclusion, the most interesting results from HMSid and HMSid2 are those obtained for unseen MWEs. Due to the well-known phenomenon of overfitting, deep learning models often have problems with unseen data, which suggests that a hybrid approach combining deep learning and our model may be useful for future research.

References

Ricardo Baeza-Yates and Berthier Ribeiro-Neto. 1999. *Modern Information Retrieval*. ACM Press / Addison Wesley, New York.

Marco Baroni, Silvia Bernardini, Adriano Ferraresi and Eros Zanchetta. 2009. The WaCky Wide Web: A collection of very large linguistically processed Web-crawled corpora. *Journal of Language Resources and Evaluation*, 43: 209–226.

Colson. 2017. The IdiomSearch Experiment: Extracting Phraseology from a Probabilistic Network of Constructions. In Ruslan Mitkov (ed.), *Computational and Corpus-based phraseology, Lecture Notes in Artificial Intelligence 10596*. Springer International Publishing, Cham: 16–28.

Colson. 2018. From Chinese Word Segmentation to Extraction of Constructions: Two Sides of the Same Algorithmic Coin. In Agatha Savary et al. 2018: 41-50.

Zellig Harris. 1954. Distributional Structure. *Word*, 10(2-3):146–162.

Thomas Hoffmann and Graeme Trousdale (eds.). 2013. *The Oxford Handbook of Construction Grammar*. Oxford University Press, Oxford/New York.

Gabriella Lapesa and Stefan Evert. 2014. A large scale evaluation of distributional semantic models: Parameters, interactions and model selection. *Transactions of the Association for Computational Linguistics*, 2:531–545.

Agata Savary, Carlos Ramisch, Jena D. Hwang, Nathan Schneider, Melanie Andresen, Sameer Pradhan and Miriam R. L. Petruck (eds.). 2018. *Proceedings of the Joint Workshop on Linguistic Annotation, Multiword Expressions and Constructions, Coling 2018*, Santa Fe NM, USA, Association for Computational Linguistics.

John Sinclair. 1991. *Corpus, Concordance, Collocation*. Oxford, Oxford University Press.

---

[3] https://idiomsearch.lsti.ucl.ac.be

Seen2Unseen at PARSEME Shared Task 2020: All Roads do not Lead to Unseen Verb-Noun VMWEs

Caroline Pasquer
University of Tours, LIFAT
France
`first.last@etu.univ-tours.fr`

Agata Savary
University of Tours, LIFAT
France
`first.last@univ-tours.fr`

Carlos Ramisch
Aix Marseille Univ, Université de Toulon,
CNRS, LIS, Marseille, France
`first.last@lis-lab.fr`

Jean-Yves Antoine
University of Tours, LIFAT
France
`first.last@univ-tours.fr`

Abstract

We describe the Seen2Unseen system that participated in edition 1.2 of the PARSEME shared task on automatic identification of verbal multiword expressions (VMWEs). The identification of VMWEs that do not appear in the provided training corpora (called *unseen* VMWEs) – with a focus here on verb-noun VMWEs – is based on mutual information and lexical substitution or translation of *seen* VMWEs. We present the architecture of the system, report results for 14 languages, and propose an error analysis.

1 Introduction

The identification of multiword expressions (MWEs) such as ***spill the beans*** is a challenging problem (Baldwin and Kim, 2010; Constant et al., 2017), all the more so for verbal MWEs (VMWEs) subject to morphological (***spill the bean***) and syntactic variability (***the beans*** were ***spilled***). The PARSEME shared task (PST) provided training, development and test corpora (hereafter Train, Dev, and Test) manually annotated for VMWEs.[1] Our system aimed at identifying every VMWE in Test which also appears in Train or Dev, including possible morphological or syntactic variants (henceforth *seen* VMWEs) or not present in Train/Dev (*unseen* VMWEs). Unseen VMWE identification, the main focus of this PST edition, is harder than seen VMWE identification, as shown by previous results (Ramisch et al., 2018).

We submitted two systems: Seen2Seen (closed track) and Seen2Unseen (open track). Seen2Unseen relies on Seen2Seen for the identification of seen VMWEs and has an additional module for unseen ones. Its best global unseen F-score (i.e. not only for verb-noun constructions) was obtained for Hindi (42.66) and it reached 25.36 in French, which was our main focus. Despite the lower global MWE-based F1-score of Seen2Unseen (63.02) compared to Seen2Seen (66.23), we describe the former (Sec. 2), analyse its interesting negative results (Sec. 3), and conclude with ideas for future work (Sec. 4).

2 System Description

While describing the architecture of our system, we use the notions of a VMWE *token* (its occurrence in running text) and a VMWE *type* (abstraction over all occurrences of a given VMWE), as introduced by Savary et al. (2019b). We represent VMWE types as multisets of lemmas and POS.[2] Our system uses a mixture of discovery and identification methods, as defined by Constant et al. (2017). Namely, VMWE *discovery* consists in generating lists of MWE types out of context, while VMWE *identification* marks VMWE tokens in running text. The system is freely available online (`https://gitlab.com/cpasquer/st_2020`).

[1] `http://hdl.handle.net/11234/1-3367`

[2] VMWEs are represented as multisets (i.e. bags of elements with repetition allowed), since the same lemma and/or POS can occur twice, as in ***appeler un chat un chat*** '*to call a cat a cat*' ⇒ '*to call a spade a spade*'.

Joint Workshop on Multiword Expressions and Electronic Lexicons, pages 124–129
Barcelona, Spain (Online), December 13, 2020.

Seen2Seen in a nutshell Seen2Seen is a VMWE identification system dedicated to only those VMWEs which have been previously seen in the training data. Its detailed description is provided in Pasquer et al. (2020), but a brief overview is included here to make the current paper self-contained. Seen2Seen extracts lemma combinations of VMWEs seen in Train, looking for the same combinations (within one sentence) in Test, with an expected high recall. To improve precision, up to eight independent criteria can be used: (1) component lemmas should be disambiguated by their POS, (2) components should appear in specific orders (e.g. the determiner before the noun), (3) the order of "gap" words possibly occurring between components is also considered, (4) components should not be too far from each other in a sentence, (5) closer components are preferred over distant ones, (6) components should be syntactically connected, (7) nominal components should appear with a previously seen inflection, and (8) nested VMWEs should be annotated as in Train. We select the combination of criteria with maximal performance on Dev among all $2^8 = 256$ possibilities. The candidates remaining after applying the criteria are annotated as VMWEs. This relatively simple system relying on morphosyntactic filters and tuned for 8 parameters was evaluated on 11 languages of the PARSEME shared task 1.1 (Ramisch et al., 2018). Seen2Seen outperformed the best systems not only on seen (F=0.8276), but even on all seen and unseen VMWEs (F=0.6653).[3] In edition 1.2 of the PARSEME shared task, Seen2Seen scored best (out of 2) in the global ranking of the closed track and second (out of 9) across both tracks. It outperformed 6 other open track systems, notably those using complex neural architectures and contextual word embeddings. We believe that these competitive results are due to carefully taking the nature of VMWEs into account (Savary et al., 2019a). Since Seen2Seen, by design, does not account for unseen VMWEs, its score in this category is very low (F=1.12).[4] Therefore, it was later extended with a VMWE discovery module. Seen2Unseen is precisely this extended system. It relies on Seen2Seen for seen VMWEs and on discovery methods described below for unseen VMWEs.

From Seen2Seen to Seen2Unseen We assume that seen VMWEs could help identify unseen ones by using (i) lexical variation, tolerated by some VMWEs (e.g. *take a **bath/shower***), and (ii) translation, e.g. (FR) ***prendre décision*** 'take decision' = (PL) ***podejmować decyzję*** = (PT) ***tomar decisão*** = (SV) ***fatta beslut***.[5] We also expect seen and unseen VMWEs to share characteristics, such as the distance between components or their syntactic dependency relations, e.g. nouns often being objects of verbs. The categories that should benefit from our strategy are, mainly, light-verb constructions (LVCs) containing nouns and, in some cases, verbal idioms (VIDs). These categories are universal, so our method can be applied to the 14 languages of the PST. Since LVCs are often verb-noun pairs, Seen2Unseen quasi-exclusively focuses on them.[6] Consequently, we do not aim at exhaustively identifying unseen VMWEs, but at determining to what extent seen verb-noun VMWEs can help us discover new unseen ones.

Resources In addition to the PST Train, Dev and Test corpora, we used the CoNLL 2017 shared task parsed corpora, hereafter CoNLL-ST (Ginter et al., 2017).[7] The CoNLL-ST corpora were preferred over the PST-provided parsed corpora because they are conveniently released with pre-trained 100-dimensional word2vec embeddings for the 14 languages of the PST, which we used to generate lexical variants. Additionally, we used a free library to implement translation towards French and Italian.[8] We automatically translated all VMWEs in the other 13 languages into French (resp. Italian), privileged due to the availability of two Wikitionary-based lexicons in the same format for both languages.[9] These lexicons were used to lemmatize and POS-tag automatic translations, e.g. (PT) ***firmar contrato*** 'sign contract' $\xrightarrow{translation}$ (FR) *a **signé** un **contrat*** $\xrightarrow{lemma,POS}$ ***signer***$_{\text{VERB}}$ ***contrat***$_{\text{NOUN}}$.[10]

---

[3] In this paragraph we refer to macro-averaged MWE-based F-scores.

[4] The score is not null due to different implementations of unseen VMWEs in the evaluation script and in Seen2Seen.

[5] Languages are referred to with their PST identifier: e.g. FR for French.

[6] We also model inherently reflexive verbs with cranberry words, i.e. verbs which never occur without a reflexive pronoun, e.g. (FR) *s'évanouir* vs. **évanouir*. With 1 VMWE discovered in Portuguese and 3 in French, this module is omitted here.

[7] http://hdl.handle.net/11234/1-1989

[8] Googletrans: https://pypi.org/project/googletrans, implementing the Google Translate API.

[9] For French: http://redac.univ-tlse2.fr/lexicons/glaff_en.html, for Italian: http://redac.univ-tlse2.fr/lexiques/glaffit.html

[10] In case of multiple POS or lemmas, the most frequent verb-noun combination in CoNLL-ST was selected.

Unseen VMWE identification   To support identification of unseen VMWEs we use a combination of semi-supervised discovery and identification methods: lexical replacement, translation and statistical ranking. For a language L, let $SeenVN^L$ be the set of all seen LVC and VID types having exactly one verb and one noun (and any number of components with other POS tags). Let each type in $SeenVN^L$ be linked with its manually annotated occurrences in Train. This set is used in the following steps:

① *Lexical replacement*: The idea is to observe lexical variability of seen VMWEs and to generate on this basis new potential VMWEs. Let LVC^L_{Vvar} contain LVC types in $SeenVN^L$ that tolerate variation in verbs, e.g. **accomplir/effectuer**$_\text{VERB}$ **mission**$_\text{NOUN}$ 'fulfil/perform mission'. Similarly, let LVC^L_{Nvar} contain LVCs types with variation in nouns, e.g. **accomplir**$_\text{VERB}$ **mission/tâche**$_\text{NOUN}$ 'fulfil mission/task'. Then we define two sets of candidates:

- MIX^L combines each verb in LVC^L_{Vvar} with each noun in LVC^L_{Nvar} to predict new combinations. e.g. **effectuer tâche** 'perform task'.
- SIM^L contains VMWEs from LVC^L_{Vvar} (resp. LVC^L_{Nvar}) where we replace the verb (resp. noun) by its closest verb (resp. noun) according to cosine similarity in CoNLL-ST word embeddings.[11]

② *Translation*: By translating seen VMWE types in one language we obtain a list of VMWE type candidates in another language:

- $TRANS^L$ is built only for French and Italian, and is empty for other languages. $TRANS^{FR}$ (resp. $TRANS^{IT}$) contains automatic translations of each VMWE in $SeenVN^{L'}$, with $L' \neq$ FR (resp. $L' \neq$ IT), into French (resp. Italian). We eliminate translations which do not contain exactly one verb and one noun (and possible components of other POS), e.g. due to a wrong translation. For the remaining translations, we keep only the verb and the noun lemmas.

③ *Statistical ranking*: This approach is based on statistical characteristics of both seen VMWEs and unseen VMWE candidates. We first calculate 3 sets of features for the whole $SeenVN^L$ list:

- $Dist^L$ is the maximal verb-noun distance for all VMWE tokens occurring at least twice in $SeenVN^L$. This should help eliminate candidates whose components are too distant in a sentence.
- $P^L_{Dep}(Dep_V, Dep_N)$ is the ratio of VMWE tokens in $SeenVN^L$ in which the incoming dependencies of the verb and of the noun are Dep_V and Dep_N. For instance, $P^{FR}_{Dep}(root, obj)$ is higher than $P^{FR}_{Dep}(root, nsubj)$ because, in French, active voice (e.g. **rendre** une **visite** 'pay a visit') is more frequent than passive voice (e.g. **malediction** fut **lancée** 'curse was cast'). We thus favour the most commonly observed VMWE dependencies.
- $P^L_{Dist}(i)$ is the ratio of VMWE tokens in $SeenVN^L$ in which the number of words inserted between the verb and the noun is i. For instance, $P^{FR}_{Dist}(0) = 0.46$, i.e. occurrences in which the verb and the noun are contiguous represent 46% of $SeenVN^{FR}$. This ratio tends to decrease as i increases: $P^{FR}_{Dist}(2) = 0.11$, $P^{FR}_{Dist}(5) = 0.006$, etc. Candidates whose number of intervening words i has higher $P^L_{Dist}(i)$ likely are true VMWEs.

Given these characteristics of seen VMWEs, we proceed to extracting and ranking unseen VMWE candidates. Namely, $Cand^L$ is the list of all occurrences of verb-noun pairs in Test such that: (i) the verb and the noun are directly connected by a syntactic dependency, (ii) the distance between the verb and the noun does not exceed $Dist^L$, and (iii) the verb and the noun never co-occur with a direct dependency link in Train or in Dev. The latter condition excludes both seen VMWEs (already covered by Seen2Seen) and verb-noun constructions not annotated as VMWEs in Train or Dev, i.e. being no VMWEs, e.g. (FR) *avoir an* 'have year' in *elle a quinze ans* 'she is 15 years old'. $Cand^L$ is then ranked by considering statistical properties. For each candidate c in $Cand^L$, we calculate three measures:

- $P(c)$ is the estimated joint dependency- and distance-based probability. Suppose that i is the number of words inserted between c's verb and noun, and their incoming dependencies are Dep_V and Dep_N, respectively. Then, $P(c) = P^L_{Dep}(Dep_V, Dep_N) \times P^L_{Dist}(i)$.

---

[11]In this way, we limit the lexical replacement to only these components whose variability within VMWEs is attested in Train. We previously applied this method to all seen VMWEs but the results were too noisy.

List	DE	EL	EU	FR	GA	HE	HI
MIX^L	0 (0)	0.31 (42)	0.34 (41)	0.57 (21)	0 (0)	0 (0)	0 (0)
SIM^L	0 (0)	0 (0)	0.45 (11)	0.17 (6)	0 (0)	0 (0)	0 (0)
$RANK^L$	0.19 (101)	0.05 (228)	0.09 (329)	0.19 (159)	0.21 (137)	0.04 (129)	0.46 (273)

List	IT	PL	PT	RO	SV	TR	ZH
MIX^L	0 (0)	0.40 (20)	0.29 (35)	0 (0)	0 (2)	0.48 (21)	0.29 (7)
SIM^L	0 (0)	0.33 (3)	0.20 (20)	0 (0)	0 (0)	0.33 (6)	0 (0)
$RANK^L$	0.11 (163)	0.14 (164)	0.08 (225)	0.03 (422)	0.21 (100)	0.15 (214)	0 (32)

Table 1: Unseen MWE-based precision (and number of predicted VMWEs) in Test for the 14 languages L, when using only MIX^L, SIM^L or $RANK^L$ lists.

- $AMI(c)$ is the augmented mutual information of c's type in the CoNLL-ST corpus. MWEs are known to have a Zipfian distribution and to often mix very frequent words with very rare ones. AMI is designed specifically to address this phenomenon, so as to leverage the rarely occurring expressions or components (Zhang et al., 2009): $AMI(x, y) = log_2 \frac{P(x,y)}{P(x)P(y)(1 - \frac{P(x,y)}{P(x)})(1 - \frac{P(x,y)}{P(y)})}$

- $RR(c)$ is the reciprocal rank combining the two indicators above. Let $rank_P(c)$ and $rank_{AMI}(c)$ be the ranks of c in $Cand^L$ according to the values of $P(c)$ and $AMI(c)$ with $P(c) > 0$ and $AMI(c) > 0$. Then $RR(c) = \frac{1}{rank_P(c)} + \frac{1}{rank_{AMI}(c)}$.

$Cand^L$ is then ranked by $RR(c)$. We keep n top-ranked candidates, where n is estimated by scaling the number (provided the organizers) of VIDs and LVCs in Test – when all the expressions annotated as seen during the Seen2Seen phase have been eliminated – by the recall of our method on Dev on the target constructions (unseen verb-noun LVCs and VIDs).[12] This n-best list is called $RANK_n^L$.

④ *Identification proper*: In step ③ we obtain a list of unseen VMWE candidate tokens $Cand_L$ extracted from Test. The aim of identification is to discriminate among true and false VMWEs on this list. Statistical ranking and retaining top-n candidates is one possible statistically-based criterion. But we hypothesise that some candidates whose rank is worse than n, notably due to data sparseness, can still be correct if they result from lexical replacement or translation of seen VMWEs. Therefore, every c in $Cand^L$ is annotated as an LVC if c belongs to $RANK_n^L$ or if c's type belongs to $MIX^L \cup SIM^L \cup TRANS^L$.

3   Results

Although Seen2Unseen uses 4 lists of candidates, here we analyse their contribution separately, that is, we use one list at a time in step ④ above. We report unseen MWE/token-based precision.[13] Sec. 3.1 analyses the impact of MIX^L, SIM^L and $RANK_n^L$, while Sec. 3.2 discusses $TRANS^L$ for French.

3.1   Impact of MIX^L, SIM^L and $RANK_n^L$

As shown in Table 1, using MIX^L alone leads to precision values above 0.29 for 7 languages out of 14. Conversely, $RANK^L$ alone mostly leads to values below 0.22 (except for Hindi with $P = 0.46$). The precision using SIM^L alone reaches a maximum of 0.45 for Basque. The error analysis below suggests ways to improve precision.

In French, using MIX^{FR} alone yields 21 candidates in Test. Among the 5 false positives, there is one literal reading (*faire dessin* 'make drawing'), one omitted VMWE (***recevoir aide*** 'receive help') and three other verb-noun pairs that could have been disregarded (being coincidental occurrences) if we had taken into account not only the existence of the syntactic dependency but also its nature (e.g. *nous avons*$_{\text{VERB}}$ *cinq points à l'ordre*$_{\text{NOUN.xcomp}}$ *du jour* 'we have five items on the agenda').

This major problem for MIX^L is shared by SIM^L, but a specific drawback with SIM^L is that not all words that occur in similar contexts are actually similar. Indeed, we obtain relevant generated unseen

---

[12] When the proportion of VIDs and LVCs in Test is unknown, it can be approximated by the analogous proportion in Dev.

[13] Shortly before submitting the final version of this paper the definition of a seen VMWE was updated by the PST organizers. Initially, a VMWE from Test was considered seen if a VMWE with the same (multi-)set of lemmas was annotated at least once in Train. Now, it is considered seen if it is annotated in Train or in Dev. In this paper we report on the evaluation results conforming to the previous definition. The change in definition probably (slightly) impacts the results on seen VMWEs but does not impact the general scores (cf. Sec. 1).

verb-noun pairs, including synonyms, antonyms and hyponyms, but also irrelevant ones. We should therefore either use more reliable resources, such as synonym/antonym dictionaries, and/or disregard frequent verbs (*to have, to do*, etc.). For these frequent verbs, the more reliable equivalences obtained by MIX^L compared to SIM^L should be preferred (*faire* 'do' $\overset{MIX^{FR}}{\approx}$ *subir* 'suffer' vs. *faire* 'do' $\overset{SIM^{FR}}{\approx}$ *passer* 'pass'). Indeed, as shown in Table 1, over 5 languages with MIX^L and SIM^L candidates, 4 exhibit a better precision and higher number of candidates for MIX^L.

In French, by dividing n by 4 in $RANK_n^{FR}$, the precision would have increased from 0.19 to 0.45 (18 VMWEs over 40 candidates). In other words, using $RANK_n^L$ in step ④ can slightly increase recall but causes a drop in precision, unless n is low. Hindi appears as an exception: no negative impact is observed with $RANK_n^{HI}$ due to a bias in the corpora (*compound* mentioned in the dependency label).

3.2 Impact of $TRANS^L$: (IT) *Traduttore, traditore* 'translator, traitor'?

With translational equivalences, we hypothesized that $TRANS^L$ would lead to situations such as:

- exact matches: (PT) **cometer crime** 'commit a crime' → (FR) **commettre crime** ,
- partial matches leading to VMWEs nonetheless: (PT) **causar problema** 'cause problem' → (FR) **causer ennui**, instead of **causer problème**,
- no match, but another VMWE: (PT) **ter destaque** 'highlight' → (FR) **mettre en évidence**.
- literal, non-fluent or ambiguous translations (Constant et al., 2017): (PT) **jogar o toalha** 'throw the towel' ⇒'give up' → (FR) *jeter la serviette* instead of **jeter l'éponge** 'throw the sponge',
- non-existing VMWEs in the target language: (TR) **el atma** → (FR) *lancer main* 'throw hand'

We focus on French due to the high number of candidates in $TRANS^{FR}$. In Test-FR, among the 44 annotated verb-noun candidates using $TRANS^{FR}$ alone, 18 are actually VMWEs and 3 partially correspond to VMWEs due to omitted determiners, yielding an unseen MWE-based precision of 0.41 and an unseen token-based precision value of 0.48. These 21 candidates are mainly provided by Greek (10 vs. 6 from PT and 0 from IT or RO). Thus, the size of the training corpora may have more influence on the probability to obtain good translations than the source language family.

The 23 false positives include (i) 13 candidates that can be VMWEs or not depending on the context, including coincidental co-occurrences, literal readings and errors in the manually annotated reference Test corpus, and (ii) 10 candidates that are not VMWEs, whatever the context, e.g. the inchoative *commencer recherche* 'start research' (from Hebrew) or *payer taxe* 'pay tax'(from (PL) **uiszczać opłatę**).

Consequently, translation may be a clue to discover unseen VMWEs, since 78% of $Cand^{FR} \cap TRANS^{FR}$ are VMWEs out of context, but barely half of them were manually annotated in context. As highlighted above, a restriction to the most frequent VMWE syntactic relations could help filter out coincidental occurrences corresponding to 39% of false positives (e.g. *lancer la balle à la main*$_{\text{OBL:MOD}}$ 'throw the ball with the hand').

4 Conclusions and Future Work

We proposed an error analysis for our system Seen2Unseen dedicated to unseen verb-noun VMWE identification. It reveals that lexical variation and translation can produce valid unseen VMWEs but their ambiguity in context must be solved: we should take into account both the dependency labels (to avoid coincidental occurrences) and the probability of the verb to be light in Train (to avoid frequent co-ocurrences like *fumer cigarette* 'smoke cigarette'). Using contextual rather than non-contextual word embeddings might also be helpful, even if computationally more intensive. We could also combine $TRANS^L$ and $MIX^L \cup SIM^L$ by applying lexical substitution to the translated VMWEs.

Acknowledgements

This work was funded by the French PARSEME-FR grant (ANR-14-CERA-0001). We are grateful to Guillaume Vidal for his prototype, and to the anonymous reviewers for their useful comments.

References

Timothy Baldwin and Su Nam Kim. 2010. Multiword expressions. In Nitin Indurkhya and Fred J. Damerau, editors, *Handbook of Natural Language Processing*, pages 267–292. CRC Press, Taylor and Francis Group, Boca Raton, FL, USA, 2 edition.

Mathieu Constant, Gülşen Eryiğit, Johanna Monti, Lonneke van der Plas, Carlos Ramisch, Michael Rosner, and Amalia Todirascu. 2017. Multiword expression processing: A survey. *Computational Linguistics*, 43(4):837–892.

Filip Ginter, Jan Hajič, Juhani Luotolahti, Milan Straka, and Daniel Zeman. 2017. CoNLL 2017 shared task - automatically annotated raw texts and word embeddings. LINDAT/CLARIAH-CZ digital library at the Institute of Formal and Applied Linguistics (ÚFAL), Faculty of Mathematics and Physics, Charles University.

Caroline Pasquer, Agata Savary, Carlos Ramisch, and Jean-Yves Antoine. 2020. Verbal multiword expression identification: Do we need a sledgehammer to crack a nut? In *Proceedings of the Joint Workshop on Multiword Expressions and Electronic Lexicons (MWE-LEX 2020)*, online, December. Association for Computational Linguistics.

Carlos Ramisch, Silvio Ricardo Cordeiro, Agata Savary, Veronika Vincze, Verginica Barbu Mititelu, Archna Bhatia, Maja Buljan, Marie Candito, Polona Gantar, Voula Giouli, Tunga Güngör, Abdelati Hawwari, Uxoa Iñurrieta, Jolanta Kovalevskaitė, Simon Krek, Timm Lichte, Chaya Liebeskind, Johanna Monti, Carla Parra Escartín, Behrang QasemiZadeh, Renata Ramisch, Nathan Schneider, Ivelina Stoyanova, Ashwini Vaidya, and Abigail Walsh. 2018. Edition 1.1 of the PARSEME Shared Task on Automatic Identification of Verbal Multiword Expressions. In *Proceedings of the Joint Workshop on Linguistic Annotation, Multiword Expressions and Constructions (LAW-MWE-CxG-2018)*, pages 222–240. ACL. `https://aclweb.org/anthology/W18-4925`.

Agata Savary, Silvio Cordeiro, and Carlos Ramisch. 2019a. Without lexicons, multiword expression identification will never fly: A position statement. In *Proceedings of the Joint Workshop on Multiword Expressions and WordNet (MWE-WN 2019)*, pages 79–91, Florence, Italy, August. Association for Computational Linguistics.

Agata Savary, Silvio Ricardo Cordeiro, Timm Lichte, Carlos Ramisch, Uxoa I nurrieta, and Voula Giouli. 2019b. Literal Occurrences of Multiword Expressions: Rare Birds That Cause a Stir. *The Prague Bulletin of Mathematical Linguistics*, 112:5–54, April.

Wen Zhang, Taketoshi Yoshida, Tu Bao Ho, and Xijin Tang. 2009. Augmented mutual information for multi-word extraction. *International Journal of Innovative Computing, Information and Control*, 5(2):543–554.

ERMI at PARSEME Shared Task 2020: Embedding-Rich Multiword Expression Identification

Zeynep Yirmibeşoğlu and Tunga Güngör
Boğaziçi University
Department of Computer Engineering
34342 Bebek, Istanbul, Turkey
{zeynep.yirmibesoglu, gungort}@boun.edu.tr

Abstract

This paper describes the ERMI system submitted to the closed track of the PARSEME shared task 2020 on automatic identification of verbal multiword expressions (VMWEs). ERMI is an embedding-rich bidirectional LSTM-CRF model, which takes into account the embeddings of the word, its POS tag, dependency relation, and its head word. The results are reported for 14 languages, where the system is ranked 1st in the general cross-lingual ranking of the closed track systems, according to the Unseen MWE-based F_1.

1 Introduction

Multiword expressions (MWEs) are lexical items that consist of multiple lexemes. The challenge of identifying MWEs comes from the fact that their properties cannot directly be deducted from the lexical, syntactic, semantic, pragmatic, and statistical properties of their components (Baldwin and Kim, 2010). Addressing this challenge, the PARSEME shared task 2020 is a campaign that encourages the development of automatic verbal MWE (VMWE) identification models in a multilingual context. In this third edition of the PARSEME shared task, the focus is on identifying VMWEs that are unseen in training data. For this task, dev, test, train and raw corpora have been provided for 14 languages.

ERMI (Embedding-Rich Multiword expression Identification) is a multilingual system with a bidirectional LSTM-CRF architecture, which can take as input the embeddings of the word, its POS tag, dependency relation, and its head word. Since the main focus of the shared task is to identify unseen VMWEs, we experiment with how the addition of the head word embedding affects the prediction results for different languages. In addition, we also take advantage of the raw corpora in a semi-supervised teacher-student neural model carrying the same LSTM-CRF architecture for two languages (EL, TR). We use no external resources in the training of our system, thus participating in the closed track.

The results for all 14 languages in the closed track have been submitted where language-specific combinations of the above-mentioned embeddings have been used as input to the system. The system has been ranked 1st in the general cross-lingual ranking of the closed track systems for the Unseen MWE-based F_1, and 2nd for the Global MWE-based and Global Token-based F_1 metrics.

2 System Description

Named entity recognition (NER) and MWE detection can be considered similar tasks, thus encouraging similar architectures. Neural models have been preferred frequently for NER (Lample et al., 2016; Güngör et al., 2019), and for detecting VMWEs in the previous edition of PARSEME (Ehren et al., 2018; Boros and Burtica, 2018; Berk et al., 2018; Taslimipoor and Rohanian, 2018; Stodden et al., 2018; Zampieri et al., 2018).

In order to detect VMWEs, we develop a system[1] consisting of three (two supervised, one semi-supervised) neural network models, all of which carrying the same, bidirectional LSTM-CRF architecture, as proposed by Huang et al. (2015) for sequence tagging tasks. All models consist of three layers:

---

[1]ERMI is freely available at https://github.com/zeynepyirmibes/ERMI

Joint Workshop on Multiword Expressions and Electronic Lexicons, pages 130–135
Barcelona, Spain (Online), December 13, 2020.

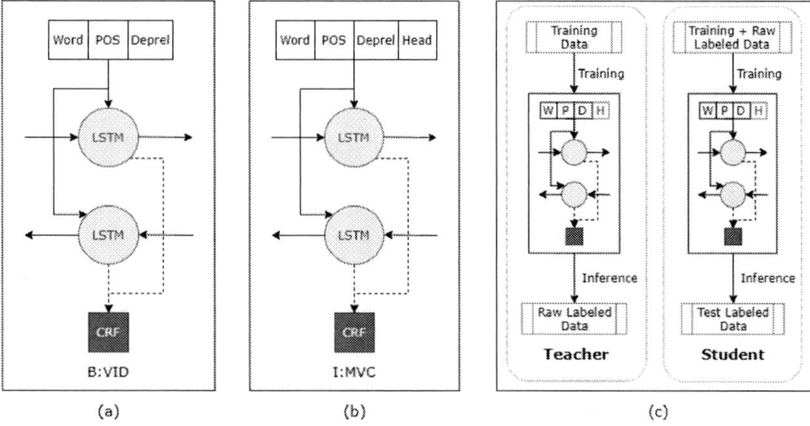

Figure 1: Our bi-LSTM-CRF models (**a**) ERMI; (**b**) ERMI-head; and (**c**) TeachERMI. For TeachERMI, the input layer may or may not contain the head word embedding, decided according to validation results per language.

the input layer, LSTM layer, and CRF layer, implemented using Keras (Chollet and others, 2015) with Tensorflow backend (Abadi et al., 2015). The architecture of each model is shown in Figure 1.

The input of our neural networks is an embedding layer, where we provide the model with the concatenation of the embeddings of the word, its POS tag, its dependency relation to the head, and the head of the word (for some languages). We do not use a pre-trained word embedding model. Instead, we exploit the provided raw corpora [2], which are gathered specifically for this task and are in the same domain as the annotated corpora[3]; and train FastText word embedding models for each of the 14 languages separately, using Gensim's Fasttext implementation (Řehůřek and Sojka, 2010). The embedding vector dimension for all languages is 300 (for word and head word embeddings), whereas the vocabulary size of the embedding models vary due to different sizes of raw corpora. Due to computational limitations, we only use a portion of the raw corpora for FR, PL and SV languages.

2.1 Supervised ERMI

We develop two supervised neural models (ERMI, and ERMI-head) differing only in the input layer. For the input (embedding) layer, word and head word embeddings each of dimension 300 are extracted from the Fasttext embedding models that we pretrained from the raw corpora. Dependency relation and POS tag embeddings are represented as one-hot encodings, and then converted into embeddings during training. Hence, the dimension of the dependency relation embedding for each language is the number of unique DEPREL tags encountered in the training data plus one, for unknown tags in the test data. The same logic holds for the POS tag embedding.

For our basic ERMI model, we use as input the concatenation of the embeddings of the word (CoNLL-U's FORM), its POS tag (UPOS), and its dependency relation to the head word (DEPREL). For our second supervised model, ERMI-head, we also concatenate the embedding of the head of the word (CoNLL-U's HEAD) to the input layer, in order to incorporate the relationship the word has to its dependent word, which, as we observe for some languages (EU, FR, HE, HI, PL, TR), aids in the decision of whether a word is to be annotated as part of a VMWE.

Differing only in the input layer, both models pass the input features to the bidirectional LSTM layer, where past (via forward LSTM states) and future (via backward LSTM states) information are taken into account. The output of the LSTM layer is then passed to the CRF layer, which connects consecutive output layers to produce the final output. With this approach, we incorporate both past and future information using the bi-LSTM architecture, and also the sentence level tag information using the CRF

---

[2] http://hdl.handle.net/11234/1-3416
[3] http://hdl.handle.net/11234/1-3367

layer.

2.2 Semi-supervised ERMI

In the third edition of PARSEME, raw (unlabeled) corpora are provided for all languages, thus enabling the possibility of semi-supervised learning. Hence, we exploit a portion of the raw corpus in addition to the annotated training corpus, and propose a teacher-student model (TeachERMI). The aim is to be able to also train on unlabeled data, as suggested by Wu et al. (2020), where they train a teacher-student cross-lingual Named Entity Recognition (NER) model.

In this approach, we first train a teacher model for every language separately, on the labeled training set. The teacher model is one of ERMI, or ERMI-head, depending on the validation results per language. Afterwards, we take a portion of the unlabeled raw corpus (corresponding to the half of the size of the training corpus for that language), and label it using the teacher model that we trained. Then, we combine the annotated training corpus with the raw corpus labeled by the teacher model, and train a student model. We observe that this approach only performs better than the teacher model (ERMI or ERMI-head) for Greek (EL) and Turkish (TR). Thus, we employ this approach (TeachERMI) for only two languages.

3 Experimental Setup

Tagging Scheme: During pre-processing, we adopt the bigappy-unicrossy tagging scheme proposed by Berk et al. (2019) to better represent overlapping (nesting and crossing) and discontinuous MWEs.

Datasets: During the validation runs (results of which are explained in Section 4.1), we concatenate the training and development corpora for each language, and randomly split 90% for training and 10% for testing. For the teacher-student model, we also use a portion of the raw corpora (roughly half the size of the training sets). After selecting the best system (out of ERMI, ERMI-head, and TeachERMI) for each language, we train our final models using the combined training and development sets, and use the blind test data for testing. For Turkish (TR) and Greek (EL), we develop a teacher-student model, using 10,796 and 9,510 sentences, respectively, of the provided raw corpora in addition to the development and training sets.

Hyperparameters: We choose the mini batch size and number of epochs with respect to the size of training sets for each language (ref. Table 1). We limit the mini batch size between 8-32, drawn from the conclusions of Reimers and Gurevych (2017), where they experiment with five sequence tagging tasks with LSTM architectures, and deduct the optimal mini batch size for large training corpora. We use a fixed dropout rate of 0.1 for all bi-LSTM layers.

4 Results and Discussion

We make validation runs on the training and development data, and compare our three neural models for each language. Afterwards, we report the official results of the selected systems on the blind test set.

4.1 Validation Results

The validation results of our three systems (ERMI, ERMI-head, TeachERMI) are compared for all languages, and the best-performing system (with respect to Unseen MWE-based, Global MWE-based, and Global Token-based F_1) for each language is selected for the final submission. In Table 1, we report the validation results together with the hyperparameters used during training.

For us, the most interesting part of evaluating the validation runs is the comparison between ERMI and ERMI-head. We observe that the addition of head word embeddings to the input layer improves the Unseen MWE-based F_1 score significantly for the EU, FR, HE, HI, PL and TR languages (4.98% on average for these languages). We also have the opportunity to observe that the teacher-student model enables the enlargement of the training corpus by around 50%, thus enabling better generalization for EL and TR.

	System	Batch Size	Epochs	Unseen MWE-based F_1	Global MWE-based F_1	Global Token-based F_1		System	Batch Size	Epochs	Unseen MWE-based F_1	Global MWE-based F_1	Global Token-based F_1
DE	**ERMI**	16	20	**21.93**	**52.59**	**57.51**	IT	**ERMI**	16	15	17.18	**43.12**	**44.73**
	ERMI-head			20.49	47.27	55.13		ERMI-head			7.74	31.63	33.96
	TeachERMI			21.89	48.70	53.71		TeachERMI			**18.40**	38.40	40.35
EL	ERMI	32	20	30.77	60.07	**66.02**	PL	ERMI	32	20	25.45	69.94	72.13
	ERMI-head			30.51	55.13	59.76		**ERMI-head**			**32.03**	**70.85**	**72.23**
	TeachERMI			**33.33**	**60.11**	64.82		TeachERMI			22.97	63.61	64.57
EU	ERMI	16	15	39.39	77.55	80.12	PT	ERMI	32	20	22.64	**57.89**	**58.23**
	ERMI-head			**42.42**	**77.81**	**80.50**		ERMI-head			**25.59**	53.57	55.18
	TeachERMI			28.57	69.16	72.01		TeachERMI			21.05	54.12	54.16
FR	ERMI	32	20	24.83	59.62	**66.31**	RO	ERMI	16	15	24.24	**82.88**	**84.38**
	ERMI-head			**27.18**	**62.75**	66.15		ERMI-head			**28.57**	80.57	81.20
	TeachERMI			20.39	57.39	63.10		TeachERMI			27.91	81.85	83.59
GA	**ERMI**	8	12	**4.82**	**9.80**	**27.23**	SV	**ERMI**	8	12	**30.23**	**60.16**	**60.41**
	ERMI-head			2.27	1.92	23.08		ERMI-head			25.00	55.85	58.26
	TeachERMI			~0	~0	~0		TeachERMI			27.50	51.33	50.28
HE	ERMI	32	20	10.67	**27.87**	31.02	TR	ERMI	32	20	42.86	64.95	64.92
	ERMI-head			**14.18**	27.19	**34.65**		ERMI-head			45.71	65.98	66.50
	TeachERMI			7.21	13.04	11.76		**TeachERMI**			**52.25**	**67.32**	**68.72**
HI	ERMI	8	12	42.11	54.84	69.35	ZH	**ERMI**	32	20	**42.99**	**62.39**	**66.67**
	ERMI-head			**53.66**	**63.64**	**74.63**		ERMI-head			39.30	59.43	63.83
	TeachERMI			35.90	53.12	70.97		TeachERMI			39.44	59.61	61.96

Table 1: Validation results and hyperparameters of our three models for each language.

		Unseen MWE-based				Global MWE-based				Global Token-based			
Language	System	P	R	F1	Rank	P	R	F1	Rank	P	R	F1	Rank
DE	ERMI	24.02	20.27	21.98	1	63.23	44.66	52.35	2	76.14	42.66	54.68	2
EL	TeachERMI	28.70	31.00	29.81	1	67.20	56.16	61.19	2	75.19	58.82	66.00	2
EU	ERMI-head	21.13	37.33	26.99	1	75.95	70.35	73.04	2	80.10	72.25	75.97	2
FR	ERMI-head	18.54	35.67	24.40	1	61.52	61.30	61.41	2	70.86	65.53	68.09	2
GA	ERMI	14.79	6.98	9.48	1	32.62	13.99	19.58	2	69.71	21.15	32.45	1
HE	ERMI-head	11.49	6.62	8.40	1	41.81	24.85	31.17	2	46.72	26.22	33.59	2
HI	ERMI-head	37.09	41.67	39.25	1	63.48	56.32	59.69	1	79.48	62.00	69.66	1
IT	ERMI	17.44	10.00	12.71	1	66.27	32.75	43.84	2	75.45	32.55	45.48	2
PL	ERMI-head	23.28	29.24	25.92	1	73.92	64.91	69.12	2	77.87	65.86	71.36	2
PT	ERMI	24.63	33.33	28.33	1	68.84	59.46	63.81	2	73.62	58.80	65.38	2
RO	ERMI	16.45	30.10	21.28	1	85.67	81.57	83.57	1	88.69	82.97	85.74	1
SV	ERMI	31.16	28.67	29.86	1	72.68	55.73	63.08	2	77.24	52.53	62.53	2
TR	TeachERMI	37.28	35.67	36.46	1	67.11	61.86	64.38	1	69.11	62.42	65.60	1
ZH	ERMI	47.49	34.67	40.08	1	66.67	55.98	60.86	1	70.92	58.99	64.41	1
Total		25.25	27.23	26.20	1	64.78	52.85	58.21	2	73.65	54.48	62.63	2

Table 2: Official Language-specific Results of ERMI

4.2 Test Results

We evaluate the validation runs (Table 1), and train the ERMI system for DE, GA, IT, PT, RO, SV and ZH languages; the ERMI-head system for EU, FR, HE, HI, and PL languages. For Turkish (TR), we train TeachERMI using the ERMI-head input layer (including the head word embedding), and for Greek (EL), we train TeachERMI using the ERMI input layer (excluding the head word embedding), judging from these languages' validation results. Having selected the most appropriate system for each language, we present the official results in the closed track for all 14 languages on the blind test data in Table 2.

4.3 Discussion

We have been able to observe from the validation results that the addition of head word embeddings to the input layer significantly aided in detecting unseen VMWEs for EU, FR, HE, HI, PL and TR. In order to observe the effect of head word embeddings on VMWE detection in the final test set, we removed the head word embeddings from the input layer for one of those languages (EU), and obtained a 24.64% Unseen MWE-based F1 score from the ERMI model, as compared to the 26.99% that we've obtained in the official results with ERMI-head.

For DE, GA, IT, PT, RO, SV and ZH, our ERMI model (without head word embeddings in the input layer) performed better than ERMI-head and TeachERMI during the validation runs. To examine this phenomenon in the blind test set, we also trained the ERMI-head system for one of those languages (IT). The 43.84% Global MWE-based F1 score of ERMI for IT drops to 36.88% when head-word embeddings are added to the input layer.

Analyzing the presence and absence of head-word embeddings in the embedding layer for each language, we deduct that feeding a language-specific input layer to the neural models increased our overall performance. Using also the raw corpora for EL and TR languages with the teacher-student model, we have been able to benefit from training on unlabeled data, which may be preferable for low resource scenarios. For TR, the validation results show the superiority of ERMI-head over ERMI, and of TeachERMI over ERMI-head. Hence, the final system for Turkish is TeachERMI with the ERMI-head input layer. We also run ERMI-head for the final test set, where we obtain a Global MWE-based F1 score of %63.47, whereas the official score of TeachERMI for TR is %64.38, showing us the benefit of using the teacher-student model for this language.

When we look at the performance of our system for the MWE-based F1 score per VMWE category, we can see that our system outperforms the other closed track system in the LVC.full category for HI, TR and ZH, and is ranked 2nd among all seven (open and closed track) systems for HI. Our system also predicts MVCs better than other systems that submitted their results for IT and PT.

Our overall system ranked 1st among 2 systems in the closed track, and 3rd among 9 systems in both open and closed tracks with respect to Unseen MWE-based F1, which was the focus of this edition of PARSEME. It is worth noting that, although we did not make use of any external resources (participating in the closed track), we outperformed most of the systems in the open track that exploit such resources. Our system also ranked 1st in the closed track for the HI, RO, TR and ZH languages in the Global MWE-based F1 metric and 5th for all 14 languages among all systems in the Global MWE-based and Token-based F1 metric.

5   Conclusion

In this paper we proposed an embedding-rich bidirectional LSTM-CRF system. In addition to word, POS and dependency relation embeddings, we exploited head word embeddings, especially to tackle the issue of predicting unseen VMWEs. Within the closed track, we have used the raw corpora to train word embeddings, as well as proposing a semi-supervised teacher-student model, providing the opportunity of training on unlabeled data for VMWE identification. These methods have increased the generalisation power, enabling our system to perform best in predicting unseen VMWEs in the closed track.

Acknowledgements

The numerical calculations reported in this paper were partially performed at TUBITAK ULAKBIM, High Performance and Grid Computing Center (TRUBA resources).

References

Martín Abadi, Ashish Agarwal, Paul Barham, Eugene Brevdo, Zhifeng Chen, Craig Citro, Greg S. Corrado, Andy Davis, Jeffrey Dean, Matthieu Devin, Sanjay Ghemawat, Ian Goodfellow, Andrew Harp, Geoffrey Irving, Michael Isard, Yangqing Jia, Rafal Jozefowicz, Lukasz Kaiser, Manjunath Kudlur, Josh Levenberg, Dandelion Mané, Rajat Monga, Sherry Moore, Derek Murray, Chris Olah, Mike Schuster, Jonathon Shlens, Benoit Steiner, Ilya Sutskever, Kunal Talwar, Paul Tucker, Vincent Vanhoucke, Vijay Vasudevan, Fernanda Viégas, Oriol Vinyals, Pete Warden, Martin Wattenberg, Martin Wicke, Yuan Yu, and Xiaoqiang Zheng. 2015. TensorFlow: Large-scale machine learning on heterogeneous systems. Software available from tensorflow.org.

Timothy Baldwin and Su Nam Kim. 2010. Multiword expressions. In Nitin Indurkhya and Fred J. Damerau, editors, *Handbook of Natural Language Processing, Second Edition*, pages 267–292. CRC Press, Taylor and Francis Group, Boca Raton, FL. ISBN 978-1420085921.

Gözde Berk, Berna Erden, and Tunga Güngör. 2018. Deep-BGT at PARSEME shared task 2018: Bidirectional LSTM-CRF model for verbal multiword expression identification. In *Proceedings of the Joint Workshop on Linguistic Annotation, Multiword Expressions and Constructions (LAW-MWE-CxG-2018)*, pages 248–253, Santa Fe, New Mexico, USA, August. ACL.

Gözde Berk, Berna Erden, and Tunga Güngör. 2019. Representing overlaps in sequence labeling tasks with a novel tagging scheme: bigappy-unicrossy. In Alexander Gelbukh, editor, *20th International Conference on Computational Linguistics and Intelligent Text Processing (CICLing)*, La Rochelle, France.

Tiberiu Boros and Ruxandra Burtica. 2018. GBD-NER at PARSEME shared task 2018: Multi-word expression detection using bidirectional long-short-term memory networks and graph-based decoding. In *Proceedings of the Joint Workshop on Linguistic Annotation, Multiword Expressions and Constructions (LAW-MWE-CxG-2018)*, pages 254–260, Santa Fe, New Mexico, USA, August. ACL.

François Chollet et al. 2015. Keras. `https://keras.io`.

Rafael Ehren, Timm Lichte, and Younes Samih. 2018. Mumpitz at PARSEME shared task 2018: A bidirectional LSTM for the identification of verbal multiword expressions. In *Proceedings of the Joint Workshop on Linguistic Annotation, Multiword Expressions and Constructions (LAW-MWE-CxG-2018)*, pages 261–267, Santa Fe, New Mexico, USA, August. ACL.

Onur Güngör, Tunga Gungor, and Suzan Uskudarli. 2019. The effect of morphology in named entity recognition with sequence tagging. *Natural Language Engineering*, 25:147–169, 01.

Zhiheng Huang, Wei Xu, and Kai Yu. 2015. Bidirectional LSTM-CRF models for sequence tagging. *arXiv preprint arXiv:1508.01991*.

Guillaume Lample, Miguel Ballesteros, Sandeep Subramanian, Kazuya Kawakami, and Chris Dyer. 2016. Neural architectures for named entity recognition. In *Proceedings of the 2016 Conference of the North American Chapter of the Association for Computational Linguistics: Human Language Technologies*, pages 260–270, San Diego, California, June. ACL.

Radim Řehůřek and Petr Sojka. 2010. Software framework for topic modelling with large corpora. In *Proceedings of the LREC 2010 Workshop on New Challenges for NLP Frameworks*, pages 45–50, Valletta, Malta, May. ELRA.

Nils Reimers and Iryna Gurevych. 2017. Reporting score distributions makes a difference: Performance study of LSTM-networks for sequence tagging. In *Proceedings of the 2017 Conference on Empirical Methods in Natural Language Processing*, pages 338–348, Copenhagen, Denmark, September. ACL.

Regina Stodden, Behrang QasemiZadeh, and Laura Kallmeyer. 2018. TRAPACC and TRAPACCS at PARSEME shared task 2018: Neural transition tagging of verbal multiword expressions. In *Proceedings of the Joint Workshop on Linguistic Annotation, Multiword Expressions and Constructions (LAW-MWE-CxG-2018)*, pages 268–274, Santa Fe, New Mexico, USA, August. ACL.

Shiva Taslimipoor and Omid Rohanian. 2018. SHOMA at parseme shared task on automatic identification of VMWEs: Neural multiword expression tagging with high generalisation. *arXiv preprint arXiv:1809.03056*.

Qianhui Wu, Zijia Lin, Börje F Karlsson, Jian-Guang Lou, and Biqing Huang. 2020. Single-/multi-source cross-lingual NER via teacher-student learning on unlabeled data in target language. *arXiv preprint arXiv:2004.12440*.

Nicolas Zampieri, Manon Scholivet, Carlos Ramisch, and Benoit Favre. 2018. Veyn at PARSEME shared task 2018: Recurrent neural networks for VMWE identification. In *Proceedings of the Joint Workshop on Linguistic Annotation, Multiword Expressions and Constructions (LAW-MWE-CxG-2018)*, pages 290–296, Santa Fe, New Mexico, USA, August. ACL.

TRAVIS at PARSEME Shared Task 2020: How good is (m)BERT at seeing the unseen?

Murathan Kurfalı

Linguistics Department, Stockholm University
Stockholm, Sweden
`murathan.kurfali@ling.su.se`

Abstract

This paper describes the TRAVIS system built for the PARSEME Shared Task 2020 on semi-supervised identification of verbal multiword expressions. TRAVIS is a fully feature-independent model, relying only on the contextual embeddings. We have participated with two variants of TRAVIS, TRAVIS$_{multi}$ and TRAVIS$_{mono}$, where the former employs multilingual contextual embeddings and the latter uses monolingual ones. Our systems are ranked second and third among seven submissions in the open track, respectively. Thorough comparison of both systems on eight languages reveals that despite the strong performance of multilingual contextual embeddings across all languages, language-specific contextual embeddings exhibit much better generalization capabilities.

1 Introduction

Multiword expressions (MWEs) are, most commonly, defined as a group of words which act as a single lexical unit and display idiomaticity at lexical, syntactic, semantic or pragmatic levels (Baldwin and Kim, 2010). As the name suggests, verbal MWEs (VMWEs) are MWEs with a verb as the head in their canonical form. Identification of VMWEs tend to be more challenging than that of other MWEs, as they exhibit more syntactic/morphological variation (due to inflection of the verb), their components can be interrupted by other words (he **made** a serious **mistake**) and furthermore their order may vary (the **decision** was hard to **take**) (Savary et al., 2017). Yet, their identification is equally important as it is a prerequisite to fully address a number of downstream tasks, such as machine translation, information retrieval or syntactic parsing.

This year's shared task is built upon the observation that the existing models fail when it comes to identify the VMWEs which are not seen during the training. Hence, the aim of this year's shared task is updated to identify the *unseen* VMWEs in running text and the organizers provide annotated corpora with varying sizes in 14 different languages.

In this paper, we present two variants of TRAVIS, TRAVIS$_{multi}$ and TRAVIS$_{mono}$, which were submitted to the open track of the shared task, where additional resources were allowed. TRAVIS follows the tradition of approaching VMWE identification as a token classification task. To this end, it employs the, now standard, contextual embeddings model, BERT (Devlin et al., 2019), which has seen very limited application to this task. Due to the multilingual nature of the shared task, we also pay special attention to the performance on different languages. The variants of TRAVIS are named after this concern, highlighting the type of the contextual embeddings in terms of their pre-training languages: TRAVIS$_{multi}$ only uses the multilingual-BERT, which is trained on 104 languages, whereas TRAVIS$_{mono}$ uses the available language-specific BERT model for each language. Hence, the aim of the current submission is twofold: (i) we investigate the generalizability capabilities of pre-trained language models on identification of VMWEs (ii) we provide a thorough comparison of the multilingual-BERT against language-specific BERTs to understand the limitations of the former, if there is any, hoping to guide the future multilingual research on VMWEs.

Joint Workshop on Multiword Expressions and Electronic Lexicons, pages 136–141
Barcelona, Spain (Online), December 13, 2020.

2   Background

Treating MWE identification as a sequence tagging problem has been one of the most popular approaches (Zampieri et al., 2019). To this end, Schneider et al. (2014) propose new tagging schemes for VMWE by extending the BIO format to allow the annotation of discontinuous and nested MWEs. Gharbieh et al. (2017) constitutes the first study which adopts this approach and applies deep learning models including feedforward, recurrent and convolutional networks. Later, a number of studies adopting a recurrent neural network with an optional CRF classifier have been proposed (Klyueva et al., 2017; Taslimipoor and Rohanian, 2018; Zampieri et al., 2018; Berk et al., 2018). Zampieri et al. (2019) further study the effects of different word representations on this architecture by using the Veyn model of (Zampieri et al., 2018). Rohanian et al. (2019) specifically target the challenge caused by discontinuity of verbal MWEs and propose a neural model which combines convolutional network and self-attention mechanism to deal with long-range relations.

3   System Description

Below, we briefly introduce the BERT language model, which constitutes the backbone of our model, followed by the introduction of the proposed models.

3.1   BERT

Bidirectional Encoder Representations from Transformers (BERT) (Devlin et al., 2019) is a transformer-based deep bidirectional language model which has quickly become a new standard in NLP. It is pre-trained on a large unannotated corpus with two training objectives: (i) prediction of the missing words in a context (ii) given a sentence pair, determine if the second sentence follows the first one. These general pre-training objectives allow BERT to learn general enough representations which can be adjusted to any particular task through *fine-tuning*. In fine-tuning, a task-specific classification layer is added on the top of BERT and the whole model is, further, trained on the target task, updating the parameters of the BERT as well.

Originally, two different BERT models were released with different number of layers in their architecture: BERT-base (12-layer, 768-hidden, 12-heads, 110M parameters) and BERT-large (24-layer, 1024-hidden, 16-heads, 340M parameters). Additionally, a multilingual BERT (henceforth mBERT) was released, sharing the same architecture with the BERT-base model but trained on the concatenation of Wikipedias of 104 languages. Yet, since mBERT does not have any cross-lingual objectives nor trained on aligned data, its cross-lingual abilities and its limitations have, since, become a research topic (Karthikeyan et al., 2019).

3.2   Proposed Model(s)

We approach identification of VMWEs as a token classification problem. Our architecture follows the standard fine-tuning strategy employed for similar sequence tagging problems as described in the original BERT paper (Devlin et al., 2019). Briefly, we use BERT as our encoder with a linear layer connected to its hidden states on top to perform token level classification. In cases where the input token is split into several sub-tokens by the BERT's internal tokenizer, we pass the representation of the first sub-token to the linear layer classifier as the representation of the input token.

As stated earlier, there are two variants of TRAVIS where the only difference between them is the BERT model employed, otherwise completely identical. The first variant, *TRAVIS-multi*, uses mBERT as the encoder whereas the second variant, *TRAVIS-mono*, employs language specific BERT models and covers the following 8 languages:DE, FR, IT, PL, RO, SV, TR, ZH [1].

The motivation behind these two variants is the general finding that the monolingual models usually outperform mBERT (Nozza et al., 2020); yet, most languages still lack their own monolingual model

---

[1]Our original sshared task submission for TRAVIS$_{mono}$ also included predictions for EL and HI. However, we later discovered that the predictions for these languages were completely erroneous due to an error in the tokenization process. Therefore, we confine ourselves to the remaining eight languages in the current system description paper and we ask reader to dismiss the published results on the web-site for these two languages.

System	Langs	Unseen MWE-based			Global MWE-based			Global Token-based		
		P	R	F1	P	R	F1	P	R	F1
MTLB-STRUCT	14/14	36.24	41.12	38.53	71.26	69.05	70.14	77.69	70.9	74.14
TRAVIS-multi	13/14*	28.11	33.29	30.48	60.65	57.62	59.1	70.39	60.08	64.83
TRAVIS-mono	10/14	24.33	28.01	26.04	49.5	43.48	46.3	55.92	45.01	49.88
Seen2Unseen	14/14	16.14	11.95	13.73	63.36	62.69	63.02	66.33	61.63	63.89
FipsCo	3/14	4.31	5.21	4.72	11.69	8.75	10.01	13.26	8.51	10.37
HMSid	1/14	1.98	3.81	2.61	4.56	4.85	4.7	4.74	4.84	4.79
MultiVitamBooster	7/14	0.05	0.07	0.06	0.19	0.09	0.12	3.49	1.26	1.85
TRAVIS-multi	13/13	30.27	35.85	32.83	65.31	62.05	63.64	75.81	64.70	69.82
TRAVIS-mono	8/8[1]	43.86	49.91	46.69	74.87	74.77	74.82	80.76	76.94	78.80

Table 1: The official results of the all participating teams in the open track, ranked according to the F-score on unseen MWE identification. The bottom part presents our results when averaged over the languages covered. *The missing language is Portuguese, for which we failed to submit a result by the time of the shared task deadline due to a bug in the script.

as training such a language-specific BERT is computationally expensive. Hence, we believe that it is important to compare these models to gain insight regarding their performance for the future multilingual research, especially on low resource languages.

As for labelling, we follow a procedure similar to (Taslimipoor and Rohanian, 2018) and convert the PARSEME annotations into IOB-like labels. The PARSEME labels consist of VMWE's consecutive number in the sentence and its category, e.g. *2:LVC.full* denotes that the token with this tag is the first token of the 2nd VMWE in that sentence, which is a light verb construction, whereas the other components of that VMWE are labeled with merely 2. We modify these labels so that the initial token receives *B-* and the respective category and other tokens receives *I-* plus that category. All other tokens, which are not a part of any VMWE, receive *O* tag.

4 Experimental Design

Our implementation is based on the Transformers library of Huggingface (Wolf et al., 2019). All monolingual BERT models as well as mBERT are obtained through Huggingface's model hub[2]. In languages with several available BERT models, we opted for the most downloaded cased one. The complete list of the models used in the first submission are provided in Appendix A.

We train all models for four epochs using the Adam optimizer (Kingma and Ba, 2014) with a learning rate of 5e-5. The sequence length is set to 400 during training, but at the time of the inference we use BERT's maximum sequence limit which is 512. As the fine-tuning procedure is prone to high variance, we run all our models four times and used the run with the best development performance to obtain the final predictions for the test sets.

5 Results and Discussion

TRAVIS variants ranked 2nd and 3rd in the general ranking, according to the target metric of the unseen MWE-based F-score. Table 1 summarizes the official results of all participating teams in the open track. Additionally, global MWE- and token-based scores are presented in order to give an overall idea about the participating teams[3]. In what follows, we discuss our results with a focus on performance in the discovery of the unseen VMWEs, following the main aim of the shared task.

Although TRAVIS$_{multi}$ ranks higher than TRAVIS$_{mono}$ in Table 1, it is because the official results are obtained by averaging the performance of the systems over all languages, independent of the number of the languages covered in the submission. When the results are averaged only over the languages

---

[2]https://huggingface.co/models

[3]The details of each measure can be found in (Savary et al., 2017).

System	Langs	Unseen MWE-based			Seen MWE-based			Global MWE-based		
		P	R	F1	P	R	F1	P	R	F1
TRAVIS-multi	8	35.22	40.19	37.54	90.44	81.42	85.69	73.30	71.03	72.15
TRAVIS-mono	8	40.28	48.27	43.91	90.98	83.68	87.17	74.87	74.77	74.82

Table 2: Average performance comparison of our two submissions on the following set of languages: DE, FR, IT, PL, RO, SV, TR, ZH. Following the updated definition of the shared task, any VMWE in the training *or* development set are regarded as seen.

covered in each submission (last two rows of Table 1), it becomes clear that TRAVIS$_{mono}$ performs better on average, achieving an increase of 14 F-score. However, to draw a more healthy comparison, we also compared the averaged performances of these variants on the same set of languages, which is provided in Table 2. The results show that TRAVIS$_{mono}$ still significantly outperforms TRAVIS$_{multi}$ by 6 F-score even when evaluated on the same set of languages. It must also be noted that this difference in performance is not due to a significant increase in one or several languages but consistent across all the common eight languages where TRAVIS$_{multi}$ only achieves better performance for Swedish by 1.4 F-score, otherwise outperformed by 8 points in F-score on average.

These results are in line with the previous findings that language specific BERT models perform better on the respective language. However, it must be highlighted that the biggest gain of the language-specific models is in the discovery of the unseen VMWEs. As far as those eight languages are concerned, both models show similar performance for the seen VMWEs with TRAVIS$_{mono}$ 87.17 and TRAVIS$_{multi}$ 85.69 F-score, respectively (Table 2). Hence, it is evident that language-specific BERTs are particularly better at generalizing to unseen VMWEs.

However, the performance of mBERT cannot be simply dismissed, as the TRAVIS$_{multi}$ also achieves consistent results across languages. Although the results are not directly comparable as the set of the languages is different and the datasets have, possibly, been modified over time, TRAVIS$_{multi}$ achieves an average of 10% increase in F-score over SHOMA (Taslimipoor and Rohanian, 2018), the best performing system of the previous PARSEME Shared Task (2018), in the identification of the unseen MWEs.

Language-wise, TRAVIS$_{mono}$ achieved the best performance in the open track of the shared task for the six of the eight languages it covers which are: FR, IT, PL, RO, TR, ZH. These languages represent various language families suggesting that the performance of TRAVIS is stable typologically. As for TRAVIS$_{multi}$, Irish (GA) turns out to be the most challenging language with only 2.6% F-score. However, that is probably due to the size of the dataset that contains only 100 VMWEs in the training portion which is too limited to fine-tune mBERT in a meaningful way. The language-wise comparison of our submissions with the best performing system is provided in Figure 1.

Finally, a general advantage of employing contextual embeddings is being completely feature-independent. Hence, the proposed model only requires a training data annotated for the positions of the target VMWEs, rendering it easily adaptable to other low resource languages where obtaining other linguistics features, such as POS-tags or dependency trees, can be challenging.

6 Conclusion

In this paper, we try to answer two questions: (i) how generalizable is the performance of contextual embeddings in VMWE identification, and (ii) if the pre-training language plays an important role or, in other words, the multilingual contextual embeddings are good enough. To this end, we offer a computational model, TRAVIS, which treats VMWE identification as a sequence classification task and employs various BERT models.

The results indicate that language-specific models perform particularly well on the identification of the *unseen* VMWEs by outperforming the multilingual embeddings by 6% in F-score when compared on the same set of languages. Yet, the multilingual-BERT also exhibits strong multilingual abilities, suggested by the average of 32% F-score in identification of the unseen VMWEs which is significantly higher than results obtained in the previous editions of the PARSEME shared tasks.

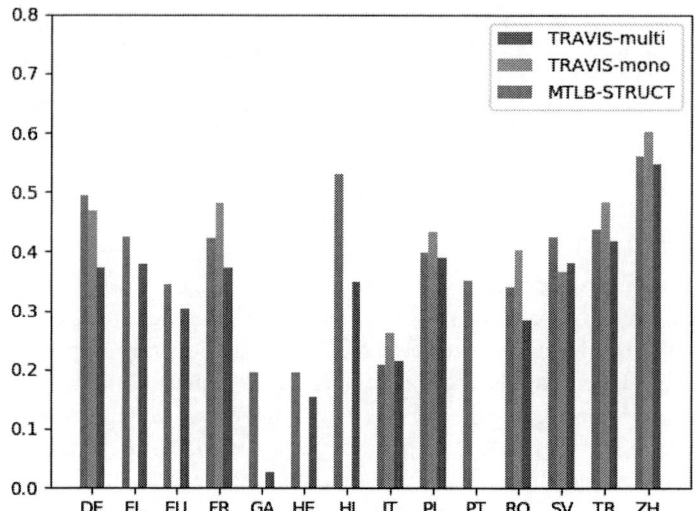

Figure 1: Language-wise comparison of our submissions and the first-ranked system (MTLB-STRUCT) on unseen MWEs.

Acknowledgments

I would like to thank Johan Sjons and anonymous reviewers for their valuable comments and NVIDIA for the GPU grant.

References

Timothy Baldwin and Su Nam Kim. 2010. Multiword expressions. *Handbook of natural language processing*, 2:267–292.

Gözde Berk, Berna Erden, and Tunga Güngör. 2018. Deep-bgt at parseme shared task 2018: Bidirectional lstm-crf model for verbal multiword expression identification. In *Proceedings of the Joint Workshop on Linguistic Annotation, Multiword Expressions and Constructions (LAW-MWE-CxG-2018)*, pages 248–253.

Jacob Devlin, Ming-Wei Chang, Kenton Lee, and Kristina Toutanova. 2019. Bert: Pre-training of deep bidirectional transformers for language understanding. In *NAACL-HLT (1)*.

Waseem Gharbieh, Virendrakumar Bhavsar, and Paul Cook. 2017. Deep learning models for multiword expression identification. In *Proceedings of the 6th Joint Conference on Lexical and Computational Semantics (* SEM 2017)*, pages 54–64.

K Karthikeyan, Zihan Wang, Stephen Mayhew, and Dan Roth. 2019. Cross-lingual ability of multilingual bert: An empirical study. In *International Conference on Learning Representations*.

Diederik P Kingma and Jimmy Ba. 2014. Adam: A method for stochastic optimization. *arXiv preprint arXiv:1412.6980*.

Natalia Klyueva, Antoine Doucet, and Milan Straka. 2017. Neural networks for multi-word expression detection. In *Proceedings of the 13th Workshop on Multiword Expressions (MWE 2017)*, pages 60–65.

Martin Malmsten, Love Börjeson, and Chris Haffenden. 2020. Playing with words at the national library of sweden–making a swedish bert. *arXiv preprint arXiv:2007.01658*.

Louis Martin, Benjamin Muller, Pedro Javier Ortiz Suárez, Yoann Dupont, Laurent Romary, Éric Villemonte de la Clergerie, Djamé Seddah, and Benoît Sagot. 2019. Camembert: a tasty french language model. *arXiv preprint arXiv:1911.03894*.

Debora Nozza, Federico Bianchi, and Dirk Hovy. 2020. What the [mask]? making sense of language-specific bert models. *arXiv preprint arXiv:2003.02912.*

Omid Rohanian, Shiva Taslimipoor, Samaneh Kouchaki, Ruslan Mitkov, et al. 2019. Bridging the gap: Attending to discontinuity in identification of multiword expressions. In *Proceedings of the 2019 Conference of the North American Chapter of the Association for Computational Linguistics: Human Language Technologies, Volume 1 (Long and Short Papers),* pages 2692–2698.

Agata Savary, Carlos Ramisch, Silvio Ricardo Cordeiro, Federico Sangati, Veronika Vincze, Behrang Qasemi Zadeh, Marie Candito, Fabienne Cap, Voula Giouli, Ivelina Stoyanova, et al. 2017. The parseme shared task on automatic identification of verbal multiword expressions. In *The 13th Workshop on Multiword Expression at EACL,* pages 31–47.

Nathan Schneider, Emily Danchik, Chris Dyer, and Noah A Smith. 2014. Discriminative lexical semantic segmentation with gaps: running the mwe gamut. *Transactions of the Association for Computational Linguistics,* 2:193–206.

Shiva Taslimipoor and Omid Rohanian. 2018. Shoma at parseme shared task on automatic identification of vmwes: Neural multiword expression tagging with high generalisation. *arXiv preprint arXiv:1809.03056.*

Thomas Wolf, Lysandre Debut, Victor Sanh, Julien Chaumond, Clement Delangue, Anthony Moi, Pierric Cistac, Tim Rault, Rémi Louf, Morgan Funtowicz, et al. 2019. Huggingface's transformers: State-of-the-art natural language processing. *ArXiv,* pages arXiv–1910.

Nicolas Zampieri, Manon Scholivet, Carlos Ramisch, and Benoit Favre. 2018. Veyn at parseme shared task 2018: Recurrent neural networks for vmwe identification. In *Proceedings of the Joint Workshop on Linguistic Annotation, Multiword Expressions and Constructions (LAW-MWE-CxG-2018),* pages 290–296.

Nicolas Zampieri, Carlos Ramisch, and Géraldine Damnati. 2019. The impact of word representations on sequential neural mwe identification.

Appendix A

Language	Model name
German	bert-base-german-cased
French (Martin et al., 2019)	camembert-base
Italian	bert-base-italian-cased
Polish	dkleczek/bert-base-polish-cased-v1
Romanian	bert-base-romanian-cased-v1
Swedish (Malmsten et al., 2020)	bert-base-swedish-cased
Turkish	bert-base-turkish-128k-cased
Chinese	bert-base-chinese

Table 3: The list of the monolingual BERT models used in the experiments. The model name denotes the model identifier of the corresponding model on Huggingface's model hub (huggingface.com/models)

MTLB-STRUCT @PARSEME 2020: Capturing Unseen Multiword Expressions Using Multi-task Learning and Pre-trained Masked Language Models

Shiva Taslimipoor
ALTA Institute
University of Cambridge, UK
st797@cl.cam.ac.uk

Sara Bahaadini
Microsoft
Sunnyvale, CA, USA
sabahaa@microsoft.com

Ekaterina Kochmar
ALTA Institute
University of Cambridge, UK
ek358@cl.cam.ac.uk

Abstract

This paper describes a semi-supervised system that jointly learns verbal multiword expressions (VMWEs) and dependency parse trees as an auxiliary task. The model benefits from pre-trained multilingual BERT. BERT hidden layers are shared among the two tasks and we introduce an additional linear layer to retrieve VMWE tags. The dependency parse tree prediction is modelled by a linear layer and a bilinear one plus a tree CRF on top of BERT. The system has participated in the open track of the PARSEME shared task 2020 and ranked first in terms of F1-score in identifying unseen VMWEs as well as VMWEs in general, averaged across all 14 languages.

1 Introduction

In addition to other challenges in multiword expression (MWE) processing that were addressed in previous work, such as non-compositionality (Salehi et al., 2014), discontinuity (Rohanian et al., 2019; Waszczuk, 2018), and syntactic variability (Pasquer et al., 2018), The PARSEME shared task edition 1.2[1] has focused on another prominent challenge in detecting MWEs, namely detection of unseen MWEs. The problem with unseen data is common for many NLP tasks. While rule-based and unsupervised ML approaches are less affected by unseen data, supervised ML techniques are often found to be prone to overfitting. In this respect, the introduction of language modelling objectives to be added to different NLP tasks and their effect on generalisation have shown promising results (Rei, 2017). Further improvements brought by pre-trained language models made them a popular approach to a multitude of NLP tasks (Devlin et al., 2019). One particular advantage of such models is that they facilitate generalisation beyond task-specific annotations (Pires et al., 2019).

MWEs are inherent in all natural languages and distinguishable for their syntactic and semantic idiosyncrasies (Baldwin and Kim, 2010; Fazly et al., 2009). Since language models are good at capturing syntactic and semantic features, we believe they are a suitable approach for modelling MWEs. In particular, our system relies on BERT pre-trained language models (Devlin et al., 2019). Additionally, we render the system semi-supervised by means of multi-task learning. The most promising feature to be jointly learned with MWEs is dependency parse information (Constant and Nivre, 2016). Accordingly, we fine-tune BERT for two different objectives: MWE detection and dependency parsing. MWE learning is done via token classification using a linear layer on top of BERT, and dependency parse trees are learned using dependency tree CRF network (Rush, 2020). Our experiments confirm that this joint learning architecture is effective for capturing MWEs in most languages represented in the shared task. [2]

2 Related Work

In earlier systems, MWEs were extracted using pre-defined patterns or statistical measures that either indicated associations among MWE components or (non-)compositionality of the expressions with regard to the components (Ramisch et al., 2010). For example, Cordeiro et al. (2016) employed such a

---

[1] http://hdl.handle.net/11234/1-3367

[2] The code for the system and configuration files for different languages are available at https://github.com/shivaat/MTLB-STRUCT/

Joint Workshop on Multiword Expressions and Electronic Lexicons, pages 142–148
Barcelona, Spain (Online), December 13, 2020.

system for identifying MWEs. While these models can be effective for some frequent MWEs, their main disadvantage is that they capture MWE types (as opposed to tokens) and they are unable to take context into account in running texts.

The use of supervised machine learning was facilitated by the availability of resources tagged for MWEs (Schneider et al., 2014; Savary et al., 2017; Ramisch et al., 2018). Al Saied et al. (2017) proposed a transition-based system based on an arc-standard dependency parser (Nivre, 2004) which ranked first in the first edition of PARSEME shared task on automatic identification of verbal MWEs (VMWEs) (Savary et al., 2017). Taslimipoor and Rohanian (2018) proposed a CNN-LSTM system which exploited fastText word representations and ranked first in the open track of the PARSEME shared task edition 1.1 (Ramisch et al., 2018). Previous systems such as TRAVERSAL (Waszczuk, 2018) (ranked first in the closed track of the PARSEME shared task edition 1.1), and CRF-Seq/Dep (Moreau et al., 2018) employed tree CRF using dependency parse features in non-deep learning settings. They showed strengths of this approach particularly in the case of discontinuous VMWEs. In SHOMA (Taslimipoor and Rohanian, 2018), using a linear-chain CRF layer on top of the CNN-biLSTM model did not result in improvements. In this work, we use tree CRF, implemented as part of the Torch-Struct library (Rush, 2020), to model dependency trees, and we show that when it is jointly trained with a transformer-based MWE detection system, it improves MWE prediction for a number of languages.

Recently, Savary et al. (2019) proposed that learning MWE lexicons in an unsupervised setting is an important step that can be used in combination with a supervised model, especially when the latter is trained on a small amount of data. While we do not specifically learn MWE lexicons from external unannotated data, we believe that state-of-the-art pre-trained language representation models can capture crucial information about MWEs similar to other NLP phenomena (Peters et al., 2017). For instance, Peters et al. (2017) showed how a semi-supervised system may benefit from pre-trained language model-based embeddings for named entity recognition (NER) and chunking. The joint learning of MWEs and dependency parsing has been proved effective in Constant and Nivre (2016). They proposed an arc-standard transition-based system which draws on a new representation that has two linguistic layers (a syntactic dependency tree and a forest of MWEs) sharing lexical nodes. The closest to our work is Taslimipoor et al. (2019) where they have trained a multi-task neural network which jointly learns VMWEs and dependency parsing on a small English dataset and uses ELMo pre-trained embeddings. Our work here is different in that we fine-tune the BERT architecture and we use a tree CRF for dependency parsing.

3   System Description

We use pre-trained BERT for language representation (Devlin et al., 2019) as the basis for our neural network. The BERT architecture is based on standard transformers involving self-attention layers of encoders and decoders.[3] What makes it different from other transformer-based pre-trained language representation models is its capability in encoding the representation in a bidirectional way through a masked language model schema. The reason that we choose BERT among other pre-trained models is the availability of multi-lingual pre-trained BERT.[4]

Our model is set up to learn MWEs and dependency trees simultaneously. BERT weights are shared among the two tasks. A fully connected layer that performs sequence tagging is added as the final layer for MWE objective. Parallel to that, linear layers and a dependency CRF module are introduced to perform structured prediction for dependency trees. [5] The whole model is trained in an end-to-end manner. Figure 1 depicts the overall architecture of the system.

We use Torch-Struct (Rush, 2020) for dependency parsing where Tree CRF is implemented as a distribution object. We first apply a linear followed by a bilinear layer on BERT's output to obtain the adjacency matrix structure of the dependency tree. The outputs from these layers are considered as log-potentials (l) for the CRF distribution. The distribution takes in log-potentials and converts them into

---

[3] There are 12 layers (transformer blocks) following the implementation of `http://nlp.seas.harvard.edu/2018/04/03/attention.html`, with the hidden dimension size of 768 and 12 attention heads.

[4] `https://huggingface.co/bert-base-multilingual-cased`

[5] In this work, we only focus on dependency arcs (tree structures) and we do not model dependency relation labels.

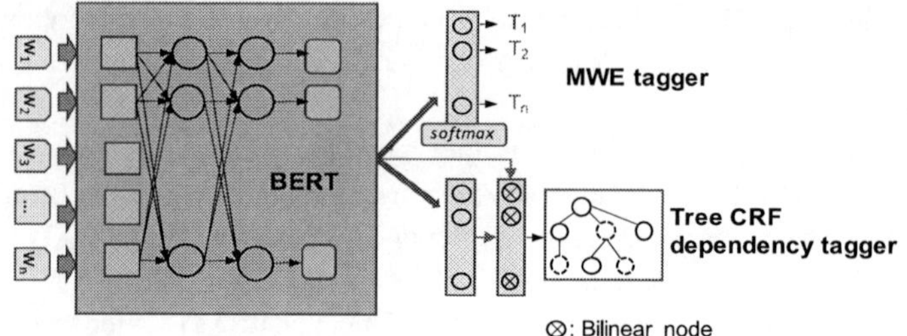

Figure 1: The overall architecture of the multi-task learning model with two branches on top of BERT. One is a linear classifier layer for MWE tagging and the other consists of a linear layer, a bilinear layer and a tree CRF dependency tagger.

probabilities $CRF(z; l)$ of a specific tree z. We query the distribution to predict over the set of trees using $argmax_z CRF(z; l)$. The cost for updating the tree is based on the difference between the tree probability and the gold standard dependency arcs.

The MWE classification layer is optimised by cross-entropy between the ground truth MWE tags and the predicted ones, while the cost for CRF is estimated using log probabilities over the tree structures. Note that log probabilities (*logprobs*) for CRF are large negative values which should be maximised, so we multiply them by -1 to get the dependency loss values compatible with MWE ones: $Loss_{dep} = -logprobs$. The overall loss function to be optimised by ADAM optimiser is a linear combination of the two losses, $Loss_{mwe}$ and $Loss_{dep}$ which are the losses for multi-word expression and dependency parse tree, respectively, with α being a constant value which is empirically set to $0.001 \leq \alpha \leq 0.01$.

$$Loss = Loss_{mwe} + \alpha * Loss_{dep} \tag{1}$$

4 Experiments

We adapted the sequential labelling scheme of Rohanian et al. (2019) which is similar to IOB with the difference that it introduces a new soft label o− for the tokens that are in between components of an MWE. We preserved MWE categories by suffixing the label with the category name. In this case, the annotations for the idiomatic verbal expression (of type VID) in the sentence *I would **give** this job **a go**, would be: $I_{[O]}$ *would*$_{[O]}$ *give*$_{[B-VID]}$ *this*$_{[o-VID]}$ *job*$_{[o-VID]}$ $a_{[I-VID]}$ *go*$_{[I-VID]}$ with the labels shown as subscripts in brackets. [6]

In the development phase of the shared task, we trained various configurations of our system and evaluated the performance on development sets. Specifically, we examined the performance of our model in two settings: (1) the model is back-propagated only based on $Loss_{mwe}$ (*single-task*), and (2) the learning is based on the multi-task $Loss$ (*multi-task*). We decided on the setting to be used for each language separately based on the performance on development sets. We used *bert-base-multilingual-cased* as the pre-trained model for all languages.[7] Due to lack of time and resources, we did not perform any extensive hyper-parameter search. We empirically chose learning rate 3×10^{-5} and batch size 10 (except for GA where the selected batch size is 1). We trained the models for 10 epochs, and the maximum lengths of sentences for training were chosen for each language separately based on the word piece tokenisation of multilingual BERT. [8]

Table 1 shows results on the development sets. According to the shared task criteria, we report MWE-based precision, recall and F1 measures for all VMWEs and unseen ones in particular. We also consider the scores on the expressions which are syntactic variants of their occurrences in the training data useful to be reported. We chose the best setting for each language based on F1 scores on unseen VMWEs (in bold). The systems marked by * (in Table 1) are trained after the evaluation period; therefore, their scores on test are not available in the official evaluation report. In the multi-task setting we tried two α values:

---

[6]Embedded MWEs can be detected only if the nested MWE is not part of the nesting one and their categories are different.

[7]We tried uncased multilingual models, for FR and PL in particular, but we didn't observe any improvements.

[8]When tokenisation splits words into multiple pieces, we took the prediction for the first piece as the prediction for the word. We masked the rest in the learning process.

	System	Global MWE-based			Unseen MWE-based			Variant
		P	R	F1	P	R	F1	F1
DE	single-task (bert German cased)	79.45	75.28	77.31	53.00	53.00	**53.00**	90.32
	multi-task (bert German cased)	74.81	75.66	75.23	46.61	55.00	50.46	90.91
	single-task (bert multilingual)	73.06	74.16	73.61	45.45	55.00	49.77	86.96
EL	single-task	70.28	72.06	71.16	37.01	47.00	41.41	81.98
	multi-task	72.38	72.38	72.38	40.68	48.00	**44.04**	82.30
EU	single-task	76.82	78.54	77.68	28.10	43.00	33.99	81.20
	multi-task	79.04	80.22	79.63	29.08	41.00	**34.02**	83.78
FR	single-task	83.17	79.06	81.06	48.57	50.50	**49.51**	87.05
	multi-task	81.53	80.00	80.76	44.92	52.48	48.40	87.46
	*single-task (camembert)	79.61	85.41	82.41	45.32	62.38	52.50*	91.16
GA	single-task	26.15	13.49	17.80	16.07	9.00	11.54	32.00
	multi-task	25.00	14.29	18.18	18.18	12.00	**14.46**	25.00
HE	single-task	52.76	40.36	45.73	23.94	16.67	19.65	73.91
	multi-task	57.14	38.55	46.04	31.15	18.63	**23.31**	58.54
HI	single-task	71.78	62.90	67.05	50.55	46.00	**48.17**	83.12
	multi-task	64.09	62.37	63.22	39.62	42.00	30.78	87.50
IT	single-task	70.53	62.04	66.01	32.35	32.67	**32.51**	76.02
	multi-task	71.84	61.42	66.22	29.90	28.71	29.29	78.90
PL	single-task	83.22	81.72	82.46	42.24	49.00	**45.37**	91.51
	multi-task	83.92	80.14	81.99	42.59	46.00	44.23	90.30
PT	single-task	78.82	74.06	76.36	33.64	36.00	34.78	87.85
	multi-task	80.11	73.05	76.42	40.40	41.00	**40.59**	84.08
RO	single-task	91.41	85.82	88.52	39.13	36.00	**37.50**	85.39
	multi-task	91.07	86.06	88.50	39.53	34.00	36.56	85.29
SV	single-task	68.99	65.93	67.42	39.83	47.00	43.12	77.92
	multi-task	70.37	70.37	70.37	41.13	51.00	**45.54**	81.53
TR	single-task	62.59	69.75	65.98	37.41	52.00	43.51	68.23
	multi-task	66.06	69.48	67.73	43.31	55.00	**48.46**	66.43
	*multi-task (+ extra data)	67.89	70.84	69.33	45.08	55.00	49.55*	70.79
ZH	single-task	72.39	73.21	72.80	59.13	60.18	59.65	71.43
	multi-task	72.45	72.45	72.45	60.36	59.29	**59.82**	71.43
	*single-task (bert Chinese cased)	73.14	78.11	75.55	61.07	70.80	65.57*	71.43
	*multi-task (bert Chinese cased)	70.92	75.47	73.3	50.68	65.49	62.45	80.00

Table 1: Global, Unseen and Variant MWE-based scores on validation datasets.

$\frac{1}{300}$ and $\frac{1}{700}$. We used the value that worked best for each language ($\frac{1}{300}$ for EL, RO, SV and TR, and $\frac{1}{700}$ for DE, EU, FR, GA, HE, HI, IT, PL, PT and ZH). The best model for each language was trained on both train and dev sets. The results obtained on test data are reported in Section 5.

After the evaluation period, we also fine-tuned the dependency-CRF branch of the model on some portions of extra data for several lower-resource languages (e.g. GA, HI, HE and TR). We saw no notable improvement except for TR as reported in Table 1 (multi-taks + extra data). We only fine-tuned the model to learn unlabeled trees for dependency arcs, which are made available for additional data as part of the shared task. Due to being limited by the amount of computational power, we only partially used the extra unannotated data; therefore we leave the experiments on their effects to future work.

5 Results and Analysis

Table 2 shows the summary results of our system MTLB-STRUCT on test sets. For each language, we report the employed system (single or multi-task), the ratio of unseen data in the test set, global and unseen MWE-based F1 scores, and finally the system's rank (#) in the open track of the shared task.[9]

---

[9]More detailed results (including precision and recall values, and token-based performance measures) are available on the shared task web page: `http://multiword.sourceforge.net/PHITE.php?sitesig=CONF&page=CONF_02_MWE-LEX_2020___1b__COLING__rb__&subpage=CONF_50_Shared_task_results`

Lang	System	unseen %	Global F1	Unseen F1	#	Lang	System	unseen %	Global F1	Unseen F1	#
DE	single	37%	76.17	49.34	1	IT	single	29%	63.76	20.81	3
EL	multi	31%	72.62	42.47	1	PL	single	22%	81.02	39.94	2
EU	multi	15%	80.03	34.41	1	PT	multi	24%	73.34	35.13	1
FR	single	22%	79.42	42.33	2	RO	single	7%	90.46	34.02	2
GA	multi	69%	30.07	19.54	1	SV	multi	31%	71.58	42.57	1
HE	multi	60%	48.30	19.59	1	TR	multi	26%	69.46	43.66	2
HI	single	45%	73.62	53.11	1	ZH	multi	38%	69.63	56.2	2
						Overall	-	-	70.14	38.53	1

Table 2: The percentage of unseen expressions (unseen %), and Global and Unseen MWE-based F1 results for all languages (Lang) in test. Column # indicates the ranking of our system in the shared task.

Our system is applied to all 14 languages and achieves the highest F1 score overall.

The amount of MWEs seen in the training data is the largest contributing factor, as the percentage of seen-in-train gold MWEs is highly linearly correlated ($r = 0.90$) with the global MWE-based F1 score across the languages. We achieve the highest performance in terms of MWE-based F1 score on unseen data for 8 out of 14 languages, with the largest gaps in performance observed on PT, where our system outperforms Seen2Unseen by 21.59 points, and on HI, where the gap between our system's F1 and that of Seen2Unseen equals 10.45 points. We note that our system works significantly better than the second best systems for smaller datasets (GA, HE, and HI) which also happen to have larger amount of unseen expressions. At the same time, TRAVIS-mono outperforms our system on FR, IT, PL, TR, and ZH, with the largest gap of 5.68 points observed on FR.

In addition, our system's performance is balanced across *continuous* and *discontinuous MWEs*, with the exceptions of HI and TR, where discontinuous MWEs amount to 7% and 4% of all MWEs, respectively, and our system's performance drops by as much as 30 F1 points compared to its performance on continuous MWEs. The distinction between *multi-* and *single-token MWEs* is only applicable to 3 languages, on two of which (DE and SV) our system achieves an F1 score above 0.80 on *single tokens*.

Finally, the shared task data shows a wide diversity of VMWE categories present in different languages: from just three in EU and TR up to eight in IT. Once again, we note that our system is applicable to detection of all categories: for instance, it achieves the highest F1 scores among all systems in identification of LS.ICV, a rare language-specific category of inherently clitic verbs used only in Italian. At the same time, we identify LVC.cause, light-verb constructions with the verb adding a causative meaning to the noun, as the most problematic category on which our system achieves comparatively poorer results, especially on DE, EL, FR, HI, PT, and SV.

It is worth noting that no language specific feature is used in our system and the authors were not involved in the creation of the datatsets. Overall, we note that our system is not only cross-lingual, but also robust in terms of its performance and is capable of generalising to unseen MWEs.

6 Conclusions and Future Work

We described MTLB-STRUCT, a semi-supervised system that is based on pre-trained BERT masked language modelling and that jointly learns VMWE tags and dependency parse trees. The system ranked first in the open track of the PARSEME shared task - edition 1.2 and shows the overall state-of-the-art performance for detecting unseen VMWEs. In future, we plan to augment the dependency parsing architecture to train on dependency relation categories (labels) as well as dependency arcs. We also plan to improve our system by making it more efficient in order to train the dependency parsing module on the extra available unannotated datasets.

Acknowledgments

This paper reports on research supported by Cambridge Assessment, University of Cambridge. We are grateful to the anonymous reviewers for their valuable feedback. We gratefully acknowledge the support of NVIDIA Corporation with the donation of the Titan V GPU used in this research.

References

Hazem Al Saied, Matthieu Constant, and Marie Candito. 2017. The ATILF-LLF system for PARSEME shared task: a transition-based verbal multiword expression tagger. In *Proceedings of the 13th Workshop on Multiword Expressions (MWE 2017)*, pages 127–132.

Timothy Baldwin and Su Nam Kim. 2010. Multiword expressions. In *Handbook of Natural Language Processing, second edition.*, pages 267–292. CRC Press.

Matthieu Constant and Joakim Nivre. 2016. A transition-based system for joint lexical and syntactic analysis. In *Proceedings of the 54th Annual Meeting of the Association for Computational Linguistics (Volume 1: Long Papers)*, pages 161–171.

Silvio Cordeiro, Carlos Ramisch, and Aline Villavicencio. 2016. UFRGS&LIF at SemEval-2016 task 10: rule-based mwe identification and predominant-supersense tagging. In *Proceedings of the 10th International Workshop on Semantic Evaluation (SemEval-2016)*, pages 910–917.

Jacob Devlin, Ming-Wei Chang, Kenton Lee, and Kristina Toutanova. 2019. BERT: Pre-training of deep bidirectional transformers for language understanding. In *Proceedings of the 2019 Conference of the North American Chapter of the Association for Computational Linguistics: Human Language Technologies, Volume 1 (Long and Short Papers)*, pages 4171–4186, Minneapolis, Minnesota, June. Association for Computational Linguistics.

Afsaneh Fazly, Paul Cook, and Suzanne Stevenson. 2009. Unsupervised type and token identification of idiomatic expressions. *Computational Linguistics*, 35(1):61–103.

Erwan Moreau, Ashjan Alsulaimani, Alfredo Maldonado, and Carl Vogel. 2018. CRF-Seq and CRF-DepTree at PARSEME shared task 2018: Detecting verbal mwes using sequential and dependency-based approaches. In *Proceedings of the Joint Workshop on Linguistic Annotation, Multiword Expressions and Constructions (LAW-MWE-CxG-2018)*, pages 241–247.

Joakim Nivre. 2004. Incrementality in deterministic dependency parsing. In *Proceedings of the workshop on incremental parsing: Bringing engineering and cognition together*, pages 50–57.

Caroline Pasquer, Agata Savary, Jean-Yves Antoine, and Carlos Ramisch. 2018. Towards a variability measure for multiword expressions. In *Proceedings of the 2018 Conference of the North American Chapter of the Association for Computational Linguistics: Human Language Technologies, Volume 2 (Short Papers)*, pages 426–432, New Orleans, Louisiana, June. Association for Computational Linguistics.

Matthew Peters, Waleed Ammar, Chandra Bhagavatula, and Russell Power. 2017. Semi-supervised sequence tagging with bidirectional language models. In *Proceedings of the 55th Annual Meeting of the Association for Computational Linguistics (Volume 1: Long Papers)*, pages 1756–1765.

Telmo Pires, Eva Schlinger, and Dan Garrette. 2019. How multilingual is multilingual bert? *arXiv preprint arXiv:1906.01502*.

Carlos Ramisch, Aline Villavicencio, and Christian Boitet. 2010. mwetoolkit: a framework for multiword expression identification. In *Proceedings of the Seventh International Conference on Language Resources and Evaluation (LREC'10)*.

Carlos Ramisch, Silvio Cordeiro, Agata Savary, Veronika Vincze, Verginica Mititelu, Archna Bhatia, Maja Buljan, Marie Candito, Polona Gantar, Voula Giouli, et al. 2018. Edition 1.1 of the PARSEME shared task on automatic identification of verbal multiword expressions. In *the Joint Workshop on Linguistic Annotation, Multiword Expressions and Constructions (LAW-MWE-CxG-2018)*, pages 222–240.

Marek Rei. 2017. Semi-supervised multitask learning for sequence labeling. In *Proceedings of the 55th Annual Meeting of the Association for Computational Linguistics (Volume 1: Long Papers)*, pages 2121–2130, Vancouver, Canada, July. Association for Computational Linguistics.

Omid Rohanian, Shiva Taslimipoor, Samaneh Kouchaki, Le An Ha, and Ruslan Mitkov. 2019. Bridging the gap: Attending to discontinuity in identification of multiword expressions. *arXiv preprint arXiv:1902.10667*.

Alexander Rush. 2020. Torch-Struct: Deep structured prediction library. In *Proceedings of the 58th Annual Meeting of the Association for Computational Linguistics: System Demonstrations*, pages 335–342, Online, July. Association for Computational Linguistics.

Bahar Salehi, Paul Cook, and Timothy Baldwin. 2014. Detecting non-compositional MWE components using Wiktionary. In *Proceedings of the 2014 Conference on Empirical Methods in Natural Language Processing (EMNLP)*, pages 1792–1797, Doha, Qatar, October. Association for Computational Linguistics.

Agata Savary, Carlos Ramisch, Silvio Cordeiro, Federico Sangati, Veronika Vincze, Behrang Qasemizadeh, Marie Candito, Fabienne Cap, Voula Giouli, Ivelina Stoyanova, et al. 2017. The PARSEME shared task on automatic identification of verbal multiword expressions. In *Proceedings of the 13th Workshop on Multiword Expressions (MWE 2017)*, pages 31–47.

Agata Savary, Silvio Ricardo Cordeiro, and Carlos Ramisch. 2019. Without lexicons, multiword expression identification will never fly: A position statement. In *Joint Workshop on Multiword Expressions and WordNet (MWE-WN 2019)*, pages 79–91. Association for Computational Linguistics.

Nathan Schneider, Emily Danchik, Chris Dyer, and Noah A Smith. 2014. Discriminative lexical semantic segmentation with gaps: running the mwe gamut. *Transactions of the Association for Computational Linguistics*, 2:193–206.

Shiva Taslimipoor and Omid Rohanian. 2018. SHOMA at Parseme shared task on automatic identification of VMWEs: Neural multiword expression tagging with high generalisation. *arXiv preprint arXiv:1809.03056*.

Shiva Taslimipoor, Omid Rohanian, and Le An Ha. 2019. Cross-lingual transfer learning and multitask learning for capturing multiword expressions. In *Proceedings of the Joint Workshop on Multiword Expressions and WordNet (MWE-WN 2019)*, pages 155–161.

Jakub Waszczuk. 2018. TRAVERSAL at PARSEME shared task 2018: Identification of verbal multiword expressions using a discriminative tree-structured model. In *Proceedings of the Joint Workshop on Linguistic Annotation, Multiword Expressions and Constructions (LAW-MWE-CxG-2018)*, pages 275–282.

MultiVitaminBooster at PARSEME Shared Task 2020: Combining Window- and Dependency-Based Features with Multilingual Contextualised Word Embeddings for VMWE Detection

Sebastian Gombert and Sabine Bartsch

Corpus- and Computational Linguistics, English Philology

Institute of Linguistics and Literary Studies, Technische Universität Darmstadt

`sebastiang@outlook.de`

`sabine.bartsch@tu-darmstadt.de`

Abstract

In this paper, we present *MultiVitaminBooster*, a system implemented for the *PARSEME shared task on semi-supervised identification of verbal multiword expressions - edition 1.2*. For our approach, we interpret detecting verbal multiword expressions as a token classification task aiming to decide whether a token is part of a verbal multiword expression or not. For this purpose, we train gradient boosting-based models. We encode tokens as feature vectors combining multilingual contextualized word embeddings provided by the *XLM-RoBERTa* language model (Conneau et al., 2019) with a more traditional linguistic feature set relying on context windows and dependency relations. Our system was ranked 7th in the official open track ranking of the shared task evaluations with an encoding-related bug distorting the results. For this reason we carry out further unofficial evaluations. Unofficial versions of our systems would have achieved higher ranks.

1 Introduction

Multiword expressions (MWEs) are an object of research in various areas of linguistics and NLP. On the one hand, areas such as lexico-semantics and construction grammar have a distinct research interest in the form and semantics of different classes of multiword expressions (Masini, 2005); their automatic detection makes them accessible to large-scale corpus analyses. On the other hand, various NLP-systems, especially in the area of machine translation where the detection of MWEs prevents spurious literal translations, can benefit from detecting MWEs (Zaninello and Birch, 2020), as well.

In this paper, we present an approach to the automatic detection of verbal multiword expressions (VMWE), MWEs which form around a head verb, which was our contribution to the *PARSEME shared task 2020 on verbal multiword expressions* (Ramisch et al., 2020a). The data set provided for the shared task (Ramisch et al., 2020b) distinguishes 7 general categories of VMWEs, some with additional subcategories:

VMWE category	Tag	Example
Verbal idioms	VID	to let the cat out of the bag.
Light-verb constructions	LVC.full, LVC.cause	to make a decision
Verb-particle constructions	VPC.full, VPC.cause	to go on
Multi-verb constructions	MVC	to make do
Inherently reflexive verbs	IRV	sich beschäftigen (to deal with; to be concerned)
Inherently adpositional verbs	IAV	to stand for s. th.
Inherently clitic verbs	LS.ICV	se ne frega (he does not care)

Table 1: The different categories of VMWEs dealt with during the shared task.

Past approaches in the area of MWE detection rely on the usage of statistical association measures (Evert et al., 2017; Pecina, 2005; Ramisch et al., 2008; Tsvetkov and Wintner, 2010) and machine learning (Klyueva et al., 2017; Moreau et al., 2018; Stodden et al., 2018; Waszczuk, 2018), sometimes combining

Joint Workshop on Multiword Expressions and Electronic Lexicons, pages 149–155

Barcelona, Spain (Online), December 13, 2020.

both (Mandravickaitė and Krilavičius, 2017). Our approach follows this tradition while paying tribute to the latest developments in the area of multilingual transformer-based neural language modeling.

Transformer-based language models such as *BERT* (Devlin et al., 2019) or *RoBERTa* (Liu et al., 2019) are pre-trained on large-scale corpora and are able to achieve state-of-the-art results for various standard tasks in NLP. They can either be fine-tuned to solve a specific task or used to provide contextualised word embeddings. The difference between such contextualised embeddings and the static ones based on traditional methods such as *GloVe* (Pennington et al., 2014) or *word2vec* (Mikolov et al., 2013) is that the former can account for different local word contexts and encode a given word individually with regard to the observed local context as well as global distributional information.

By intuition, this aspect should make contextualised word embeddings a feasible candidate for the detection of MWEs, as they should encode a word differently when observed as part of an MWE compared to an occurrence in open distribution, given both cases were reflected during pre-training. As this aspect can, however, not be guaranteed in all cases, we complement the embeddings with regular window- and dependency-based features to make the results of our systems less dependent on the pre-training of the language model used, and, thus, more robust. To be able to account for the multiple languages represented in the shared task without providing a distinct transformer language model for each language, we use the multilingual *XLM-RoBERTa* (Conneau et al., 2019) which was trained on *Common Crawl* data in 100 languages (including all languages represented in the shared task) and is, as a consequence, able to generate contextualised word embeddings for all of them.

2 System Description

For our system, *MultiVitaminBooster*, we interpret detecting MWEs as a binary token classification task whose goal is to decide whether a token is part of a given MWE or not. We train respective binary classifiers per language and MWE category to account for the phenomenon of overlapping MWEs from different categories using the *train* and *dev* sets provided for the shared task. For re-assembling single tokens into coherent MWEs, we calculate sub-graphs of the dependency tree of a given sentence where all nodes not marked as being part of a given MWE category are filtered out. We interpret the remaining connected components within them as coherent MWEs and tag the tokens accordingly.

2.1 Feature Encoding

XLM-RoBERTa-based contextualised word embeddings: we represent each token by the contextualised word embedding generated by XLM-RoBERTa by itself as well as for its parent within the dependency tree of a sentence and the root of the respective sentence. To this end, we add the averages of the contextualised embeddings of all children and siblings of a given token. For acquiring the embeddings, we rely on the version of *XLM-RoBERTa* provided by *huggingface.co* (Wolf et al., 2019) and use the *base model*. As this language model requires a more fine-grained segmentation of tokens than present in the training data (e. g. highly productive morphemes are regarded as independent tokens to save input dimensions) and because, as a consequence, a token within the training set might correspond to multiple sub-tokens and, thus, to multiple contextualised embeddings, we average these embeddings in such cases.

XLM-RoBERTa attention values: as transformer-based language models use attention during the calculation of representations (Vaswani et al., 2017), they provide numerical values directly indicating the importance of tokens for the semantics of each other. Our intuition is that the question whether two tokens are part of a given MWE, or not, could be reflected in the attention they show for each other. We encode each token with the attention it pays its parent and the root of a given sentence as well as the attention both of these pay to the token itself. Analogous to the embeddings themselves, we average the attention values in cases where multiple sub-tokens correspond to a token from the training data.

Linguistic features (window- and dependency-based): the training- and evaluation corpora of the shared task (Ramisch et al., 2020b) comply to the format of the *universal dependencies* project (McDonald et al., 2013). The majority of them were either automatically annotated with lemmata, *UD* POS tags, language-specific POS tags, *universal features*[1] and *UD* dependency relations using *UDPipe* (Straka and Straková, 2017) or taken directly from official *UD treebanks*.

We encode each token with its corresponding lemma (we filter out all lemmata not observed as being part of an VMWE within the training corpus), its language-specific POS tag, its *universal features* and its dependency tag. To this, we add the corresponding annotations of the parent, siblings and children of a token within the dependency tree of a given sentence, the respective annotations of the root token of this sentence within this tree, and the corresponding annotations of neighbouring tokens given a size of two for the left and the right context. We encode these features as one-hot respectively *n*-hot-vectors.

2.2 Classification

Gradient Boosting: for *MultiVitaminBooster*, we use gradient boosting (Mason et al., 1999) relying on the implementation provided by *CatBoost* (Dorogush et al., 2018; Prokhorenkova et al., 2018). Gradient boosting creates an ensemble of weak learners in the form of regression trees in order to create a strong one. The logit parameters predicted by these trees are combined into final prediction scores using a variant of logistic regression. We chose gradient boosting as an algorithm as it is able to create complex and powerful classification models for heterogeneous feature sets. We use the default parameters and train for 1000 epochs. Per language and VMWE category present for this language, we train a binary token classifier whose goal is to decide whether a token is part of a VMWE of the respective category.

2.3 VMWE re-assembly

This leaves us with tagged tokens. However, the task requires VMWEs to form connected units indicating relations between the different corresponding tokens within the output data. To reconnect the single tokens tagged as VMWE within a given sentence into such complete units, we implemented the following heuristics which is executed per language and VMWE category:

- We instantiate the dependency tree of a sentence as a graph.

- Within this graph, we delete all nodes corresponding to tokens without a respective VMWE tag.

- We interpret the remaining connected components (= remaining sub-graphs consisting of one or more connected nodes) as coherent VMWEs.

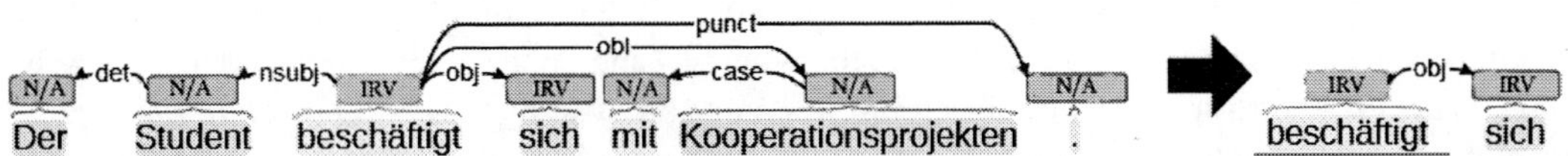

Figure 1: An example illustrating this heuristic. Translation of this utterance: *the student is concerned with cooperation projects.*

3 Results and Analysis

As already stated, our official system (*MVB*) was ranked last in the official shared task evaluations with an output encoding-related bug distorting results (under a common condition, it was likely that multiple sentences were assigned the same VMWE tags). For this reason, we evaluated a bug-fixed system (*MVB (bug free)*) for seven out of the 14 languages represented in the shared task (*DE, EU, GA, HI, IT, SV* and *TR*; due to time-related reasons, we only managed to evaluate our system for these languages for the official shared task which is why we decided to focus on them throughout all other evaluations).

In addition to our bug-fixed system, we trained a system exclusively on the contextualised embeddings and attention values (*Emb. Att. B.*), another system exclusively on the window- and dependency-based linguistic features (*Ling. Feats. B.*) and a third system which relies on the same feature set as *MVB* but

---

[1] https://universaldependencies.org/u/feat/index.html

uses *logistic regression* as classification algorithm (we rely on the implementation provided by *scikit-learn* (Pedregosa et al., 2011) for this and train for 1000 iterations) as additional baselines.[2]

The official evaluations of the shared task were separated into two tracks. Systems participating in the closed track were obliged to only rely on the data sets provided directly by the organisers (Ramisch et al., 2020b), while systems participating in the open track were allowed to use external resources such as external corpora or lexical resources, as well. All our systems except for the one relying solely on window- and dependency-based linguistic features would have participated in the open track due to the usage of the external contextualised embeddings if submitted for the official shared task. The systems were evaluated with regard to different categories with the three most important ones being *unseen MWE-based*, a category that evaluates the performance of systems in respect to VMWEs not observed within the training data, *global MWE-based*, a category that evaluates the general detection of VMWEs as connected units, and *global token-based*, a category evaluating the detection of VMWEs on a token level.

System	Unseen MWE-based				Global MWE-based				Global Token-based			
	P	R	F1	Rank	P	R	F1	Rank	P	R	F1	Rank
MVB	0.05	0.07	0.06	7	0.19	0.09	0.12	7	3.49	1.26	1.85	7
MVB (bug free)	3.74	3.48	3.61	6*	52.21	30.02	38.12	5*	**84.10**	35.16	49.59	5*
Ling. Feats. B.	14.88	10.03	11.98	2**	56.62	35.72	43.80	3**	**82.52**	41.49	55.22	3**
Emb. Att. B.	13.44	0.42	0.81	7*	25.81	0.89	1.72	7*	67.11	1.73	3.37	7*
MVLR	3.65	21.12	6.22	5*	21.60	46.89	29.58	5*	37.87	70.76	49.34	5*
MTLB-STRUCT	*36.24*	*41.12*	*38.53*	*1*	*71.26*	*69.05*	*70.14*	*1*	*77.69*	*70.9*	*74.14*	*1*
SEEN2SEEN	*36.47*	*0.57*	*1.12*	*2*	*76.21*	*58.56*	*66.23*	*1*	*78.64*	*57.02*	*66.11*	*1*

Table 2: The overall results of our evaluations for the seven languages. ** = unofficial rank in the open track. ** = unofficial rank in the closed track. MTLB-STRUCT and SEEN2SEEN are the winning systems of the two tracks of the shared tasks. We provide their results for reasons of comparability.* **Bold** *marks the highest score reached within a category throughout all shared task results within a given track.* <u>Underline</u> *marks the best score reached among our systems.*

The bug-free version of *MultiVitaminBooster* would have been ranked fifth within the *global MWE-based* and *global token-based* evaluation categories and sixth within the *unseen MWE-based* category if it had participated in the official shared task. While this is a huge improvement over the bugged version, these results can be considered subpar, especially in comparison to the winning systems *MTLB-STRUCT* and *SEEN2SEEN*.

Two further observations which speak against our form of usage of multilingual contextualised word embeddings for the given task can be made here, as well: on the one hand, the system which was trained solely on them (*Emb. Att. B.*) performed by far worst out of all our unofficial systems, and, on the other hand, the system which was trained solely on the window- and dependency-based linguistic feature set (*Ling. Feats. B.*) performed best out of all our systems and even manages to put *MultiVitaminBooster* into place. If submitted to the shared track, it would have been ranked second in the *unseeen MWE-based* category and third in the *global MWE-based* and *global token-based* categories for the closed track. Here, the question whether these results would have turned out more successful if another language model had been used instead of *XLM-RoBERTa* (Conneau et al., 2019) or if our results reflect a general inadequacy of the approach to use transformer-based word embeddings for detecting VMWEs remains.

Our model based on logistic regression (*MVLR*) achieved lower precision but higher recall scores than all our systems based on gradient boosting and, by average, lower F1-scores than the best gradient boosting-based models. This raises the question to what extent the results would differ when applying other classification algorithms.

One other important finding is that for all our systems, there is a discrepancy between the precision scores observed for *global MWE-based* and *global token-based*. While the precision achieved for the *global MWE-based* category turned out subpar, *MultivitaminBooster* and the system relying solely on the linguistic feature set achieve the best precision scores out of all our unoffical and all official systems within the *global token-based* category. We attribute this discrepancy to our heuristics used for re-assembling VMWEs.

---

[2]Our code and our full evaluation results can be found under `https://github.com/SGombert/MultiVitaminBoosterResults`

A closer look onto an example can explain this: *"'Es **tut weh**, die **Sprache** derer **benützen** zu müssen, die **dich schinden'**, **heißt es** da beispielsweise schon am **Anfang** [...]."* ("*'It hurts having to use the language of those who maltreat you', it says, for example, at the beginning."*) In this German sentence, all tokens marked as bold were recognised as one large VMWE instead of multiple ones, illustrating a problematic pattern which is observable for our systems throughout all languages evaluated. Tokens of multiple VMWEs of the same category can form connected components within the dependency tree of a given sentence which our heutristics is not able to resolve in a correct way. A solution to this would be to further inspect the dependency relations for which this phenomenon is observable and to try to identify criteria to filter them out under given circumstances.

System	Unseen MWE-based				Global MWE-based				Global Token-based			
	P	R	F1	Rank	P	R	F1	Rank	P	R	F1	Rank
MVB (bug free)	0.65	2.27	1.02	4*	65.14	50.82	57.10	3*	87.07	59.50	70.69	2*
Ling. Feats. B.	1.63	4.55	2.40	2**	70.50	56.46	62.71	1**	86.09	64.16	73.52	1**
MTLB-STRUCT	*48.75*	*58.33*	*53.11*	*1*	*72.25*	*75.04*	*73.62*	*1*	*81.20*	*77.24*	*79.17*	*1*
ERMI	*37.09*	*41.67*	*39.25*	*1*	*63.48*	*56.32*	*59.69*	*1*	*79.48*	*62*	*69.66*	*1*

Table 3: The results of two of our systems for the langugage *Hindi*. * = *unofficial rank in the open track.* ** = *unofficial rank in the closed track. MTLB-STRUCT and ERMI are the winning systems of the two tracks of the shared task for this language. We provide their results for reasons of comparability.*

A further observation is that in the case of the language *Hindi*, the results achieved by our systems show positive outliers. Here, *MultiVitaminBooster* would have ranked third in the *global MWE-based* category and second in the *global token-based* category. The unofficial system trained solely on window- and dependey-based features even manages to achieve unofficial first ranks in the closed track.

4 Conclusion and Future Work

We presented *MultiVitaminBooster* and three unofficial systems implemented for the *PARSEME shared task 2020 on verbal multiword expressions*. We evaluated our systems for seven languages. The best of our systems would have ranked fifth in the official shared task. A positive outlier can be observed for the language *Hindi*, where our systems achieved more competitive results. The usage of multilingual contextualized word embeddings for our systems can be considered a failure, as the same deteriorated results and our system relying solely on the linguistic feature set achieved superior results. It is, however, to explore if this would have turned out differently with another language model.

To summarise, there remains room for improvement. Using statistical association measures induced from large scale corpora as additional features may be a route to further explore this. An improved redesign of the heuristics used for assembling tokens into VMWEs built on a more complex rule set could lead to improvements in *MWE-based* precision scores and close the gap to the *token-based* ones. Different classification algorithms, such as CRFs or SVMs, could be explored as alternatives to gradient boosting and logistic regression, as well as different variations and combinations of training hyperparameters to aim for better regularisation.

References

Alexis Conneau, Kartikay Khandelwal, Naman Goyal, Vishrav Chaudhary, Guillaume Wenzek, Francisco Guzmán, Edouard Grave, Myle Ott, Luke Zettlemoyer, and Veselin Stoyanov. 2019. Unsupervised cross-lingual representation learning at scale. *CoRR*, abs/1911.02116.

Jacob Devlin, Ming-Wei Chang, Kenton Lee, and Kristina Toutanova. 2019. BERT: Pre-training of deep bidirectional transformers for language understanding. In *Proceedings of the 2019 Conference of the North American Chapter of the Association for Computational Linguistics: Human Language Technologies, Volume 1 (Long and Short Papers)*, pages 4171–4186, Minneapolis, Minnesota, June. Association for Computational Linguistics.

Anna Veronika Dorogush, Vasily Ershov, and Andrey Gulin. 2018. Catboost: gradient boosting with categorical features support. *CoRR*, abs/1810.11363.

Stefan Evert, Peter Uhrig, Sabine Bartsch, and Thomas Proisl. 2017. E-VIEW-Alation – a Large-Scale Evaluation Study of Association Measures for Collocation Identification. In Miloš J Jelena K Simon K Iztok K, Carole T and Vít B, editors, *Electronic Lexicography in the 21st Century. Proceedings of the eLex 2017 Conference*, page 531–549, Brno. Lexical Computing.

Natalia Klyueva, Antoine Doucet, and Milan Straka. 2017. Neural networks for multi-word expression detection. In *Proceedings of the 13th Workshop on Multiword Expressions (MWE 2017)*, pages 60–65, Valencia, Spain, April. Association for Computational Linguistics.

Yinhan Liu, Myle Ott, Naman Goyal, Jingfei Du, Mandar Joshi, Danqi Chen, Omer Levy, Mike Lewis, Luke Zettlemoyer, and Veselin Stoyanov. 2019. Roberta: A robustly optimized BERT pretraining approach. *CoRR*, abs/1907.11692.

Justina Mandravickaitė and Tomas Krilavičius. 2017. Identification of multiword expressions for Latvian and Lithuanian: Hybrid approach. In *Proceedings of the 13th Workshop on Multiword Expressions (MWE 2017)*, pages 97–101, Valencia, Spain, April. Association for Computational Linguistics.

Francesca Masini. 2005. Multi-word expressions between syntax and the lexicon : The case of italian verb-particle constructions. *Sky Journal of Linguistics*, 18:145–173.

Llew Mason, Jonathan Baxter, Peter Bartlett, and Marcus Frean. 1999. Boosting algorithms as gradient descent. In *Proceedings of the 12th International Conference on Neural Information Processing Systems*, NIPS'99, page 512–518, Cambridge, MA, USA. MIT Press.

Ryan McDonald, Joakim Nivre, Yvonne Quirmbach-Brundage, Yoav Goldberg, Dipanjan Das, Kuzman Ganchev, Keith Hall, Slav Petrov, Hao Zhang, Oscar Täckström, Claudia Bedini, Núria Bertomeu Castelló, and Jungmee Lee. 2013. Universal Dependency annotation for multilingual parsing. In *Proceedings of the 51st Annual Meeting of the Association for Computational Linguistics (Volume 2: Short Papers)*, pages 92–97, Sofia, Bulgaria, August. Association for Computational Linguistics.

Tomas Mikolov, Kai Chen, Greg Corrado, and Jeffrey Dean. 2013. Efficient estimation of word representations in vector space. In Yoshua Bengio and Yann LeCun, editors, *1st International Conference on Learning Representations, ICLR 2013, Scottsdale, Arizona, USA, May 2-4, 2013, Workshop Track Proceedings*.

Erwan Moreau, Ashjan Alsulaimani, Alfredo Maldonado, and Carl Vogel. 2018. CRF-seq and CRF-DepTree at PARSEME shared task 2018: Detecting verbal MWEs using sequential and dependency-based approaches. In *Proceedings of the Joint Workshop on Linguistic Annotation, Multiword Expressions and Constructions (LAW-MWE-CxG-2018)*, pages 241–247, Santa Fe, New Mexico, USA, August. Association for Computational Linguistics.

Pavel Pecina. 2005. An extensive empirical study of collocation extraction methods. In *Proceedings of the ACL Student Research Workshop*, pages 13–18, Ann Arbor, Michigan, June. Association for Computational Linguistics.

Fabian Pedregosa, Gaël Varoquaux, Alexandre Gramfort, Vincent Michel, Bertrand Thirion, Olivier Grisel, Mathieu Blondel, Peter Prettenhofer, Ron Weiss, Vincent Dubourg, Jake VanderPlas, Alexandre Passos, David Cournapeau, Matthieu Brucher, Matthieu Perrot, and Edouard Duchesnay. 2011. Scikit-learn: Machine learning in python. *J. Mach. Learn. Res.*, 12:2825–2830.

Jeffrey Pennington, Richard Socher, and Christopher Manning. 2014. GloVe: Global vectors for word representation. In *Proceedings of the 2014 Conference on Empirical Methods in Natural Language Processing (EMNLP)*, pages 1532–1543, Doha, Qatar, October. Association for Computational Linguistics.

Liudmila Ostroumova Prokhorenkova, Gleb Gusev, Aleksandr Vorobev, Anna Veronika Dorogush, and Andrey Gulin. 2018. Catboost: unbiased boosting with categorical features. In Samy Bengio, Hanna M. Wallach, Hugo Larochelle, Kristen Grauman, Nicolò Cesa-Bianchi, and Roman Garnett, editors, *Advances in Neural Information Processing Systems 31: Annual Conference on Neural Information Processing Systems 2018, NeurIPS 2018, 3-8 December 2018, Montréal, Canada*, pages 6639–6649.

Carlos Ramisch, Paulo Schreiner, Marco Idiart, and Aline Villavicencio. 2008. An evaluation of methods for the extraction of multiword expressions. In *In Proceedings of the LREC Workshop Towards a Shared Task for Multiword Expressions (MWE 2008*, pages 50–53.

Carlos Ramisch, Bruno Guillaume, Agata Savary, Jakub Waszczuk, Marie Candito, and Ashwini Vaidya. 2020a. Shared task on semi-supervised identification of verbal multiword expressions - edition 1.2. `http://multiword.sourceforge.net/PHITE.php?sitesig=CONF&page=CONF_02_ MWE-LEX_2020___lb__COLING__rb__&subpage=CONF_40_Shared_Task`. Accessed: 2020-09-09.

Carlos Ramisch, Bruno Guillaume, Agata Savary, Jakub Waszczuk, Marie Candito, Ashwini Vaidya, Verginica Barbu Mititelu, Archna Bhatia, Uxoa Iñurrieta, Voula Giouli, Tunga Güngör, Menghan Jiang, Timm Lichte, Chaya Liebeskind, Johanna Monti, Renata Ramisch, Sara Stymme, Abigail Walsh, Hongzhi Xu, Emilia Palka-Binkiewicz, Rafael Ehren, Sara Stymne, Matthieu Constant, Caroline Pasquer, Yannick Parmentier, Jean-Yves Antoine, Carola Carlino, Valeria Caruso, Maria Pia Di Buono, Antonio Pascucci, Annalisa Raffone, Anna Riccio, Federico Sangati, Giulia Speranza, Renata Ramisch, Silvio Ricardo Cordeiro, Helena de Medeiros Caseli, Isaac Miranda, Alexandre Rademaker, Oto Vale, Aline Villavicencio, Gabriela Wick Pedro, Rodrigo Wilkens, Leonardo Zilio, Monica-Mihaela Rizea, Mihaela Ionescu, Mihaela Onofrei, Jia Chen, Xiaomin Ge, Fangyuan Hu, Sha Hu, Minli Li, Siyuan Liu, Zhenzhen Qin, Ruilong Sun, Chenweng Wang, Huangyang Xiao, Peiyi Yan, Tsy Yih, Ke Yu, Songping Yu, Si Zeng, Yongchen Zhang, Yun Zhao, Vassiliki Foufi, Aggeliki Fotopoulou, Stella Markantonatou, Stella Papadelli, Sevasti Louizou, Itziar Aduriz, Ainara Estarrona, Itziar Gonzalez, Antton Gurrutxaga, Larraitz Uria, Ruben Urizar, Jennifer Foster, Teresa Lynn, Hevi Elyovitch, Yaakov Ha-Cohen Kerner, Ruth Malka, Kanishka Jain, Vandana Puri, Shraddha Ratori, Vishakha Shukla, Shubham Srivastava, Gozde Berk, Berna Erden, and Zeynep Yirmibeşoğlu. 2020b. Annotated corpora and tools of the PARSEME shared task on semi-supervised identification of verbal multiword expressions (edition 1.2). LINDAT/CLARIAH-CZ digital library at the Institute of Formal and Applied Linguistics (ÚFAL), Faculty of Mathematics and Physics, Charles University.

Regina Stodden, Behrang QasemiZadeh, and Laura Kallmeyer. 2018. TRAPACC and TRAPACCS at PARSEME shared task 2018: Neural transition tagging of verbal multiword expressions. In *Proceedings of the Joint Workshop on Linguistic Annotation, Multiword Expressions and Constructions (LAW-MWE-CxG-2018)*, pages 268–274, Santa Fe, New Mexico, USA, August. Association for Computational Linguistics.

Milan Straka and Jana Straková. 2017. Tokenizing, pos tagging, lemmatizing and parsing ud 2.0 with udpipe. In *Proceedings of the CoNLL 2017 Shared Task: Multilingual Parsing from Raw Text to Universal Dependencies*, pages 88–99, Vancouver, Canada, August. Association for Computational Linguistics.

Yulia Tsvetkov and Shuly Wintner. 2010. Extraction of multi-word expressions from small parallel corpora. In Chu-Ren Huang and Dan Jurafsky, editors, *COLING 2010, 23rd International Conference on Computational Linguistics, Posters Volume, 23-27 August 2010, Beijing, China*, pages 1256–1264. Chinese Information Processing Society of China.

Ashish Vaswani, Noam Shazeer, Niki Parmar, Jakob Uszkoreit, Llion Jones, Aidan N. Gomez, Lukasz Kaiser, and Illia Polosukhin. 2017. Attention is all you need. *CoRR*, abs/1706.03762.

Jakub Waszczuk. 2018. TRAVERSAL at PARSEME shared task 2018: Identification of verbal multiword expressions using a discriminative tree-structured model. In *Proceedings of the Joint Workshop on Linguistic Annotation, Multiword Expressions and Constructions (LAW-MWE-CxG-2018)*, pages 275–282, Santa Fe, New Mexico, USA, August. Association for Computational Linguistics.

Thomas Wolf, Lysandre Debut, Victor Sanh, Julien Chaumond, Clement Delangue, Anthony Moi, Pierric Cistac, Tim Rault, Rémi Louf, Morgan Funtowicz, and Jamie Brew. 2019. Huggingface's transformers: State-of-the-art natural language processing. *CoRR*, abs/1910.03771.

Andrea Zaninello and Alexandra Birch. 2020. Multiword expression aware neural machine translation. In *Proceedings of the 12th Language Resources and Evaluation Conference*, pages 3816–3825, Marseille, France, May. European Language Resources Association.

Association for Computational Linguistics
209 N. Eighth Street
Stroudsburg, Pennsylvania 18360